THE MOST INTERESTING LEAGUE IN THE WORLD

HOW THE NFL EXPLAINS AMERICA

CHRIS CHAMPAGNE

NLP

NEXT LEFT PRESS
NEW ORLEANS, LA

Published by Next Left Press, New Orleans, LA.
www.nextleftpress.com

Design: Geoff Munsterman

ISBN-13: 978-0-9962374-8-2

Printed in the United States of America.

Title: The Most Interesting League In the World / by Chris Champagne.
Publisher: New Orleans, LA : Next Left Press, 2020. |
ISBN: 9780996237482 (pbk.)
Subjects: Professional Football. | Humor. | Memoir.

This book is dedicated to

Ed Champagne

LSU, 1942 and 1946
Los Angeles Rams, 1987-1950

THE PLAYBOOK

PRE-GAME PREDICTIONS

In the early 60s when football was in its homestretch run gaining on baseball as America's game of choice, my family would find itself in our car riding through the night from my dad's summer job at a racetrack in Maine toward Chicago for his autumn job at Hawthorne Race Course.

Our ritual was to try to find pro football preseason games on the radio. My mom, me, and my sister were football fans and my dad, well, as a former Los Angeles Rams player from 1947 to 1950, he had an interest.

We were among those sports fans who were hooked on the game and those nighttime radio searches were anticipated highly in my young life.

I suppose you could say I started collecting tales early on and that was the true beginning of this book.

Football is now unquestionably America's game.

The National Football League at over 100 years old is at the center of our popular culture which culminates every year in the Super Bowl which has become, for all practical purposes, a national holiday.

I am lucky enough to have a radio show in which I get to decide the content and I developed a feature that I call "Pro Football Subjective."

What is that exactly?

It was a vehicle to explore unexpected and eccentric stories that are in some way connected to NFL franchises: history, celebrity; connections to music, film, politics; current events, what have you.

I noticed over time that the NFL extends itself into almost every aspect of our culture.

Music, theater, literature, art, film, and the entire marketplace of our lives reaches both ways, toward the league and away.

There are lesser known events that have transpired in the game itself and some offbeat occurences on and off the field in 100 years. I have tried to gather as many as I could find and they create quite an interesting eclectic mosaic. The premise in a quirky way finds the exuberance, strength, whimsy, and even the weaknesses of whatever it is that informs the culture of the United States.

You'll find, among others: Princess Di, Prince, Marvin Gaye, *Game of Thrones* author George R. R. Martin, Julie Andrews, Bob Dylan, Frank Sinatra, Jane Russell, and even Lisbeth Salander (*The Girl with the Dragon Tattoo*); names that, admit it, you wouldn't associate with the NFL off the top of your head who connect to the NFL in surprising, interesting, and fun ways.

I look upon this book as a museum in the modern sense. There are historical gems, tales of societal growth, oddball tidbits, celebrity sightings, a video and audio link here and there. And even a few on-the-field tales.

Modern book writing faces a new task, a lot of information is available to all online.

As such I consider myself a curator as much as an author and I did the easy-chair work as opposed to the leg work.

It would take someone a lot of time to distill the info in this book into one whole with an eye toward the unusual. And that is what I have tried to do.

Another way to look at this book is "NFL as Roadside Attraction."

We will use the creative definition of truth coined by *The Moth*, the popular public radio show: "these stories are truthful to the teller."

I cannot vouch for the veracity of all of these tales and anecdotes but I do strive to deliver them true to the sources.

So, we've got a *Ripleys' Believe It or Not* situation.

This calls for critical thinking. You must believe it or not. That seems like a fair bargain.

There are stories in which I interject my own observations, stories my father, an NFL player in the 40's, told me and I offer my opinion as a fan.

How's this for a curve ball in a football book—stories that include Gerald Ford, Richard Nixon, Barack Obama, Donald Trump, John F. Kennedy, Lyndon Johnson, Harry Truman, and Rutherford B Hayes.

Music is represented by Eminem, James Brown, Hank Williams, Michael Jackson, Ozzy Osbourne, Bob Dylan, Frank Sinatra, and others.

The criterion for my "Pro Football Subjective" was a link to an NFL team if only ever so slight. And because it's my book I got to choose. There are even a couple of entries that really have almost nothing to do with the team in which chapter they appear.

I am a Baby Boomer, I have lived through an ever-changing America and I was all of my life a sports fan in the American sense, meaning baseball, football, basketball.

I remember many of the stories in this book as a fan and as a fan I was lucky enough to actually attend some of the early Super Bowls and I, like many or even most of American sports fans, experienced these times as a TV spectator in my own living room.

There are also all but forgotten stories that give a time travel aspect at times.

I'm also a New Orleans Saints fan and yes, I was there when John Gilliam ran back the opening kickoff in 1967. In the North End Zone to be precise.

This book I hope will be fun, will be enlightening, will be interesting and will showcase how in some foundational way we, the citizens of the United States as the ultimate authors of our culture have much in common, maybe more so than we have differences. Our differences are profound at this moment in time but our shared experiences of our fandom are perhaps deeper than we imagine.

We often recreate across political divides.

Nonetheless, I want this to be a fun read. Even a fascinating scrapbook of unlikely by products.

You will find failure, perseverance, rich people ,poor people, victory, defeat, war, death, romance, nostalgia, humor, darkness, luck, injustice, and a whole lot of sociology going on.

What does it all mean?

That's for someone like Malcom Gladwell to decide.

Before we move on, I'd like to say a few words about my dad, Ed Champagne, or #86 of the Los Angeles Rams.

He was a great father. He was always kind to me.

He told me that when he was 8 years old he knew he wanted to be a football player. That would be 1929, pro football was a struggling enterprise then at best. He was about the size of a goat but his mother fashioned a path on the side of their home so he could run wind sprints. America was truly a land for dreams. The odds were astronomical against him succeeding, but he did.

Every pro team has many players on its roster and only a few are considered stars but it is a fact that almost every player on an NFL roster was once a star in college or surely in high school. Every one of these guys is a superior athlete.

In my dad's case he was an All City and All State performer in New Orleans at S.J. Peters High, on a team that didn't win too many games.

Yet he received a scholarship to LSU where he excelled and was a teammate of, among others Y.A. Tittle, Steve Van Buren and Alvin Dark.

In 1979 Peter Finney, an award winning journalist for the *Times Picayune*, wrote a book: *Fighting Tigers :75 Years of LSU Football*.

In that book he asked Bud Montet, a journalist at the Baton Rouge *Advocate,* to name an all time LSU team as Montet had covered the team since the '30s.

We're talking thousands of players had played at LSU at that point.

Montet chose twelve players.

Tittle and Van Buren of course both in the Pro Football Hall of Fame and two tackles, one of those tackles was Ed Champagne— "Quickest tackle I ever saw."

My dad, like most men of his generation, served in World War II and by virtue of that played a split time at LSU lettering in 1942 and 1946.

He gave up his senior year to turn pro because of financial and family obligations and his intentions to stay or leave were the subject of speculation in the local press. It was a consensus feeling that if he played his senior year at LSU he would be an All-American. We'll never know that *what if.*

He went to Los Angeles where he joined a team with a lot of star power, Bob Warefield, Norm Van Brocklin, Tom Fears, "Crazy Legs" Hirsch (all Hall-of-Famers), Kenny Washington, Tank Younger, and Glen Davis to name a few outstanding players. Coaches on the team were Clark Shaughnessy, Joe Stydahar (HOF) and George Trafton (HOF). The team doctor was another Hall-of-Famer, Dr. Danny Fortman. Pete Rozelle (HOF) and Tex Schramm

(HOF) were in the Rams front office. Bob Hope was an owner of the team. It was an exciting time to be a Ram

He was named a starter on the Rams 11 in 1949, a year in which they went to the NFL Championship Game only to lose to his friend Steve Van Buren and the Philadelphia Eagles 14-0 on a rain-soaked field in Los Angeles.

He played 59 minutes of that championship game in 1949 when players played on both sides of the ball. That would be every minute but 1. They again lost the NFL championship in 1950 to the Cleveland Browns on a last second field goal by Lou Groza (HOF). The teams my dad played on in L.A., were at the top of the NFL food chain.

He was offered a 20% raise in salary to jump to Canada in 1951 and he did so, playing for the Calgary Stampeders at a high level until he broke his neck in the first half of the game and played the rest of the game with the broken neck. He discovered the neck was broken a day or two later and that ended his football career.

I've added a few anecdotes he passed along to me in this book. Just a few and I hope you'll forgive a proud son this indulgence.

Researching this book I was, as an ardent fan—struck—by how many of the giants of the games were friends and contemporaries of my father.

My dad didn't dwell on his football past and went on to a distinguished career as an official in thoroughbred racing. When he retired he would regale me with stories of his glory days. He told me these stories over and over and I listened gladly and if I could sit and listen to him tell them to me again and I would gladly a thousand times over.

He was a great and good man.

One last thing—teams move. It was up to me to decide which stories go where: Baltimore Colts stories are divided up between Indianapolis and Baltimore because I feel that ultimately the history of these teams belongs more to the fans and citizens of the city in which they happened. Ravens get some old and some new. Tennessee Titans get Bud Adams. Houston Texans chapter gets Houston Oilers stuff mostly. Rams get a bit of St. Louis, not much. My apologies to St. Louis Ram fans. Cardinals get three cities: Chicago, St. Louis, and Phoenix. Browns get old and new. Just wanted to explain these choices.

Chris Champagne
New Orleans, Louisiana, 2020

THE MOST INTERESTING LEAGUE IN THE WORLD

BUFFALO

SayBrah

DONALD J. TRUMP

BUFFALO

FB

TRUMP, TERRORISM, AND THE SUPREMES

THE MOST INTERESTING LEAGUE IN THE WORLD

BUFFALO

"I believe in the jury system."
—O.J. Simpson
Buffalo RB ('69-77)

SayBrah

One of the original AFL franchises awarded in 1959, the Buffalo Bills started play in 1960.

The Bills are the only team to go to four consecutive Super Bowls.

Original owner Ralph Wilson owned team until his death at ninety-five.

His estate sold team to Terry and Kim Pegula in 2014.

Super Bowl Appearances: 4
Super Bowl Record: 0-4
Super Bowl Losses: 1990, 1991, 1992, 1993

The NFL is a juggernaut of American culture that emerged as such in the 1960s. Its visibility is front and center. It brushes up on all aspects of our society in many ways.

On June 18, 1965, such an intersection of divergent royalties spoke to diverse currents that shape who or what we are, for better or worse.

This particular snapshot of America was sponsored by Ralph Wilson, the founder and long-time owner of the Buffalo Bills.

Wilson was from Detroit and of its moneyed class. The fashion among the rich families of Detroit was to throw lavish coming out parties for its young daughters.

Mr. Wilson was described as a scion of an insurance fortune in the New York Times article that reported on this slice of life. As such, he was a member of the tribe that also included American luminaries as the Fords and Fishers.

The bar had been set for debutante shindigs, it is said, by soirées thrown for the Ford sisters. The entertainment for one Ford daughter in 1959 was Nat King Cole, a huge star. In 1961 the next Ford daughter had Ella Fitzgerald as her musical entertainment.

This was 1965 when Ralph Wilson, owner of the Buffalo Bills, paid $85,000 for the party for his daughter Christy Cole Wilson. Musical styles were changing in America. And this was Detroit, or more precisely Grosse Pointe—a neighborhood of the rich and famous, but more to the point a suburb of Motown.

The musical guests were the Supremes, just one week from their fifth number one hit on the charts, "Back in My Arms Again." Just a month earlier they had been on the cover of *Time* magazine.

The Supremes were from about ten miles away geographically from Grosse Pointe but, as the *New York Times* article points out, perhaps light years away in socioeconomic terms.

There were no black families living in Grosse Pointe in 1965. At the time of this snapshot of the passing parade, this coming together of the Wilsons and the Supremes was an interesting juxtaposition of American race relations and wealth.

MYSTERIOUS WAYS

November 27, 2010, the Bills were on the threshold of defeating the Steelers. A pass right on the money to wide receiver, Steve Johnson. They hit him in a bad spot—right in his hands—and he dropped the game winner. The Bills lost. We all know these things happen.

What came next? Not so much.

Steve Johnson then went for an outlet for his frustrations-Twitter.

I PRAISE YOU 24/7!!!!!! AND THIS
IS HOW YOU DO ME?!!!!! YOU EXPECT
ME TO LEARN FROM THIS??? HOW???!!!"
I'LL NEVER FORGET THIS!! EVER!!!" THX THO.

That God has a Twitter account is a given. God is everywhere. The nuns told me. So, God is on Twitter. Slam dunk. And God—she, he, or a 3rd choice—has been put on notice. The part that I like the best is the "THX THO." A nice touch.

And there's more to this story.

On November 28, 2010, Johnson dropped his pass and posted the infamous tweet. Some time later (which in the internet or tweet post world is its own small eternity), Adam Schefter, NFL guru-esque commentator, helped send the tweet out to the larger world.

A Bills fan named Del Reid, who is, by the way, universally recognized as the Godfather of what has come to be knowns as the Bills Mafia (a name given to Buffalo Bills fandom), decided to go on Twitter and make fun of the world just catching up to Johnson's epic tweet with the hashtag, #SchefterBreakingNews.

It took off. The rest is history. The Bills Mafia was up and running.

REAL SACRIFICE

Bob Kalsu, an offensive guard for the Bills for one season, is honored on the Bills Wall of Fame.

He has a plaque in his honor in Canton at the Pro Football Hall of Fame.

Maybe you never heard of him.

Listen up.

Bob Kalsu was an All-American at Oklahoma and he was drafted by the Bills in the 8th round and not by the NFL even though he was 1st team All-American.

He had participated in ROTC while at Oklahoma and that's a clue.

He had an obligation to report for military service due to his ROTC participation. This put off teams because it was the late 60's and the United States was in the throes of the Vietnam War.

Bob didn't have to go right away so he played with the Bills and was rookie of the year for the Bills and started 9 games.

Then Uncle Sam came calling.

The team and his family both urged him to get an appointment to the National Guard which would mean that he probably would not have to go to Vietnam. But Bob said that he had given his word to serve when he joined the ROTC.

So, he went to Vietnam as a First Lieutenant.

The Kalsus were devout Catholics, his wife later said she prayed to God asking that if he was to take Bob from her to at least give her a son.

The Kalsu's already had a baby girl and, right after Bob shipped out, his wife Judy found out that she was pregnant.

Bob Kalsu ended up at a place called Firebase Ripcord, and after the commander of his unit helicoptered out with a neck injury in July 1970, Bob was given command of his unit.

Firebase Ripcord was, at that time, one of the most dangerous posts in a dangerous warzone. Up to 600 mortars were pounding the hilltop redoubt a day. The American position was manned by 300 soldiers and was surrounded by 5000 NVA or 10 to 12 battalions.

At night his fellow soldiers could hear the enemy, the North Vietnamese Army, shouting to them, " G.I. die tonight. G. I. die tonight." It was a highly stressful place. But his fellow soldiers said that Bob Kalsu was up to the task of leadership at a demanding time and place.

One of his friends who was there with him said of him: "A fearless guy, smart, brave and respected by his troops."

The story turns terribly tragic as one mortar shell, in an instant, took Bob's life.

His buddies said that he had just read a letter from his wife that informed him that the due date of their baby was that very day.

As Bob was killed in action, his son was being born.

Word came to Judy while still in the hospital.

Before she left the hospital she had their son's name officially changed to Robert James Kalsu, Jr.

It took the Bills a while to honor Bob, but they did and many awards have been renamed in his honor. In 2018, the Buffalo-based 105th Military Police Company National Guard Unit in Iraq named their base Forward Operation Base Bob Kalsu (or Camp Kalsu) in his honor.

His wife, who has been left with a lifetime of sorrows, said of the honors her husband received posthumously, "Please, please know that any honor that is given to Bob is given to all of them."

AUTHOR NOTE: *Bob Kalsu has been given credit for being the only NFL player killed in action in Vietnam, but Don Steinbrunner—who played for the Cleveland Browns in the 1950's—was a navigator flying in a UC-123 over Kontum Province in the Central Highland when it was struck by enemy fire and crashed, killing all four members of the crew.*

THE ACCIDENTAL FAN

Amanda Perino, a resident of the Netherlands, was visiting New York state for a business opportunity and decided that she might need a phone that could be compatible with United States cell towers. She bought a SIM card.

That's when the trouble started.

Her phone started to ping and ping and ping and ping some more.

She had stumbled into a fantasy football chat group of Buffalo Bills fans.

If you've ever been on a fantasy football thread it's pretty testosterone-rich and bro-friendly, to put it mildly. And annoyingly ping happy.

She texted the group and informed them that she was not the former owner of the SIM card, KG.

She asked to be dropped from the chat group.

They, being fantasy football kind of guys, informed her that no, she was stuck for at least life.

At first annoyed, she started to get used to it as a break from her routine. Plus, as a woman, it gave her a peek into the minds of men in a way that women don't often get.

Oh yeah, they assumed she was a guy. A fact she did not share with them.

She even got a nickname: NKG or New KG.

She went back to the Netherlands but stayed in touch via the group texts. At some point she was planning a trip back to New York City and her new-found phone pals invited her to Buffalo for a Bills game. Free ticket and all.

She accepted, but not before she had her mom do a computer search of the group members. The group surprisingly (they are Bills fans after all) passed Mother's muster.

Ms. Perino still did not tell them she was a woman.

When she showed up it was a surprise, but the guys turned out to be good guys whose girlfriends and spouses were also along for the Bills ride.

All's well that ends well.

Now Ms. Perino is a Bills fan for life.

FLYING BEER

Beer bottles thrown through the air in displeasure at American sporting events is a cliché that no longer applies generally as precautions have been made to deal with this natural reflex.

Yet, in 1962, at the Rockpile (as War Memorial Stadium was lovingly referred) home of the Buffalo Bills, these modern sensibilities were not in vogue.

Old school beer tossing still loomed on occasion.

The Jets were in town and the Jets had a quarterback problem. The starting quarterback for that day actually joined the Jets late that week before he could even practice with the team. That's right, the starting QB for a pro football team had never practiced with the team he would lead onto the field. The Jets won the game anyway,

Bills fans were not in the mood. At the end of the game a shower of beer cans crashed down on the field, the Jets, the Bills—what have you. Bills players shielded themselves from the fusilade of cans as they raced to safety.

Press and police reports indicated that more than 3,000 beer cans rained down onto the field.

Curious then that as the deed was transpiring, the concession manager of the Bills was in the press box watching the bombardment and remarked something to the effect of *Man, we must have sold a lot of cans of beer today.*

Then it dawned on him.

They didn't sell beer in cans.

So, this begs the question: where did the cans come from? Two sources, it turns out. The fans were walking across the street to local bars, buying beer, and returning with it to the stadium. The best of multiple worlds—you drink a beer at a cheaper price, you have a souvenir empty to flex your free speech rights, and you get to try out your own athletic ability to boot.

In those days you were allowed to bring your own six packs into the stadium.

COMMUNIST MANIFESTO

In 1956 when the Soviet Union rolled its tanks into Hungary to put down the Hungarian revolution they of course had no idea that they would have a hand in changing pro football in America.

Pete Gogolak and his family fled Hungary for America as a result of the revolution.

They settled in New York state and Pete, a soccer player in Hungary, enrolled at Ogdensburg High School but there was no soccer team. Pete then did what numerous immigrants have always done as in "When in Rome..." and he went out for football.

One day the coach asked for kickers and Pete tried his foot at kicking an American football but with a twist. He lined up to the side at about a 45 degree angle and kicked that baby with the side of his foot. It didn't go too well. About three feet in the air and everyone laughed.

Pete thought it would work. He practiced and refined the process. He made it work.

Even though he was successful with his new invention no college would give him a scholarship. He walked on at Cornell and in his first game he kicked three field goals against Yale. The soccer style of kicking a football was born.

After college a scout from the Buffalo Bills came to take a look. He must have been impressed because the Bills took a chance on Gogolak in the 12th round.

He kicked a 57 yard field goal in an exhibition game against the Jets and he made the team and history. Later he was signed by the NFL in a break of an unwritten protocol between the leagues to not to raid each other's rosters.

Pete Gogolak, one of the more curious results of the Columbian Exchange.

RON PINTO

An especially deserving Bills fan, Ron Pinto, is the fulcrum of another strange Bills tailgating tradition.

There are special tailgating sections outside the Bills Stadium and one of them claims Ron Pinto, who, for reasons unknown, is squirted by other Bills fans with mustard and ketchup until he is covered in the stuff.

So important and so iconic is Ron Pinto's Passion Play-esque antics that his tailgating performances were banned from Bills stadium property at the request of the National Football League.

See for yourself on YouTube.

CITY OF NEIGHBORS

And if you are still not convinced of the "special-ness" of the Bills fans, I submit this for your perusal.

This was posted on Craigslist in "Buffalo date."

"I sat down next to you at today's game. I was with my boyfriend. When he went to get food and drinks you put your hand on my leg. At first I was weirded out, but that quickly passed. Instead of moving your hand I let you touch my leg. Idk why...I never did anything like this before especially since I have a bf, but I slid my hand down your pants. I was too nervous to make eye contact with you, tho, so I don't really know what you look like. You didn't move my hand or freak out, so I grabbed your d#*k and gave u a hand job until u creamed in your pants, as soon as I felt your cream explode all over my hand my boyfriend came back and sat down. I was so nervous cause u had to act like nothing happned (sic). I didn't see your face cause I was looking down the whole time. Besides you had that face paint on your face that was kind of cute. I'd kinda like to give you another h*#d job, but i gotta make sure it's really you. So, if you see this tell me what color paint you wore, and if you were wearing any underwear to prove it"

BUFFALO 66

Released in 1998, *Buffalo 66* revolves or hovers around Bills fandom on a personal level.

The protagonist, Billy, is named after the Buffalo Bills. His mother has never missed a Bills game except one, the Championship game of 1966 when she gave birth to Billy. And Billy is released from prison at the beginning of the film for a crime necessitated by not being able to pay off a debt he incurred from a last-minute Super Bowl loss by the Bills, a plot device supplied by Scott Norwood's missed field goal in real life, that Billy, in Buffalo 66, will eventually exact revenge to no one's satisfaction.

Meanwhile, the film, a highly-regarded independent feature length film which got a 76 from Rotten Tomatoes website with an 88% from viewers, boasts an all-star Hollywood cast. Besides its director and star Vincent Gallo, it has Christina Ricci, Mickey Rourke, Ben Gazzara and Angelica Huston as Billy's Bills-obsessed mother.

WE TALKING ABOUT PRACTICE

Sharece Wright, like most American children who play football, dreamed about making it in the NFL. Few get the chance.

Sharece, however, was good enough to get invited to Buffalo Bills OTAs.

So when Wright missed his flight connection in Chicago he wasn't going to just throw in the towel. He had to find a way. He needed to get to Buffalo the next morning at 7am.

He called Uber. The first two drivers, when they realized his destination, declined the fare. Third Uber was the charm.

One American striver story meets another.

The third Uber driver was Hadi Abdollahian, an Iranian immigrant, who came to America via Turkey, his memories of the journey from Iran to Turkey to the good ole USA so fraught with trauma and unpleasant memories that he declined to share details when the story got, as they say, some traction.

Abdollahian had promised to take Wright to Buffalo, although he thought it was Buffalo Wild Wings. But as a man of his word, he took Wright to Buffalo, New York.

Hours later, with about an hour to spare, they pulled up to Buffalo OTA camp.

By that time, hurtling across the open road of the USA, they had bonded and, when word got out of the unusual nature of the journey, they had become somewhat famous for the proverbial fifteen minutes of American fame (coined by a true American success story, Andy Warhol).

The bill was $632.08 and with a generous $300 tip from Wright added up to a cool $932.08 which was matched by Blue Rock Energy-a sponsor of the Bills. Abdollahian's American dream is to parlay the computer science degree he is pursuing into becoming an astronaut.

It's reassuring to imagine a prospective Astronaut and would-be pro football player driving through the night in the American icon automobile on America's byways in pursuit of dreams.

CHEATING

Conspiracy is a slice of American life.

The sporting world is of course full of these suspicions—Deflategate, bounty scandals, steroid abuse et cetera, et cetera, et cetera...

So it is almost refreshing to find in the sporting world a clear concession to these nefarious deeds.

On page fifty-seven of his book, *Ineffective Habits of Financial Advisors*, Bills special teams coach John Steven Moore—with NFL coaching stints in Seattle, LA and Buffalo over a twelve-year career—sandwiches (in between talk of changes in social environments and government regulations) a confession.

He goes on to say that the wind blows hard from the easterly direction over the rim of Ralph Wilson Stadium during Bills games. And his idea was to signal equipment managers to open the gates to create an east-west wind tunnel when the other team was punting. He describes a game in which the Bills won, when the New England punter kicked the ball nicely but claims his signal to the equipment managers and the opening of the gate caused the wind to push the ball basically all the way back to the punter. He also confesses that it worked so well he almost felt sorry for the Patriots punter.

There is a beauty in this story, methinks.

THREE DAYS OF THE PIGEON

The Bills were to host the San Diego Chargers in a nationally televised game and they wanted to put their best foot forward.

War Memorial Stadium where they played their home games was affectionately and otherwise dubbed "The Rockpile."

It was basically a stadium built for baseball and as such had a dirt infield that had to be negotiated during football games and was less than photogenic. They also practiced there so this also tore up any grass that might be in the outfield.

The team decided to seed the field with fast growing grass and hope to have it ready for its closeup on national TV.

DAY ONE: The day after the grass seed was spread on the field the Bills showed up to practice and there were hundreds of pigeons munching on the new bird buffet.

They tried to scare them off but basically the birds would all just flock to different parts of the field and the practice had to be called off.

DAY TWO: The pigeons were still there. As practice was attempted Bills employees or municipal employees armed with pellet guns shot at the birds to chase them off. No dice, practice again halted due to pigeons.

Since the pellet guns didn't work the next idea was to put poison into the grass.

DAY THREE: The Bills showed up for practice and sure enough the field was filled with dead pigeons. The players spent the day not practicing but picking up dead pigeons.

Ed Abramoski, the trainer of the Bills for thirty-seven years and eventual member of the Bills Wall Of Fame was also a member of the Buffalo Homing Pigeon Association and raced pigeons. He was considered one of the best pigeon trainers in the country. When he saw the dead pigeons, he frantically ran around checking leg bands to see if any of the pigeons were his.

The Bills ended up spray painting the field green for TV. No practice for three days.

Final score: San Diego 34, Buffalo 3.

POSTER BOY

He grew up in Buffalo. He was a Buffalo Bills fan when they were in their golden years of 1990-1994 and the unprecedented four consecutive Super Bowl appearances. Alas, they lost all four. Yet four Super Bowl appearances in a row is quite an accomplishment.

The first of those Bills Super Bowls ended in a painful loss by one point after a missed field goal by Scott Norwood.

Perhaps the most famous moment in Buffalo Bills history is one filled with misery.

The Buffalonian of which this piece is about was, by that time, a member of the U.S. military and serving in the Middle East during Desert Storm—with distinction.

He came home from Desert Storm, after seeing war and death, the destruction and waste of it. By the time he was back in Buffalo (and still a Bills fan) at the age of twenty-four, his life had taken a negative turn by all accounts.

He had a nervous breakdown, had considered suicide and had a job as a security guard at the Buffalo Zoo on the night shift. It would be a good guess to think he was suffering from PTSD as many do after living in a war zone.

The Bills, however, were on a roll, in the midst of their four-year Super Bowl run. In a city like Buffalo—a working class, down-to-earth community—zeal for its NFL team is strong.

The twenty-four-year-old decorated army veteran was—doubtless—no different than thousands of other Buffalo residents who lived and died on the fortunes of the Buffalo Bills.

On the Bills' third bite at the Super Bowl apple, he bet $1,000 with a bookie on the Bills to win the Super Bowl against the Dallas Cowboys, America's Team. The Bills not only lost, they were creamed 51-13.

He paid his gambling debt with a credit card. Soon, he left Buffalo for good.

He traveled south to pursue his new obsession with the confrontation at Waco, Texas, between the Federal Government and the Branch Davidians in which seventy-six members of the Davidians would die.

Four weeks after his departure from Buffalo he went to investigate the events at Waco.

He started disseminating conspiracy literature from his car.

His obsession led this Buffalo Bills fan to perpetrate the biggest home-grown act of terrorism in American history.

The young, decorated soldier known by his fellow soldiers for, among other things, his unbelievable marksmanship, who lost $1,000 on his beloved Buffalo Bills, money he could probably ill afford to lose, was Timothy McVeigh.

HAIL TO THE CHIEF

Buffalo, as it is reminded ad infinitum, is a small TV market.

NFL franchises, only thirty-two in all the world, are the ultimate civic trophy of the rich and famous. If you don't count, say, the White House. For our purposes let's not, but funny that we mentioned it.

The Buffalo Bills had the same owner since day one and the formation of the AFL. Ralph Wilson, a very successful businessman from Detroit, he got the Bills franchise and held on to it until his death.

In 2014 Mr. Wilson passed away and the team hit the market. Anxiety in a small market like Buffalo, with a working-class base, at times of transition like this is almost palpable.

I know. I live in New Orleans and after Katrina the prevailing thought of Saints fans was that our team was all but gone. It was an all-too real possibility—but this is a story about the Bills.

Two of the major players in the competition to buy the Bills were Terry Pegula, already the owner of the other major league team in town, the Buffalo Sabres of the NHL, and Jon Bon Jovi—a New Jersey rocker and part of a group of wealthy Canadians from Toronto.

Toronto. That's another country. Fears were that if the Toronto group got the team it would move to Canada. Toronto to be exact. A huge market.

There was a third, very interested party, who many people believe has coveted an NFL franchise for decades. You may have heard of him: Donald Trump.

Mr. Trump's strategy it seems was to sour the heirs of Mr. Wilson on one of his rival groups in the bidding. That would be the Canadian group. A grassroots neighborhood group called the "12th Man Thunder Bills Backers" was formed by Michael Caputo, an associate of other Trump associates such as Paul Manafort and Roger Stone.

This group, populated by citizens who lived near the neighborhood of Ralph Wilson Stadium—home of the Bills—were used in what is commonly called "Astroturfing." It's a process by which nebulously authentic rank and file citizens are presented with money to espouse a civic cause or position. They help raise awareness or, in some cases, mislead the powers that be or public at large on the grass roots support for or against public policy.

Mr. Caputo had helped or worked with, among others, Boris Yeltsin, Vladimir Putin, Oliver North—to drop just a couple names.

The purpose of the 12th Man group (fronted by a Buffalo Bills fan who was a double amputee) was to, so the theory goes, scare off the opposition—in this case, the Canadians.

Trump eventually made an official $1 billion offer to purchase the Bills and had to inform Caputo he needed to sever ties with him and his group. After Trump went public with his bid, the gloves came off—so to speak—with a radio campaign to portray the Bon Jovi group in a less than favorable light.

At some point Texas A&M then entered the fray, issuing a cease and desist order to the 12th Man Thunder Bill Backers for unauthorized use of the 12th Man appellation, to which Texas A&M claimed a copyright. Keith Olberman, then on ESPN and later a well-known Trump detractor, took up the cause against Texas A&M by calling the president of Texas A&M "The Worst Person in Sports" on his ESPN show.

A&M demurred and Caputo got $25,000 from A&M to change the name of the 12th Man to Bill's Fan Thunder. Terry Pegula got the franchise. Bills fans sighed a huge sigh of relief.

Michael Caputo issued a statement gloating claiming that the efforts of his group were designed to stop Bon Jovi and his Toronto henchman and as such was a labor of love.

Donald Trump didn't get his team.

So, instead, he decided to run for President of the United States.

EPILOGUE: *Trump won the Presidency, Keith Olbermann went on to write a book called* Trump is F*cking Crazy *and the Bills Fan Thunder, started perhaps to help Trump, now has twenty season tickets they award to underprivileged children in Buffalo. It's a funny world.*

OJ

On October 3, 1995 the day the OJ Simpson verdict was announced in the trial that captivated America an edgy crowd at Kelly's Sports Grill was glued to the ten TVs.

The atmosphere described as tense and full of anxiety

When the jurors returned a "Not guilty" verdict, the crowd erupted in joy, relief, and in some cases vindication in the hope of OJ's innocence.

This crowd was in a mostly all-white sports bar in Buffalo.

OJ was an icon in Buffalo. He was Buffalo's Mickey Mantle or Lebron James.

From day one, most Bills fans said they wanted to believe that OJ didn't do it. Such is the gravity of sports fans loyalty.

Things changed.

OJ was not named to the 50th anniversary Bills team.

His Bills Hall of Fame plaques have been removed and the common thinking is that most Bill fans now believe he was guilty.

And if all of that is not bad enough, OJ is given credit for one other by-product of his murder trial and infamy.

OJ's friend Robert Kardashian renewed his expired law license to help defend his old friend OJ Simpson.

You can find magazine articles that give credit or blame to OJ Simpson for helping or giving impetus to the creation of the Kardashian reality TV phenomena.

The Kardashians, Robert and Kris Jenner, as most people know her, were very close to OJ and Nicole Brown Simpson.

The Kardashian girls grew up calling the *If I Did It* author, "Uncle OJ."

Kris was Nicole's best friend and a constant presence in the courtroom during trial in support of Nicole and her family.

On the day OJ was to surrender to the police, he was holed up at Robert Kardashian's home and Kardashian as his representative read a letter that was penned by OJ to the press.

"The Trial" has a million retellings.

You be the judge.

DETROIT

SayBrah®

MARVIN GAYE

DETROIT

CB

MARVIN GAYE, A CURSE, AND DEATH IN THE AFTERNOON

DETROIT

"When I die I want to come back as Bobby Layne's chauffeur."
—Don Meredith, Cowboys QB ('60-68)

SayBrah®

Detroit Lions franchise started out as the Portsmouth Spartans in 1930.

Portsmouth is a small city on the Ohio River. The Spartans had a brief and somewhat successful tenure on the field before a radio station owner in Detroit bought the team and moved it to Detroit in 1943 and renamed them the Lions.

The Lions have never been to the Super Bowl.

"I am a human being!"
—The Elephant Man

Keep that in mind as you read this tale of failure.

Matt Millen says that when William Clay Ford Jr. hired hired him, he told Mr. Ford that he didn't have any experience being a general manager. Ford told him, "You're a smart guy, you'll figure it out." Millen was the GM of the Detroit Lions for too long. I think we can all agree on that.

Despite an abysmal 31-84 record during his time as general manager, Matt Millen received a contract extension. He was reportedly the second-highest-paid GM in the NFL.

Anyway, at some point the Lions fans had had enough. "Fire Millen" chants broke out all over the place: Patriots games, Red Wings games, Lakers games in LA, U. of Michigan games. All over the world.

Rasheed Wallace of the Pistons, who was playing in an NBA game at Auburn Hills, joined the crowd in chanting "Fire Millen." In front yards throughout Michigan, snowmen held "Fire Millen" signs under their carrot noses.

In 2005 a Detroit radio show encouraged by callers and others organized what they called a "Millen Man March." Nine in the morning on game day, Lions fans dressed in orange hunting gear, which was the same color as that day's opponent (Cincinnati Bengals), showed up at a bar and walked to Ford Field. Soon the crowd was about 1,000 strong. Their chant was reminiscent of union marches in a union town.

The Bengals won 41-17. Nothing changed.

Green Bay Packers fans held up "KEEP MILLEN" signs. This was bad.

Finally in 2008, Millen was fired.

He said at some point, "It was a little bit of a tactical error on my part. I had a fleeting dream that I thought I could run a team. Sorry, Detroit, it didn't quite work out."

He was hired by ESPN as a football analyst almost immediately after his firing. So, the lesson here? Never listen to a thing an ESPN analyst says or at least take the opinion with a large grain of salt.

HISTORY

In 1934 the Portsmouth Spartans were sold to a Detroit radio station owner, moved to Detroit and became the Detroit Lions.

A rich short NFL history was left behind in Portsmouth, a city on the banks of the Ohio River.

Stadiums were a bit of a factor in the NFL even in the 1920s.

Portsmouth built what today still stands as Spartan Municipal Stadium and after the stadium was built for pro football, Portsmouth was awarded a franchise in the NFL. It was the same month as Black Thursday on Wall Street that sent the world into the Great Depression yet sixty-seven people in Portsmouth, Ohio ponied up at least $100 to buy shares in the team. Such was the importance of football in Ohio.

The Spartans had a brief run in the NFL punctuated by teams that boasted stars and Hall of Famers like Potsy Clark, Dutch Clark, Ace Gutowsky, and Glenn Presnell. In 1931 they were tied for the league lead but the Green Bay Packers reneged on playing a late season game and the NFL awarded the title to Green Bay.

1932 saw the Packers play the Portsmouth squad and the Spartans defeated the defending champs 19-0 in what has gone down in history as the Iron Man game, as the Spartans only used 11 players who all played the entire game. The 1932 Spartans went on to play the Chicago Bears for the NFL championship that year, the first NFL championship game which led to a championship game becoming a regular occurrence.

The Spartans and Bears played that game in Chicago Stadium. an indoor venue, because of the weather in Chicago. The Bears won 9-0, however Portsmouth diehards will tell you that their star quarterback Dutch Clark didn't play in the game. Why? Because he couldn't get off work.

He was head basketball coach at Colorado and the chancellor of Colorado wouldn't let him off for the weekend.

The Spartans left Portsmouth, yet the stadium still stands and all these years later is a rallying point for a small city reeling from an opioid epidemic like so many small towns in America. But a group in Portsmouth is using the renovation of Spartan Municipal Stadium as a rallying point. Its renovation and restoration along with a new semi-pro team, the Portsmouth Stealth, are focal points of a small city fighting for its identity and the soul of its residents. All these years later the legacy of the Spartans lives on. Fights on.

They have a Facebook page thanks to a group of men inspired by the town's NFL pedigree. Portsmouth Spartans Historical Society keeps the fire burning.

SEASON TIX

Ralph Wilson, went through a divorce in the early 70's. His wife got the house in Grosse Pointe. He had to pay attorney's fees. He gave her $1 million and had to pay her $1.5 million a year for ten years.

The owner of the Buffalo Bills, Wilson was a rich man.

His wife got one more thing of note. It was stipulated in the settlement that she would get the couple's two Detroit Lions 50 yard line season tickets for life.

Priorities.

BASEBALL

In the winter of 1965 I recall this story from a national sports magazine.

The big news in that time on the American calendar between the end of the NFL season and the rite of spring, the beginning of baseball season, was the dual holdout of the Los Angeles Dodgers star pitchers Sandy Koufax and Don Drysdale. The two had linked their contract negotiations to each other. One would not sign unless the other did.

On a desolate stretch of America's highways an NFL player said he was looking for a gas station when a bright light came out of the night sky. He goes on to say that it was beings from another planet. A UFO sighting.

What did the alien have to say?

They told the NFL player that he needed to alert the Dodgers or anyone whom it may concern that if the Dodgers did not soon sign Koufax and Drysdale to contracts then the Earth would be destroyed.

My recollection is the NFL player was a member of the Detroit Lions.

WORDS

In the song "Just Don't Give a F#@&!" penned and performed in 1998 by Eminem, you'll find this lyric that refers to a former Lions football coach:

I'm buzzin'. Dirty Dozen, naughty rotten rhymer
Cursin' at ya players worse than Marty Schottenheimer

Eminem has said when he wrote this song and lyric things weren't going so well for him and this is kind of how he felt in those days. He and his girlfriend had a one-year-old, were living with his mom and his record producer was thinking about giving up on him.

Seamus Heaney, a Nobel laureate poet, noticed Emienm's use of words and had this to say: "There's this guy, Eminem. He has a sense of what is possible. He sent a voltage around a generation. He has done things just not through subversive attitude but also high voltage energy."

From the coach of the Lions to the music of Detroit to Nobel poet. The NFL is a part of the Earth.

DEATH IN THE AFTERNOON

Chuck Hughes was a wide receiver with the Detroit Lions in the 70's. He caught a total of 15 passes in the NFL, or 3 per season. So it was of no note at all when he caught a pass in a Lions game with a minute on the clock in a game they lost by 5 points.

Yet Chuck Hughes will go down in history for something I'm sure he'd rather not.

Coming back to the huddle, he collapsed on the field. It became apparent something was wrong when doctors ran onto the field and feverishly administered to him. Long story short, on October 4,1971,Chuck Hughes died on the field—the only player in NFL history to have done so.

Years later, a story reported that Hughes had what now appears to be a first heart attack earlier that season but it is thought that it may have been misdiagnosed at the time. His family sued the hospital and doctors for malpractice and received an out of court settlement,

The entire Detroit Lions team attended Hughes' funeral in San Antonio. People who listened to the game on the radio and who were in attendance still vividly remember the game.

Hughes is still the only NFL player to have died on the field in a regular season game. Rest In Peace, Chuck.

MORE COWBELL

Roger Zatkoff was an All-American at Michigan and he was an All-Pro player at Green Bay more than once and played in several Pro Bowls. Zatkoff had game.

Most people don't know him as Roger though. No most fans would remember him if at all by his nickname, Zany.

Zany Zatkoff was a good player, not just some guy passing through.

Yet he got his name because of his intensity or singleness of purpose.

His trademark was his kick coverage skills or attitude.

Spearing of course was allowed in the 1950's NFL along with other dubious techniques were long ago banished in our more 21st century enlightenment.

Let Zany explain his philosophy in his own words: "My goal was always to see how many guys I could take out at one time during a kickoff."

He would run down and with abandon throw himself though the air sideways to take out two men at a time. The most he ever got on one play was three. His dream was four. But he never got to four.

"I even hit some of my own guys if they got in the way," said Roger...I mean Zany.

He was also a terror in practice. He demanded a trade from Green Bay to be closer to his Michigan home and ended up on the Lions. His teammates were a little bit leery of Zany and his habit for always playing for keeps even in practice.

He even injured a few of his fellow Lions teammates in practice. (We talking about practice!)

One day before practice was to start, the team leader Bobby Layne approached Zany. Layne huddled up the team around Zany and told Zany the only way they would allow him to practice with them was if he wore a necklace of cow-bells that Layne put around his neck.

The Lions reasoned that maybe if they couldn't see him coming they could at least hear him coming.

And Layne wasn't kidding.

GERALD FORD

Gerald Ford, the 38th President of the United States, was from Michigan, served nine terms in Congress for Michigan before being appointed to the Vice Presidency and eventually rose to the office of the President when Richard Nixon resigned.

He was also an All-American football player at Michigan. Offered contracts by the both the Detroit Lions and Green Bay Packers, Ford received a letter from Curly Lambeau with an offer of $110 a game to play for the Packers. The Lions offered $200 a game.

Instead, he went to Yale to pursue his law school ambitions.

It worked out.

MONKEY BUSINESS

In 1934 the Detroit Zoo had a celebrity chimpanzee named Jo Mendi.

Jo had been a star on Broadway, vaudeville, and the movies. You can find a video of Jo driving a car and changing a tire on YouTube.

The Lions signed Jo Mendi to an NFL contract as a publicity stunt in 1935, the year the team moved from Portsmouth to become the Lions. The Detroit papers wrote many articles about it.

The coach of the Lions is quoted as saying about Jo, "He looks like good material but he needs discipline, we don't want any Prima Donnas on this club."

Pictures were taken of Jo Mendi wearing a Lions jersey with the number 0.

Jo was a star. Known as "the gentleman chimpanzee" in the national press, he had appeared in Dayton, Tennessee dressed up in a morning coat, bowler hat, and cane for the entire Scopes Monkey Trial. While there, he played the piano, posed for photographers, and even drank a coke at the local soda fountain.

When Jo died in 1935, h ewas replaced by other "Jo Mendi's." Jo had built a strong brand in Detroit.

Joe Millen, the guy who led the Detroit Zoo said this about Jo Mendi, a chimpanzee who once drew a bigger crowd than a speech by Franklin Delano Roosevelt: "[He was] the greatest doggone monkey that ever lived."

And he was a Detroit Lion.

Jo Mendi for Commissioner of the NFL!

In the early 50's, chlorophyll was ubiquitous in America.

Research had shown, or so the scientist claimed, that chlorophyll—the basic thing that makes plants green—had some amazing properties. One being that it made things smell good.

It soon was used in a variety of products like Clorets, the green gum that is still around. It was used in toothpaste, cigarettes, mouthwash, the formula for Palmolive (which had been around for decades but was changed to add chlorophyll.)

In the early 1950s, the green supplied by chlorophyll was everywhere in the American popular consciousness.

Such a sensation was chlorophyll that the *Detroit Free Press* had an article with the headline "The Year of Green" about the chlorophyll craze. The Lions players adopted a slogan that 1953 season: "Chlorophyll will put more sock in your jock."

In 1953 the Detroit Lions played the Cleveland Browns for the NFL Championship. Bobby Layne, the Lions starting quarterback, said that the Lions wives (as a paen or spoof of chlorophyll and the Lion slogan) did something interesting.

Up in the stands that day of the 1953 NFL Championship game—a game the Lions won—the Detroit Lions wives all wore hats fashioned out of jockstraps that they had dyed green.

Yes, you read that correctly.

GENIUS AT WORK

Hunk Andeson has quite a football resume.

Hunk played and was named All-American at Notre Dame under Knute Rockne and Hunk was named Rockne's successor after the tragic plane crash that took Rockne's life.

Hunk also was appointed head coach of the Chicago Bears during World War II while George Halas was serving his country in the Pacific as a member of the United States Navy.

Hunk was the coach who, while with the Bears, enticed Bronko Nagurski out of retirement (with help from a bigger paycheck by Halas).

Halas called Hunk Anderson, "the greatest line coach of all time."

Hunk is credited with pioneering the new blocking techniques required to address changes wrought by the adoption of the T Formation offense and for innovating many defensive other tactics.

When my dad, Ed, was playing for the LA Rams in the late 40's they played against Hunk Anderson's defense when he was with the Bears. The Rams had George Trafton as their line coach at that time and he had coached in Chicago.

My dad told me that Trafton told the Rams before the Bears game that he knew what Hunk Anderson was telling his defensive squad before they went onto the field to battle the Rams that day, as Hunk always gave the same succinct pep talk to his defense.

Tarfton said it went like this, "If you go out on that field don't come back to this bench unless you have an eyeball in one hand and a left nut in the other!"

So, with that in mind, let us wade into a glimpse of defensive genius.

Detroit Lions center great Alex Wojiehowicz gives us an eyewitness peek into one of the great strategies of a defensive genius.

Hunk was the coach of the Lion defense this fateful day that the awesome Chicago Bears—the fabled "The Monsters of the Midway"—came to town to play the Lions.

Wojiehowicz told this story to Myron Cope in his fabulous book, *The Game That Was*.

The Bears were a rough tough team with a reputation to match and Hunk Anderson, a former Bear himself, had a special strategy waiting for them.

After the kickoff went into the endzone, setting the Bears up at their own 20 yard line, Hunk told his defensive players to line up 7-on-7 at the line of scrimmage. He told his men to, as soon as they snap the ball, just hit all seven members of the line right in the face.

And so they did.

Hunk surmised that the officials would only give them one 15 yard penalty. He was right.

Wojiehowicz said it sounded like "bang, bang, bang" all the way down the line. Kind of like synchronized swimming without the water.

But Hunk wasn't finished. He also instructed his defense to hit the Bears in the face on the first three plays. After three snaps and three' 15 yard penalties the Bears were on the Lions 35 yard line.

One thing to remember is that in the NFL at that time the linemen did not have facemasks. So the punches were received "right in the puss." In fact, HOF Bears lineman Joe Stydahar, a big dude, went to the bench after the first play bleeding profusely from his face, according to Wojiehowicz.

The Bears never made it past the Lions 35 for the rest of the game and the Lions won the game 10-0.

Genius?

You be the judge.

THE CURSE

Bobby Layne is in the Pantheon of truly great NFL quarterbacks. When he retired he held the NFL record for attempts, completions, yards and touchdown passes among other records. He was the starting quarterback on three Lions NFL Championship teams in six years (1952 to 1957).

He was traded in 1958 to the Pittsburgh Steelers.

Layne was traded, among other reasons, for his reputation of hard drinking and such. It was also widely believed he was involved in gambling and shaving points, something never proven and that he always steadfastly denied.

It is rumored he was not too happy about the trade to Pittsburgh and said the Lions, because of the trade, would not win again for fifty years.

Hence the Curse of Bobby Layne.

There is no confirmation of him actually saying this, but...

In the next fifty years the Lions had the worst winning percentage of any NFL team and are still one of the only 4 NFL franchises never to have played in a Super Bowl.

In 2008, on the 50th anniversary of the curse, the Lions were the first team in NFL history to go 0-16.

The next year they drafted Matthew Stafford with the first overall pick in the draft. Stafford graduated from the same high school as Bobby Layne.

Voodoo symmetry?

Layne was the last player to play in the NFL without a face mask. *Sports Illustrated* called him the toughest QB who ever lived. Bobby Layne is also given credit for inventing the 2 minute drill. HOFer Doak Walker, fellow Texan and opponent at SMU turned teammate, said of Layne: "Bobby Layne never lost a game...time just ran out on him."

OUT OF THIS WORLD

In the 11th round of the 1986 NFL draft, the Detroit Lions selected Melvin Leland, WR, Richmond.

Leland was the all-time leader in receptions at Richmond and was a two-time honorable mention All-American. He was injured in Lions camp. The following year he came back and was injured again. He went to training camps with the Dallas Cowboys and the Toronto Argonauts but injuries ended his playing career.

So, what's he doing here?

Leland received a BS in Chemistry from Richmond and went on to become an engineer. His research led him to a job that only 555 people in the history of the Earth and only 362 Americans have ever held.

That's right, the Detroit Lions drafted an astronaut.

Leland flew on two space shuttle flights on STS-122 and STS-129 as a space station mission specialist. He logged 565 hours in space. His career as an astronaut was almost scuttled by a training injury that caused him to completely lose his hearing. A small device made out of Styrofoam called a Valsalva was not put into his training vehicle when it was lowered into a five-million gallon water tank to simulate space walks. The pressure damaged his hearing.

He was rushed to a hospital and it took two full years for his hearing to be restored. His brain had somehow severed its connection to his ears and according to Leland, who is a scientist after all, he attributes his hearing restoration to the brain's unbelievable ability to adjust to injury.

Leland is described as "...one of the most inspiring and influential NASA astronauts of all time."

JOHN HANCOCK

The Detroit Silverdome is no more.

There was an auction of various and sundry things at the former home of the Detroit Lions, a place where Barry Sanders ran amuck as possibly the greatest running back in NFL history.

Before the Siverdome was demolished a guy named Mike Kozan was struck by perhaps you could call it inspiration. Let's.

He bid $23 for a urinal from the Detroit Lions locker room. He later carried it down to a mall where Barry Sanders was signing autographs. Earlier Sanders had tweeted that he would not sign a urinal.

But Barry Sanders is a nice guy. He said he had a change of heart when he saw the guy had brought the urinal all the way down to the event and stood in line. Barry signed the urinal. He says he won't do that again.

Kozan sold the urinal for $3000 on eBay.

GOLD RECORD

Lem Barney, the all-time great Lion, was playing golf. He had a thought that Marvin Gaye, one of his favorite Motown artists, lived nearby. He had some time to kill before practice. He asked around if anyone could point him toward Gaye's home. A hometown guy, Gaye was very famous and so sure, a lot of people knew where he lived. Barney drove over and knocked on the door. Gaye answered and recognized Barney. After all, he was famous too.

Gaye was a big Lions fan. They hit it off and had a great visit when Barney realized he had to race to practice. He told Mel Farr about just meeting Gaye and hanging out. Farr was blown away.

Gaye, at that time, was going through some tough times. Tammy Terrell, his partner on tour and on some great Motown hits, had collapsed in his arms at a concert and was diagnosed with a brain tumor that would debilitate her and, sadly, end her life. Gaye was in a deep funk around the time he met Barney.

He started hanging with Barney and Mel Farr.

Record executives were hounding Gaye to record, but he was depressed—not only by his personal problems but by the state of the world: Vietnam, protests, civil rights activism...the country was in turmoil.

Eventually Barney and Farr convinced Marvin Gaye to go back into the studio and he did, recording one of his greatest hits, 1971's *What's Going On.*

However, Gaye insisted he wouldn't do it unless Barney and Farr sang backup on the record. Even though they had little musical experience (or talents) they did it. They even both received gold records.

Gaye had other ideas that included his new buds Barney and Farr. He wanted them to get him, Marvin Gaye, a tryout with the Lions.

Barney and Farr were of course skeptical but went to Joe Schmidt, the GM and a Hall of Famer who, as it turned out, was a big Gaye fan.

Schmidt said, "No." Then Schmidt changed his mind.

Gaye had thrown himself into the idea: he quit drugs, started working out, and even put on thirty pounds of muscle.

He was serious.

The Lions had a tryout for about twenty guys one day and Schmidt decided that, yes, Marvin Gaye could come out and try out. He did.

The Lions decided that he just wasn't a candidate. He accepted this and at least he got his chance to show what he could do.

Gaye revived his recording career and the bad habits that a musical star falls prey to: hangers on, drugs, and a lot of destructive things. Barney and Farr, still friends, saw it coming.

A music legend with some of the most soulful and impactful music of his time and beyond, Gaye was tragically shot and killed by his father. But not before he got gold records for two fans—Lions legends Lem Barney and Mel Farr—and not before he got to try out for the Detroit Lions.

TAMPA BAY

SayBrah®

GREAT WHITE SHARK

TAMPA BAY

LB

**INDENTURED SERVANTS,
A PARROT, CARLI LLYOD**

TAMPA BAY

When asked about his team's execution:
"I'm in favor of it."

—John McKay,
Bucs Head Coach ('76–84)

SayBrah®

The NFL awarded Tampa an expansion franchise in 1974 and the Buccaneers (who are billed as playing in Tampa Bay because pirates, water...you get it) began league play in 1976.

They suffered through a winless season in their first year in league play. in fact they lost 26 straight games before winning their first NFL game.

Super Bowl Appearances: 1
Super Bowl Record: 1-0 (2002)

Tampa Bay, under the ownership of Hugh Culverhouse, could not be called a success where it counts most—on the field.

All you have to do is look at some of the moves Tampa made off the field to figure out why the issues added up in Tampa.

The Bucs were in position to get the number one overall pick in 1986. And not only that, they were in position to choose perhaps the greatest athlete of his generation, Bo Jackson.

Somehow, if you are to believe Bo, Culverhouse found a way to screw it up.

Jackson was in the middle of his senior baseball season at Auburn and tearing it up. Speculation was that he could play either sport at the highest level.

Culverhouse invited him to come to Tampa for a visit to have him checked medically and to get acquainted—pre-draft due diligence. That was against NCAA and SEC rules if Tampa paid for the visit. They did. But not before telling Bo that they had had it cleared with the NCAA. They didn't.

Bo thought they had lied to him so he would become ineligible to play baseball and that way he was more likely to sign with Tampa Bay to play football.

He was immediately declared ineligible to play baseball at Auburn, ending his college baseball career in the middle of the season.

He was so angry that he warned the Bucs and Culverhouse that if they drafted him he would not sign.

All smiles on draft day, the Bucs selected Bo Jackson with the first overall pick in the draft. True to his word, Bo refused to sign and played baseball with the Kansas City Royals instead.

After a year had passed and with Bo still not signing with the Bucs, his name was re-entered into the pool of eligible players for the NFL draft. A star baseball player by that time, the Oakland Raiders drafted him in the 7th round.

Bo Jackson went on to become the only player in history to be an All-Star in both MLB and the NFL.

Good job, Mr. Culverhouse.

Keeping your brand out there.

OHFER

When a city receives an NFL team it is a reason for civic celebration.

Sometimes however there are growing pains.

1976 Tampa Bay gets the call to the NFL and into legend.

Unfortunately it was the 0-14 season and the 26 losing games in a row before their first NFL win that branded the Bucs in the beginning.

It started off quickly.

The first regular season game in Tampa Bay Bucs history was in the Houston Astrodome.

Coach John McKay, who had made a name for himself with Collegiate National Championship teams at Southern Cal led his team from the field after pre game warmups into the bowels of the Astrodome. They got lost. The whole team: the coaches, the players, the trainers. Everyone. A security guard found them and led them to the locker room.They almost didn't make it to the field in time to lose 20-0.

Things just got worse. They were shut out five times.They became punchline fodder on *The Tonight Show*.

Quarterback Steve Spurrier said that once there were thirteen players in the huddle during a game and Coach McKay screamed for the extra idiots to get off the field. When the huddle broke there were only 4 players left on the field.

McKay bristled at the failure. He was combative with the press. Once telling the Tampa press that they didn't know the difference between a football and a bunch of bananas.

After his next press conference someone left a bunch of bananas at his office door.

His reaction? At the next press conference he told the press that they didn't know the difference between a football and a Mercedes Benz.

At the end of the season McKay, one of the funnier guys to ever coach in the NFL, told the departing players that he hoped to see them next season and to the ones who were planning to stay in Tampa for the off season that they should stop by this office to get fake noses and mustaches so no one would recognizes their sorry asses.

McKay said during the season that his team would be back. "Maybe not this century but we will be back."

They made the playoffs in 1979.

MONEY MONEY MONEY

Phillip Buchanon was drafted number 17 overall in the 2002 NFL draft by the Oakland Raiders and was given a contract with a bonus in excess of $4 million. That's when his troubles started.

Buchanon went on to have a pretty successful career on the field. However, after a nine-year NFL career in which he earned $20 million bucks he left football, by his own account, $500,000 in the hole.

Buchanon chalks his financial bottom line to being too easy of a touch when it came to friends and family. Right after he signed his first contract his mother informed him he owed her one million dollars for raising him.

Buchanon claims this was news to him as he asserts that he actually moved out of his mother's house when he was seventeen and still in high school because he did not feel secure there. He moved in with a friend.

He did purchase a house for his mother.

As time went on his mother, who did not pay the mortgage, maintenance or upkeep on the home, complained she could not afford to keep the place up.

Philip blames himself for buying a home that was too extravagant. He told his mom he could no longer pay all her bills but he would buy her another more modest home. She balked, saying among other things, that she would not move into a house unless it had two living rooms. Finally she accepted a $15,000 payment in lieu of a new home. Eventually her home was foreclosed on.

Buchanon has turned out to be quite the entrepreneur. After his playing days he wrote a book, *New Money: Staying Rich*, a guide to explain and give advice to those, like him, who come into quick windfalls of cash. He tells his reader that if they, like him, come into huge amounts of money overnight, "your fun friends and family will view you as a walking ATM."

He seemed to know from which he speaks here as he also says that his family and friends were constantly coming to him with problems that needed to be fixed. He would always oblige them with a check, "...only thing is, the problems would never get fixed but the checks would always get cashed."

This is sadly an all too common story in professional athletics. Family and friends and unscrupulous or incompetent financial advisors destroy or purloin the money of the player.

Buchanon says he wrote *New Money: Staying Rich* to give a blueprint or a warning to others. The promotional materials for the book say, "This book is on a mission to teach the youth of today an important lesson in financial literacy."

He also invented a board game by the same name that is described as a modern day Monopoly. And still another game, this one a party game version of Twister entitled "Twerkin' It," a game with a purpose of spicing up your next party.

All in all, I guess Phillip Buchanon's mother didn't raise no fool.

TWEET THIS!

T witter is a window to the soul.

Miko Grimes' husband Brett Grimes, played cornerback, and very well, for the Miami Dolphins before his wife, Miko, helped get him traded to the Tampa Bay Bucs by, according to her, a calculated move via use of Twitter.

Is it possible Donald Trump noticed the power of Twitter from Miko? Maybe not. Others of course did notice. Headlines blared in the *New York Post*: "EPIC ANTI-SEMITIC RANT." In a little capsule we'll call "If Words Could Talk."

Miko Grimes:

> "Gotta respect ross for keeping
> his jew buddies employed but
> did he not see how tannenbaum
> put the jets in the dumpster

w/that sanchez deal?"

NFL commentator Jay Glazer :
"At this point I'm asking @iheartmiko
please SHUT THE F#$K UP! Sincerely
the Jew buddy of your husband
who first got him to train in MMA."

Miko Grimes:
"@JayGlazer "Suck my d^*k!"

Stephen Ross, owner of the Miami Dolphins commented, "I think everybody knows what she represented. I thought it was best that the Dolphins move on from Brett and Miko."

Other analysis from Mrs. Grimes: Miko went on a radio show to claim that the Oakland Raiders offensive line, which is all black, allowed Derek Carr to be injured because they had disputes over the National Anthem protests. Offensive tackle Donald Penn and other Raiders went on Twitter to say that it was BS in no uncertain terms.

Miko was arrested at a Dolphin game and charged with disorderly conduct, battery of a police officer and resisting arrest with violence upon a police officer.

Another tweet she made was in reference to 9/11:

> "Jet fuel can't melt steel beams
> because I'm a scientist now"

SAPP THE KNIFE

Warren Sapp, Tampa Bay all time great and Hall-of-Fame player, was lobstering in the Florida Keys. A shark bit him. That's right, a shark bit him.

In his own words, "I was sticking my hands in a hole and a monster locked on me. You gotta be careful sticking your hand down some holes down here."

He got a nasty bite on his arm.

PETA, the animal rights group, sent Sapp a vegan lobster.

BOOK COOKING

The Tampa Bay Bucs, an NFL franchise worth just south of two billion dollars according to *Forbes,* filed a claim with the BP oil administrators that they should be paid $20 million due to negative impact from the BP oil spill in the Gulf of Mexico.

The court ruled that the claim was dubious because of "an unjustified departure from an established accounting practice."

The team used different fiscal dates than they usually used to calculate some of the claims and the court found this to be according to press reports, "dubious, bogus, accounting chicanery" and other uncomplimentary descriptions of the Bucs arguments.

Nonetheless the Tampa Bay Bucs appealed the decision and lost again.

Not a good look.

ALMOST GONE

One thing leads to another.

Professional sports teams are fond of calling the team we root for as *Your* Cleveland Browns or *Your* Baltimore Colts.

Sure.

In 1995 the NFL was in flux as teams were moving and threatening to move mostly over stadium issues.

Raiders were moving back to Oakland and Los Angeles to St. Louis. The Colts had abandoned Baltimore for Indianapolis in 1983 and the Cardinals had moved to Arizona, and the Cleveland Browns announced they were leaving Cleveland in 1996 for Baltimore.

Musical franchises, suddenly, *Your* team was somebody else's.

NFL franchises are sought after commodities for cities. They are brand rich assets of almost incalculable value. When moves are afoot the blood is in the water.

When the Browns or more to the point Art Modell decided to move to Baltimore it set off a lot of maneuvering.

In Cincinnati the Bengals were angling for a new stadium. The NFL was scrambling to mollify the city of Cleveland with promises of an expansion team or relocation of *Your* team.

Right after the Browns announced the move WBAL of Baltimore had a report on what was going on behind the scenes.

The Bengals and Mike Brown were holding the possibility of moving out of Cincinnati by demanding a ballot referendum to finance a new stadium.

The threat included moving the Bengals to Cleveland. Yep.

As it turns out it was like an action thriller with an atomic bomb on red integer clock ticking off and with literally only two minutes to go before Mike Brown pulled the trigger on the move the city of Cincinnati came up with its offer to put the stadium initiative on the ballot. It passed and the Bengals got the new stadium.

The NFL meanwhile promised Cleveand a new team in 1999. The league also proposed to Cleveland they could keep the Browns history and name for any new team.

Modell then needed a new name. If the Bengals moved to Cleveland that name could have been, now wait for this—Baltimore Bengals.

The city of Cleveland would rather have a existing team and there were candidates.

The most logical choice because of franchise availability and lack of fan support was the Tampa Bay Buccaneers.

Yes, the Tampa Bay Buccaneers almost became the Tampa Bay Browns or new Cleveland Browns.

Whoa!

Of course all involved claimed this was nonsense but for the silence of Buccaneer owner Malcolm Glazer who had no comment.

SHADE

Rookie place-kicker Matt Gay missed a 34 yard field goal as time expired against the Carolina Panthers on September 22, 2019. The Tampa Bay Bucs lost the game 34-33.

Gay had also missed a PAT and had another PAT blocked that game. Not a good day.

Then the next week Secret Deodorant swung into action with a bit of pointed shade. Secret, put out an ad featuring Women's Olympic Soccer Team Captain Carli Lloyd kicking a field goal.

The copy of Secret's ad said "Hey Bucs fans, do you sweat 34 yard field goals? Carli Lloyd doesn't."

Lloyd had during the preseason practice between the Philadelphia Eagles and Baltimore Ravens demonstrated her field goal kicking skills by drilling a 55 yard field goal.

Some teams have said to have interest in Lloyd as a possible field goal kicker after her Olympic career winds down.

MATCHMAKER

Steve Young in an interview with "MMQB" of *Sports Illustrated* tells this strange tale.

In 1985 Young was quarterbacking the Tampa Bay Bucs against the Colts.

At some point in the game one of the referees taps him on the shoulder. He asks Young if he can have a word with him.

The referee, during the game now, on the field, takes him out of the huddle, tells Young that his daughter is attending BYU—Young's alma mater—and that he thinks Young should date her. Young asks her name, the ref tells him, and back to the huddle Young goes.

As game progresses, Young is hit in what he describes as a brutal hit near the end of the game. Young fumbles. Then a yellow flag appears. The ref calls a personal foul on the Colts. The Bucs retain possession. Otherwise they lose the ball and the game is over.

As the ref passes Young after the call he whispers to Young, "She likes Italian food."

BRAD JOHNSON GATE

In a story in *The Tampa Times*, Brad Johnson, starting quarterback in Tampa Bay's 48-21 win in Super Bowl XXXVII, admits to paying some guy or guys $7,500 to scuff up and break in the 100 footballs the league supplied for the Super Bowl. He did this to make the balls more simpatico for him.

The NFC Championship game was played in inclement weather and Johnson had trouble gripping the balls. They were cold, wet and, even those that came out of the box new and shiny, Johnson didn't find those to his liking either.

This was like twelve years before the celebrated ball tampering hoopla of Deflategate.

In 2006 the league changed a rule that would allow quarterbacks to scuff up the balls before games. Before 2006, only the home team quarterback was allowed to do this.

But when Johnson paid $7,500 to doctor the balls to suit him, it was against the rules.

PARROT GM

On the third day of the NFL Draft 2018, the Tampa Bay Bucs went to Twitter to introduce, "Zsa Zsa, a catalina macaw parrot, who will announce our 4th pick."

Anticipation was high as the third day of the NFL draft can drag on.

The parrot was brought out onto the deck of the Tampa Bay Buc pirate ship at Raymond James stadium on the arm of a young lady dressed in pirate gear.

The parrot didn't say a damn thing. Maybe on advice of its lawyer.

The young lady announced the pick, which turned out to be Jordan Whitehead of Pitt.

The internet was not amused. They were pissed. They felt jobbed by the Bucs who seem to have a way of screwing up the draft in ever more creative ways as time goes on.

One choice Tweet from @LeviDamien: "Parrot is clearly a glaring need for Bucs. Look for them to trade up for one in this round."

It may be pointed out that the previous year's NFL draft featured a draft pick executed by an orangutan. (see Colts chapter 16).

INDENTURED SERVANTS

W hat?

Yep.

It was reported by the *Tampa Bay Times* in December of 2014 and also chronicled in *Atlantic Magazine* that the Tampa Bay Buccaneers were using a group called New Beginnings to have homeless destitute men work in concessions selling hot dogs and beers and not paying them.

New Beginnings called it "work therapy" in which the money earned went to New Beginnings to compensate the church group for the $600 cost of rent. Labor experts called it "legal human trafficking" and also characterized it as "indentured servitude."

Investigations ensued and the Tampa Bay Bucs and other sports teams like the Rays and Lightning also distanced themselves from New Beginnings and its director, Tom Atcheson, who was once honored as a "community hero" and was, at that time, the pastor of New Life Pentecostal Church of Tampa.

FUBAR

P erhaps the most notorious screw up in Tampa Bay Buccaneer history involves the unprecedented actions of the team during the NFL draft of 1982. What transpired that day in the first round had never happened before and has never happened since.

When it was the Tampa Bay Bucs' turn to hand in their first-round pick, equipment manager Pat Marcucillo, who was in New York as the team's representative tasked with handing in the official draft card, gave the card with the wrong name on it.

No? Yes.

The Bucs brain trust, GM, owner, scouts, coaches were in a draft war room in Tampa, watching. When the pick was announced as Sean Farrell, guard out of Penn State and a highly rated player, there was, at first, a prolonged silence in the room. Followed closely by a tirade of cursing and such.

The Bucs had narrowed down their first pick to either Farrell, the guard from Penn State, or a raw freakish athlete out of Bethune Cookman, a small HBCU by the name of Booker Reese. GM Ken Herock made the call to go with Reese.

But, the communication equipment was, by today's standards, primitive. Marcucillo had been given two cards, one with Farrell's name, the other with Reese's name. The arguing over who to pick went down to the wire, Herock called New York, told Marcucillo something to the order of "We are not going with Farrell we want you to give the card with Reese's name."

Only problem, in the confusion and excitement of the moment and the less than favorable sound quality, Marcucillo only heard Farrell's name.

One of the contributing factors probably was that the draft was held in New York City with a live crowd on hand. The NY Giants pick was up next, which caused a large and growing hub-bub among Giant fans in anticipation of the Giants imminent pick.

The Bucs tried to get the NFL to change the pick. They wouldn't.

For the record, Sean Farrell turned out to be a fine player in the league, playing 11 seasons and making the Pro Bowl.

He had been called just minutes before he was picked by the Bucs to tell him that they were high on him but had decided not to pick him. Then, as he watched TV a few minutes after, came the call that the Bucs picked him. He was confused and surprised.

The draft continued and the plot, at least for the Bucs, thickens.

As the draft continued, Herock realized that his first choice, the freakish athlete Booker Reese, was still available. Herock moved into action trading his number one in the 1983 draft to get the pick to pick Reese.

Well, beside the fact that the 1983 NFL draft turned out to be one of the most talent rich hauls of all time—John Elway, Jim Kelly, Dan Marino, Eric Dickerson, Bruce Matthews, and Darrel Green, to name a few—Reese turned out to be not ready for prime time, on the field or off the field.

As an example, Reese, who was described as a nice affable guy, was given a $150,000 signing bonus. The day he got his check the Bucs got a phone call from a car dealer who told them they had a problem.

The problem turned out to be that Reese had stopped at the dealership and purchased a Firebird for himself and a truck for his mother.

So far, so good.

When asked how he would pay for the cars, the salesman was given the $150,000 check and told by Reese, "Take it out of here and give me the change."

Reese just never panned out as a player; he got involved in drugs, would eventually end up in prison, and was out of the league in short order.

His whereabouts after prison are listed as unknown.

A very sad story.

Meanwhile, Sean Farrell went on to prosper.

His stay in Tampa was not enjoyable and is a window as to why the Bucs didn't perform too well on the field in those early years.

After playing in Tampa Bay, where players were docked between $40-50 for the game balls they were awarded and were also required to fork over 35¢ to buy Cokes while at the training facility, he was quoted as saying, "I know what I want for Christmas. I want to get the hell out of Tampa Bay."

He did.

TENNESSEE

SayBrah®

Fox

TENNESSEE

WR

KURDISTAN, CUPCAKES, VEGANS

TENNESSEE

"Whether its one play in the NFL or 1000 plays in the NFL, your pads will come off eventually."

—Myron Rolle,
Rhodes Scholar

SayBrah

Tennessee Titans were born as the Houston Oilers one of the original AFL franchises with Bud Adams as the owner.

The Oilers left Houston and relocated to Memphis for a year then played in Nashville at Vanderbilt University Stadium while awaiting the construction of a new stadium.

Bud Adams owned the team until his death and his family retains ownership of the team.

Super Bowl Appearances: 1
Super Bowl Record: 0-1
Super Bowl Loss: 1999

It all started by going to practice. Teams give away stuff. Stuff you don't need and ya don't want.

But, aha, the Crazy Titan Lady thought, "What can I do with these flags?" And her new identity emerged and it is as her daughter says, "Something that makes her happy." And what's the matter with that? Edwin Starr: "Absolutely nothing."

Lorrita Turnley took those giveaway Titans flags and in the best traditions of American primitive folk art, and sewed them together with a Titans pillow she had gotten at Goodwill and went with it.

Now her bedroom is a Titans Cave filled with her creations. It seems like every inch of it. Four times a week she goes "Goodwillering," as she calls it, to collect new material for her passion.

She has a Facebook page but she only accepts the worthy, real Titans fans. Those committed to her team. She has a motto: "Titan up but don't lighten up."

Ms. Turnley is a prime example of the human face and heart of NFL fandom.

What if you had a pro football league and nobody came? Indeed.

MEMPHIS

When the Oilers moved to Tennessee from Houston they played their first season in Memphis. To hear Memphis talk about this, it was not a good thing.

Memphis had tried to get into the NFL many times and failed. They were in the WFL, and had Larry Csonka. They were in the USFL. They, along with Carolina, Jacksonville, Baltimore and St. Louis, all vied for NFL expansion in 1998. Only Memphis, of those cities, has failed to ever secure its own NFL franchise.

Along comes Bud Adams and the Oilers. The team played in Memphis but lived and trained in Nashville, traveling to Memphis to play each home game.

Titans, as they were renamed, planned a parade in Memphis to welcome the team. According to Eddie George, the team's star running back, about 150 people showed up for the parade. Attendance was never good because they were just using Memphis, according to long time Memphians.

There is a rivalry between the two cities and this didn't help. But mostly it was that the Oilers/Titans did little to ingratiate themselves to Memphis. After one year they left for Nashville even though the stadium wasn't finished. They played in Vanderbilt's stadium that second year.

NAME GAME

Some reports are that Bud Adams when he moved the Oilers to Tennessee wanted to keep the Oilers name but found out that that was not a good idea after the move to Memphis. He had a change of heart and suggestions were entertained as Adams thought eventually the people of Tennessee at least the football fans should have a voice in the name.

According to *Houston Chronicle* sports writer John McLain Bud Adams had chosen Pioneers as the new name but before he could announce it the name was leaked, some people believe by a source in Memphis, at that point Adams withdrew the name and replaced it with Titans.

Why? There is no answer as to why this was an issue with Adams that I could find.

The Titans name was problematic because the Jets used to be called the New York Titans when the league first formed in 1959 and there was thought that permission would be needed to use the name or something,

Other names that were in consideration were Tornadoes, Stars, Copperheads and Cherokees.

Owner K. S. "Bud" Adams was a member of the Cherokee Nation for those wondering about that last one.

Nonetheless, the Tennessee Titans were almost named the Tennessee Pioneers.

BUD ADAMS THE YOUNGER

Bud Adams moved the Houston Oilers to Tennessee which of course did not endear him to the football fans of Houston.

Adams' image in Tennessee was that of an elderly team owner perhaps whose day had come and gone, yet there was another side of Adams, one of the main architects of the AFL or "The Foolish Club" as the AFL owners called themselves. That the AFL even existed was due to Mr. Adams efforts.

It was only business that led to Nashville.

In the 1960's Al Davis had been named the Commissioner of the AFL and at an owners meeting at the Shamrock Hotel in Houston Mr. Davis was introduced.

Houston sports writer Jack Gallagher walked in and Bud Adams who was smarting from an assertion in print, by Mr. Gallagher, that the Oilers were run with the efficiency of the Cuban government—which at that time was not in favor in U. S. popular opinion—greeted Gallagher who was bald with "Hello, Skinhead." One thing led to another and soon as it was described in *Sports Illustrated* a "rolling slugfest" and it was rollicking across the floor with Bud Adams on top of Gallagher.

New Commish Al Davis and Buffalo Bills owner Ralph Wilson broke it up.

A photo of Adams on top of Gallagher with appendages at strange angles went out on the national wire. The good ole days when pro football owners meetings were the MMA of their day.

VEGANS

It's a new world, brah.

The Tennessee Titans have a cabal, fifteen by my last count, of players who are on a vegan diet and swear by it.

Football is a tough game and the conventional wisdom is or was that you need to eat meat. "Not so," say the vegan advocates.

Titans cornerback Derrick Morgan's wife is a cordon bleu trained chef and she started preparing Derrick meals and other players saw them, smelled them and one by one Charity Morgan started cooking vegan meals for as many Titans who signed up.

The players think it works to their advantage, claiming that it helps speed recovery, decreases inflammation and increases their energy. It also helps keep their weight down. Which is a problem for some players.

Tom Brady uses a vegan regimen as of late, although he does add some meat during the colder weather.

If some of the Titans get to the Super Bowl with this new dietary course in a copycat league soon you may see a lot more Jackfruit cheese steaks and seitan burgers at NFL training tables.

VINCE YOUNG

Vince Young was a hero, is a hero.

He led Texas to a College Championship win against the juggernaut USC team of Reggie Bush and Matt Leinart in one of the most classic National Championship games ever.

And you can't take that away from him.

Chosen third overall by the Titans and paid somewhere between $25 and $35 million, guaranteed, you'd think he was on his road to success.

Well, it didn't work out like that.

Shakespeare could write a tragedy about it. Maybe even Arthur Miller.

NFL offensive Rookie of the Year and a winning record as Tennessee starting QB notwithstanding, Vince Young's pro career was an opportunity missed. A few years later Young ended up out of football and in debt. Some reports of his earnings in the NFL were as high as $50 million.

How can this happen?

Well the theories are, according to him and his family, betrayal by unscrupulous financial advisers. One of them was his uncle.

Or...

Jeff Fisher didn't like him. He was the head coach of the Titans. Or... it could be his lavish lifestyle. Reportedly spending $15,000 at Cheesecake Factory, or buying all the seats on a Southwest airliner for a trip back home or borrowing $300,000 to throw himself a birthday party when his financial advisor told him he couldn't afford it.

He now says he didn't pay attention to his money until his career was over. Okay. Vince Young, as an NFL prospect at the pre-draft combine, scored a reported 5 out of 50 on the dreaded Wonderlic test. The Wonderlic test is supposed to measure something that is of some interest to NFL teams about players coming out of college.

One thing is clear, all too many of these young athletes are often not anywhere near ready for the infusion of cash they receive overnight. It is estimated that 78% of all NFL players are broke 5 years after their playing days.We're talking about a job that has a minimum pay of several $ 100,000 a year.

MYRON ROLLE

Myron Rolle was drafted by the Tennessee Titans in the 6th round of the 2010 NFL draft.

He never played a down in a regular season NFL game.

Rolle was attempting to be only the third player in league history to be both a Rhodes Scholar and an NFL player. The only other player, Byron "Whizzer" White, ended up Justice on the Supreme Court of the United States.

Rolle is an extraordinary man who graduated with a BA from Florida State after only two and half years. He went on to letter at Florida State in football and become third team All-American and, of course, become a Rhodes Scholar.

When he was offered the Rhodes Scholarship, which would be a great step toward his goal of becoming a neurosurgeon, he had to make a tough decision: to accept the scholarship meant he would have to step away from football for a year and put his other great dream of being an NFL player on hold. Plus this would be seen with suspicion by the NFL as a sign he didn't want football enough.

Rolle graduated from Florida State's College of Medicine in 2017 and was matched with a neurosurgery residency with Massachusetts General Hospital and Harvard Medical School.

Dr. Rolle, with family ties to the Bahamas, went to the Bahamas in 2019 to help with the recovery from the devastation of Hurricane Dorian.

BROADWAY

A Heisman Trophy winner is in the spotlight.

Eddie George, 1995 Heisman Trophy Winner and Tennessee Titan (a star running back) has always, from his perspective, thought that life gives numerous opportunities to express your talents.

He has a landscaping business, the result of a landscaping degree from Ohio State University. He has a financial business and he is an actor.

Yes, George pursued an acting career after football. He auditioned for Nashville Community Theater and eventually landed some choice roles, even as Shakepeare's Julius Caesar.

He took this endeavor seriously, as he does most things, and he took acting lessons two or three times a week as well as improv classes.

When the Broadway touring version of *Chicago the Musical* came to Nashville, where he and his wife made their home, his name came up and the producer gave him a look-see.

It paid off for both of them and George got the role of Billy Flynn, a starring role in the musical and ended up appearing in a seven-week run with the company on Broadway.

George doesn't know where his acting chops will bring him but he loves challenges and for this former NFL player there seems to be no limit to his talents.

CUPCAKES?

Many NFL players don't know what to do with themselves after football.

Many start or try to start a business and the high profile provided by the NFL connection usually presents opportunities to come knocking on your door.

Brian Orakpo, a star LB with the Tennessee Titans, got together with former player Michael Griffin and a friend to brainstorm what they might do for an entrepreneurial enterprise. The answer? Cupcakes.

They love Gigi's Cupcakes, a Nashville chain with over a hundred stores nationwide. They, being NFL players, had some money but not much business acumen.

They were diligent learners, immersing themselves in all aspects of the business: opening the shop, decorating the cupcakes, baking the cupcakes, cashiering and closing the shop—the whole nine yards, as it were.

Orapko, the 6' 4", 247 NFL linebacker, called the ordeal of opening and learning and running the cupcake shop, "a grueling process."

COMMUNITY SPIRIT

The Tennessee Titans offensive line, plus Marcus Mariota, can be seen in this video displaying a camaraderie with the Nashville Predators NHL team by... well...pounding tall boys, wearing Predator jerseys, and catfish, too.

It is Nashville.

See for yourself, courtesy of NBC Sports:

⊕ @NHLonNBC on Twitter: "the @Titans are here to paaaaaaaarta-aayyyyyyy..."

BIRYANI Y'ALL

Immigration is a hot button issue in 21st century America as it has often been.

One of the things that seems to be overlooked while the arguments and counter-arguments rage doesn't take into account the strong allure of American culture.

Some of my most educated friends in fact scoff at the idea of "American Culture" as opposed to the easily accepted concept of culture as it pertains to older societies like Italian Culture or Japanese Culture, pick your own fav.

Yet every society young and old has a shared culture just by the fact that we live in the same area are exposed to the same foods, have the choices of whatever the "street" offers, and experience life wherever our particular hineys seem to be at over a given time.

In Nashville these days this is manifested by the burgeoning Kurdish population that now lives in Nashville and the embrace by many Kurds in Tennessee Titan football or more pointedly Titan tailgating.

The young of any ethnicity are drawn to the same things as their peers and add an ethnic mix and you get that spice of variety of life we always refer to.

At a Kurdish tailgate at a Titans game you'll often find a Titan banner alongside the flags of Kurdistan and the USA.

You'll also find unsurprisingly, unfamiliar football fare at a Kurdish tailgate like biryani(a mixed rice dish). kutlik, koftu (a central asian meatball) or stuffed grape leaves on the menu just to name a few of the choices.

The Kurds' in recent times have been one of the staunchest American Allies in the Middle East and Nashville is now the home of the biggest colony of Kurds in the country.

And the NFL now has a notable new Kurdish foothold.

AUTHORS NOTE: *Moslems have been emigrating to America in the last forty years in larger numbers than ever before and as my theory on the strong influence of American culture takes into account newcomers often embrace the new culture in surprising ways.*

Dearborn, Michigan which abuts Detroit has the largest Arab American population in the USA and thus 97% of the students at Fordson High are Arab American and heavily of the Muslim faith and it is not surprising as these new citizens move to the country their children adapt to their new home. One of the results of this meeting of cultures is that the Fordson High football team has become one of the most successful football programs in Michigan high school competition having only four losing season in thirty-eight consecutive years.

A documentary film Fordson: Faith, Fasting, Football *has made the rounds at independent film fests and chronicles the very interesting story of football, America and the adaptation of our institutions. Kind of how that melting pot thing is supposed to work.*

If you were watching the 2020 Super Bowl you might have seen a guy named Robert Saleh who was the defensive coordinator of the San Francisco 49ers.

He played football at Fordson High School in Dearborn, Michigan.

TALLY HO!

When Bud Adams died the ownership of the Tennessee Titans went to his three children. After a brief interlude the team ended up in the hands of Amy Adams Strunk, one of Mr. Adams' daughters.

Ms. Strunk injected a new direction and vigor into the running of the team.

Like many owners Ms. Strunk is a sportswoman herself.

Her sport of choice is not football or tennis or swimming or ...well, if I gave a few guesses it might take you awhile to come up with her sporting passion.

Fox hunting.

Ms. Strunk, an avid horse woman, got the fox hunting bug and is the driving force behind Kenada Fox America, one of the few sanctioned fox hunting clubs in the United States.

It should be noted that North American fox hunting rules are geared toward the hunt and not to killing the fox. Fox hunting if it was on *Star Trek*.

As Kenada is located in Texas, the hunted are often not foxes at all but coyotes.

Coyotes are said to be not as intelligent a quarry as the fox and therefore run a more linear path of escape and as such are not considered as wily an adversary. Yet the coyote brings other attributes to the game. It is more aggressive than the fox and a more able combatant when cornered than your average fox.

A story that goes around Kenada, is of a coyote running into a pond with a row boat in which the coyote jumped into the row boat and one of Ms. Strunks's fellow fox hunters was obliged to wade into a freezing pond to save not only the capsized coyote but the dogs that had followed the adversary into the drink.

Ms. Adams Strunk, her Titans players might like to know, is described thusly by one admirer: "She can ride like the wind and is fierce." She is known by still others in the fox hunting racket as "The Annie Oakley of Texas."

Fox hunting?

The rich are not like you and me.

SIGN LANGUAGE

Bud Adams, the founder of the Houston Oilers and the guy who moved them to Nashville, had quite a life. He was a member of the Cherokee Nation (his uncle, in fact, was the Chief of the Cherokee), he played college football at Kansas with Bob Dole, he was a successful oil wildcatter and prolific art collector.

The most enduring image of him may be, however, his brief post game performance after a 41-17 victory by his Tennessee Titans over the Buffalo Bills in Nashville in 2008. Adams, then eighty-six years old, reacted to the Bills bench or fans by shooting them the bird with both fingers.

Roger Goodell, who at Adams' death a few years later was quoted as saying "Bud had a terrific sense of humor that helped lighten many tense NFL meetings" was at that game and slapped a $250,000 fine on the billionaire owner.

Adams said, "Oh, I knew I was going to get in trouble for that. I was just so happy we won."

It might be noted: Bud Adams: Exuberant filthy gestures. FINE: $250,000. Ray Lewis: Indicted for murder after a Super Bowl. FINE: $250,000.

Anyway.

TOP TEN LIST

After the infamous hand gesture episode at Tennessee Titan game Bud Adams made the Letterman Top Ten list.

As a comedian myself I must say that this Letterman Top Ten List is pretty lame.

Advantage Bud Adams.

BALTIMORE

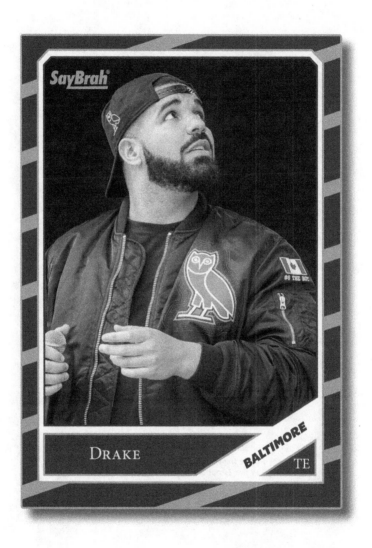

SayBrah®

DRAKE

BALTIMORE

TE

DRAKE, QUEEN ELIZABETH, A MILLION DOLLAR BET

BALTIMORE

SayBrah®

"[Owner Carroll] Rosenbloom gave you the feeling that if you crossed him. He was capable of slitting your throat, then donating the blood to the Red Cross."

—Gene Klein,
Chargers owner (1966-1984)

Baltimore Ravens, formerly the Cleveland Browns, were moved from Cleveland in 1996 by owner Art Modell after he failed to get a new stadium.

An agreement with the league and Cleveland stipulated that the Browns would relinquish the Browns name, logo, and all team records achieved as the Cleveland Browns in Cleveland to be owned by a new Cleveland franchise to be awarded later.

**Super Bowl Appearances (as Ravens): 2
Super Bowl Record: 2-0 (2000, 2012)**

THE DEAL OF THE ART

Art Modell owned the Cleveland Browns for thirty-five years.

Art Modell is given credit for creating the modern NFL prosperity as he negotiated the first lucrative TV deal which, of course, is the lifeblood of the financial success of the league.

Art Modell was also instrumental in the creation of *Monday Night Football*, inarguably an American institution.

Art Modell was a critic of the Baltimore Colts and Oakland Raiders abandonment of their fan bases by relocating to Indianapolis and Los Angeles respectively.

Art Modell moved the Cleveland Browns to Baltimore in 1996.

Art Modell was nominated for the Hall of Fame numerous times.

Art Modell is not in the NFL Hall of Fame.

Art Modell died at the age of 87 in 2001.

There are three stories in this book about bowel movements and Art Modell.

THE DEAL OF THE ART PART 2

It was a stadium deal, or lack thereof, that eventually led Modell to leave Cleveland and never return.

Modell had asked for a referendum to approve taxes to improve Municipal Stadium or he would move the Browns.

About a week before the vote on the referendum he announced he had a deal to move the team to Baltimore.

There is some speculation that Modell wanted the information of the deal made public before the vote so that the vote would fail and he would have an excuse to move.

The referendum passed by a large margin. He moved the team anyway.

When Modell died, the NFL held a moment of silence for him at each league game the week of his death, to acknowledge his long time pivotal role in league business. At the request of his family the Cleveland Browns at their game pretty much ignored the fact of his death to avoid Mr. Modell's death being booed.

EPILOGUE: *Drew Carey is from Cleveland. He had a popular network TV show. One episode featured cameos by notable Clevelanders including former starting quarterback for the Browns Bernie Kosar. At one point in the episode, Kosar asks for directions to the bathroom. Drew Carey obliges with directions but adds, "Just don't take a Modell."*

GRANPAW OF THE BALTIMORE
PRO FOOTBALL TEAM

A brief on the history of the Dallas Texans, the team that would one day become the Baltimore Colts.

In no particular order.

Giles Miller buys the remnants of the Baltimore Colts and moves them to Dallas naming them the Texans. He ends up losing his entire fortune in the process.

The Texans franchise in 1952 is a disaster and ends up as a Hershey, PA-based road team which eventually makes the franchise again available at the end of season for relocation.

Baltimore, which lost its team in the early 50's holds a fundraiser to bring pro football back to town. One of the celebrity fundraisers was Morey Amsterdam of *The Dick Van Dyke Show*.

NFL Commissioner Bert Bell challenged the City of Baltimore to sell 15,000 season tickets in six weeks if it wants in.

Baltimore, under Mayor Thomas D'Alessandro rose to the occasion and bought the tickets in four weeks.

Question: Mayor D'Allessandro is the father of which politician?

Answer: Speaker of the House Nancy Pelosi.

Bert Bell, Carroll Rosenbloom's college football coach at Penn, suggests Rosenbloom buy Colts. Rosenbloom buys Colts.

The city of Baltimore got the Colts back.

Dallas Texans highlights? Lowlights?

Art Donovan who would be one of the few Texans players to end up in Baltimore in 1953 and other players started fires on the field to stay warm.

At the final game the players went into the stands and thanked each fan personally with hand shakes. This is an indication of attendance numbers.

The Coach of the Texans had his players instead of practicing football on game week play volleyball or go to the racetrack after short practices.

Weirdest NFL scouting report ever. Scout reports to the coach of the next opponent: "You won't believe this but he has them playing volleyball over the crossbar."

They would ride into the stadium on game day in full cowboy regalia for a brief time.

Free seats to Texans games were given to any fan who gave a pint of blood.

One Dallas newspaper implored the Texans to trade its black players to Cleveland.

In response to this blatantly racist request by the newspaper, owner Giles Miller—the son of a millionaire and who lost his entire fortune on the Texans—responded with a press release that said "Places on our team are open strictly on the basis of ability without regard to race or creed." This was seen at the time as an impossibly brave and radical statement in Dallas.

Before moving to Hershey, Miller paid his team and he told them: "I'm not telling you your checks are no good. But if I were you I'd run to the bank."

The Tavern on Chocolate Avenue in Hershey, PA became a watering hole of note in the Texans' short life and player lore as fights and drunken shenanigans were the order of the day. Or night. Whatever the case may be.

Carroll Rosenbloom bought the Baltimore franchise and he made his entire investment back in a matter of weeks by selling season tickets. Baltimore is a football town.

GOD SAVE THE QUEEN

The Ravens were to play a regular season game in London in 2017. For a brief moment in time the Ravens, on their official Twitter feed, posted a photo of Queen Elizabeth II with what appeared to be a face painted with the Raven logo. They deleted it quickly but you can still find it on the internet.

The Ravens had an app that allowed you to superimpose faux face paint of either Ravens colors black and purple or a version that looks just like the Raven logo.

We don't know from the Queen so much in NFL fandom but I did read once that, when QEII visited Canada, the press was not allowed within fifteen feet of her.

Silly me. I didn't even know she was dangerous.

TAGLIABUE

Baltimore lost the Colts but the pursuit of an NFL franchise was always on the front burner for Baltimore football fans. Twice NFL expansion loomed and, if you're to believe some informed sources, the fix was in to prevent Baltimore from securing the prize.

Why? The conspiracy theory involves: Jack Kent Cooke, owner of the Washington Redskins, who supposedly didn't want the competition from a team so close to his own.

He had planned a new stadium to be located in Maryland and, more importantly, Cook and NFL Commissioner Paul Tagliabue were old friends.

The first expansion teams that might have gone to Baltimore ended up in Charlotte and Jacksonville.

The second chance to snap up a coveted NFL franchise by moving the LA Rams to Baltimore (ironic since the Rams had been swapped for the Colts) ended with the team relocating instead to St. Louis (from where they would eventually move back to LA).

Tagliabue gets the blame in some circles both times.

After one disappointing chance to get a team, Governor William Schaefer of Maryland (former mayor of Baltimore and a key player in the dramatic loss of the Colts move controversy) is quoted as saying that if Tagliabue ever showed up at Camden Yards to attend a Baltimore Orioles game, "I'm going to have it announced on the loudspeaker that we have the commissioner of football in seat 10 row 14."

There is also a fabulous article written by Ken Rosenthal in the *Baltimore Sun* that sheds quite a bit of light on the attitude of some Baltimore football fans regarding commissioner Tagliabue.

STADIUM OF THE FUTURE

A modern stadium called the Baltodome was proposed but, again, there was no political will to get the money and the project was abandoned in 1974.

The most curious stadium proposal, one that has been mostly lost to history, was all the way back in 1945 when aviation pioneer Glen L. Martin—of Lockheed Martin fame—designed and backed a $100,000 multi-purpose domed stadium that was to have an ⅛ th inch aluminum dome roof to be held up by air pressure from electric fans.

This stadium, which had the backing of many of the civic and business leaders of Baltimore, never got off the drawing board.

This would have been the world's first domed stadium, predating the Houston Astrodome by twenty years. But it did not catch the public's fancy and never came to fruition.

What could have been?

CURSES

There is something about sports fandom that requires some supernatural reason for their teams failures.

The most famous specific curses in sports belong to baseball: "The Curse of The Bambino" in Boston and the "Billy Goat Curse" in Chicago. Both of these have come to and end with recent Red Sox and Cub World Series victories.

And of course there is the "*Sports Illustrated* curse" which goes to anyone who is lucky (or unlucky) enough to appear on the cover and therefore become jinxed and the video game inspired "Madden Cover" curse.

The NFL is peppered by team curses. Among others there are the Saints, Lions, Cardinals, and Dolphins which all claim curses of some kind.

The curses keep on coming.

Lamar Jackson and the Baltimore Ravens entered the 2020 playoffs heavily favored over the Tennessee Titans only to be foiled by the latest sports curse or some would lead you to believe.

This curse is supplied by the popular rapper Drake—a huge sports fan, as he pops up at a lot of sporting events.

Drake is from Toronto and showed up at a Maple Leaf playoff game clad in a Leafs jersey. They lost to the Bruins.

He attended the U.S. Open tennis championships in support of all-time great Serena Williams, the favorite. She lost.

He went on Instagram in an Alabama Crimson Tide sweatshirt before the Tide lost to Clemson in the CFP in 2019.

He is a big Kentucky basketball fan. Since he's become a highly visible Kentucky U fan. Despite top ranked recruiting classes, they have not won a title since 2012.

He appeared at a Conor McGregor weigh-in in support or the UFC champion. McGregor was beaten handily by Kahbib Nurmagodmedov.

This dude, if you believe such things, is not just bringing teams and sports personalities down—he's sinking the cream of the crop: Kentucky Wildcats, Alabama Crimson Tide, Serena Williams, and Conor McGregor.

Drake even went as far to wear four different jerseys during the NFL playoffs in 2019 to dispel this "curse" thing. He wore Patriots, Saints, Rams, and Chiefs gear before the games. Only thing is none of the teams won the game in regulation. The games ended in ties and went into overtime. Even the Cosmos was confused.

So, it wasn't Derrick Henry and the Titans who brought down Lamar Jackson, the de facto MVP of the NFL, in January of 2020.

No, it was the "Drake Curse."

Ravens safety Earl Thomas tweeted after the Ravens-Titans game: "Drake curse is real LOL."

PERSEVERE

Johnny Unitas is from Pittsburgh.

The Steelers drafted him but cut him.

He then played semi-pro for the Bloomfield Rams for $3 a game.

His efforts paid off when he and another teammate were asked to travel to Baltimore to try out for the Colts.

He had to borrow gas money to drive to Baltimore.

They signed him to a $7,000 contract and the rest, after a George Shaw leg injury and a rocky start, is football history. His first pass was a pick 6 and his second series was a missed hand-off to Alan Ameche that resulted in a fumble. It went better from there.

To Canton.

Sports lends itself to legend—Babe Ruth, Michael Jordan, Muhammad Ali, Tiger Woods, Ted Williams—icons all.

It also, in the 20th century, gives us a pipeline of business types who, in our capitalistic system, own the teams and come by money in various ways, becoming stars in the firmament of American popular culture.

Winning racehorse bets (Billy Sullivan, Tim Mara, Art Rooney), industrialists (Ford family), football prowess (George Halas, Al Davis, Paul Brown), the law (Hugh Culverhouse), business success (Arthur Blank, Tom Benson, Daniel Snyder), oil (Jerry Jones, Pat Bowlen, Bud Adams, Lamar Hunt) and the way of royalty to the manor born (Mark Davis, Mike Brown). All of these roads often lead to larger than life personalities.

None more so than Carroll Rosenbloom, whose remarkable life was touched, with varying degrees of separation, to a gallery of the passing American parade of celebrity.

Check out this virtual album of associates and friends.

Rosenbloom, who grew up in Baltimore, claimed to have lived down the street from H.L. Mencken, and that Mencken gave him his first hard crab. Johnny Unitas, one of the greatest QBs ever, was Rosenbloom's employee. LBJ stayed at one of Rosenbloom's properties when running for president because Johnson believed his hotel was being bugged by the Kennedys, who were also friends of Rosenbloom (golfing partners), supping and playing golf with Joseph P. Kennedy. He was in Hyannis Port the day JFK won the presidency playing touch football with the Kennedys, He sent RFK an autographed ball after the Colts victory in the NFL championship game in 1958. He turned down Knute Rockne who wanted him to transfer to Notre Dame to play football (Rosenbloom was a player at Penn at the time), he was part owner of Atlantic City Race Course with, among others, Jack Kelly, Princess Grace's father. Fidel Castro confiscated a casino in Havana that Rosenbloom partly owned and, it is alleged, anyone owning a casino in Cuba in those days had to get the OK of Meyer Lansky. He was a golfing, gambling, and casino partner with Mike McLaney, linked by some Kennedy conspiracy aficionados to CIA training at his property in Louisiana three months before the Kennedy assassination.

When Rosenbloom mysteriously drowned in Florida at the age of seventy-two, foul play was suspected by some.

At the memorial service for Mr. Rosenbloom Jonathan Winters was the emcee with attendance by Hollywood types like Ross Martin and Ricardo Montalban. The memorial ended with Don Rickles performing his act. Quite a send off for a remarkable life that in NFL terms went from coast to coast, Baltimore to Los Angeles to Indinapplois to St. Louis—all across the fruited plain.

By any measure Mr. Rosenbloom had quite a life.

THE SUN ALSO RISES

Haloti Ngata was an inside presence for the Ravens on the defensive line and a very popular player. One thing about being an NFL player who plays awhile is that you end up with a lot of coin. This affords you things that regular people can't have, like expensive things or great experiences. Ngata announced his retirement on Instagram from atop Mount Kilimanjaro.

That's truly going out on top.

THE TRADE

Carroll Rosenbloom owned the Baltimore Colts from 1953 to 1972. They won NFL championships in 1958, 1959 and Super Bowl V. He, along with the owners of the Baltimore Orioles, the MLB team, shared Municipal Stadium, which became older and creakier as time went on and new stadiums became a perk of professional sports owners.

Rosenbloom, by all accounts a can-do guy, decided he had enough and wanted to move to the west coast.

Dan Reeves, long time owner of the Los Angeles Rams, died. His heirs wanted to sell. In fact, Reeves had told Rosenbloom, a friend in Reeves' waning days, that he would be pleased if Rosenbloom ended up with Rams after he had left this mortal coil.

Rosenbloom went into negotiations with the heirs and came up with a brilliant idea: he would find someone to buy the Rams, and he would swap even-up the Colts for the Rams. That way he could avoid the huge capital gains taxes from a sale.

Someone else had a deal to buy the Rams, or so they thought—Hugh Culverhouse, an attorney from Jacksonville, was waiting in the lobby of a hotel while Rosenbloom and his buyer of the Rams. Robert Irsay, an air-conditioning and heating magnate from Chicago, made a deal with the Reeves estate and, with NFL permission, swapped teams. (Culverhouse sued and eventually was awarded the Tampa Bay expansion franchise)

Rosenbloom and his new wife, Georgia Frontiere, moved to LA and immersed themselves in the Hollywood scene. Frontiere later moved the team to St. Louis after she was given the team in Rosenbloom's will over his son Steve.

AUTHORS NOTE: *Rosenbloom had an alternate idea before the "swap" and that was that he would just give the Colts to his son Steve and then just purchase the Rams himself.*

PERSONNEL TOUCH

Your brother is about to be inaugurated as President of the United States. What is your biggest worry the night before the swearing in?

The day of the inauguration of JFK is less than twenty-four hours away. You're his brother, Ted and you are at brother RFK's place in McClean, Virginia and as the snow is falling you are sweating the touch football game.

Carroll Rosenbloom, a close friend of the Kennedys was there and he was talking with Ted about the next day's touch football game between teams captained by Bobby and Ted.

Teddy laments that he will lose because Bobby had chosen the better players. Rosenbloom volunteered himself telling Teddy that he was good. This didn't seem to cheer Teddy up.

Rosenbloom was the owner of the Baltimore Colts. He made a call and the next day Teddy's team won with the help of a few ringers. The ringers looked suspiciously like members of the Baltimore Colts.

THIS PARROT IS NO MORE

Ray Lewis tore his triceps muscle during the season and it was of great concern that it would keep him out of the playoffs. Athletes, especially at the highest levels of competition, are always on the cutting edge of therapeutic frontiers to keep them on the field.

Lewis was reported to have gone to deer antler spray to help with his recovery.

Deer antler spray is pretty much what it sounds like, a substance that is made from the velvet like tissue cover of a deer antler. This particular velvet like tissue came from a New Zealand deer.

The antler byproduct is ground up and put into pill form or a spray. The spray is squirted under the tongue. This seems, at least to me, to be in *Monty Python* sketch territory.

The antler therapy has some link to Chinese traditional medicine. Chinese traditional medicine would make a frontier snake oil salesman blush. According to the *New York Times Magazine* article in 2019, it's on the rise with the help and encouragement of the Chinese government. This leads to, among other things, illegal animal trafficking. Indeed, illegal animal trafficking is the fourth most lucrative illegal market on Earth behind drugs, arms, and human trafficking.

Chinese medicine prescribed such things as ground tiger penis, bear bile and pangolin parts for what ails you.

Think—you're at your doctor's office and he or she gives you a prescription for ground tiger penis. Yeah.

It turns out that deer antler spray is supposed to contain human growth hormone and is used to treat a rare condition named Laraon dwarfism.

How many dwarfs do you spot in the NFL?

There is no test to detect the pertinent ingredient in deer antler spray.

It remains to be seen if the NFL had a test to detect peyote from the look of this story—but I don't know.

MURDER?

NFL players live in the fast lane.

Ray Lewis and two of his friends were charged with murder after a Super Bowl shindig.

His two friends were acquitted of the charges but not until Lewis flipped on them at the trial. He copped to a lesser charge to save his skin and his NFL career.

The case was ruled self defense by the justice system.

Self defense means that lawfully there was no murder.

Still two people are dead.

There is a lingering cloud over Lewis from this incident even though no one was convicted and he made a deal with the law and was fined $250,000 by the NFL and he later paid damages to the victim's families to avoid a civil trial.

Asked by Sterling Sharpe about the payment he made to the families, Lewis rambled on about God. Something to the effect that God makes no mistakes and does not allow people like Lewis, for instance, to achieve great things if they are guilty, or something like that.

Boomer Esiason was on the broadcast with Sharpe and took exception to Lewis' non-answer.

Esiason said "He knows what went on there (at the scene of the altercation) and he can obviously just come out and say it."

There are always two sides to every story.

But, God was not charged as an accessory in the murder.

BALTIMORE SCHOOL FOR THE ARTS

The Baltimore Raven circa 2016-19 have a PBS-y element.

Let's start with Alex Collins, the leading rusher in 2018. He attributes some of his athletic success to a kind of dare he received from the daughter of his high school football coach. She suggested he try the physical regimen and dexterity advantages of Irish river dancing.

He did and, much to his embarrassment at first, he was sweating while the others just danced away. Dancing gets short shrift often from an athletic perspective but it is arduous, as Collins found out fast.

Justin Tucker was a kicker on the University of Texas football team but Justin had always had musical talent, teaching himself to play guitar as a kid.

He wanted to pursue both football and music at Texas but the band director would not have it. The band director demanded Tucker had to quit football to be in his band.

Football won. But Justin also applied and auditioned for the Butler School of Music in Texas and was accepted. It is there that he became a bass-baritone opera singer.

Justin can sing opera in at least eight languages, including Czech and Latin.

His voice coach, a Russian and former pro hockey player, introduced Justin to a technique called *bel canto* which the voice coach claims gives athletes an advantage because it uses a full array of different muscles. It takes a lot of physicality to sing loud for hours, says the voice coach.

Tucker has such a beautiful strong voice that he will pursue a career as a professional opera singer when he hangs up his football cleats.

He is a classically trained singer who has a huge musical soul and, when he shares his gift, he connects to people, says a prominent conductor.

In fact, at the traditional rookie show where rookies are expected to perform, usually the college fight song, Tucker blew the team away with his booming world class voice.

You can check out Tucker's impressive pipes on YouTube.

Jim Urschel is 6'3" and 313 lbs, now a former offensive lineman for the Baltimore Ravens. He has retired from football because of the threat of CTE problems any player faces after football, but also to pursue his other passion, which is mathematics.

Urschel, a Canadian-American, grew up in the United States and played football at Penn State where he was awarded the William V. Campbell Trophy, known as "the academic Heisman."

Urschel has a PhD from MIT for—among other things—the study of integral vectors, calculus, and trigonometry. He co-authored an academic paper entitled, "A Cascadic Multigrid Algorithm for Computing the Fiedler Vector of Graph Laplacians."

Something to do with machine learning. How to teach your toaster to pick winners at the track or something else?

He has written a book about his dual passion for football and mathematics, *Mind and Matter.*

As you can see, NFL rosters often conceal a whole range of talents.

DA PLANE! DA PLANE!

December 19, 1976 the Baltimore Colts lost an AFC Championship game to the Pittsburgh Steelers, 40-14. Thank God.

Because ten minutes after the game a small plane, a Cherokee Piper that had buzzed the field, and had come as close as ten feet above the 50 yard line by some accounts stalled as it tried to flyout of Memorial Stadium and crashed into section 1 and 2 of the Upper Deck, wiping out several rows of seats that had previously been filled with football fans literally only minutes before.

A Baltimore City policeman Joe Scacco was injured and spent ten days in the hospital.

No one else, except the pilot of the plane, Donald N. Kroner, was injured.

There to cover the game, Dave Ailes—a reporter for the *Greensburg* (PA) *Tribune Review*—was an eyewitness. At one point the plane was coming toward him before it crashed into the stands.

Joe Gordon, the Steelers communication director later said it was the most bizarre thing he ever saw in his twenty-eight years in football.

The pilot, Mr. Kroner, had told a friend earlier in the week that he was going to land on the field and give the Colts a Christmas present.

Mr. Kroner had been ejected from a restaurant owned by former Colts LB Bill Pellington at an earlier date and had been arrested for dropping, from his plane,two bottles and some toilet paper on Pellington's restaurant in retaliation. Kroner also called in a bomb threat to the restaurant.

Mr. Kroner was out on $2,100 bail at the time of the crash.

Mr. Kroner it was reported had recently lost his job as a bus driver with Maryland Transit Authority and was evidently a Colts fan as he had a note in the plane's cockpit when it crashed addressed to Colts quarterback Bert Jones that said "to Bert Jones QB, from Blue Max, Good Luck, ya B-Colts."

"Blue Max" was Mr. Kroner's nickname. Kroner also had some yellow spray paint and something called snow spray and toilet paper in the cockpit.

Mr. Kroner it was reported in the press at the time of the incident had previously been arrested for stealing two buses from Dulles International Airport, and had been grounded for four years by the FAA for psychiatric reasons and was alleged to have been an unpaid representative working for the U.S. Customs Service to fly cocaine from South America to the United States in an arranged drug bust.

Some people have very interesting lives.

Coupled with Kroner being out on $2,100 bond for illegally using his plane to harass Bill Pellington—how could anything go wrong?

Thankfully the Colts got slaughtered in the game and subsequently the stands emptied out early or perhaps hundreds could have been injured or worse.

As it was, the Baltimore policeman, Scacco, was hospitalized and other patrons are quoted as saying. "We couldn't duck, we couldn't run, we didn't know what to do."

On YouTube, you can find a report of the Baltimore Colts radio announcing team (that included Hall of Fame announcer Chuck Thompson and Colts great Art Donovan) describing the scene for WCBM radio.

Mr. Kroner, who died in 2013, got a two-year sentence for malicious destruction of property and violation of aviation ordinances. He only served three months of the sentence before being released.

Ok. Sure. Whatever.

$3 MILLION BET

There is a persistent rumor that Carroll Rosenbloom was in on a large bet on his team, the Baltimore Colts, in the famous NFL Championship game known widely as "The Greatest Game Ever Played."

The idea is of course pooh-poohed by NFL purists as the NFL is gambling averse. The suspensions of Paul Hornung and Alex Karras, two of the biggest stars in the prime years of their careers in 1961, for allegedly betting on games was a statement that the league was serious about any gambling noise. Enter the great game of golf.

Al Besselink was a successful professional golfer in the 50's and 60's and he tells this tale that lends a lot of credence to the idea that this legendary bet was real.

We will take a slight detour here...

Reading Besselink's tale, I was struck by the appearance of a semi-mythological person from my life. This name was not on any sports page that I ever read in the late 50's or early 60's.

This person was Al Besselink's best friend and, as it turns out, was a friend of the guys I worked with at the Fairgrounds Race Track in New Orleans. They would talk of him once in a while as they spun the tales of their somewhat colorful lives.

These two guys—let's call em "Nervous Nick" and "Dawlin" because that is what we called them up in the Turf Club. They had this shadowy friend, as far as I could tell, from New Orleans whose name was Mike McLaney.

McLaney was Besselink's friend. According to "Dawlin," he was a renowned golf hustler. He also ended up owning casinos in the Caribbean. One day while I was sitting at my window at the track, "Dawlin" said to me: "Hey, I think that's Mike McLaney." And so it was. It was like a sighting of Robin Hood or Amelia Earhart.

...Now back to the Colts.

Besselink claims that McLaney, a guy named Lew Chesler, and Carroll Rosenbloom had a $3 million dollar bet on the Colts giving up 3 ½ or 5 ½ points to the Giants.

Watching the game in California with Besselink was NFL quarterback John Brodie.

The score tied at the end of regulation, Brodie (who knew of the bet) told Besselink that the bet was probably lost as they went into Sudden Death overtime because one of the teams would probably win the game with a field goal. Besselink scoffed. He told Brodie, "They won't kick a field goal." Remember this is $3 million dollars in 1958. An NFL team was worth less than that.

Sure enough, on 2nd down from the 7yd line Unitas threw a pass to Mutscheler down to the one. Brodie was amazed by the call, according to Besselink. On 3rd down, Alan "The Horse" Ameche ran through a huge hole to win the game and the bet.

Besselink said that the next week he was in New Orleans where he picked up a bag containing $300,000 to $400,000 for McLaney.

Besselik also said that McLaney cut Besselink in on the action for nothing. Besselink wouldn't divulge what his share was.

According to Wikipedia, McLaney was a tennis champion and as my friends "Nervous Nick" and "Dawlin" told me, a great golfer who became a golf hustler instead of going pro because that is where the money was in those days. He is said to have once beat Carroll Rosenbloom out of a $250,000 bet on the golf course.

McLaney went on to own casinos in Cuba, the Bahamas (where it is believed he helped Linus Pindling get elected Prime Minister) and Haiti, where he had a monopoly to run casinos under the Duvallier family.

He also is alleged to have concocted a scheme to blow up Cuban oil refineries after Castro confiscated his and Rosenbloom's casino but was stopped from doing so by a personal visit from the U.S. Attorney General Bobby Kennedy, who stuck a digit in his chest and told him he would do no such thing.

After losing his casino in Havana, McLaney is believed by some Kennedy assassination buffs to have hosted a crew of anti-Castro commandos at his Lacombe, Louisiana property three months before the Kennedy assassination—a group said to have at some point included Lee Harvey Oswald. The camp was said to have been run by the CIA.

The camp was raided by the FBI.

A film of the purported camp mysteriously disappeared from the U.S. House of Representatives committee investigating the Kennedy assassination after it was viewed by the committee, seemingly showing a commando training facility run by the CIA on U.S. soil. Allegedly.

So McLaney is also tied by some to activity dealing with the Kennedy assassination. I guess that somehow there is a normal progression here. All roads lead to the Colts. Christ! Robin Hood might want this guy's autograph.

Paul S. Serbu was videoed urinating on Art Modell's grave.

The charges were dropped, according to authorities, after consulting Mr. Modell's family and the allegation that a medical condition may have led to Mr. Serbu's actions.

You can find it on YouTube. If you must.

CAROLINA

SayBrah

JULIE ANDREWS

CAROLINA

LB

JULIE ANDREWS, MURDER, HAMBURGERS

CAROLINA

SayBrah®

"I see myself as more than a football player but as an entertainer and icon."
—Cam Newton

Carolina was awarded a franchise in 1993 and began play as The Panthers in 1995.

The founder of the franchise, Jerry Richardson, played wide receiver for 1958 NFL champion Baltimore Colts. Richardson used the bonus money he received as member of the 1958 Colts team to start the fast food chain Hardee's.

After sexual misconduct allegations surfaced in 2016, Richardson was forced by the NFL to sell the team, which was eventually bought by hedge fund manager David Tepper.

Super Bowl Appearances: 2
Super Bowl Record: 0-2
Super Bowl Losses: 2003, 2015

The NFL is such a popular part of culture in the United States and sometimes we forget it has an increasing global reach. This reach extends to an incredibly feel-good story that gives one pause to think about the place opportunity or fate plays in our successes or failures.

Efe Obede, a defensive lineman for the Carolina Panthers, took a most unusual path to the National Football League.

At the tender age of ten, Efe and his sister were trafficked to London from the Netherlands where they were abandoned on the streets of London. Efe remembers only feeling fear at that time but also remembering he had to be strong to protect his sister.

His family had come from Nigeria to Europe and his mother found it preferable to send her children to England.

They found their way into child welfare programs available in the UK but Efe eventually ended up back living on the street. He joined a gang and after seeing some of his friends die, decided he would take a different path.

He went to work on a loading dock where his size and strength led a fellow worker to suggest Efe try out for the London Warriors, an American style football team.

NFL Europe was a short-lived league that was abandoned by the NFL. But the league has not totally given up on the European market, as evidenced by the regular season games it plays in London every year.

The culture of the United States—its music, films, and even its own style of football—are alluring to young people all around the world.

The NFL started a program to help players of promise in Europe make it into the league with special exemptions. This program started in the NFC South.

Efe was signed by the Dallas Cowboys, played briefly with Kansas City, Atlanta, and finally made it onto the 53-man roster of the Carolina Panthers, making him the first such European player to make it under this program.

Efe has an incredibly unique perspective on life by way of his inspiring journey from trafficked ten-year-old to NFL player.

With the insatiable appetite for content in the press and online, his story screams out for a Hollywood treatment. Yet the serious nature of his path to the NFL will have to wait as Efe continues to hold back details of his rough existence and is only just recently starting to share his life story.

In his first game as a member of the Carolina Panthers he recorded a sack and an interception and was awarded the game ball.

During the first game his teammates remember him screaming at the Cincinnati Bengals opponents, "They don't know me! They don't know me!"

He says that what he meant was, "They don't know how hard I'd had to work or went through to reach that moment."

NFL players often make headlines for a variety of criminal and personal transgressions. Yet inspiring stories such as Efe's are also a part of the landscape of NFL football, examples of success in the face of obstacles most of us can only imagine in a nightmare.

And this is a story the league should at some point spotlight and be proud.

The NFL has further recognized Efe's achievement as they have named the office of the NFL's UK headquarters after him.

GOD

In 1996 The Reverend Billy Graham was called to dedicate Ericsson Stadium, the brand new home of the NFL''s Carolina Panthers.

Graham not long after that held one of his Christian Crusades for four days with attendance of over 65,000 every night at Ericsson Stadium.

Jerry Richardson the owner of the Panthers said of the Crusades: "How do you put a value on the Billy Graham Crusade being in that stadium for four days. I don't think you can. But I knew in my mind it is far greater than a winning season."

Graham, who is believed to have preached in front of more live humans than anyone in history, was born in Charlotte, NC and was a well known Dallas Cowboys fan for many years as he was a close friend of coach Tom Landry— a very public Christian.

But with Charlotte getting the Panthers he quickly became a fan of his hometown's team.

After the Panthers first playoff victory in 1996 he wrote a letter to Jerry Richardson that said in part:

"What you all have done this past year is a miracle from God. You have put Charlotte on the map and shown the world the strength that Christianity gives to a city, state, team."

ABLE TO LEAP SMALL BUILDINGS

October 23, 2011 one of the most well received NFL rituals was unveiled.

Cam Newton had debuted his after TD celebration of mimicking unveiling his phantom Superman costume to accentuate his unique super athletic talents.

His QB coach Mike Shula had urged him to add a more humbling touch to the celebration.

On this particular day after the TD Shula (via the helmet mic) urged Newton to hand the ball to a kid.

A gentle urging via radio.

Like a conquering Roman hero entering Rome in triumph, a voice at his shoulder whispering: *Give it to a kid. Give it to a kid.*

Newton says he looked up into the face of a kid gleaming from ear to ear and he gave the ball to that kid. A new tradition was started and it was a winner.

GROSS TONGUE

Jordan Gross was a first round pick of the Carolina Panthers and turned out to be a Pro Bowl performer and all-time great Panther offensive lineman.

Rookie OL, especially those who sign large contracts, are expected to take the veteran offensive linemen out to dinner and the vets usually try to stick the rookie with a huge bill as a welcome to NFL hazing.

Another rookie was paying for the meal when Gross screamed and said that he had bitten into a foreign object. His teammates scoffed, calling him a wuss. Then they saw the blood. A one-inch object of some kind in his appetizer had stuck all the way through his tongue. They couldn't remove it. It turned out to be a lobster or crab claw that somehow got into his appetizer and Mother Nature had designed it to play for keeps.

One lineman had a pocket knife. They tried to get the broken claw out of his tongue. Bad idea.

Luckily a team physician for the Panthers was at a nearby table and he was called to take care of Gross' tongue.

They went off to the doctor's office. The doctor fixed the problem and Gross returned to finish his dinner.

His food was gone; consumed by another Panther in his absence.

Growing boys don't ya know.

COFFEE BREAK

In the ebb and flow of success in the history of any pro football team there are key pivot points.

Fumbles, bad clock management, dumb personnel decisions, bad calls, etc., etc.

These whys and wherefores are debated ad infinitum on talk radio and in barrooms.

One thing you probably didn't think of when you were contemplating betting a few hundred on the home team or just betting with your heart whether your beloved team can get over the hump and finally win that coveted Super Bowl—the office coffee machine.

Coffee machine issues? Yes.

In 2003, the Carolina Panthers went to the Super Bowl against the daunting New England Patriots and lost 32-29 at a time when the Patriots were in the midst of an unprecedented run of success. How many points does your average bookmaker factor in for coffee machine peace? But for a cappuccino machine, things could have been different.

Or could they?

Jordan Gross was a rookie at the time and, as many rookies before or after, was dealing with hazing. Todd Steussie, a fellow offensive lineman and veteran, demanded that Gross purchase a new cappuccino machine for the OL meeting room. Relying on his own instincts and an assist in the form of advice of fellow Utah grad (and notorious bad-ass) Steven Smith, Gross drew the line at buying the cappuccino machine.

Then of course the veterans, the adults in the OL room in this million-dollar business, would just go on in a wholly professional manner. There are games to be won and stuff. Not so fast my friend.

The Househusbands of Charlotte? No, the Carolina Panthers.

Steussie was reportedly pissed and stayed pissed. Other linemen on the Panthers took sides. Kevin Donnalley took Gross' side. The problem festered and led to a bit of alleged bad feelings among the line.

Gross years later admitted he may have made an error in not buying the machine. Gross, along with three other Panthers lineman, later wrote a book, *Handbook For Rookies*, detailing what you should do and not do as a rookie to avoid such awkward and petty misunderstandings.

Gross, who went on to a very productive career as an NFL player, even later purchased a cappuccino machine and was given the nickname "Barista" after he learned to make coffee just as each lineman liked it. On a radio interview Gross was asked about the rift he caused by not buying the damn machine. He answered tongue sturdily in cheek, "Yes, I upset the lads."

While on that radio show he actually called Todd Steussie to confront the by now picayunish historical event in Panther history. The call went well. Kind of an alls well that ends well.

HASH MARK

The Carolina Panthers had a secret weapon when they went 15-1 and to the Super Bowl in 2015.

Waffle House, the southern restaurant chain.

Many of the players swear by Waffle House, in fact Cam Newton the star QB of the Panthers after a key MNF win against the Patriots in 2015 didn't go to Disneyland to celebrate the big win, no he went to the Waffle House to get his usual, scrambled eggs, hash browns, and cheese in a bowl with a light waffle.

The Panthers cite the advantage of the Waffle House because of many reasons. One is that it is open 24-hours a day and pro players are up often at odd hours when they are training. And the place serves breakfast 24-hours a day. This allows them to load up on cheap caloric content.

Many NFL players are well acquainted with Waffle House especially those who played at ACC and SEC schools.

Kevin Norwood who played with the Panthers but who was drafted into the league by the Seattle Seahawks said that one of the first things he did when he got to Seattle was search on the web for the nearest Waffle House.

He was crestfallen to find that there were no Waffle Houses at all in the state of Washington the closest being in Colorado.

DE Mario Addison says that yes, the proximity of Waffle House to the Panther facility is definitely an advantage the Panthers have. There are twenty Waffle Houses within a twenty-five mile proximity of Bank of America Stadium in Charlotte.

Which makes it easy to get your hash browns scattered, smothered, covered, chunked, peppered, capped (that's with mushrooms), or tipped. That last one is covered in chili.

BUSINESS

Jaylin Clyburn, twelve years old, started a lawn mowing business to help out his mom to pay for his college dreams. He went on Facebook to advertise. Local TV got wind of the feel good story of the young entrepreneur and with the media play he was gifted by strangers to the tune of, a newer lawn mower, a leaf blower, an electric hedge cutter and contribution to his college fund from a state senator.

Lowe's Home Improvement and the Carolina Panthers also saw the TV spot and invited Jaylin, a huge Panthers fan, to come to the game as their guests, Ron Rivera the Panthers head coach and Lowe's also gifted Jaylin with a brand new $500 blue lawnmower and a Cam Newton autographed football.

Panthers social media channels put a 92-second piece up and the Twitter-verse exploded with a debate about the gift and whether it was enough. Criticism to Lowe's and Panthers for not doing enough for Jaylin roiled social media.

Eventually, after a storm of criticism, David Tepper the owner of the Panthers quietly stepped up to contact the Clyburns and gave what is described by Mrs. Clyburn as a substantial gift toward Jaylin's college education.

No good deed.

BLAKE EDWARDS' MAIN SQUEEZE

Derrick Moore scored the Panthers' first TD ever. He was the leading rusher in 1995, the first season. Derrick was known by his teammates for one other signature thing. Three guesses? You'll never guess.

He was obsessed with *The Sound of Music* and Julie Andrews' character Maria.

Derrick was known to break spontaneously into song with a tune from *The Sound of Music*. "My Favorite Things" seemed to inspire Derrick. *The Sound of Music* in an NFL locker room. Ja.

Music is, of course, a big part of the lives of professional athletes—after all, they are young men and are like all young people immersed in the popular culture of their contemporaries. But show tunes?

So obsessed was Derrick that one computer literate teammate superimposed Derrick's head onto a *Sound of Music* poster of Julie Andrews' torso romping and singing through the Alps. Julie Andrews heard about Derrick somehow and sent him an autographed photo. Sweet.

GNOME

In 2016, a Super Bowl year for the Carolina Panthers, security firm CPI Security aired a commercial in which Luke Kuechly intercepts a burglar who is using a garden gnome to break into a house. At the end of the commercial Keuchly replaces the stolen gnome with a Luke Kuechly gnome.

Soon, the Luke Kuechly gnome which had been simply a prop in a TV commercial became the most sought-after tchotchke around.

One was sold at auction for $16,000 and social media was afire with discussions on how one could get one.

CPI finally had the guy who created it make a mold and made a limited edition available. But not for sale to the general public. They were sold at fundraisers.

The power of celebrity.

DISGUSTING

There is a photo of Rae Carruth you can find online in which he looks every bit like a Conehead, one of the characters from the classic *SNL* sketch.

However, that Rae Carruth, he just ain't funny.

To attempt to make the long, tawdry, disgusting tale of Rae Carruth (which let us hope and pray is the darkest chapter in Carolina Panther history) short if not sweet, we'll start with this.

On November 16, 1999, Rae Carruth—1st round draft choice, star wide receiver for the Panthers—made a date with Cherica Adams (a sometime girlfriend who was pregnant with his child) to go to a movie. According to Carruth they were not a couple and had only hooked up about five times just for the sex. Ms. Adams seems to have seen the relationship differently. Carruth didn't want Ms. Adams to have the baby.

That night according to Ms. Adams' words on a 911 tape, she was following Carruth's car in hers, on the way to her place to spend the night together. He stopped or slowed his car to the point Ms. Adams had to stop her car. Then another car sped up and Carruth had her blocked in. Shots were fired into her car. Four of these shots hit her and she was left to die. The shooter's car and Mr. Carruth sped off.

She wasn't dead. She called 911 and told her story. Eight months pregnant, she was rushed to the hospital where she was expected to live.

She didn't.

The child, Chancellor Adams, was delivered, born with severe brain damage.

Four people were arrested for the crime. Carruth was one of them. He posted $3 million dollar bond and, after Ms. Adams died, was arrested and charged with murder.

This is when the tale takes a buffoonish turn. Carruth convinced a friend, Wendy Cole, to bring him along on a trip to California as he was not going to stick around to face the charges. He hid in her trunk the whole ride to their first stop, a motel in Tennessee.

Ms. Cole called Carruth's mother as he hid out in the trunk with energy bars and two plastic drink bottles in which to do his business. His mother, fearing for his safety, called authorities.

Mr. Carruth spent the entire time locked in the trunk. The FBI popped the trunk and he surrendered.

Watkins, the admitted shooter, a man who had claimed to have already murdered four others for money, implicated Carruth in the conspiracy as having hired him to do the deed. Carruth says it was a drug sale gone bad.

Another guy, the driver of the car from which the shots were fired, said otherwise and corroborated the murder for hire scenario.

Carruth spent eighteen years in prison.

His son, Chancellor, nineteen on the day of Carruth's release, was raised by his grandmother, Sharonda Adams, and is significantly impaired because of the nature of his birth.

Despite this he is a straight A student who enjoys horseback riding.

It is painful to recount the brutality and waste of this tale but it is such a significant factor in Carolina Panther history I felt compelled to include it.

Your team is on its first Super Bowl run at home playing a divisional opponent. Fourth quarter you are up 20-14. What would be your next move if you are Carolina Panther management?

During a timeout, give the stadium microphone to a guy dressed up in black fur, maybe with two small panthers attached to his shoulders like a pirate with a parrot, and let him wax poetic? Not your first choice? You made the right call.

However, in 2003 the Carolina Panthers had this very feature at home games, allowing a fan to say a few words on the stadium PA at a timeout during the game.

Leading up to the game Simeon Rice, a DE for the Tampa Bay Bucs, had guaranteed a win against the Panthers. The fan chosen to get the mic at that game was no ordinary fan. No, Joe Mucscarello, known as the Carolina Prowler, is a Hall of Fame fan.

Indeed, his photo has been displayed at the Pro Football Hall of Fame in Canton and he was invited to come to Canton for a get together of "Hall of Fame" fans. So he has skins on the wall. Once given the mic, Mr. Muscarello proceeded to go down in Carolina Panther history by calling out Rice and Warren Sapp. "Let me tell you something, Warren Sapp and Simeon Rice, you guaranteed a win. We guarantee to kick your ass."

Sapp and Rice could clearly hear the smack and reacted by preening and pointing to the scoreboard. Rice also reacted by sacking the Carolina quarterback on two of the next three plays.

Clearly Muscarello's exhortation had riled up the Bucs. Other fans reacted to the announcement favorably, at first. After the sacks and Bucs taking the lead, popular opinion in the stands shifted palpably. Muscarello started to sense a negative vibe and since he was at the game with his nine year-old son, decided to take a powder.

The Panthers won the game on a TD pass from Jake Delhomme to Steven Smith with 1:06 seconds on the clock. Muscarello's *bon mots* did not go unnoticed by the home team.

Quarterback Jake Delhomme: "It was good that he thought that but we needed to say it with thirty seconds on the clock when we are up by 10."

Center, Jeff Mitchell: "That guy, we need to seek him out and revoke his season ticket privileges."

Coach John Fox: "Don't sweat that. You were fired up. I like people who are fired up."

Muscarello himself said later, "If I offended anyone and especially the team or coaching staff, I apologize."

FIZZ

This was not the first brush with media relations that concerned the Panthers by Super Fan, Joe Muscarello.

Not by a long shot.

If you are thinking negatively of Mr. Muscarello as some of his beloved Panthers seemed to after that Bucs game consider this.

In 1993 the NFL was in the process of expanding and Charlotte did not yet have a team. Carolina, Jacksonville, Baltimore, Memphis, St. Louis, and Baltimore were all vying for entry into the exclusive American club and only two cities would come out winners. There was a fan contest and guess who won the contest?

If you guessed anything but Joe Muscarello you are wrong.

Mr. Muscarello, in an effort to help Charlotte obtain the franchise, won first prize when he taped 216 Alka Seltzer tablets to his person and jumped into a pool. He jumped out after a lot of fizzing. He pumped his fist and screamed, "Carolina Panthers!" The team did not yet exist.

They got the franchise. An executive of the Panthers, which had already decided upon the name Panthers even before they got the team, said it was such an impressive effort by Mr. Muscarello, the future Carolina Prowler don't-ya-know, that the team considered changing the mascot name to the Effervescent. They probably didn't really.

FUZZ

One of the more memorable moments in Panther history was accomplished by its mascot Sir Purr. This is not necessarily a good sign.

In 1996 against the Pittsburgh Steelers a punt hit at the four and bounced into the end zone.

As it bounces around, Sir Purr, the mascot, jumps on it and basically downs it. Sir Purr is penalized. Bill Cowher laughs about it and that's that.

SEX

The scene: women's room of a Tampa Bay nightclub. A long line of female patrons waiting by the door, steamed.

Why? The only stall available is occupied by two women allegedly having sex.

The two young ladies, engaging in a bit of recreational sex in a limited space, wanted privacy in the public restroom. Angry words are exchanged. Nasty words, by some reports.

Turns out the two allegedly sexually engaged women are members of the Carolina Panthers cheerleading squad.

Court records show that one of the Carolina cheerleaders punched a complaining lady in the face. The other cheerleader, who may have been underaged, gave police the ID of still another cheerleader who resembled her and was subsequently charged with a felony.

And no, this is not a Woody Allen movie treatment.

The cheerleaders' attorneys deny these allegations.

The story did in fact become the most posted story on ESPN.com that week.

Football plus sex equals clicks.

CINCINNATI

SayBrah®

HARAMBE

CINCINNATTI

LB

A GORILLA, A COMPUTER, AND A HOLOGRAM TO BE NAMED LATER

CINCINNATI

"You don't live in Cleveland! You live in Cincinnati!"

—Sam Wyche
Bengals Head Coach (1984–1991)

SayBrah®

The Cincinnati Bengals were the final expansion team in the AFL awarded in 1967 to Paul Brown the former head coach of the Cleveland Browns. They started league play in 1968.

Mike Brown assumed ownership responsibilities upon his father's death in August 1991 and has remained in the ownership position since.

In 2008, the Bengals set a record for the most games needed under one specific owner to attain 100 wins.

Super Bowl Appearances: 2
Super Bowl Record: 0-2
Super Bowl Losses: 1981, 1988

FOUNDER 2.0

Paul Brown, usually described as "the legendary Paul Brown," was the first coach of the Cleveland Browns and he was kind of the Belichick of Pro Football for a brief epoch, in the late 40's and early 50's.

The Browns were quite successful, but all good things come to an end and it's a "what have you done for me lately" world. When Art Modell bought the Browns he soon jettisoned Paul Brown, legendary or not.

Paul Brown owned the team's equipment, so he took it with him when he left.

Paul Brown owned all the team's stuff: uniforms, shoulder pads, blocking dummies—like that.

So, when Paul Brown—still legendary, mind you—started the Cincinnati Bengals as an expansion team in the AFL he brought the Browns' stuff with him to Cincinnati.

He must have had an interesting garage.

NAME THAT TEAM

Paul Brown, when he founded the Cincinnati team in the AFL, wanted to have a historic connection with football from Cincinnati's past. Cincinnati has had many teams—after all Canton, the birthplace of Pro Football, is just up the road. So he chose the name Bengals, which was a successful pro franchise in Cincinnati's past.

But that would mean that someone else named the team, because someone had originally named it back in the day.

As it turns out, the Cincinnati Bengals are named after a stove.

Hal Pennington was coach of the original Cincinnati team in 1937 that would become the Bengals. A name was needed and his mother's stove was a Bengal stove. He didn't know what a Bengal was but the tiger was right on the stove manufactured by Floyd, Wells & Co. and it looked fierce to him.

Voila!

Cincinnati Bengals.

The Chicago Whirlpools?

IVY LEAGUE

Paul Brown valued intelligence in his players and this paid off not only for the Bengals but also for Cincinnati.

Reggie Williams was drafted by Brown out of Dartmouth.

Williams went on to play more than twelve years with the Bengals and excelled, leading them to their first Super Bowl and playing on the second Super Bowl team.

Williams was a force off the field as well, using his Dartmouth education to contribute to his community. Williams was named recipient of the Byron "Whizzer" White Humanitarian Award in 1985, the Walter Payton NFL Man of the Year Award in 1986, and was *Sports Illustrated*'s co-Sportsman of the Year in 1987.

Then, in 1988, he was appointed to the City Council of Cincinnati to finish the term of an elected council person. In 1989, he ran for that seat and was elected in his own right, finishing with the fourth top amount of votes in a unique system where the top nine vote totals are elected.

Williams worked on the City Council to have Cincinnati divest itself of investments in South Africa during the Apartheid era. It is an interesting note that Williams ran not as a Democrat or Republican or Independent, but as a Charterite.

Charterite is a party that had been started in Cincinnati fifty years before Williams' election to fight corruption in the major parties.

Williams later went on to work for Disney Corporation where he was CEO of Wide World of Sports Complex in Orlando.

Paul Brown's desire for smart players brought Williams to Cincinnati and such was Williams' impact that he, Reggie Williams, was chosen as one of the pallbearers for Paul Brown.

PIANO MAN

Mike Reid was an All-American defensive lineman for an undefeated Penn State teams in 1968 and 69. He won the Maxwell Trophy, given to the best college football player every year, and was drafted with the 7th pick in the first round of the NFL draft in 1970. Reid led the Bengals in sacks and made the Pro Bowl five times in his brief, injury-shortened career.

His degree from Penn State was in music and he was an accomplished pianist, playing with numerous symphonic orchestras including the Cincinnati Symphony.

After his playing days he pursued a music career as a singer and songwriter.

A cassette recording from a session that ended at 3 am (as many music sessions do) found its way to country star Jerry Jeff Walker.

The song "Eastern Avenue River Railway Blues," penned by Reid, was recorded by Walker.

Reid moved to Nashville and ended up writing songs recorded by Conway Twitty, Tonya Tucker, Marie Osmond, Alabama, Larry Gatlin, Bonnie Raitt, and Ronnie Milsap, among others. In fact, Reid's song "Stranger in My House," recorded by Milsap, was the Grammy winner for best country song in 1984.

Reid wrote twelve #1 singles and recorded seven *Billboard* chart-hitting songs as a singer songwriter and was inducted into Nashville's Songwriter Hall of Fame in 2005.

PROTEST

Tommie Smith was at the center of one of American sports most enduring moments of protest.

In 1968 Smith won the gold medal in the 200-meter sprint in world record time and John Carlos another American sprinter had won the bronze at the Mexico City Olympics. They both bowed their heads and raised black gloved hands during the national anthem to bring a message to the world that highlighted racial inequality in the United States.

Smith and Carlos were dismissed from the Olympic Team and sent home. That was 1968.

In 1969 Tommie Smith the world record holder in the 200-meters was trying out for the Cincinnati Bengals as a WR.

The legendary Paul Brown gave him a chance and it seems there was little fanfare in the press. Brown was quoted as saying that other teams wanted him and that he was certainly fast enough.

He had been drafted by the Rams in 1966 but cut in training camp.

Smith was on the Bengals taxi squad for three years catching only one pass for 41 yard gain in 1969. He injured his knee on the play and that pretty much ended his football career. He went onto a career as a college professor.

He issued a statement when he joined the Bengals to address the controversial nature of his very public protest to clarify his position first hand.

"I'm a citizen of this country who happens to be black and regardless of my skin color I wore red white and blue in Mexico and represented all America. I'm proud to be an American, yet I firmly believe we have problems that must be met. I've been misquoted and misunderstood many times by those who had to have a story and refused to see the truth."

For the record, Smith said his protest was not a Black Power salute as many interpreted it but he saw it as a "Human rights salute."

NUMBER CRUNCHING

Virgil Carter became the starting quarterback in Cincinnati and even though he was small and did not have a strong arm, he led them to the division title his first year with the team.

Off the field Carter, who was drafted by the Bears out of BYU, attended graduate school at Northwestern in Chicago. He developed, using the Northwestern mainframe computer, an early version of football analytics, a concept that took the NFL over thirty years to begin to embrace.

When Carter got to Cincinnati, he taught math at Xavier University and did seminars for A.O. Smith Corporation, using its computers to further his number crunching to see a different NFL game through analytics.

He wrote a newspaper column on the subject that was run by thirty-five newspapers. His column, *The Computerized Quarterback*, would answer questions sent in by readers.

Questions like whether or not it is a good idea to go for it on 4th and 1. It is,by a large margin,with a success rate of over 80% if you are in your opponent's side of the field but only at the above 80% if you are between your opponent's 49 and 10. once inside the 10 yard line the success drops.

Another finding of *The Computerized Quarterback* was that fumbles are most likely to occur in the first two plays of a series.

Carter also claims that the number crunching debunks the existence of momentum in a football game.

Carter was also instrumental in Bill Walsh's development in what came to be known as The West Coast offense. After QB Greg Cook went down with an arm injury,Walsh, who went on to success in San Francisco with the offense he developed in Cincinnati, went to Carter whose arm strength caused Walsh to change his offense to a short passing model which became the West Coast offense.

The cerebral Carter, just the kind of smart player Paul Brown liked, had a run of the mill NFL career but was a trailblazer in computer analytics of NFL football in his off-time and was an inspiration, in a sense, for Walsh's innovative offense which some contend should be called the Ohio River Offense.

WONDERLIC TEST

Every year around draft time, you hear about the Wonderlic test, described as "a group intelligence test used to assess the aptitude of prospective employees for learning and problem solving in a range of occupations."

It is to give teams a measuring stick for the intelligence of incoming players.

Some Hall of Fame quarterbacks have scored rather low—15 and 16 respectively for Hall of Fame QBs Dan Marino and Terry Bradshaw—so you might want to take the Wonderlic with a grain of salt.

But the lowest rungs of Wonderlic are often talked about ad infinitum and live on in history. So, who got the highest score?

The perfect score is 50. It's a 50-question test to be taken in twelve minutes.

A 50 was the reported score of Pat McInally, punter for the Cincinnati Bengals who went to Harvard.

The Wonderlic Test's use in the NFL, as would be apropos, was the idea of the legendary Paul Brown.

INSIDER TRADING

In 1971, Bengals fan Judy Carter bet the guys sitting around her $5 that she could predict the Bengals first offensive play. She got it right. The guys doubled down.

She ended up predicting the first eight Bengals offensive plays accurately, much to the amazement of the guys and to the benefit of her bankroll.

Turns out she was the wife of Bengals quarterback Virgil Carter. He had helped her memorize the first eight Bengals plays which were scripted. Insider trading?

ALL YOU CAN EAT

Some members of the Cincinnati Bengals found out about an offer they could not refuse.

Pete Perreault in *Sports Illustrated*, 1969: "We found out about this all-you-can-eat seafood restaurant outside Cincinnati, the Imperial House, and Steve Chomyszak (a 280 lbs DT) ate fifteen whole lobsters, eight dozen shrimp, a platter of every kind of fish they had, another platter of roast beef, two bottles of wine and two whole pies. John Matock, a center on the team, was with us, and he got so embarrassed that he went out in the lobby and waited for us. The maitre d' came over to the table three times. The third time he asked Steve, please, to leave. He said he didn't even have to pay anything if he'd just leave. Chomyszak did leave. He was finishing his second pie, anyway, so he didn't care."

Perreault prefaces this account with this statement: "I'll take a lie detector test on this."

INSIDE PAUL BROWN'S HEAD

Clive Rush was the offensive coordinator of the 1969 New York Jets and he parlayed that success into the head coaching job of the Boston Patriots in 1969.

Clive's tenure in Boston got off to an unusual start when at his first press conference as coach the microphone gave him a five second shock that almost electrocuted him.

His career was freckled with episodes that questioned Clive's mental stability.

He among other things gave his Patriots the game plan in detail while shaking his head "no" when they were in the locker room before playing the Jets because he believed the Jets had bugged his locker room.

In his last head coaching job at the Merchant Marine Academy he was dismissed during the season with a record of 6-1, because of a player revolt and it was reported that when he left the Patriots job he had a nervous breakdown.

Nonetheless Clive did have some success,

Which brings us to the inside of the "legendary" Paul Browns' head.

Clive's Patriots were going to play Brown and his new Bengals team in Cincinnati. Clive game-planned to get inside of the head of Paul Brown.

How?

It was a multi-faceted plan. Kind of like Chaos theory.

He tells his place-kicker right before the game that when they get into field goal range they will kick a field goal on third down.

The kicker asked *Why?*

The answer? *Because we're going to destroy Paul Brown's mind.*

Clive told his kicker, Gino Cappelletti, *Paul Brown will be wondering the same thing as you.* "Why are they doing that?"

Another part of Clive's plan that day against the "legendary" Paul Brown, who Clive considered the greatest football coach of all time, was to send in running back Charlie Frazier to the huddle with plays from the sideline like they had always done with Clive's Patriots, but with a twist.

Frazier would run out to the huddle. The quarterback would ask "What's the play?"

There was no play. Frazier was told by Clive to run into the huddle, stand there a bit and not do anything or say anything then run back to the sideline. He did it about four times then Frazier asked "Why am I doing this?" Clive told him that he was trying to distract Paul Brown. Clive said that Brown will be asking himself, "Why are they doing that?"

Clive told his quarterback to run a man in motion even though it was not part of their offense.

The Patriots won the game.

That's how you beat Paul Brown. You get into his head. You get *Monty Python's Flying Circus* to call the plays.

FUTURAMA

Paul Brown Stadium is a controversial project. It has been called the "most fiscally disastrous stadium deal in American history." Just being in that, if-you'll pardon the expression, "ballpark" is saying something.

The contract obligated Hamilton County to spend eleven percent of its general fund of expenditure to satisfy the terms in 2008. And 16.4 percent in 2010.

The contract has a clause that the county must pay to keep the stadium up to the state-of-the-art of modern stadiums. This clause is also found in a few other NFL stadium contracts.

If fourteen other NFL stadiums have something, then taxpayers must buy the Bengals that thing. Like the latest model JumboTron for instance.

One thing included in the Bengals' contract is this: if and when a holographic replay system—something that has yet to be invented—is available, the Bengals get that with most of the bill going to the taxpayers of Hamilton County.

GORILLA

A petition was started in 2016 to change the name of the Cincinnati Bengals to the Cincinnati Harambes. It was a joke, I think.

It did show up on Change.org, a place where self-proclaimed important people with so-called important ideas surface to inform you of their superior enlightenment. Thousands of people signed the petition.

Harambe was a sixteen-year-old lowland gorilla who was shot by zoo officials after a three-year-old boy fell into the gorilla enclosure at the Cincinnati Zoo, and Harambe, curious, agitated or confused, grabbed the boy and kind of tossed him around.

After zoo officials made the decision that the boy was in mortal danger, they ordered the shooting. It caused an international stir.

Jane Goodall, famous primate researcher, among others, came to the defense of zoo officials.

The team name remains the Bengals.

YOUR CHEATIN HEART

Hazing of rookies in the NFL is a time tested ritual and some players take it seriously.

To choose the best or most insidious depending on your point of view would be a difficult task.

However many would agree that Lyle Blackwood, a player who played with the Cincinnati Bengals and many other NFL teams is at least a candidate for the honor of best in show.

Blackwood would choose a rookie and during preseason games would point out a great looking woman in the stands and Blackwood would tell the rookie that the lady in the stands had the hots for the rookie. Blackwood said he could set the rookie up but there was one problem, the lady was married.

The plan was to set up the tryst when her husband was out of town.

If the rookie fell for it the game was afoot.

They would approach the house where the lady waited and when they got close an irate gentleman with a shotgun would burst out screaming that he knew what was going on and would fire the shotgun toward Blackwood.

The shotgun was loaded with blanks. Blackwood would feign that he had been shot and hurt badly. The rookie would head for the hills.

The perps of the prank would then search for the rookie who they would find cowering in shrubs, crying in brambles all cut up or running for miles. Just running away.

Monstrous in its conception, devious in its engineering, and brutal in its implementation.

Yet, it is pretty awesome in its genre.

THE AMERICAN DREAM

This is a very incomplete list.

Wide receiver Chad Johnson (#85) played for the Cincinnati Bengals for ten years in what will surely be a Hall of Fame career. He caught a lot of passes and played in a number of Pro Bowls. Among other things, Chad Johnson:

Wore a Mohawk haircut

Legally changed his name to Chad Javon Ochocinco

Was a contestant on Dancing with the Stars

Rode a bull in a professional Bull Riding Competition (1.5 seconds)

Played in both Mexican and Canadian Professional football leagues

Is a professional soccer player

Has hosted TV shows

Has his own app

Was going to change his name to Hachi Go (8+5 in Japanese). He changed his mind.

Raced a thoroughbred horse a furlong with a 100 meter head start and won.

Changed his name back to Chad Johnson because "he wanted to reconnect with his former self."

His most recent marriage broke up after he head-butted his wife.

Endorsed Bernie Sanders for President in 2016.

Interviewed by reporters when neighbor Roger Stone was arrested by the FBI in a case that involves Donald Trump shenanigans with Russians or-Wikileaks or something (you may have read about it in the papers).

Named United States Ambassador to the Moon by President Donald Trump in 2019...(this last one about the Moon isn't true)

Author's note: *If you are a citizen of Austria and just read this entry then, yes, as a citizen of the U.S. and an NFL fan, I am embarrassed.*

JACKSONVILLE

SayBrah®

Since 1968
IT AIN'T A PO-BOY
IF IT DON'T GOT

Numa's
Real
"My-Nayz"

SMOOTH ON DA BREAD, BRAH

8 FL. OZ

MAYONNAISE

JACKSONVILLE

C

AN UNDERTAKER, AN AXE, AND FONDUE

8 THE MOST INTERESTING LEAGUE IN THE WORLD

JACKSONVILLE

"I love it. In the NFL you win or you lose and the money still shows up."
—Shahid Khan, Jaguars owner

SayBrah

Jacksonville was awarded a franchise with Wayne Weaver as the owner in 1993 as an expansion team in the NFL. They started league play in 1995.

Jacksonville, a small TV market, had been actively seeking an NFL team for years without success coming ever so close.

In 1993 they were an upset winner of the franchise over St. Louis and Baltimore.

In 2012, the Jaguars were purchased by Shahid "Shad" Khan.

The Jaguars have never been to the Super Bowl.

In 1995, the Jaguars took the field for the first time.

Coach Tom Coughlin is known as old school. He wanted to set a tone in his first year and had a lot of rules that probably wouldn't fly in today's game.

He wanted players on time for meetings, which meant early. If you weren't early you were late. You were required to have both feet on the floor during meetings, no sunglasses, and you wore ties, like on the road when dress was required, tied tightly.

One concession seemed to be that the Jaguars would do summer training camp in Stevens Point, Wisconsin, to spare the team the summer heat of Florida. It was the only time the Jags have trained outside of Florida and it was the hottest summer in Wisconsin history.

The camp is legendary for its heat and brutal byproducts.

Two-a-days in NFL summer camp are now *verboten* due to the collective bargaining agreement. Jaguars in 1995 at Stevens Point sometimes had 4-a-days, in pads.

They constantly ran out of ice and players were required to sit in plastic garbage cans filled with ice instead of the usual cold tubs.

It was so hot that cows were dying in the fields around them. 750 cows died by one count. The *Chicago Tribune* reported that dairy production was down by 25% that summer in Wisconsin and in nearby Iowa, 1.2 million chickens died because of the heat wave.

Still the Jaguars practiced in what one player described as "The Bataan Death March of NFL practices."

And it all seemed to pay off.

They went 4-12 that first year but in their second year they came within one victory of the Super Bowl by defeating the four time AFC champ Bills in Buffalo and the Elway-led Broncos in Denver to get to the AFC Championship game, losing to the Patriots and up-and-comer Tom Brady. An unprecedented run for a second-year team.

LONDON

The NFL has this idea to expand to London. The scenario most talked about is to move a franchise. That franchise mentioned is usually the Jacksonville Jaguars.

The Jags had played seven regular season games in London as of the 2019 season and lost four of them.

In 2018 a new twist livened up the game narrative when four Jaguars (all defensive backs by the way, three safeties and one cornerback) got in a row, as they say in "Merry Ole England," over a bar tab.

This, however, was just not any old bar tab. This baby was a 50,000 pounds of bar tab. Converted to American that would be just shy of $64,000.

The club in question, The London Reign Club, is described as having burlesque, circus performers, a waterfall, jellyfish in a tank, and confetti cannons—among other things.

Drinking goes on.

Players contend that bottles—expensive bottles—were sent their way all night by the establishment and, being NFL players, they thought the booze was being comped.

At four in the morning (after all, they were playing a game in about twelve hours) they left. Needed their sleep or something? Or, I should say, tried to leave.

There was the little matter of the $64,000 bill. They balked—a baseball term.

Security, bouncers that is, stopped them.

One source described what happened then as "The West End version of *King Kong Meets Godzilla*."

Police were called, players arrested, questioned, released, no charges filed.

Game goes on. Jaguars lose another in London.

FUNERAL DIRECTOR

Jacksonville was desirous of an NFL team for years. The NFL is a keystone for American cities to be considered "Big Time."

It is usually a team of civic boosters, the business community and politicians who do the heavy lifting.

And so it was in Jacksonville but with a twist.

A story in the *Sporting News* in 1979 that said Bob Irsay was interested in moving the Colts if he didn't get a new stadium caught the eye of Jacksonville businessman Doug Peeles, a funeral director. He wrote Irsay a letter telling him how much Jacksonville loved football and was ready, willing and able to get the Baltimore Colts.

Then.

The mayor of Jacksonville, John Godbold, gets a phone call from Irsay and tells him he's interested in coming to Jacksonville in two weeks, to see what Jacksonville's got.

Godbold excuses himself from the phone and asks if anybody ever heard of Bob Irsay. His aide says, "Yeah, he's the guy who owns the Baltimore Colts."

Godbold tells Irsay, "Come on down."

Then.

Two weeks?

Godbold and his staff, some of whom thought it was a ridiculous idea, hatched the plan which, among other things, included obligatory elements of civic pride,a VIP tour of Duval county for Irsay, a Gator Bowl event with free hot dogs and beer, and a helicopter entrance for Irsay.

Two weeks?

It all came together, without free beer, and a call to a state senator in a trade for a political endorsement from the mayor in order to get special permission from the FAA to land a helicopter in a football stadium which had never been done up to that time and fingers crossed that anyone would show up to impress Irsay.

They thought 5,000 people would be acceptable. They got 50,000 and national press notice of the event. With that, they did NOT get a team, but did put the NFL and America on notice that Jacksonville was a player for an NFL team.

TEAL FOOD

Sports concession food can get kind of out there. All you have to do is check out the offerings each year at Minor League baseball games from sea to shining sea to see the limitless possibilities of American culinary madness.

In 2018 The Jacksonville Jaguars were hosting their first NFL playoff game in 19 years and the concessionaires went into action.

Teal is the signature Jaguar color that sets them apart from other teams.

So, teal ice cream served in inverted plastic Jaguar helmets were on the menu. But it didn't stop there.

Teal hamburger and hot dog buns were available. Right, teal bread.

And there's more. Teal beer. Created by no less a brand name than Anheuser Busch, I'll have you know.

Teal beer? Oh yeah.

Critics are always on the ready to *kepple*, as my Austrian friend would say. That's to complain.

I mean, they all laughed at Christopher Columbus...right?

One critic said the Jaguars, with teal bread, was "testing God's patience." Another said the Jaguars didn't get the "once a year memo," as in, it's okay to do green beer on St. Patrick's Day but not teal beer (I guess) any day?

There was also teal candy and, for diehards, a raspberry sucker that, if you put it in your mouth, turned your tongue teal.

While we're on the subject of food, one more Jaguar thing:

The head coach, Doug Marrone was asked what he would choose as his last meal. The answer?

Bologna and cheese sandwich.

He didn't say if he would take it on teal bread.

AFTERLIFE

The Good Place, an award-winning sitcom set in the afterlife that started running on NBC in 2016 starring Kristen Bell and Ted Danson, seems like a longshot to be linked to the Jacksonville Jaguars of the NFL but one of its recurring characters, Jason Mendoza, played by Manny Jacinto, was a part time DJ and drug dealer who lived in Jacksonville before his demise and his residency in *The Good Place* in 2016.

In the first season there was a Molotov cocktail thrown by Mendoza with the cry, "Bortles" as in Number one draft pick and starting Jaguar, at the time, quarterback Blake Bortles.

Joe Mande, a writer and producer on the show who had spent some time in Jacksonville, is responsible for the character being a Jacksonville resident and also for the "Bortles" cry which he claims was ad-libbed and then cut from the show. Mande protested and "Bortles" remained and in season two, "Bortles" is used no less than 300 times. Making it "a thing."

The Good Place, set in the afterlife constructed by the Ted Danson character, Michael, has received high praise from critics. The show is described as "making philosophy seem cool."

The plots often revolve around issues of ethics and philosophy. Scripts have been based on ideas formulated by Immanuel Kant, Kierkegaard, and Aristotle to drop a few names.

As the show gained in popularity and the Jaguars references became "a thing" on the show some members of the cast and production went on a trip to see the Jags play.

One of the things they did at the game was to seek out the teal food.

Mande says he ate a burger on a teal bun and it was the first time that he worried more about his bun than the burger, because "It looked radioactive."

Alas NFL quarterbacks are not immortal in real life and the Jaguars moved on from Bortles.

This had to be addressed in the show and this is how they did it:

Mendoza is told that Bortles is no longer the quarterback of the Jaguars.

"What? How? Why? Who is their QB now?"

"A man named Nick Foles."

Mendoza then says, "Nick Foles, are you kidding me? He won a Super Bowl! We're gonna be unstoppable."

BEING THE ELITE

Pro Wrestling and pro football have had a symbiotic relationship since at least the 1930's when Bronko Nagurski, one of the biggest stars in the NFL, would spend his off-season wrestling professionally. Nagurski won numerous "world" titles as a wrestler. Over time, pro football has bequeathed to pro wrestling a constellation of stars.

To name just a few: Vern Gagne, Steve McMichael, Wahoo McDaniel, and Dick the Bruiser, and Bill Goldberg all of who won multiple "World" Championships.

So it would seem in this media driven age it was only a matter of time until an NFL team took advantage of the marketing possibilities.

In 2019, All Elite Wrestling was created to compete with the WWE—the first attempt to do so in almost two decades.

The AEW was founded by Tony Khan the son of Jacksonville Jaguar owner Shahid Khan who is the chief financial backer of the enterprise.

Tony the CEO of AEW is also a senior VP of Football Technology and Analysis for the Jacksonville Jaguars.

AEW has signed many prominent pro wrestlers and received a big boost to its credibility in the wrestling world with the endorsement of Jim Ross, a truly legendary wrestling announcer.

All Elite Wrestling has also taken advantage of its Jaguars connection by having Jacksonville Jaguars cheerleaders, players, and Jaxson de Ville (the rambunctious on-field mascot) appear at its events. There is a heavy dose of teal and black (the Jags color scheme) at AEW events.

In 2020, AEW had a PPV event during the COVID-19 pandemic lockdown, and its main event, The Stadium Stampede, utilized an empty TIAA Bank Field (home of the Jaguars) as a backdrop for a wrestling "match" that used the entire stadium and all the bells and whistles the huge football stadium supplies—field, goal posts, swimming pool, refreshment stands, full-service bar, etc.

AEW has tie-ins with Mexican, Chinese, and European broadcasting entities for its weekly two-hour show on *AEW Wednesday Night Dynamite* and, by so doing, has tapped into a truly global market for its wresting product but also perhaps millions of potential new Jaguar fans.

🌐 https://www.youtube.com/watch?v=NtOZIlZucJ

LIFESTYLES

Shad Khan, owner of the Jacksonville Jaguars, moved to the United States when he was sixteen.

His first job was as a dishwasher making $1.20 an hour.

Now he owns the Jacksonville Jaguars valued at one-point-something billion dollars and growing.

He owns the yacht *Kismet*, which was voted the Super Yacht of the Year in 2015. He's building a new one that's bigger, or so it is rumored.

Kismet is over 300 feet long, has room for sixteen guests, has a crew of twenty-eight, and is valued at $200,000,000.

You can rent it for $1.6 million a week.

ENDORSE THIS

Gardner Minshew is one of those guys who comes along and becomes an overnight sensation.

Minshew was drafted in the 6th round draft in 2019 from Washington State and in his first season became the starting quarterback for the Jacksonville Jaguars.

He sports a mustache and this became his trademark.

NFL players even with a team down in the standings like the Jaguars in 2019 get a lot of ink.

Every corner of the U.S. is saturated with NFL news. Which made Gardner an instant national celebrity of some note.

Endorsement opportunities follow to starting NFL quarterbacks.

And so it came to pass that CamSoda, which describes itself as an adult webcam site, came to court Minshew.

Minshew was offered $1 million to do a weekly fitness class and become a brand ambassador of CamSoda, which is described in some press releases as a porn site.

A V.P. for CamSoda said the idea came to him after seeing that Minshew does band exercises half naked.

To earn the million, Minshew would be required to do the online fitness show either naked or wearing only a jockstrap.

CamSoda also would like Minshew to be the "face" of its puppet line.

Yes, puppet line.

The puppets are knit costumes for your private parts.

The firm was ready in 2019 at the time of the offer to Minshew to add a jaguar puppet to its stable of, er, ah, models which were of an elephant and a vampire. Minshew turned them down.

DO NOT HOLD THE MAYO

Not often do you find a story that features a convergence of engineering, democracy, love, and mayonnaise to tell the tale.

A group of Jaguars fans, Bold City Brigade, tailgate before every Jaguar home game and their "spokesgater" said they try to come up with something special for each home opener.

The Tennessee Titans, a rival due to their conference affiliation, was the opponent for the opener in question in 2017.

What to do?

At times such as this the Lord always provides.

A video of a person wearing a Tennessee Titan jersey eating mayonnaise out of the jar with a spoon was posted by a Jags fan and went viral on Jags fan threads.

A kiddy pool and forty jars of mayonnaise were purchased at Costco, and this is where the engineering comes in. The plan was to have Jags fans belly flop into a pool full of mayo, so an air mattress was purchased to make the flop less dangerous (someone at some college needs to do a study on how tailgating insanity or ingenuity impacts the community from a retail angle). Caputo, the "spokesgater" for the group, says he was not in favor of this stunt, but he was out voted by other members, hence the democracy culpability in the deed. The winner (?) of the dive competition, judged like Olympic events on a 10-point scale, proposed to his girlfriend covered in mayonnaise.

Love.

It is immortalized on YouTube,

KING OF POP

Shahid Khan purchased Wembley Stadium in London where the NFL has played most of its overseas regular season games and there is belief that if an NFL team moves to London, it will be the Jaguars.

The Jaguars have played an NFL regular season game in the British capitol every year since 2013.

Khan also had in 2013 previously purchased Fulham FC, a professional soccer team and a member of England's Premier League, located in London.

This is where it gets a bit goofy. Just a bit.

Khan bought Fulham FC from Mohammed Al Fayed. If you keep up with current events the name Mohammed Al Fayed might ring a bell.

He is the owner of the Ritz Hotel in Paris, 75 Rockefeller Plaza in New York City and he used to own the venerable Harrods department store, a London institution if ever there was one.

But his biggest claim to fame, alas, in this media celebrity-driven age is that his son Dodi was in the car with his then girlfriend Princess Diana of Wales when she and he were killed in an automobile accident.

Al Fayed for years after contended in the press and in court proceedings that the couple died because of a conspiracy spearheaded by members of the British Royal family. All of his accusations were proved false in British courts.

Anyway, Khan at the news conference to announce his purchase of the Fulham FC was asked a question about a statue that Al Fayed had unveiled in front of Craven Cottage Stadium—the home field of Fulham—of his friend, the famous pop star Michael Jackson.

It seems the local Fulham peeps didn't much care for the Michael Jackson statue in front of their stadium.

Khan, asked by the press if he would remove the statue, demurred.

Al Fayed on the other hand, who was at the press conference, chimed in that the statue would remain.

To emphasize his point, Al Fayed looked at Kahn and told him: "Are you listening to me about Michael Jackson? I promise now? Otherwise...I will take your mustache off."

Khan has a very nice mustache. Even snazzier than Jaguar quarterback Gardner Minshew.

Jacksonville is full of famous mustaches.

Khan eventually returned the statue to Al Fayed.

Khan decided that the fans didn't want the statue.

THE SWISS

Injuries are always a concern in sports. But.

Chris Hanson, the Jaguar punter was having a dinner party at his home in 2002. Fondue happened.

Yes, Hanson slipped, dropped the fondue pot on the tile floor and sustained first and second-degree burns. Jarett Holmes, the Jaguar place-kicker, was a dinner guest and sustained burns as well. Kasey, Hanson's wife, is said to have slipped in the spilled fondue and, for her troubles, sustained second and third-degree burns which required skin grafts.

All participants in the accident have completely recovered.

Hanson may be in line for what I call a "Bobby Goldsboro Award."

Goldsboro was a successful recording artist of the 60s who had the hit "Honey." I remember his story on the *Tonight Show* as to how he was once injured. He sliced his foot open on a hardened kernel of cereal on his kitchen floor.

KEEP ON CHOPPING IN THE FREE WORLD

"Someday we'll look back on this and it will all seem funny."
—Bruce Springsteen, "Rosalita"

The Jaguars got off to a bad start in 2004, losing their first few games. Coach Jack Del Rio wanted to light a fire or give some motivational focus to his team's efforts.

Football coaches are big on motivation—a high school football coach once got in trouble for biting the heads off of frogs in the locker room to boost his team's, er, focus.

Del Rio took the phrase "Keep Chopping Wood." It's an old athletic maxim that implies just keep with the program, keep working and all will be fine, keep your eye on that goal while working.

Del Rio went one step further than simply applying the slogan—he put an actual, huge stump and ax in the middle of the locker room and encouraged the players to give it an occasional whack.

Which they did.

It all came to an end when punter Chris Hanson (the only Jaguar player from the previous year to make the Pro Bowl) walked through the locker room after practice and gave the stump a whack. Only thing is, it went sideways and Hanson cut his non-punting leg to the point he had to be rushed to the hospital for emergency surgery.

He was out for the season. Although he was put on the non-football injury list, which meant the Jaguars did not have to pay his $375,000 salary, they did pay him. He recovered.

Del Rio said, "I'll find another slogan."

GOAT

There is always an argument as to who is the greatest of all time, whether it be a position like QB or a particular team.

For my money, the greatest Jacksonville Jaguar of all time is Curtis Dvorak.

"Who?" you might say. "What position does he play?"

Mascot.

That's right, for nineteen years Curtis Dvorak was Jaxson de Ville, the rambunctious cartoon-like Jaguar running around the field causing mayhem and mirth.

What makes Dvorak stand out are several things, such as standing on top of the light standards and bungee jumping onto the playing field. Or zip-lining down from the scoreboard which, by the way, is way the hell up in the air.

He also agitated the league who changed the rules to rein him in on behalf of other teams' front office and players.

Dan Rooney of the Steelers once said of Jaxson de Ville, in reference to Jaxson getting kind of close to the team on the field where he would taunt them during the game: "It's too bad that Greg Lloyd or Jack Lambert aren't still playing," During the game.

He was once reprimanded by the league and the Jaguars apologized when Jaxson displayed a Steelers Terrible Towel with a message written on it that claimed the towel caused Ebola virus.

He spent the next home game sitting in a cage as a faux penance.

He was one of a kind and if ever a mascot can get into the Hall of Fame, my vote is for Jaxson de Ville.

SAN DIEGO

SayBrah®

VANNA WHITE

LOS ANGELES (A)
SAN DIEGO
TE

TATTOOS, TACOS,
AND RATTLESNAKES

LOS ANGELES (A)
SAN DIEGO

"If you want to ring the cash register
you have to pass."

—Sid Gillman,
Chargers Head Coach (1960-1969)

SayBrah

The Chargers started out as a charter member of
the AFL in 1959.

The team was founded by Barron Hilton and started
playing in the AFL in 1960 as the Los Angeles Chargers but moved to San Diego in 1961.

In 2017, they moved back to Los Angeles.

Super Bowl Appearances: 1
Super Bowl Record: 0-1
Super Bowl Loss: 1994

FICTIONAL

Dan Jauregui was a huge Charger fan back in 1994-95, the year the Chargers went to the Super Bowl, and he made a decision that would define a greater part of his life by creating what or who would be known as Boltman, the smiling, unofficial mascot of the San Diego Chargers.

A season ticket holder, Jauregui has appeared at all Chargers games taking thousands of photos with fans for over two decades until, of course, the Chargers bolted for Los Angeles in 2017.

Many might think Boltman and the Chargers are linked and that Boltman is the official mascot of the Chargers, but Boltman is only loosely connected to the franchise by association.

The Chargers did offer him $3,900 a game or offered to buy the character for $20,000, but Jauregui wouldn't sell his "hobby," which he has bankrolled himself while becoming a San Diego icon along the way.

In fact, the relationship with Chargers higher ups, most notably Alex and Dean Spanos, depending upon who you believe, has been mostly acrimonious. To hear one report, the Chargers hate him.

He has been threatened with the loss of his two front row season tickets and he says a cameraman at the stadium once told him that the camera people were warned not to show him on the JumboTron.

Nonetheless, his Hollywood-fashioned headpiece of a smiling Max Headroomesque, muscle-bound mascot is a crowd favorite.

Jauregui even admits he has put over six figures of his own money to keep Boltman alive and that his alter ego contributed both to his divorce from his childhood sweetheart, and to bad blood between him and the other San Diego iconic mascot, Ted Giannioulis, aka the San Diego Chicken.

Giannoulis claims that Jauregui wrote a disparaging letter to the San Diego daily years ago, although the paper and Jauregui say they have no recollection of this.

When the Chargers decided to go to Los Angeles, Jauregui decided it was time to retire Boltman by selling the character, for which he owns a trademark and copyright. He auctioned the character lock stock and barrel on eBay with plans to split the proceeds with his favorite charity, Rady Children's Hospital-San Diego. The reserve figure was not reached so the rights to Boltman remain with Jauregui.

Everything under the sun is complicated.

PAUL MAGUIRE FIVE $100 BILLS STORY

Money is a defining factor in professional sports. The amounts are almost unfathomable these days.

Lest we forget the impact of making a living as a professional athlete and what a life transforming thing it can be, the NFL landscape of not so long ago is strewn with much smaller amounts that made a big difference.

Paul Maguire played in the AFL/NFL for eleven seasons, mostly with the Buffalo Bills, but he was signed out of the Citadel to his first pro contract with the Chargers.

He grew up in a modest working-class clan in Youngstown, Ohio. His father worked in a rail yard.

After graduating from college, he was drafted by both leagues and was offered a pro contract by the Chargers for $7,000 in the early 60s. The representative of the Chargers showed him the contract and ten $100 bills. He crossed out the 7 and made it an 8. If ya sign, you get this $1000 now.

He signed.

He went downstairs from the room in which he was staying, having just played in a college all star game, and found his dad. He gave his dad 5 of the $100 dollar bills for all the things he had done for Paul, his son, that had helped him to that point. His father, a hard-boiled rail-yard man from Youngstown, cried.

His father died two years later at the age of eighty. Going through his dad's wallet, his son found the five $100 bills still there.

WHEEL

Rolf Bernischke grew up in San Diego, went to high school there, college at Cal Davis and worked summers at the San Diego Zoo where his father, Kurt, was a pathologist who started the Center for Reproduction of Endangered Species at the San Diego Zoo.

After being drafted by Oakland, he was traded to San Diego, made the team as the Chargers place-kicker and retired as the all time leading scorer in San Diego Charger history.

In the middle of Bernischke's career, he developed ulcerative colitis and was so sick he had to interrupt his career, his weight plummeting down to as low as 123 pounds on his 6' frame.

He bounced back and played many more years, and today is the national spokesperson for the Crohn's and Colitis Foundation of America and for Hepatitis C awareness.

ACT TWO

Rolf also became a TV star for a short time, Jan 10 to June 30, 1989, as Pat Sajak's replacement hosting the popular game show Wheel of Fortune, when Sajak quit to be host of *The Pat Sajak Show*.

Bernischke was a long shot to get the gig as it was offered to Vanna White, who turned it down. Others vying for the job were John McEnroe, Jimmy Connors, and sportscaster Tim Brando. But Merv Griffin picked Rolf.

AIRCRAFT CARRIER

In the spring of 2012 it was announced by the NFL, trying to piggyback on the success of an NCAA basketball game being played on an aircraft carrier, that the Chargers would open the season at home on the USS Ronald Reagan aircraft carrier.

The opponent was to be announced at a future time.

The press pointed out that an NCAA basketball court required 4,700 sq feet of surface and the NFL field, measuring at 58,000 sq feet, would necessitate that no actual seating would be available, making this game a "for TV event" only. It would also kick into effect a special codicil in the team's contract with the city—and the city of San Diego would have to make up for the loss of revenue from ticket sales by paying for 60,000 tickets. The season ticket holders would be compensated with extra preseason game tickets.

Of course, it turned out that this was printed on April 1st.

But...

In 2006, the Chargers did visit an aircraft carrier and in 2013 they practiced on the USS Ronald Reagan as part of "NFL 60" initiative to encourage kids to exercise sixty minutes a day.

The team spent time practicing for the upcoming preseason game on the flight deck, also signing autographs for sailors and their families.

FREE INK

NFL teams try to connect with their fans in many ways.

The Chargers move to Los Angeles was an emotional transaction for San Diego sports fans and the LA Chargers were, of course, anxious to establish a brand beachhead in their new home. For two seasons the LA Chargers have tried a unique giveaway, a free Chargers Tattoo on a first come first serve basis. The team had partnered with the Shamrock Social Club tattoo parlor to offer the free images to its fans.

The parlor is on Sunset Strip and the offer in its second year and festivities include appearances by former Chargers players. The fans line up in West Hollywood outside the Shamrock, on select dates, from 1 pm to 1 am.

The latter, a prime tattoo time one might think.

The lines were long.

FREE TACOS

Teams love to use words like "us" and "we" and "your," as in *Your* San Diego Chargers, and "family," and the new one is "nation"—as in "Raiders Nation." Now, don't get me wrong, Raiders Nation is real, the collective fan base, and I give all props to that bunch.

But let's get real. The San Diego Chargers—the owners, the front office, the coaches, the players—are not on your side. To be crystal clear, they are not on the side of the fans. They are on their own side. And in the players' case, look, they should be on their own side. Absolutely. But that means quite often they are at odds with the side of the fans. Period. This is my belief. This is my position. And I'm sticking to it. Because I believe it to be true.

Which brings me to major kudos for Victor Lopez, life-long San Diego Chargers fan and owner of El Pollo Frillo in San Diego, who put his money where his mouth and heart are by offering free tacos to anyone who comes into his place the day after a Los Angeles (phooey!) Chargers loss, after the Chargers jilted San Diego and went north.

Lopez later said that it actually was good for his business when he started the taco giveaway and he was just hoping the Chargers would go 0-16.

To get your free taco you had to utter the secret words—Spanos Taco.

Bravo brother.

BRAIN

Junior Seau was one of the best and most beloved players in the history of the San Diego Chargers. At some point family and friends say he wasn't the same Junior they knew. He was acting erratically and in ways unfamiliar to those close to him.

This culminated, unfortunately, with him committing suicide.

By this time, CTE and its link to playing football was in the news and at the top of the NFL's agenda.

As soon as Seau was found dead the phone started ringing.

His family was urged to send or give access to his brain from several quarters.

Bennet Omalu, the forensic pathologist who found the link between football, head injury and CTE, wanted in on the autopsy. Seau's son gave him permission.

Stanley Prussiner, who won the Nobel Prize for discovering the protein that causes brain disease, urged Omalu to get to the brain as soon as possible.

The medical examiner, with Seau's son's permission, allowed Omalu in on the autopsy.

The NFL, meanwhile, had a deal in place for the brains of NFL players to go to Boston University Center for the Study of Traumatic Encephalopathy. The

San Diego team doctor, in turn, urged Seau's son not to allow Omalu to sit in on the autopsy. The son then called up the medical examiner and demanded that Omalu be banned from the autopsy.

So, we have a full-blown fight over a dead man's brain.

Think about this.

Your beloved relative and loved one has committed suicide. You, in turn, become embroiled in a tussle over his brain from numerous quarters.

Nice.

When the dust settled, the NFL donated $30 million dollars to the National Institute of Health to study concussion science.

A blind study was done on tissue from Seau's brain and the finding confirmed that he was suffering from CTE.

For a thorough account of the tale of Mr. Seau's brain, seek out Steve Fainamu and Mark Fainaru-Wada's report for PBS's *Frontline*.

PERSONAL NOTE: *My father Ed played for the Rams for four seasons and he died from dementia related issues, so I have first hand experience with the horror and struggles this disease presents. It is not a pleasant thing to see a man who is vibrant and healthy in every other way robbed of life by damage that may have occurred to his brain earlier in his life while he was pursuing his dreams.*

THE SPORTS ARTIST

Ernie Barnes was drafted by the Baltimore Colts in 1959. He didn't make the team but his artistic journey as a chronicler of sporting themes and of African-American life started a long successful career after his attendance at the 1959 NFL Championship game. As a guest of the Colts as a newly drafted member of the organization he had seen with his artist's eye the perspective from right behind the bench of the Colts.

He said he left the game and when he got home he created the painting he named "The Bench" in about an hour of quick work. He did it with a sense of urgency as he wanted to remember the images in his mind's eye from the event he had just seen.

Barnes did go on to a successful pro football career playing in the AFL with various teams.

Barnes became what some call the first famous successful athlete artist but even as his paintings sold and he received many important commissions he kept the painting "The Bench" and always refused the many offers to purchase it. He was so attached to it that he even brought it with him when he traveled and kept it under his bed.

After his death in 2009 "The Bench" was donated to the Pro Football Hall of Fame by his family.

Barnes grew up in Durham, North Carolina where his father was a shipping clerk in a tobacco company and his mother the head of a household in a prominent Durham lawyer's home.

When the young Ernest accompanied his mother to the lawyer, Frank L. Fuller's home, the prominent attorney would encourage him to delve into the artistic books in his library. In this way Barnes became somewhat versed in the art of Michelangelo, Toulouse Lautrec, Reubens, and other masters before he entered the first grade.

As a child he was described as chubby and unathletic. This led to him being bullied and he kept to himself at school. One day a teacher found him alone with his sketch pad. The teacher was a weightlifter and he encouraged Barnes to lift weights and to pursue his sketching.

By his senior year Ernest Barnes was the captain of the football team which got him a football scholarship to college where he majored in art and of course to a career as a pro football player.

Barnes first glimpse of fame for painting was on a local TV show hosted in San Diego by Regis Philbin. Barnes appeared as an artist/pro football player as he was a player for the San Diego Chargers at the time.

He played three seasons with the Chargers where he became lifelong friends with quarterback Jack Kemp who would one day become the Vice Presidential running mate of Robert Dole in 1996.

Barnes then went to Denver where he also got recognition for his art in an underhanded way.

He would sketch at practice and even on the sideline. He was once fined $100 for sketching during practice by Head Coach Jack Faulkner when playing for the Broncos.

But he was also encouraged by Red Miller, an assistant coach, who would one day be the head coach at Denver. Barnes would give Miller his sketches on scraps of paper that he would make during the game. Miller would keep them for him and give them to him after the game.

Barnes went to NFL meetings during the offseason to try and get the league to name him the official artist of pro football. At the NFL meeting he met Sonny Werblin, the owner of the New York Jets, and Werblin was so impressed with the offensive lineman's work that he signed Barnes to a pro football player's contract—not to play, but to paint.

Werblin told him, "You have more value to the country as an artist than as a pro football player."

Werblin arranged a one man show of Barnes' work at the Grand Central Art Gallery of New York City.

Unbeknownst to Barnes, Werblin had invited three New York City art critics who were duly impressed with Barnes work calling him the best painter of sport since George Bellows.

Barnes sold all of his paintings at the show.

Since that time the places Ernie Barnes and his painting have been is impressive.

Perhaps his most famous painting in America's consciousness is "Sugar Shack"—a canvas that appeared on the credits of the opening and closing of the popular sitcom *Good Times*. His painting also peppered the show's scenery as work that was supposedly created by the character J.J. played by comedian Jimmy Walker.

Barnes also supplied the artwork of more than a few prominent music albums, most notably the use of "Sugar Shack" on the cover of Marvin Gaye's album *I Want You*.

Ernie Barnes was known as perhaps the most successful and impactful artist who just also happened to be a former NFL player.

ROUGH ACRES

The San Diego Chargers only won four games in 1962. Sid Gillman, the head coach, wanted to toughen up his team. His solution was to hold training camp at a dude ranch seventy miles east of San Diego in the California desert called Rough Acres.

It was hot, it was bare bones, shacks, no outdoor showers. It was located outside of Boulevard, California a town of fifty. Only one bar in town.

The field had little if any grass and they had to put sawdust out each day onto the field in order to practice on the hard scrabble rocky terrain.

And, oh yes, there were a lot of snakes. Rattlesnakes and tarantulas and scorpions one might surmise. The usual suspects of a California desert.

They killed between seventeen and twenty rattlers during camp.

Gillman was always thinking and he added a couple of touches to the regimen of camp.

He bunked players of different races together to add to the cohesiveness of the team and it worked.

He also hired the first full-time weightlifting coach in NFL history, Alvin Roy, a trainer for the 1960 U.S. Olympic weightlifting team.

The prevailing view had always been that weightlifting would make a player muscle bound and impede his athleticism. The opposite is actually true so this was an innovative move at the time.

Roy, in the speech he gave at the beginning of camp the players recalled years later, told them that he had learned something from the Russians who had almost swept all of the Gold in the 1960 Olympics and that thing was Dianabol, a little pink pill.

Steroids.

At each of the three meals players were given a pink pill to take.

After a month some said that they were starting to look like Popeye the Sailor.

Not all of the team took the pills—notably the QBs and some skilled position players demurred. After Dave Kocurek, a TE, went to his doctor and told the doctor about the pills and the doctor showed Kocurek the label on the package that said "DANGEROUS" in big red letters and added the side effects such as, "will cause permanent bone damage, liver damage, heart damage and testicular shrinkage." Some players had second thoughts about the wonder drug.

All Pro G Ron Mix had a team meeting where he told the players of the dangers of the pills and at that point, the beginning of the regular season players were no longer required to take the pills.

Steroids, it must be pointed out, were not illegal in 1963.

The Chargers who survived Rough Acres and its heat, horrible food, and rattlesnakes won the AFL Championship. That is the only league championship that the Chargers have ever won.

SMALL PHARMA

The Chargers coming off a bad season decided on a peculiar strategy. They decided to trade and sign players who were thought to be problems.

The strategy was to wend some magic or something which is even more bizarre when you learn that at the time the new players brought in under this strategy were referred to in house as "the crazies."

Some of the problem children were Duane Thomas, Deacon Jones, Tim Rossovich.

The Chargers had another problem: drugs.

Amphetamines to be more precise.

Owner Gene Klein was blindsided by the drug problem and he had recently cashed out his business empire to enjoy life and concentrate on his football team. He got a lot more than he bargained for.

Klein decided to ask Dr. Arnold Mandell, a Distinguished Professor of Psychiatry at the University of California San Diego, to join the team as an unpaid consultant.

What Dr. Mandell found was a team inundated with amphetamine usage. He also found it was a league-wide problem. So amped up on pills were many NFL players that many would refuse to take the field unless they were under the influence and pumped up into what amounted to a chemically induced rage.

The results were players Mandell described as in a "pre-psychotic rage state" when they went out onto the field.

Or another way to put it they would embark on a five-hour temper tantrum every Sunday game day afternoon.

This chemical induced fury would result in brutal hits and a lot of injuries and lead head coach Harland Svare to declare that this game in the NFL in the late 70's was not the game he grew up on.

The NFL started to notice and sent security to shadow the Chargers players even going as far to hire prostitutes that the league purportedly wired for sound to entrap the players.

This led to the player going to Tijuana to score "black beauties" for game day. Dr. Mandell's solution was to prescribe amphetamines in lower doses to the Chargers players trying to wean them off the stuff.

This would eventually lead to Dr. Mandell losing his medical license for doing something technically that wasn't against the law.

Klein didn't see it that way and was pissed off at Mandell. Klein was summoned to Pete Rozell's office for a chat.

Rozelle fined Klein $20,000, fined Svare $5,000, and fined some of the players lesser amounts.

Rozelle demanded that Klein fire Svare. Klein refused and after Rozelle threatened to fine Klein if he did not fire Svare, Klein told Rozelle "F&%# You" and was then fined the $20,000.

Mandell eventually lost his prescription rights as they were taken away from him after a fifteen-day hearing caused by the release of medically privileged patient information Mandell had compiled of amphetamine prescriptions. Someone with access to records in possession of the California State Board of Medical Examiners leaked the info.

Mandell (again, an unpaid consultant for the Chargers) was a nationally-recognized psychiatrist, had been a past president for both the United States Society of Psychiatry and the Society of Biological Psychiatry, had twenty-three years of research dealing with amphetamine use, 18,000 hours of treating patients behind him, written six books on related subjects, published 230 articles in his field, and had been the recipient of a MacArthur Genius grant in his field of study.

He was a well-credentialed expert.

He was defended by a phalanx of colleagues from all around the country.

Nonetheless he lost his license which led him to write a book about the experience with the Chargers, *The Nightmare Season.*

Meanwhile 60% of the league's players were using amphetamines.

Mandell estimated that the Chargers were using around 10,000 amphetamines a season.

THE CURSE?

The 1994 San Diego Chargers went to the Super Bowl. They lost but are still the only Charger squad to make it to the Super Bowl.

However, there is a pall hanging over this squad.

With his untimely suicide, All-Pro and Hall of Famer Junior Seau became the eighth player from San Diego Chargers Super Bowl squad to die before his forty-fifth birthday.

According to professor Wei Zhu, the chair of the Department of Applied Mathematics and Statistics at Stony Brook University and two colleagues in a study carried out for NPR, the odds that this many men—eight in a group of fifty-three (roster size)—would die before the age of 45, is 500 to 1. Very rare.

The deaths, not in order, were reportedly Seau's suicide, drunken driving, drug overdose, airline crash, two apparent heart attacks, complications from diabetes and somewhat eerily, being hit by lightning twice. The same guy was hit by lightning twice in one day.

LB Doug Miller was hit by lightning while camping in Colorado and as he was being administered CPR, a second lightning bolt hit him and killed him.

Odds?

Just bad luck?

KNOCKED OUT

Weather is a variable in many defeats and victories, just ask Napoleon. Or the Spanish Armada and that was back in 1588.

On December 22, 1995, it snowed in New Jersey.

The next day the New York Giants hosted the San Diego Chargers. There was a lot of snow in the stadium. The Giants were 5-10 and not going anywhere that year.

As the game progressed with the Chargers winning and with a chance to make the playoffs—enter the Giants promotional services. There was an in-game promotion that season sponsored by UPS. A man in a UPS uniform was showcased on the stadium video screen with a signed football that he would hand deliver to a random winner chosen from spectators.

That day, when the winner was located, he was wearing a San Diego Chargers jersey. Then the snowballs, slush balls, and ice balls commenced raining down.

From there it was all downhill.

Charger's bench was ground zero and the players, coaches, and anyone hanging around got pelted. The most infamous casualty was Sid Brooks, the equipment manager of the Chargers. In the video, poor Mr. Brooks was hit in the head by what, presumably, was more of an ice ball. He went down like he was shot by a sniper. Knocked him out cold. He survived.

The game was salted away with an interception by Charger Shaun Gayle who returned it 99 yards for a TD. His 99-yard run was through a fusillade of snow projectiles. He later was quoted as saying, "It was the longest 99 yards of my life."

Fifteen fans were arrested, 175 were ejected and seventy-five lost their season tickets.

In case you might think this is a humorous anecdote, consider that Sid Brooks says in his book that he had to take medication the rest of his life due to the effects of the incident.

AMERICAN DREAM

At the ripe old age of twenty-five, Jerry Jones had a dream.

He was the son of an entrepreneur who had a grocery business and had started a successful insurance firm headquartered in Springfield, MO.

Jerry had gone to the University of Arkansas and played guard on the football team and was known, even as a college student, as a budding businessman dubbed by some "the Arkansas Business" for selling shoes to fraternities and other money-making endeavors.

But Jerry, as a twenty-five-year-old with a net worth that hovered around $0, had a dream. And that dream was to own a pro football team.

This was 1966 and the AFL seemed like the place that Jerry could make this happen. He was married and he told his wife to keep his idea to herself, especially not telling his boss, his dad Pat Jones.

Jerry was in Missouri. He would travel to nearby Houston where he knew AFL owners would meet and he would hang around the lobby of the hotel the owners frequented. He met some of them. Notably he became known to Joe Robbie, Lamar Hunt, and Ralph Wilson.

Jerry even traveled to Miami and literally helped move Joe Robbie's furniture into his Dolphins office.

Robbie called Barron Hilton on Jerry's behalf. Hilton was trying to sell the Chargers for, among other reasons, the fact that they were losing money. Hilton demanded a $1 million line of credit as prerequisite to speak to Jerry Jones, who he didn't know from Adam.

Jones said in those days he could get people to lend him money. He had a deal with some folks in a Shakey's Pizza franchise deal and he even asked the Teamsters—Jimmy Hoffa's union—about getting a loan. Jones got the line of credit from his pizza connection and got an audience with Hilton and made a deal to buy the Chargers for $5.8 million.

Jones met with Lamar Hunt who gave him a tutorial on the cash flow and business of the AFL.

A newspaper headline in the Little Rock paper trumpeted that Jones was going to buy the San Diego Chargers in 1966.

Jones says he had the money, or at least a promise to get a loan, to buy the team but there was only one obstacle.

Daddy.

Pat Jones got wind of the deal, called his son, and laid down the law—or gave him the facts of life spiel or whatever. Jerry didn't buy the team.

Two months later the team was sold for $10.1 million and Pat Jones would tell the story of how he talked his son out of making a $4 million profit in only two months time for the rest of his life.

The merger happened shortly after the Chargers were sold and that pro football thing kind of took off.

Jones got his team twenty years later.

Right after the failure to pull the trigger on the Chargers deal, Jones' next business venture didn't go so well. In fact, he was in Dallas trying to rent a car and the car rental place cut his credit card up right in front of him.

This was in Dallas, where one day he would be almost like a king.

Dreams.

ATLANTA

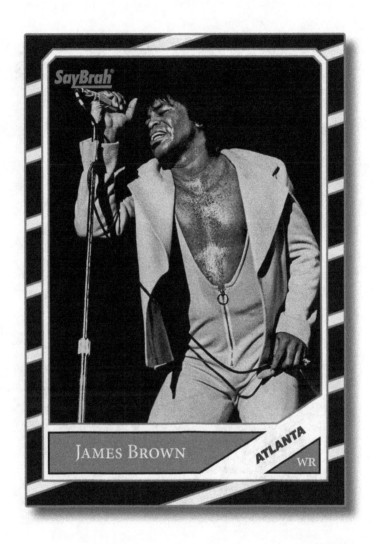

SayBrah®

JAMES BROWN

ATLANTA

WR

BURNING DOWN THE HOUSE, ALLIGATORS, AND JAMES BROWN

ATLANTA

"I don't know anything about football."

—Rankin Smith,
Falcons owner (1965-2002)

SayBrah®

Atlanta Falcons were given a franchise in the NFL in 1965 to prevent the AFL from locating a team in the capital of what at the time was referred to as "the New South."

Home Depot co-founder Arthur Blank purchased the team in 2002 from the Smith family.

In Super Bowl LI, Atlanta blew a 25-point lead to the New England Patriots in the largest collapse in the history of the Super Bowl.

Super Bowl Appearances: 2
Super Bowl Record: 0-2
Super Bowl Losses: 1998, 2016

RON MEXICO

In 2005 a website called *The Smoking Gun* reported that Michael Vick was alleged to have given herpes to a woman after engaging in unprotected sex. She sued and in the proceedings it was revealed that Vick had used the alias "Ron Mexico" when being tested and treated for herpes.

After the news broke, fans started buying Falcon jerseys with "MEXICO" on the back of the jersey where "VICK" would normally be until the NFL got wise and stopped the sale of Mexico Falcon jerseys.

In 2005, Will Leitch started the sports news and blog website *Deadspin*. Leitch admitted that this story about Vick inspired the website. Leitch said the Vick aka Ron Mexico story proved that sports reporting was hiding the best stories.

Ron Mexico became a go-to reference on *Deadspin* and "Ron Mexico" got a second fifteen minutes or more of fame when the Anthony Weiner scandal revealed that Weiner used the pseudonym "Carlos Danger."

Online the question was asked—who has the better fake name, Carlos Danger or Ron Mexico?

PROPHESY

Furman Bisher covered sports for the *Atlanta Journal Constitution* with great distinction for decades and was one of the most prestigious sportswriters ever.

He covered every Super Bowl but the first. And there is a reason he missed the first.

Bisher said his editor at the *AJC* told him of the Super Bowl: "Nothing will ever come of this game. There is no point in going out there, it's too expensive to send somebody all the way to Los Angeles."

Said Bisher of his editor, "He was a man of extraordinary vision."

SHEAR GENIUS

Rankin Smith was the first owner of the Atlanta Falcons.

He was not shy about claiming that he knew nothing about football.

This didn't stop him from putting in his two cents.

Smith had a suggestion for the owners,

His reasoning was that the 50 yard line seat was the premium seating option. So far so good.

His idea was to maximize the 50 yard line seat thing by proposing that each stadium put in two football fields. One laid out east -west and the other north- south and have the teams play on alternating fields after each quarter.

This way you would have twice as many 50 yard line seats.

I think he may have stolen the idea from DaVinci.

When Norb Hecker got the job as the first head coach of the Atlanta Falcons he was looking for veteran leadership to help mold his ragtag expansion team.

Hecker was a disciple of Vince Lombardi and he was looking for discipline and toughness in his new squad that consisted of NFL rejects and young players the Falcons had picked in the NFL draft.

One of the guys Hecker planned to look to was Alex Hawkins the special team captain of the Baltimore Colts who was one of the more accomplished NFL players the Falcons received in the expansion draft.

This is where research might have helped.

It didn't quite work out.

Hecker's scouting report on Hawkins must have been incomplete.

Hawkins did excel with the Falcons on the field and become a fixture on Falcons media coverage as a color man on TV and radio broadcasts after his playing days but Alex and Hecker did not have a meeting of minds.

Black Mountain, North Carolina was the site of the Falcons first pre-season training camp and it turned out to be one of the more legendary hell holes in NFL training camp lore known for the size and number of its mosquitoes, its austerity, and for its awful food. Not to mention Hecker's unrelenting drive to get his team in tip-top shape in the summer heat.

Black Mountain was a religious retreat run by the YMCA and the Falcons shared the camp that summer with a religious group and an Alcoholics Anonymous gathering.

The Reverend Billy Graham lived nearby and is said to have made a few appearances in camp.

On the other end of the spectrum from the reverend you'd find Hawkins, who is a legendary NFL carouser. Early in camp he showed up at five in the morning in the back of a watermelon truck only to be greeted by Hecker who fined him $2000—a princely sum for NFL players in 1966.

Hawkins would say later in life that he was fined so many times that he might be the only player who, after ten years in the league, owed the NFL money.

Hecker threatened to take Hawkins BB gun away in camp as he had a penchant for shooting out the lights. The closest liquor required a road trip. The facilities were horrible and the food caused a rebellion among the players. It is said that when the Falcons left Black Mountain, two of the players stayed behind to burn the bridge that led to the camp.

The players summed up the time at Black Mountain where Hecker's first order of business was to whip his charges into shape thusly: "It was hell."

Hawkins with his first chance to play offense in the NFL with the Falcon was a star player for them. But he and Hecker didn't get along so he was shipped back to Baltimore after less than two years with Falcons.

He played for the Colts against the Falcons and after that one game in which Hawkins caught a bunch of passes against the Falcons, Hecker said, "I don't care if he catches forty passes I don't want him."

He was a character indeed.

He became a newspaper, radio, and TV guy and worked NFL TV games as the partner to legends like Jack Buck, Vin Scully, Dan Criqui, Frank Gleber, Al Michaels, Jack Whitaker, and Lindsey Nelson—a Hall Of Fame roster there.

But Alex was an honest man and he was once told by a network exec about life in the pro football telecast booth: "There's no room for honesty."

He once opened a telecast by telling the viewers that they were about to watch a game between the two worst teams in the league.

As an announcer he was teamed with the legend Vin Scully for a Dallas Cowboy game and he said on air he was rooting for the Cowboys. After a shot of Roger Staubach running out to the field to rejoin the team in the huddle Hawkins told Scully and the listening audience," Roger runs like a sissy."

To which Scully replied, "Did you wear a helmet when you played?"

He was fired three times by CBS for undiplomatic statements.

Jake Scott, the Dolphins defensive back, had two broken hands and was still playing in the game. Hawkins observation while working behind the mic? "Jake found out who his real friends were when he went to the men's room." He was fired for that one.

He wrote two books that described his raucous NFL career, *That's My Story (And I'm Sticking To It)*, the title of which was used by country recording star Collin Raye to write a hit song that Hawkins received royalties from as he was listed as one of the song's writers.

Hecker didn't want him in Atlanta, but Baltimore welcomed him back as he brought a style that boosted morale and he was a tough hard-nosed superior athlete on the field.

After every game he would give what he called the "Cutty Sark Award" to the best special team player. The award consisted of a bottle of Cutty Sark scotch. He would make a speech and after the speech he would always bestow himself with the award. His teammates loved him.

His second book, *Then Came Brain Damage*, was cruelly prophetic as he died from dementia.

Yet he was a joker to the end, said his wife.

Quite a life he lived so let's end on a high note for a positive man.

He said of his NFL career: "I would have paid the Colts to let me play." And in reference to his NFL career: "I was the luckiest little boy in the world."

KNOW YOUR AUDIENCE

Man is accused of armed robbery in 2015 at a chain restaurant. A security guard wrestles the alleged perp and takes the black pistol he used to allegedly rob the establishment.

He goes on trial for armed robbery and other serious charges. Turns out the gun he had in his hands was also used in two murders in the same community.

At trial the prosecution claims to have found a pair of black gloves. The victim says the person who committed the crime wore a black glove. Next to the black glove was also found an Atlanta Falcon baseball cap.

The DNA of the defendant is found on the hat.

All the crimes were committed in Baton Rouge, Louisiana less than a 100 miles from New Orleans, home of the Saints and bitter rivals of the Atlanta Falcons. Sometimes fashion choices are important.

THE DUTCHMAN

Norm Van Brocklin is a Hall of Famer. You can look it up.

If you scan the top-ten passing performances of all time in NFL regular season games you'll see a who's who of modern quarterbacking excellence— Brady, Marino, Roethlisberger, Warren Moon, Matthew Stafford, and a few others, and then one outlier.

The guy who threw for more yards than anyone in NFL history did it nearly seventy years ago? That's right, Norm Van Brocklin, who threw 554 Yards versus the New York Giants in 1950.

Van Brocklin coached the Falcons from 1968 -1974. He was known for his old school quotes and for being a hard ass.

He had an operation for a brain tumor and said "I asked them to give me a sportswriter's brain because I wanted one that had never been used." This begins to explain national sports talk radio. Maybe not? Only a liberal interpretation of the Old Testament could explain that.

Earlier in that season there was speculation about whether he would quit. Later, after a sportswriter's question as to whether he was still a fighter, he answered, "Get out of that chair and find out. I mean it. Come over here and we can start stacking furniture."

In the late 40's the Rams were playing the Chicago Bears. Van Brocklin was blindsided by a guy named Ed Sprinkle, a notorious tough guy in a league of tough guys. George Halas thought that Sprinkle was the toughest player he ever coached.

In those days even defensive linemen didn't necessarily wear face masks. Sprinkle didn't that day. Van Brocklin told my father, Ed Champagne, not to block Sprinkle. "Just let him in."

My dad confirmed the request. Indeed, Van Brocklin insisted. Let him on in.

The play commenced. Sprinkle came in fast, barely touched from Van Brocklin's blind side. Van Brocklin turned and threw the ball as hard as he could into Sprinkles' nose with a greeting something like, "Eat it!" Broke his nose. Knocked him out.

Like I said, Van Brocklin was well known in NFL circles as a hard ass. He was one of the two players chosen to represent the NFL players at the first informal meeting with the league that eventually led to the players forming a union.

Van Brocklin was my father Ed's roommate on the road when he was on the Rams. After a Saints-Falcons game in New Orleans, I met Van Brocklin and I could tell he didn't much care for me. Why? My guess: because I had long hair. He was old school.

What is less well-known is that he was said to be an exemplary parent and that his wife and he, after raising their own three children, adopted and raised children whose parents had died in an automobile accident.

Humans are complex creatures, much.

Van Brocklin as a coach had feuds with players—notably with HOF quarterback Fran Tarkenton.

But, human beings are amalgamations of many things and are judged differently by equally complex other humans.

I found this story that I think paints Van Brocklin's contradictions pretty well:

Lance Rentzel was with the Vikings when Van Brockiln was the head coach in Minnesota. This particular day they were playing the Colts in Baltimore.

Rentzel had made several mistakes on special teams including a fumble that led to a Colts touchdown.

Rentzel explained that he was afraid of Van Brocklin but he goes on to say in the same breath that Van Brocklin was a terrific guy and a wonderful man. Rentzel also says he cherished his relationship with Van Brockiln. He says Van Brocklin was a great man. A kind man. The Dutchman and his wife had taken in and raised six foster children.

But he didn't want to be the brunt of Van Brocklin's wrath at that moment in time after his on-field mistakes because Norm could be brutal in his criticisms.

Baltimore Memorial Stadium was the only NFL venue where both teams' benches were on the same side of the field.

Rentzel, avoiding his head coach, went over to the Colts bench and sat between Johnny Unitas and Tom Matte to hide from Van Brockiln.

Unitas asked Rentzel what was the color of the jersey Lance was wearing? Rentzel said "Purple."

Then Unitas asked him, "What color is my jersey?"

Rentzel answered, "White."

Unitas then said, "Doesn't that tell you something?"

Rentzel said "Yes, that we are on different teams."

Rentzel then asks Unitas to lean forward and do a 90 degree turn and look down the sideline toward the Vikings bench and asks Unitas, "What do you see?"

Unitas leans forward and says "I see Norm Van Brocklin tearing the warmups off all of your teammates."

Rentzel then says, " And what do you think he's doing?"

Unitas answers, "Looking for you."

So Unitas, Matte, and other Colts gathered around Rentzel to hide him from his coach.

The Colts later scored a TD. The Colts kicked off and Rentzel had to go out to receive the kickoff.

Meanwhile Van Brocklin can't find Rentzel and is going bonkers.

Van Brocklin finally sees Rentzel on the field waiting to receive the kickoff.

Van Brocklin runs onto the field and screams, "Lets see how you can f**k up more Rentzel?!"

Rentzel ran the kickoff back 101 yards for a TD which was a Viking record.

Every year my family would receive a Christmas card from the Van Brocklin family.

Van Brocklin was fifty-seven (too young) when he passed away on his pecan farm just outside of Atlanta.

BURNING DOWN THE HOUSE

Andre Rison was a great NFL receiver and made over $19 million in salary in his pro career. He, according to press reports, blew it all.

When Rison was playing for the Falcons he dated hip-hop R&B star Lisa "Left Eye" Lopes.

One night Rison went out clubbing and came home around 5 AM to a less than pleased Lopes. Lopes is said to have hit him in the face and he said he slapped her in the face to calm her down. The same excuse that the Germans used in Poland in 1939. Then he sat on her. It didn't seem to work so he left the house.

Lopes set a pair of sneakers on fire and threw them in a bathtub. Next thing ya know the million dollar mansion of Andre Rison was on fire and, for all practical purposes, burned to the ground.

That's right. His girlfriend burned his house down.

Later in court he said he forgave her. Held her hand in court. They were to be married but she tragically died in a car crash in Central America in 2002.

GREEN PANTHER

Green Panther, the headline starts, a play on *Black Panther*, in an article describing Atlanta Falcon former fullback Ovie Mughelli's new ventures.

Mughelli, an All-Pro who played for the Falcons from 2007 to 2011, has established a foundation that focuses on environmental issues.

He has created a comic book superhero, Obami, who is the star of *Gridiron Green*, a twenty-eight page graphic novel that is aimed at reaching young people with environmental themes.

Mughelli had a partnership with the United Nations Comics Unity Nation Team as one of the purposes of the graphic novel is to reach young people in the developing world.

Mughelli, before he was a bruising fullback in the NFL, was a big fan of the animated cartoon *Captain Planet and the Planeteers*. The show had an African superhero, Kwame, as one of its Planeteers, who caught young Ovie's imagination. He is a first-generation American whose family had come to America from Africa.

As a member of the Atlanta sports community, he met Ted Turner's daughter Laura Turner Seydel at a charity event and she pushed Ovie to use his foundation for environmental causes. As it turned out, her father Ted Turner was the creator of *Captain Planet*. She even sang the theme song off the top of her head to recruit Ovie to the cause.

Mughelli had started the Mughelli Foundation in 2009 and, from that chance encounter with Laura, Ovie thought of the idea for a "green" superhero not unlike Kwame from *Captain Planet*, which had an environmental theme—as the characters derived their power from the Earth.

Ovie's family is originally from Nigeria. His dad is a doctor and his mom earned her MBA. Now Ovie is giving back to the world a message of eco-awareness he hopes will travel the world through a unique vehicle—a green superhero.

BIG BIRD

When the Atlanta Falcons built the new Mercedes-Benz Stadium in 2017 as the new home of the Falcons they contracted with the Savannah College of Art and Design to curate the art for the building.

They scoured the world it seems, for they found Hungarian artist Gabor Miklos Szoke and inquired if he was interested in doing one of his world-renowned animal sculptures to be installed outside of the stadium.

He said yes and he then started on a two-year enterprise that turned an idea and thirty-two tons of stainless steel into a four-story sculpture of a Falcon which is the largest avian sculpture in the world.

Szoke had experience with large sculpture having already created the largest avian sculpture in Europe and the world's largest equine statue "Colossus" in Slovakia.

200 people worked on the sculpture and it took four large containers sent across the Atlantic on a month and a half voyage from Europe to Savannah, Ga. to bring the sculpture in pieces to be reassembled in front of the Mercedes Benz Stadium where it soon became a landmark in Atlanta and to all NFL fans.

It gets a lot of camera time whenever an NFL game is televised.

IN ORBIT

Astronaut Frank Borman was circling the earth in a spaceship. He radioed to Earth to tell his hometown Oilers to choose Tommy Nobis of Texas with their first pick. The Falcons however picked Nobis as their first draft pick ever and Nobis opted to play in the NFL.

Borman, whose sons just happened to be Houston Oilers ball boys at that time, was a good judge of talent as Nobis became an NFL star.

The day of the draft, Nobis—still a student at Texas—was walking around campus and a coed asked him if he was Tommy Nobis. He said, "I am" and she went on to tell him that he was all over the news as Borman's advice had been heard all over the world.

Nobis went home and he turned on the TV and found that it was true, that an astronaut had mentioned his name on a transmission back to Earth. Nobis said that at the time he thought that was the coolest thing.

Nobis was so good on the field that even the jaded Dutchman took special notice.

Van Brocklin, while talking to sportswriters in the Atlanta Falcon locker room, pointed to Nobis' locker and said that is where our team dresses.

Nobis is not in the NFL Hall of Fame. The only reason it seems to me is that he is not enshrined in Canton is that the Falcons sucked as a team when he was there.

SIS BOOM BAH? or JUST BOOM?

Jim Hanifan is a distinguished longtime coach in the NFL. He has been a head coach in the league twice and has served as an interim coach, once with the Falcons. As an interim coach, he decided to motivate his team with a pre-game speech.

Game One, he brought in an unexploded stick of dynamite. Told players to touch it and be explosive out there. Game Two, he brought three unexploded hand grenades for his pre-game pep talk. Game Three, he had a diffused bomb painted in Atlanta Falcon colors and asked players to touch it.

Game 4? The terms of the Nuclear Proliferation Treaty kicked in?

SEE YOU LATER ALLIGATOR

Matt Bryant, a fine place-kicker with the Falcons, was watching a nature show on television. It was about the mating call of the alligator. Bryant decided to try and duplicate the call.

As luck would have it Bryant lived in Florida and on a body of water. He went into his back yard and tried his new skill. Sure enough, baby alligator heads popped up.

Bryant honed his new skill and decided to show it off at a team golf tournament in Florida. Sure enough, a ten foot alligator came out of the swamp and onto the course to investigate.

Scared one the coaches who ran away.

Later in Latin America at still another team golf event, Bryant was at it again. This time a 12 to 14-foot crocodile answered the call. Scared everyone including Bryant, who may have finally learned his reptile lesson.

Jerry Glanville is the NFL coach who instructed one of his players to blow up Morten Anderson after he kicked off. He's the coach who Chuck Noll—coach of the Pittsburgh Steelers—had a quiet come-to-Jesus post-game handshake with to admonish Glanville's cheap-shotty philosophy.

Glanville brought the passion.

His main claim to fame may be his leaving free tickets to every game he coached in the NFL at Will Call for James Dean and Elvis. Not for winning games.

Back in the day when Glanville was head coach of the Atlanta Falcons, he was known for his embrace of the violent nature of the game. I don't think he's welcome in the "Twenty-First Century NFL."

He rhetorically accosted a rookie referee in the heat of an NFL battle. After what Glanville thought were bad calls—and aren't they all when they are against your team—he told the new ref, "NFL—that means Not For Long if you make calls like that," or something along those lines.

So, it was a natural progression, or so it seems. When Sega Genesis came to Jerry Glanville, the man in black, to ask him to endorse a video game based on football but set in medieval times. Jerry Glanville's PigSkin Footbrawl.

In an interview with *GamePro* magazine in 1992, Glanville explained that he did not ordinarily endorse products and was very particular about where he would allow his name to be used commercially. He even claimed to have turned down McDonald's.

The idea of medieval virtual game console football intrigued him. He and his nine-year-old son and friends went to check out the game.

The game consisted of a football type format set in olden days with weapons: swords, spears, maces, axes, nooses, and such.

Think *Game of Thrones* football.

If you scored a lot of unanswered points your team could bring out a "Troll"— a big fast green dude.

Kind of what SEC Hockey might be like. Alabama vs Auburn on the ice. LSU vs. Ole Miss at high speed on skates. Frigging brutal.

Glanville, after his real commentary was cleaned up, did voice-over for the game and his image appeared at halftime and post-game with stats from the contest listed.

Stats like: stabbings 2, hangings 2, axing 1, spearing 0, spike in the face 3. Like that.

Glanville mused about rocks and weapons in the NFL. He's not getting on the rules committee any time soon.

However, all is not lost in this regard. Not in a world with Kim Jong Il.

For those in the know, North Korea has unusual basketball rules.

Three points for a dunk, subtract a point from your score if you miss a free throw, and every FG in the last three minutes counts for eight points.

So? Who knows?

Glanville was asked why he chose to do this. He said he thought the company was unusual and perhaps even crazy. Like him.

The *GamePro* folks said they were 49er fans but would now have to root for the Falcons unless they were playing the 49ers.

Glanville, who is also known for being a part of big time competitive road racing, appearing as a driver in thirty-three NASCAR events, told the folks at *GamePro* to come out to the game when they played the 49ers. He said he hoped to make them cry.

We have a saying in my hometown that applies to Glanville for better or worse.

"Go on with yourself Jerry. Live your life! Go down swinging!"

THE MURDER OF JAMES BROWN?

A lady connected to the music business had an idea: write a song about the Atlanta Falcons to raise money for charity.

She writes the song.

Members of the Atlanta Falcons were to sing backup and country star Ronnie Milsap was to be the lead singer.

The Atlanta Falcons liked the idea but they wanted James Brown, "The Godfather of Soul," to be the lead singer.

He agreed and "Atlanta Will Be Rockin'" was recorded.

The story that eventually emanates from this convergence of things could just lead to the discovery over fourteen years later that James Brown was murdered.

The story among other things includes the circus, elephant friends, beaucoup violence, the Atlanta Rhythm Section, threats, money, lawyers, Jolly Rancher candy, CNN, journalistic imperatives, lawyers, show biz, family dynamics out the wazoo, drugs, a Beverly Hills Cop, doctors, an empty crypt, and perhaps pounds of mental health.

The tale is so fraught with twists and turns a brief description in these pages cannot do it justice.

I refer you to an outstanding bit of reportage by Thomas Lake working for CNN. His three-part series is worth a read if this little snippet has whetted your appetite for more.

MIAMI

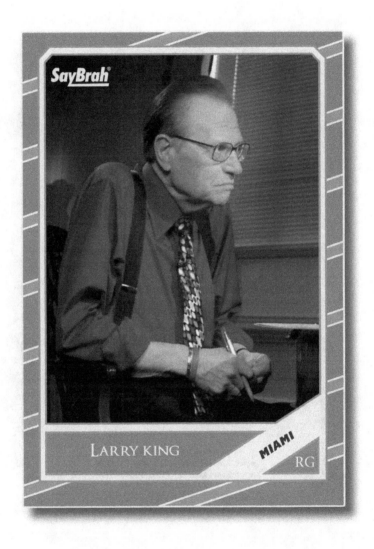

SayBrah®

LARRY KING

MIAMI

RG

THE BERING SEA, FLIPPER,
AND LARRY KING

11

MIAMI

SayBrah

"Well then I guess I have to say it. I'm not going to be the Alabama coach."
—Nick Saban,
Alabama Head Coach

Miami Dolphins entered the AFL as an expansion team awarded to attorney Joe Robbie and entertainer Danny Thomas in 1965, starting play in 1966.

In 1972, they completed the only undefeated season in NFL history.

Stephen M. Ross has been the majority owner of the Dolphins since 2008. Minority owners include latin pop singers Gloria Estefan and Marc Anthony, Black Eyed Peas frontwoman Fergie, and tennis greats Venus and Serena Williams.

Super Bowl Appearances: 5
Super Bowl Record: 2-3 (1972, 1973)
Super Bowl Losses: 1971, 1982, 1984

NO JAWS

Rob Konrad played for the Miami Dolphins from 1999-2004.

Sometimes fate brings you to certain outcomes. For instance, the episode we're about to describe maybe never happens if Konrad had been drafted by, say, Kansas City.

Konrad went fishing off the south Florida Coast in his thirty-six-foot boat. A wave hit the boat. He fell overboard. He tried to swim back to the boat but it was on autopilot and was headed out into the Atlantic. Konrad then decided his only chance was to swim west back to shore.

Nine miles and sixteen hours later an exhausted Konrad, spurred on by determination, strength and the thought of seeing his two beautiful daughters again, arrived on shore at Riviera Beach, suffering from hypothermia, dehydration, and rhabdomyolsis.

The world we live in today may be skeptical of a claim of a nine mile, sixteen-hour swim in the ocean to save your own life.

It was actually sixteen hours and twelve minutes, according to an investigation carried out by the Florida Fish and Wildlife Conservation Commission, which established that he did indeed swim back to shore just as he claimed.

He did this incredible deed between January 7-8th, 2015. And his boat? Bahamian authorities recovered it on the ninth.

TAPED TO A PALM TREE

Alfred Oglesby, all 6'3", 278 pounds of him, was kidnapped at gunpoint during training camp in 1992 by two men who forced him to drive to the Everglades where he was left on the side of the road.

Or so he told Coach Shula.

He wasn't. It didn't happen.

He went to have drinks with his friend, then went home with his friend and overslept, missing practice after his friend took a BMW Oglesby had borrowed from a fellow player.

Fearing Coach Shula's wrath, Oglesby called Shula and told him the kidnapping story.

After interrogation by police, the story quickly unraveled and he admitted that it wasn't true.

Shula's punishment?

He punished the entire team. No one was allowed to go home after practice and had to stay, two to a hotel room, for the duration of training camp.

The team was unhappy with Alfred.

Oglesby was on a pay phone when the defensive line and others kidnapped him (for real this time) and taped him to a palm tree with ankle tape. It seems worth mentioning here that ankle tape has to be cut off with scissors.

He struggled for twenty minutes before some of the guys cut him loose. There's no record as to whether Alfred was a creative writing major.

MEN OF LABOR

Near the end of the 1925 college football season, *The Miami Daily* published a scoop.

The paper claimed that Red Grange, the most famous football player in America and still playing college ball for the University of Illinois, had secretly signed a contract with C. C. Pyle, the renowned promoter, that would make Grange a pro player.

The paper came upon this story no doubt because a game between Grange's new team would bring pro football to Miami for a game that Pyle had already arranged to be played that year on Christmas Day.

Grange had one more college game against Ohio State yet to play and his amateur status would be in jeopardy if the story was true.

Grange denied it and calls for him to be declared ineligible fell on deaf ears as he went on to lead Illinois to victory against Big Ten rival Ohio State.

After the Ohio State game Grange and Pyle announced the deal.

A contract with the Chicago Bears and George Halas completed the deal and led to the 19 game barnstorming tour of the country.

Miami, or Coral Gables to be precise, history with pro football predates the Dolphins and goes all the way back to 1925 as just as the Miami Daily had reported Grange was coming to Miami or more precisely Coral Gables.

C. C. Pyle scheduled games all over the country to take advantage of his contract with Red Grange.

Pyle had promised Grange a $100,000 guarantee on the tour and Pyle was good to his word as Grange did indeed make $100,000—and we're talking in 1925!

On arrival in Miami it was discovered that there was no stadium to accommodate the crowd they were expecting.

Three weeks before the game construction was started on a stadium that would eventually hold 16,000 spectators.

400 workers in eight hour shifts would use 600,000 feet of lumber and 50,000 rivets and bolts to build the stadium in Coral Gables in time for kickoff of the game.

The tickets were pricey and attendance was not as great as they anticipated but half way through the first quarter the customers in the cheap seats were asked to fill in the premium seats if they liked. The crowd scrambled to the good seats and were rewarded with some nice runs by Grange.

The Stadium was dismantled after the game and the lumber and land used to build a housing development.

INSPIRATION

Robert Sowell wanted to be an NFL player.

He went to Richmond, was All-Conference, but had to drop out of school to help support his family.

He never gave up the dream. In fact, he was obsessed with it.

He carried a football wherever he went. He slept with a football to remind him of his dream. His wife encouraged him.

The odds against making the NFL are astronomical, so it would not be out of the ordinary for most people to roll their eyes at Robert Sowell's dream.

He tried the CFL, the USFL, and even played semi-pro ball in California where he was paid in the use of an apartment, $50 a week, and food stamps.

That's right: "WILL PLAY FOR FOOD STAMPS."

It seemed like a long shot, but Robert Sowell had a dream.

He sent out letters to every NFL team asking for a tryout.

The Dolphins sent Elbert "Golden Wheels" Dubenion, a former wide receiver standout with the Buffalo Bills, to take a look at him.

"Golden Wheels" recommended they give him a look-see and they invited him to training camp.

He eventually made the team.

Mission f@&*ing accomplished!

Sowell played for the Dolphins 1983-85 and in 1987. He even played in and won a Super Bowl ring.

He was named the Dolphins Special Team Player of the Year in 1983; a contributor to a Super Bowl team.

SUCCESS. (capital letters on purpose.)

Football is a young man's game. Transitory, one might say.

Robert went back to the world of ordinary mortals and was working for UPS when he succumbed to what some think were his football residuals, dying of a heart attack at the age of fifty-three. He had a dream.

BUSINESS

Mike Golic, the ex-NFL player who now has a regular gig on national radio, relates a story of how he came to leave the Dolphins in 1994. It sheds light to the maxim about pro football being a business.

Golic was injured and he was hankering to get back onto the field because he knew his position on the team was tenuous and a player who can't play is of no use to the team and, well, the paycheck is pretty good.

Golic went to management and told them, even though he was not fully healed, that he was ready to go out and play anyway. But first, there are rules, protocols, procedures, legal issues, and all that.

To get onto the field, a player must be medically cleared by the team doctors, otherwise there is legal vulnerability to the franchise. Golic knew this. He's a smart guy.

He signed the waiver that allowed the team to skirt responsibility if he were to be injured before being cleared to play by the medical staff.

Now "healthy," Golic said he signed the papers and opened the door to walk out onto the field, but a member of the Dolphins front office was waiting right on the other side of the door, telling him that now that he was healthy, not injured by his own admission in writing, he was eligible to be cut. So that fast, he was cut.

This is something a fan might want to ponder during salary negotiations between a player and an all-benevolent team.

FIRED

When Miami was awarded an AFL expansion team, in excess of 19,000 pieces of mail were sent in with mascot suggestions. 622 had Dolphins.

Dolphins were a pretty good fit, all things considered.

The Dolphins, the AFL kind, made an agreement with the city of Miami and the Seaquarium to have a pool for a dolphin to appear at the games and train it to jump up when the Dolphins scored a touchdown.

The dolphin was trucked in every game and trucked back to the Seaquarium after every game.

After a couple of years, the city of Miami and the Seaquarium told the Dolphins they could no longer pay to maintain the pool and pay for the dolphin's appearance.

Joe Robbie fired Flipper.

FOUND ART

1973 Dolphins are coming off their perfect season.

In this tale passed along from a fine tribute column by Peter King on *NBC Sports* in May 11th, 1973 you'll get a sense of the fiber of the man Don Shula.

The Dolphins are 1-0 in the new season and are in Oakland to play the Raiders. Because of construction at the stadium the Dolphins must use the Raiders locker room.

Larry Csonka finds himself at Art Thoms, a Raiders player's locker, after practice. Thoms was a teammate of Csonka at Syracuse. Csonka feels compelled to leave a message for Thoms. As Csonka put it a message, a dead fish, something.

Csonka looks around for something to write on. He finds the Oakland Raider game plan for the game against the Dolphins.

The cartoon angel and cartoon devil appear on Csonka's shoulder. What to do?

Csonka brings the game plan to OL coach Monte Clark who is also described as a Shula confidant.

Clark asks Csonka, "What is this?"

Csonka replies, "I don't know. I never saw it before," and drops it in Clark's lap.

The Dolphins lost the game.

After the game on the bus to the airport Clark sits next to Csonka. Csonka asks him what happened to the game plan?

Clark said he showed it to Shula who asked what it was and then told Clark to tear it up.

Said Shula, "If we can't win straight up we shouldn't win."

And you can believe this—Shula wanted to win.

As Coach Herm Edwards will tell you, "You play to win the game!"

NO MAS

In 2009, the Miami Dolphins attempted to boost attendance by commissioning rappers T-Pain and Pitbull to come up with a newer version of the Dolphin fight song.

At its debut during a Dolphins pre-season game, it was met by the faithful with a chorus of boos.

Jimmy Buffet had also been asked to do an updated version of the song.

The first song was not played again. "Fins" by Buffet was.

LITTLE NICKY

I'm an LSU fan.

Nick Saban was our coach and he left for Miami to coach the Dolphins. Which means I am not inclined to give Nick the benefit of the doubt. Just a disclaimer.

Nevertheless, Saban's tenure in Miami, 2005-06, didn't work out too good for the Dolphins.

He said he unequivocally would not leave the Dolphins to take the job as head coach at Alabama. Thirteen days later, he did.

Some think he's a liar.

It's like this: no one in America lies more than politicians except maybe head football coaches. But as we delve into a few incidents from Nick Saban's years at the helm of the Miami Dolphins, you will see he made the right choice, for him, to bolt for Alabama.

Nick wants his way as a football coach but many NFL players don't see it his way. Today's NFL, it would seem, is not for Nick Saban:

EXHIBIT A: He doesn't like to be called Nick by his players. So many Dolphins called him Nick just to goad him. One, Robert Traylor, had a contract that allowed him not to run wind sprints. Traylor called him Nick while he was not running the wind sprints with everyone else. Traylor called him Nick repeatedly and Nick screamed at him to STFU. Traylor then screamed at Nick, Who the F you think you talking to?

EXHIBIT B: Zach Thomas was a star Dolphin player who was somewhat intense. He got into it with Nick and Thomas had to be restrained by his teammates from going after Nick as Thomas called out to Nick, "I'm a grown ass man!" Meaning you can't treat me like this, dude.

EXHIBIT C: Will Muschamp was an assistant with the Dolphins under Saban. He and his wife went on a vacation in the off-season and Muschamp's mom and dad were babysitting the grandchildren. Saban calls angrily to demand that Mrs. Muschamp or someone fax him a document, like now. Mrs. Muschamp, not having a fax machine, drives to an office supply place to fax the document. Only trouble, Nick gave her the wrong phone number. Saban called again a little later to demand the document. Now! Will Muschamp's dad wanted to stick the document up Saban's ass. The hits keep coming.

EXHIBIT D: Jeno Janes was a big offensive lineman for the Dolphins. He comes off of the field one day and is in the throes of a seizure. Jeno is a big guy. Several players are trying to pick him up and move him out of a hallway. His eyes are rolling back in his head and he is vomiting. Saban walks in. Sees Jeno, steps over him and goes upstairs. Jeno is brought to the hospital in an ambulance.

That night, Saban called a team meeting. He explains: "You know the captain of the ship can never show fear or indecision. We always have to have the answer and so I had to go upstairs. I had to collect my thoughts and decide what's best for our team, that's why I walked over Jeno like that."

That explains it. There is no evidence Nick had ever taken the Hippocratic Oath.

Don Shula said Saban's quick about-face to leave the Dolphins after assuring everyone he was not going to Alabama was unbelievable. "There were four or five direct statements that were blatant lies. That tells you a little bit about the guy."

And this from sportswriter Dan Lebatard on the flight of Nick Saban to Alabama from the Dolphins, "Talks like a warrior. Acts like a weasel."

If you want to be an owner of an NFL franchise you better have a lot of coin—like a billion smackers for starters. Or marry into the family.

It was not always so.

Sure, you had to have some means but not a billion dollars.

Let's take a brief look at how the Miami Dolphins ended up in the hands of a Lebanese-Irish-American lawyer from South Dakota.

Joe Robbie was a second generation American on his dad's side. He went to college after the Navy and became a lawyer who ran for governor of South Dakota but didn't win.

He met Hubert Humphrey and moved to Minneapolis, and would support and befriend Humphrey.

He became involved with a group of investors trying to get an expansion team in Philadelphia in the AFL. Robbie served as their front man and representative. As it turned out, his Navy pal was Joe Foss, the first Commissioner of the AFL and a former governor of South Dakota.

Foss informed Robbie that the AFL was not interested in going into Philadelphia but they were interested in going to Miami.

Robbie, a lifelong sports fan, got to thinking that maybe he could put together a deal to get the Miami franchise.

Robbie is Lebanese-American and this led him to befriend Danny Thomas, the comedian and television producer and prominent Lebanese-American who started St. Jude Children's Hospital. Robbie was the budget director of St Jude's.

Robbie got Danny Thomas, the producer of many top network TV shows, *The Dick Van Dyke Show* being one, and a very rich guy, into the Miami AFL quest.

Okay, Robbie was a successful lawyer, he had some coin, but not $7.5 million in 1966 dollars. He was friends with Joe Foss, who knew everyone in the AFL and he was pals with Hubert Humphrey, Vice President of the United States.

One of the stumbling blocks that Miami faced in acquiring a pro football team was the use of the Orange Bowl so Robbie's political connections to Humphrey was key in enlisting the help of Miami mayor Robert King High to smooth the way into the Orange Bowl's availability.

He was a really smart, driven guy; he got 'er done.

But it is almost impossible to believe that this could happen without all the connecting dots involved.

The Robbies moved from Minnesota to Miami and the Dolphins went to several Super Bowls.

Robbie also put the first big NFL stadium deal using PSLs and luxury box sales to finance the deal. That became the model for future stadiums in the NFL, which is of enormous importance in the modern 21st century league dynamic.

I told you he was a very smart guy.

Joe Robbie was diagnosed with an illness that would take his life prematurely in 1990 and although he tried to plan for his family to keep the team after his death it didn't work out that way. Not at all.

He left control of the team, his biggest asset, to three of his nine surviving children. This eventually led to a rift in the family that has been reported as virtually destroying the family dynamic.

They had to sell the team, mainly because of tax purposes and family infighting.

Quite a ride from Sisseton, SD to Miami and into American sports history.

THE WORST PASS IN NFL HISTORY

The worst pass in Super Bowl history was thrown in the Super Bowl game that completed the perfect season and was thrown by an unlikely source— Garo Yepremian, a guy from Cyprus.

The FG kicker had his FG attempt blocked, he recovered and tried to pass. It fell out of his hand more than anything. The Redskins intercepted it and ran for a TD. It was their only score of the game.

It is said that after the play the other players were pissed at Yepremian. Nick Buoniconti, the MLB, went up to Garo and told him, "If we lose this game I'm going to kill you."

If the kick is good they win 17-0. Symmetry.

If the Redskins don't score they get a shutout.

The play is such an iconic Super Bowl moment that Ypremian became a motivational speaker after his NFL career. This didn't sit well with some of the players. Guard Bob Kuechenberg, for one, is said to be still angry at Yepremian because of the speaking deal.

In the aftermath of the game Yepremain said he was depressed and was relieved to get a letter from Coach Shula telling him it was okay and not to worry.

Only, Shula said he never sent such a letter.

Turns out Shula's wife Dorothy wrote and sent the letter.

TRICKY

Don Shula was old school.

He was having trouble with his team breaking curfew.

The Dolphins were on the road and as Shula was getting ready for bed he put his plan into action.

He went downstairs to have a word with the guy working valet parking that night.

Shula gave him a football and asked him to ask every player who came in after midnight to autograph the ball.

The valet guy did his job.

The next day as the Dolphins players and coaches got onto the bus for the ride to the game Shula stood at the front of the bus and read all of the names on the football.

Then said, "All of you are benched for the first half of today's game."

JOHNSON

Csonka and some of the boys went out on Bourbon Street a few nights before the big game. They had asked Shula for a looser curfew. He grudgingly granted it.

Csonka says everything was going swimmingly in the club. "We figured we had it made, that these *tall*, beautiful women were going home with us."

Then one of the players hollered out, "She's got a Johnson!"

The club had hired female impersonators to work the club for the week of the big game.

Csonka related that at that point the players pretty much tore up the place. The cops were called. It was an ugly incident all around. Very 20th Century.

The next day Shula was pissed. He fumed at some point, "What the hell is a female impersonator?"

Shula's focus on football didn't leave him much time to contemplate the social fabric.

The Dolphins got smothered by the Cowboys 24-3.

DEADLIEST CATCH

Larry Csonka, all time great Dolphin, grew up in Ohio.

But he says that from an early age he was fascinated with living in Alaska and the great outdoors.

Eventually Csonka's celebrity and love of the outdoors came together when he was asked by The Outdoor Life Network to host a reality TV show. He couldn't believe his luck. He got to hunt and fish and get paid to do it.

He and his partner and co-host Audrey Bradshaw moved to Alaska.

Over ten years he appeared in about 240 episodes.

It wasn't all peaches and cream though.

On a show on a remote island in the Aleutians, his TV crew had spent the day hunting reindeer (don't tell Santa Claus) and they embarked from the island on their small boat to return home. As things often do on the Bering Sea the weather changed quickly and seas rose, sea squalls, gale force winds, and pounding rain tossed the boat and its seven passengers around.

They were really out in the boonies, the closest town was about five miles away and it had only thirty-six inhabitants. Csonka and his crew sent out radio maydays but it was so remote that they were only heard at first by a citizen on the island of Unalaska. The Coast Guard was over ten hours away.

The people of Unalaska brought out their cars and four-wheelers and beamed their headlights toward the boat as a makeshift lighthouse. Unfortunately Mother Nature was sending them further out into the Bering Sea. After a harrowing night that resembled the worst case scenarios of the TV show *Deadliest Catch* but on a much smaller boat after about ten hours the Coast Guard showed up and rescued Csonka and his party by basketing them up to a helicopter.

All's well that ends well but that was a little too close for comfort.

One of the Coast Guardsmen came prepared. He had a football ready for Csonka to autograph. Which he did, gladly.

CURSES

Fan bases always look to every possible reason as to why their team has long dry spells.

The Red Sox had the "Curse of the Bambino" and the Cubs had the "Curse of the Billy Goat."

When builders were excavating the site of Joe Robbie Stadium they came across what appeared to be human remains. Archaeologists told them it was probably the remains of the Tequesta tribe who inhabited the area and were wiped out in the mid 1700s by European diseases. Most likely a burial ground.

The Dolphins agreed to take a great deal of care with the site as it pertained to the native remains, which archaeologists surmised could also have been Seminole as they also inhabited this area at one time.

The Dolphins promised and they carried through by carefully excavating in six-inch increments and painstakingly sifting through the dirt slowly.

Maybe they missed a big toe.

Some people were not pleased. WIOD radio got two consecutive callers one night in 1989.

The first caller said he had put a curse on the stadium and the football games. He cited no credentials.

So, there you go, radio talk show callers, good enough for say Galileo, he would certify the science, no doubt. Now we know why the Dolphins suck. Right? There must be a scientific treatise someplace that uses as the basis of its research the verity of radio talk show random callers. Right?

Nonetheless the disc jockey asked him if he was across the street from the stadium sacrificing chickens or something? He answered that yes, he was. And if that's not enough evidence for David Attenborough, the caller that followed, a lady, said an exorcism was needed because the ground the stadium was built on was an Indian burial ground.

The Curse of Tequesta.

NO SHULA?

Check this out.

There is a letter you can find online that intimates Don Shula was not the first choice to coach the Miami Dolphins.

Whom might that have been?

Well, the winningest coach in football history, that's who.

Halas? Deceased. Eddie Robinson? Nope. He's now number 2.

John Gagliardi, that's who.

Who?

John Gaglairdi, of St. John's University (Minn.), was a division III power-house winning four national titles and, at the time the offer was made, 1969, was of course not the winningest coach of all time but he was on his way.

Gagliardi retired with 489 wins or a nice 77% winning percentage.

The letter (written on official Miami Dolphin stationary that, on the left, says clearly Joe Robbie and Danny Thomas, he of TV fame and Marlo's dad) goes on to pretty much offer Gagliardi the job, "There are a few details to square away but it should all be in order within a week."

What happened?

FATE?

Larry King's success gives me pause as I think about the power or even existence of Fate. The foreordained happenings of our lives that, according to the belief in destiny, have over our paths in life. Larry King's celebrity tends to argue for this theory in my opinion.

New York born, he moves to Florida, gets a job in radio.

Jackie Gleason moves to Florida to do his TV show, visits King on the late-night broadcast, one thing leads to another. Voila! King registers in the national spotlight and his show goes national, late night, all over the country. Then at some point CNN. But before CNN and his nationally syndicated show, King, for a brief epoch, was of all things the Miami Dolphins color commentator on radio broadcasts of the games.

Yes, the Larry King, nee Zeigler, who claimed that he did not prepare for his interviews on CNN with some of the most famous humans on Earth. He was giving his opinion and better yet his analysis on NFL games. A guy who, from the look of him, never played a rough game of jacks in his life. He would have been in the booth when the Dolphins played in Super Bowl VII against the

Cowboys except for one minor detail. He was canned right at the end of the regular season when he was arrested and charged with grand larceny.

The charges, dealing with a business deal gone sideways and a check, were resolved and the rest is history.

OAKLAND

SayBrah®

ICE CUBE

OAKLAND
LAS VEGAS

RB

TOM HANKS, HELLS' ANGELS, AND FATS DOMINO

OAKLAND

"There is nothing wrong with reading the gameplan by the light of a jukebox."
—Ken "The Snake" Stabler

SayBrah®

Max Winter in Minneapolis jilted his fellow AFL owners and joined the NFL. The Minneapolis AFL franchise then ended up in Oakland.

Under Al Davis, the Raiders established a reputation as "bad boys" in the league.

In 1982, Al Davis defied the NFL and moved the team to Los Angeles. The NFL took him to court, where Davis eventually prevailed.

The Davis family now owns the Raiders and have once again abandoned Oakland, this time for Las Vegas. Thy made their debut in Vegas for 2020.

Super Bowl Appearances: 5
Super Bowl Record: 3-2 (1976, 1981, 1983 (as L.A.)
Super Bowl Losses: 1967, 2002

HILTON

After Max Winter jilted the AFL and jumped to the NFL in 1960, that left the AFL with only seven franchises.

Barron Hilton, the owner of the Los Angeles franchise, wanted a regional rival and pushed hard for a franchise in Oakland.

Hilton could therefore be considered the founding father of the Oakland Raiders.

NOT A GIRL, A RAIDER

Amy Trask cold-called the Oakland Raiders when she was in college to ask for an internship with the team.

She got the internship in the legal department in 1983.

She left to pass the bar and join a law firm in LA but, in 1987, she rejoined the Raiders in the legal department and, in 1997, she became the first female CEO in the NFL.

In her book, *You Negotiate Like A Girl*, she notes that her formula for success in a male world, as a woman, is to basically ignore gender.

Early on she got into a screaming match with Al Davis and she held her ground without being fired. She fit right in.

She was known for her abrasive manner when CEO of the Raiders, and for standing up to Commissioner Tagliabue at meetings by insisting on being heard when she had something to say.

An unnamed high-ranking executive on another team contends that Trask was despised by others in the league for her attitude and manner. A protégé of old Al it seems. She was nicknamed "The Princess of Darkness" by some.

She reveals that she had a "F^%K You" fund in which she would save a percentage of every paycheck as protection from being fired. That way she could act as she saw fit as CEO of the Raiders.

She resigned in 2013.

One of her most memorable moments with the Raiders is when at a practice Gene Upshaw, the former Raider great, was asked by the press what it was like to have a girl working on the Raiders. He replied, "She's not a girl, she's a Raider."

Trask says thinking of that moment still gives her goosebumps.

POM POMS

NFL cheerleaders are vastly underpaid and these women who dance during games have filed suit against the league for unfair labor practices with some favorable judgments.

Raiderettes were paid $1,250 a season. You read that right, $1,250 a season or about $5 an hour by their attorney's reckoning.

Some teams have no cheerleaders and some have discontinued them because of labor and other issues.

A look inside some of the language in the Raiderette Handbook gives a glimpse into what is, by 21st Century standards, a very sexist situation.

Raiderettes are expected to, among other things:

- Never to use foul language in public
- Be always camera ready in public
- And, at events outside of game day where they are hired for appearances, "The client assumes you are professional and close to perfect. Be sure you are!"

Perfect? I think this is the same language used in official North Korean government handbooks. Just a guess, though.

As far as the explosive mix of beautiful, fit young women and young, fit rich football players—it is "Strongly preferred that cheerleaders not date the players." Cheerleaders are not allowed to go to parties at the players' homes.

There was a series of unseemly incidents.

And then there is this from the *Raiderettes Handbook*: "Make it a point to find out if a player is married. In most cases they won't tell you! You can call up the Raider office with questions as to the marital status and I encourage you to do so. Again, he will not tell you he is married!"

For more, Melanie Ehrenkranz's 2017 article on mic.com:
"Leaked NFL handbook reveals the sexist rules cheerleaders endure—for abysmal pay"

FLAME

In 2011 the Oakland Raiders unveiled the Al Davis Torch, often referred to as the "Al Davis Eternal Flame."

At the inaugural lighting of the torch, a who's who of Raiders greats showed up to honor Al Davis. A partial list: Jim Otto, Willie Brown, Raymond Chester, Ted Hendricks, Jim Plunkett, Bill Romanowski, David Caspar, Tom Flores, Rod Woodson.

Quite a group.

The flame is lit before every home game by an honorary flame lighter.

Dec 26, 2018, was thought to be the final game in Oakland before the team relocated to Las Vegas. The final torch lighter was Marshawn Lynch, Raider and Oakland guy.

Why an eternal flame needs to be relit is, I guess, a semantic question.

Nonetheless Lynch, electronic igniter in hand, did his duty and then some.

The torch fires up with Lynch right there under the torch. He then maneuvers and reaches and even tries a little hop jump to try and light up a big fat joint.

He was, of course, asked about it and the man, famous for deflecting the press, answered, "Only right to send the Raiders off in the real Oakland way."

The new home of the Raiders, Allegiant Stadium in Las Vegas, is to have a 120-foot high tower for The Al Davis Eternal Torch.

THE KINDNESS OF STRANGERS

Forrest Gump is a Kenny Stabler fan.

Kenny Stabler passed away at the age of sixty-nine in 2015 and The Snake's daughters Kendra and Alexa, after finding out that Tom Hanks was a Stabler fan, sent the Hollywood actor a bit of Kenny Stabler memorabilia.

Hanks in turn wrote a personal letter on his typewriter telling the Snake's daughters of his admiration of Stabler.

Hanks grew up in Oakland during the tenure of Stabler as the QB of the Raiders.

Hanks' heartfelt letter ends with Stabler's catch phrase: "Throw deep baby."

Hanks said he always tells people who ask him about his philosophy for success and he says he's always remembered the phrase "throw deep baby," which was associated with Stabler in his Raiders days.

Hanks reportedly signs his emails "throw deep baby."

Hanks also gave a shout out to Stabler and the "throw deep" philosophy while accepting his People's Choice Award in 2017.

RAGS

Oakland Raiders gear is like a lot of other sports apparel that becomes associated with gang culture in LA and around the country.

In fact, it has been argued that one of the reasons many NFL owners preferred the Raiders not be relocated to LA and chose the Rams and Chargers instead in the big LA move scenario was the worry about Oakland Raiders gang affiliation reinvigorating in LA.

In recent years, it seems that LA Dodger caps have started to supplant the gangs' wearing of Raiders gear.

In the 70s the Crips and Bloods emerged in LA and two East Coast gangs came to LA, the People's Nation and the Folk Nation. These new arrivals have allied themselves with the local Crips and Bloods.

When the Raiders moved to LA in 1982 it would be a few years before the popularity of hip hop and the association of LA street culture would make the Raiders an international brand.

Ice Cube, of N.W.A, says the reason he wore the Raiders gear was because, as a group of individuals, N.W.A did not have a "uniform" but were seeking a unifying look and they decided to wear black. He was a Raiders fan. Mostly because of attitude and success. He once said the Raiders reminded him of his uncles, so he wore his Raiders jacket and it caught on.

Folk Nation and People's Nation, according to people who claim to know these things, have adopted the Raiders gear. In fact Folk Nation has a pseudonym for the Raiders connection.

To Folk Nation, Raiders stands for 'Ruthless Ass Insane Disciples Runnin S$%T" or "Remember After I Die Everyone Run Scared" or "Ruthless & Insane Disciple Eliminating Red Slob."

Whereas People's Nation goes with "Raggedy Ass Iced Doughnuts Everywhere Running Scared."

The NFL, aware of this, has tried to distance itself with videos it played on MTV and other media outlets. Schools in the LA region forbid Raiders apparel on campus because of suspected gang affiliation.

In the American way, it is believed that some apparel companies took advantage of the marketing opportunities to sell stuff by coming out with colors that are nontraditional for caps, such as changing a Boston Red Sox cap which would be traditionally be dark blue to a red version, red being the color of the Bloods.

AIN'T THAT A SHAME

"RIP FATS" read the scrawled note on the well-known residence of Rock 'n' Roll legend Fats Domino's devastated home in the New Orleans Lower Ninth Ward in the wake of Hurricane Katrina. Fats was thought to be dead. However, it was fake news, as Fats Domino showed up a little worse for the wear but in pretty fair shape alive. His welcomed surfacing was in Baton Rouge, LA., at the home of LSU star quarterback Jamarcus Russell.

Fats, his family, and approximately twenty guests had been staying in the three-bedroom apartment of LSU's All-American starting quarterback who was described in some press accounts as a distant friend of Fats' family. Fats stayed with Jamarcus for two days.

Jamarcus would soon be famous for something else: as the number one overall pick in the NFL draft by the Oakland Raiders, signing a contract that paid him over $50 million.

MY (OAKLAND) PRECIOUS!!

Player's who played in the AFL had a special pride in the fact that their league had defied the odds and that their game was the equal to the NFL even though most people didn't see it that way.

Jim Otto, an AFL lifer, was proud of his American Football League Championship ring he won for defeating the Houston Oilers in the game that sent the Raiders into Super Bowl II against the Green Bay Packers.

Otto gave his ring to his father for safekeeping in his Miami home.

Burglars broke into the older Ottos' home and stole the ring along with other things.

Five years later a nine-year-old boy named Chip Rapp went to the bathroom at his school in West Linn Oregon and he spied a shiny object in the shower. He picked the object up and handed it in to the principal of the school.

It was Jim Otto's AFL Championship Ring.

No one knows how it got from Miami to Oregon.

These rings get around.

COMMUNITY OUTREACH

Al Davis and his minions, the Raiders players, reached out into the Oakland community by befriending, among others, the Hell's Angels and Black Panthers.

The Angels and Panthers would be in the stands at Raiders games rooting for the home team just like teachers, waiters, lawyers, truck drivers and kids.

Al Davis would send crates of Raider gear to both the Angels and the Panthers.

Phil Villapiano used to workout with weights with the head of Hell's Angels, Sonny Barger.

One night Villapiano came out to his car and some Hell's Angels were leaning up against it. He told them something and while he was engaged in said discussion another Angel came up to him from behind and hit him in the head with a hammer.

Villapiano went back to Raiderland, and Jack Tatum and the Tooz wanted to go back and fight. Villapiano talked them out of it.

Since Villapiano was friends with Barger they worked it out and one day John Madden looked up at practice and there were the Hells Angels, guests of some of the players.

It was part of the reconciliation.

THE DARK PRINCE

Al Davis, as he appears to Hunter S. Thompson:
"A small, wiry man in a golf jacket with a greasy ducktail haircut."
"Strange looking bugger."
"Who looked like a pimp or a race track tout."
Pretty much.

If you told me that Al Davis sprinkled confetti made from pages of Niccolo Machiavelli's *The Prince* on his breakfast cereal, I'd believe you.

Al Davis, who barely played at all on his high school team, parlayed drive, manipulation, and chutzpah into becoming a billionaire through football.

In 1972, he was one of three partners in the Raiders. While managing partner F. Wayne Valley was out of the country at the summer Olympics, Davis got the other partner, Earl McGah, to sign a revised partnership agreement that he, Davis, had written up. With the signatures of Davis and McGah on the revised agreement, while the third of the general partners was in Germany, this made Al Davis basically the man in charge of the Oakland Raiders.

Valley sued but under 1972's California partnership laws the move was totally legal and binding.

The guy on the helmet? The Raider? What ya think? Al?

He basically swindled his partner, who eventually sold his share of the team in 1976 and was once sued by Eugene Klein the owner of the San Diego Chargers alleging that Davis was the cause of Klein's heart attack.

Klein won the case, Which means that a court ruled that Al Davis caused his rival owner to have a heart attack. The ruling in the case was later overturned on appeal.

But?

Al Davis was always scheming and trying to one up everyone.

Once at racetrack Davis was with Sonny Werblin, owner of the Jets, when Werblin hit a big bet on the horses. Werblin excused himself to go cash in his winning ticket, Davis told him he would cash it, Werblin told him it was a large figure. Davis asked how much. In the thousands as it turns out. Davis reached in his pocket and pulled out a roll that as they say 'could choke a horse' and peeled off Werblin's winnings.

In closing, John Rauch was the coach of the Oakland Raiders and he had decided to move on to be the head coach of the Buffalo Bills. He went in to tell Davis he was resigning to go to Buffalo.

Davis told Rauch he was under contract and the Raiders would need compensation to allow Rauch to go to Buffalo.

Rauch informed Davis that if Davis did not allow him to leave, he would hold a press conference and tell the world all he knew about AL Davis personal life.

Al Davis replied "Say no more."

WELCOME TO PITTSBURGH

The weekend that would culminate with the Immaculate Reception didn't start off too well for a certain Oakland Raider, namely TE Bob Moore.

Moore and LB Greg Slough returned to their Pittsburgh hotel Friday night to turn in early only to find a large group of Steelers fans blocking the entrance to the hotel. There was also a contingent of Pittsburgh's finest at the hotel to keep the peace.

Moore went up to one of the policeman and told him they were members of the Raiders and wanted to get to their rooms.

The cop answered, "I don't give a f^%k who you are. You're not going to jump to the front of the line."

Moore then replied, "Listen motherf#$%er, we're going to our rooms."

Upon which Moore got an experience most of us don't get in Pittsburgh. He got to find out what a baseball felt like when Ralph Kiner hit it over the left field fence at Forbes Field.

The cop hit Moore on the top of his head with a Billy club.

Bam!

Moore woke up to find a man straddling his chest trying to beat the crap out of him as another man held his legs.

The policeman got Moore into the back of a paddy wagon and the first cop came up to the wagon and Moore and he fought for a bit. Then the cop left and another took his place. The second cop told Moore they were taking him to the station to book him. Moore asked for what?

The cop looked at Moore, who was drenched in blood.

They decided to take him to the hospital instead.

On the operating table Moore said it wasn't that bad; only seven stitches and cuts on both sides of his head. The doctor told him he was lucky.

Moore in his best *Dragnet* dialogue asked, "How's that?"

The doctor replied that when they usually see guys like him it's only after they come from the morgue already dead.

Moore's head was so swollen he couldn't fit into his helmet at game time. They had to take a larger helmet from a guy with a big head and strip all the padding out to squeeze it on his head. He said he played the game in a daze.

Welcome to Pittsburgh.

THE EL RANCHO TROPICANA MOTEL

Most NFL players do not look forward to training camp.

The Raiders were different. They looked forward to training camp at El Rancho Tropicana Motel in Santa Rosa, California.

They would roll in ready to train and party. From 9 to 11 pm it was party hearty time after a long day of practicing hard. They would hit the "Circuit," five bars, and hurry home for bed check at 11.

After bed check they would sneak out for more.

It was like *Animal House* on steroids, and I guess it was.

Besides enormous amounts of sexual hijinks and drinking there were other highlights such as: C Dave Dalby, who bought two 25¢ pinball machines to set up in his room, using the proceeds from this enterprise to pay his bar bills during camp; ladies' undergarments collections nailed to the walls to measure the success of that year's camp; George Buehler's flying model airplane and remote control tanks; fireworks in the night; an annual parade at training camp's end down the main drag of Santa Rosa; and, the annual Air Hockey Tournament that featured stripper Carol Doda from San Francisco using her breasts to block the air hockey goal.

And, oh yes, T Bob Brown would bring a suitcase full of firearms with him to camp. He once shot out the TV screen in his room and another time he shot Willie Brown's mattress a few times with Willie in it to get his attention.

El Rancho Tropicana Motel.

A safe space for mayhem.

GOPPPL

The history of when something is invented is usually shrouded in the mist of time even if that thing was invented last Wednesday.

On a flight to Buffalo from Oakland, California a discussion between a limited partner of the Oakland Raiders, "Bill" Winkenbach and George Ross the *Oakland Tribune* sports editor the idea for Fantasy Football was born.

The limited partner Wilford "Bill" Winkenbach had been playing a game of his devise of fantasy golf and baseball since the late 1950's. Ross suggested that the same could be done with football stats.

The Raiders were on a sixteen-day road trip to Buffalo and New York and while the entourage of front office type,owners, and journalists were staying at a hotel in New York City over cocktails they began to work out the rules that would be used in the Greater Oakland Professional Pigskin Prognosticator League (or GOPPPL), which many would come to consider the first Fantasy Football league. The league officially started in 1963 with a draft in Winkenbach's rumpus room.

There are of course skeptics, yet the evidence for fantasy football's creation at The Row NYC Hotel, formerly the Milford Plaza, at 700 8th Avenue in New York is strong.

Back in Oakland at the first fantasy football draft George Blanda was the first player ever selected.

The game grew in the Bay Area and led to what is described as a very competitive atmosphere and to friendships being destroyed, marriages happening etc., etc., etc. Yep, things haven't changed much from the very start.

The game at some point found its way across the bay sometime in 1968 to San Francisco and a bar called the Kings X run by Andy Mousalamis, a charter member of the GOPPPL, and it caught on with business types in downtown San Francisco and after a few years Moustamia and Winkenbach's groups had a schism over rules and procedures but the game prospered.

Calls would come in from all over the country in relation to the league. It was good for the bars business as players would congregate at the bar and you had to come in person to change your lineup in this pre-internet world of the late 60's

In some circles the creator of Rotisserie Baseball, Daniel Okrent, is given the designation as the creator of fantasy sports but that is because Okrent is at the top of the journalistic food chain and a member of the tribe that writes the history, the East Coast swells, the writers of the *New York Times*, *The Atlantic*, *The Washington Post*, *Sports Illustrated*, *Inside Sports*, *The Wall Street Journal*, the big house publishing houses, the journalistic glitterati.

Okrent one of the first inductees to the Fantasy Sports Hall of Fame, Winkenbach not being among that number, certainly gets a lion's share of the credit for making fantasy sports as widespread as it is because of the popularity and circulation of his book, but...

It's pretty clear Winkenbach's league the GOPPPL with his history of golf and baseball games he played in the 50's was first.

The passion of the game can be seen in an anecdote from the first all ladies league. At the draft of the GOPPPL ladies division the commish had a heart attack and after he was whisked away in an ambulance, Moustalamis asked if the ladies wanted to continue the draft and they said of course.

To all you Walter Mitty fantasy owners one of the founders of GOPPPL was Scott Stirilng who went on to be the GM of the San Francisco Warriors (now the Golden State Warriors) and GM of the New York Knicks.

In the first year of the GOPPPL teams had an owner and a coach. One of the coaches in that first year was a young dude named Ron Wolf.

You may have heard of him. He went on to be a distinguished GM in the NFL and was the GM of the Green Bay Packers the last time they won the Super Bowl.

Andy Moustalamis at the age of eighty-eight participated in his last fantasy draft.

He said in fifty years of playing he had a lot of fun.

SWEET HOME ALABAMA

Bob Pedecky covered the Raiders beat for the *Sacramento Bee* in the 70's and reported this story of the vicissitudes of interviewing professional athletes.

1978: Stabler's career appears to be in decline. The Snake decides he will no longer speak to the press. He says after the season he will entertain questions from the media.

Pedeckey found himself in New Orleans to cover the Sugar Bowl. The NFL season was over and Pedecky is only about 160 miles away from Stabler's off-season home at Gulf Shores, Alabama.

Pedecky shows up in Gulf Shores. He calls Stabler who will still not speak with Pedecky. Pedecky then tells Stabler if he doesn't talk to him he'll just have to interview the people of Gulf Shores. Stabler thinks this is not a very good idea.

Pedecky interviews the townspeople of Gulf Shores and writes a three-part article for the *Sacramento Bee*.

Stabler's neighbors didn't reveal any bombshells. Their thoughts ranged from—he needed to get in better shape, should go to bed earlier, and they really wished he would marry his girlfriend.

Not much earth shaking news.

Pedecky goes to the Super Bowl in Miami and gets a call from Stabler to fly up to Gulf Shores after the Super Bowl and he says he'll give him the interview. The offer: "I'll spill my guts."

Pedecky is told to meet Snake at Lefty's, a bar in Gulf Shores. They meet. Stabler says, "You're the first reporter to come and try to dig up dirt." Stabler clearly was not happy with the three-part series.

Stabler is called away and says he will call Pedecky later.

He calls and summons Pedecky to a place named BJ's.

Stabler is there but still close-mouthed. Stabler has to leave again. He will call Pedecky later.

He calls. This time they meet at the Silver Dollar Lounge.

Stabler is still not happy. No real interview. Stabler goes on a ten-minute diatribe aimed at Pedecky. Stabler has to leave again. Tells Pedecky to meet him back at BJ's.

Pedecky gets in his car. He pulls out onto the Alabama highway and is surrounded immediately by two cop cars and a motorcycle cop. They search under the left front fender of his rental car. The police found cocaine. He is arrested.

Pedecky soon finds himself inside an Alabama jail. Half naked, handcuffed, in a stinking jail cell and told they will be facing a maximum sentence. He makes one phone call to his editor at the *Bee*.

Deputy eventually informs him that he was probably set up. They bring him back to his hotel room. Pedecky calls Stabler, at the suggestion of the police and tells Snake that Pedecky has been arrested for DUI. The cops hope to smoke out the cocaine planters this way.

Police Chief Jimmy Maple, packing a .357 magnum, sits in a hotel with Pedecky. Chief tells Pedecky we have five cars staking out the hotel. He says if they show up and want a war the police are prepared to take care of an army.

Cocaine dudes are a no-show after ninety minutes.

The Police Chief informs Pedecky that his life may be in danger.

Suggests he might want to leave town and go back to Florida.

An idea whose time has come.

They ride to the airport in Pedecky's rental. Chief Maple, riding shotgun, has a sub machine gun on his lap and tells Pedecky, "If anyone tries to stop us you brake the car hard, swerve to the shoulder, and I'll take care of them."

Pedecky makes it to the airport and to Ft. Lauderdale where he stays under an assumed name until the coast is clear and writes his story.

The FBI, state of Alabama, and the NFL all investigate the incident. No arrests are made, In fact Pedecky's "arrest" is no longer on the books.

Leigh Steinberg, super agent, calls; movie deal for the story available. Michael Douglas is interested. John Belushi pegged to play Pedecky. Pedecky declines.

At El Rancho Tropicana that summer Pedecky approached Stabler. Stabler says ."#uck Off."

Or something like that.

Time passes.

Thirty years later in 2009, Pedecky and Stabler ran into each other at Sonoma Raceway. Pedecky says, "Hi Kenny." Stabler says, "Hi Bob." They shake hands.

No actual journalist seems to have been harmed in this story.

Not physically anyway.

MURDERS

Anthony Smith, first round draft choice of the Raiders out of Arizona by way of Alabama, recorded 57 and half sacks in his Raider career and signed a $7.6 million contract. A long way from Elizabeth City, North Carolina, and life where his mother died when he was three and his father's identity was nebulous at best.

He abruptly quit football while in Denver Broncos training camp, calling his personal assistant to get the Hummer and come pick him up.

He was once married to Vanity, a member of Prince's all-girl band, and when things started to go south on Anthony, he was married to a lawyer and the assistant district attorney for San Bernardino, California.

But...

A man described as "a big old teddy bear, generous, a mentor to kids, charitable, loving heart, enthusiastic and courteous" was also characterized as someone who "would choke you out for thirty cents" and "an obvious liar." He seemed to harbor unrelenting inner turmoil.

After football, he was involved in a dispute with a furniture store owner. He got a $615 check from her. He then had an assistant call her and say he lost the check and needed a replacement. She cut him a new $615 check and he tried to cash the new one after the first had already been cashed. Soon after, the furniture store was torched. In the charred debris detectives found 30 pieces of mail addressed to Anthony Smith and his wife. Tried twice for the crime, both times led to a hung jury. The case was dismissed and Smith sued the furniture owner.

Later he was charged with four murders in different episodes. He was a good witness, all agreed.

This time, however, he was found guilty of murder in three of the deaths. The victims all were tortured before they were killed. Smith was ID'd on the stand as the man who masqueraded as a cop to kidnap one of the dead men who was never again seen alive after the abduction. In searches of Anthony's property police badges and other paraphernalia were found.

Along the way he was found to have umpteen weapons, books in his possession with titles like *Professional Killer: An Inside Look*, *Kill Without Joy*, and

Ultimate Revenge Techniques from the Master Trickster, and, by coincidence, the Lincoln Navigator of one Maurilo Ponce, the vehicle Ponce was driving the night he was killed after swapping numerous cell phone calls with Anthony Smith. Smith was not found guilty in that case.

As a player, Smith showed a tendency to fib. He told reporters he was raised in New York City where he was on drugs at the age of nine. He said he had stolen and crashed a car with two other kids and that the two kids died in the accident. He claimed to have done cocaine, PCP, heroin and LSD as a nine-year-old on the streets of New York.

Only thing, he grew up in Elizabeth City, North Carolina.

His teammates at Alabama remember him as an intimidating presence, something not quite right about him.

At his trials for murder, members of a local gang were ever present in the courtroom and the corridors of the courthouse wearing Raiders gear.

He is serving three life sentences after being convicted of three murders.

Writing for *GQ* in 2013, Kathy Dobie fleshed out his pathetically fascinating story: "Ex-Raider Anthony Smith's Murder Trial and Violent Past."

KANSAS CITY

SayBrah™

THOMAS HART BENTON

KANSAS CITY

FB

MICKEY MOUSE, A GHOST,
THE SEXIEST MAN ON EARTH

KANSAS CITY

"[After eleven knee surgeries] my knees look like they lost a knife fight with a midget."

—E. J. Holub

SayBrah®

The Kansas City Chiefs are the original AFL team started by AFL founder Lamar Hunt as the Dallas Texans and started play in the AFL in 1960.

Hunt, realizing Dallas could not support two pro football teams, moved the team to Kansas City in 1963 and renamed them the Chiefs.

The Chiefs played in the first Super Bowl after the NFL/AFL merger as representatives of the AFL. They lost to the Green Bay Packers, 35–10.

The Hunt family has maintained ownersip after Lamar Hunt's passing in December 2006.

Super Bowl Appearances: 3
Super Bowl Record: 2-1 (1969, 2019)
Super Bowl Loss: 1966

Len Dawson, starting QB for the Kansas City Chiefs in Super Bowl IV in 1970 and Hall of Famer, was linked to a notorious gambler named "Dice" Dawson, no relation, on a report carried on NBC's nationally televised news program, *The Huntley-Brinkley Report*. It caused a s#!t storm.

Dice had Len's phone number on a piece of paper in his pocket when the FBI nabbed him.

"Dice" is on record as claiming to have been in on the fixing of up to thirty-two NFL games. This is a disturbing story due to the fact that "Dice" Dawson was known to have hung out with many notable athletes in Detroit at the Fox and Hound Club.

He was a well-known gambling fixture described as "a massive bookmaker, and savvy racketeer."

Talk is cheap. So, just because "Dice" said it happened doesn't mean it did. Or didn't, for that matter. But is somewhat worrisome for those who worry about such things because of "Dice" Dawson's proximity to Detroit athletes.

Dick "Night Train" Lane also told a tale of how he believes "Dice" Dawson was feeling him out to perhaps shave points. So there is some smoke here, if no fire.

Len Dawson was interviewed by Jack Danahy, the chief of NFL security, in his hotel room in New Orleans, site of Super Bowl IV, about the allegations which were getting beaucoup attention in the nation's press leading up to the big game. Len denied the allegations. Len said he knew "Dice" and that "Dice" had called him on the phone twice, once when Len's dad had died and again when Len was in the hospital. Len offered to take a polygraph test.

Danahy wrote a report on Dawson's hotel room testimony for him to sign. The report was to be given to NFL Commissioner Pete Rozellle.

Rozelle asked Danahy whether he believed Len Dawson. Danahy said he did.

The reason he believed him he said was because while Danahy was writing the report of what Dawson said to Danahy under interrogation, Dawson fell asleep. He had to wake him up to sign the document. Danahy said that he had interrogated spies, gangsters, criminals of all stripes, and he never had one fall asleep on him.

Len Dawson and DB Johnny Robinson had been hounded by rumors of point shaving before and in 1968 both took polygraph tests that they both passed.

And Kansas City is reputed to have been a key city in mafia casino skimming operations, which raises a few eyebrows.

Experts on gambling like Mort Olshan, publisher of the legendary *Gold Sheet*, doubted that most of the rumors of fixed games were true.

Olshan said that mob and gambling interests actually wanted games to be on the up-and-up so they can accurately post point spreads in what, for the gambling interests, was a successful and lucrative enterprise. Gambling at this level is structured so that the house never loses. And Olshan said if the fix was in, money would come in patterns that would be noticed, and bookies would notice the peculiar action and in Olshan's words, "News would spread faster than a nuclear attack."

The story was big news that weekend.

Right before the game Lenny Dawson received a telephone call of encouragement from none other than Richard Nixon, who was President of the United States at the time. Nixon told Dawson not to worry about the "noise" and concentrate on the matter at hand. The game.

GEORGE NOORY'S TEAM?

For what it's worth, The Dallas Texans, the team that became the Kansas City Chiefs, held their first training camp in Roswell, New Mexico, site of the notorious alleged extraterrestrial or UFO crash landing in 1947 and the subsequent attempts to deny that space aliens were aboard the craft.

The event comes with its conspiracy and cover up whisperings that linger to this day.

I'm not saying.

I'm just saying.

KID'S STUFF

The Kansas City Chiefs were in the first Super Bowl. They lost.

In the Green Bay Packers locker room an eleven-year-old pushed his way hither and yon between the behemoths of the Green Bay Packers celebrating victory. He had a pen in hand and was in search of autographs.

Lucky kid.

He gets Jim Taylor, Paul Hornung and others to sign.

He approaches Vince Lombardi who signs his autograph. Vince knows who he is.

"You think your Daddy is going to spank you for coming in here?" Vince asks.

Nah.

It was Chiefs head coach Hank Stram's son, Neal.

UP IN THE SKY

The Dallas Texans and Dallas Cowboys (nee Rangers) both started in 1960.

A rivalry was inevitable and both owners pulled out all the stops.

Lamar Hunt, among other things, had female school teachers travel around Dallas in bright new red cars to sell season tickets door to door. The top seller was to be awarded one of the new cars.

One of the more unusual promotions in Dallas was the Texans stuffing bags of Fritos with Texans tickets and attaching them to helium balloons and launching them into the sky where they would eventually fall to earth. A resident of the Dallas area could come home and find a pair of Texans tickets that had landed on his or her lawn, theoretically.

QUAINT

Hank Stram had some what now seem almost archaic rules as coach of the Chiefs.

He had the Chiefs players dress in custom made duds to travel. Gray blazers with the team logo on the breast pockets, white shirts, black pants and black ties.

It was a bit Felix Unger-ish in an *Odd Couple* kind of way.

There was the Chiefs' choreographed huddle: interior lineman stood with his back to the line of scrimmage with receivers and running backs bent over at the waist in front of the lineman in two rows of five all facing the quarterback.

And this one, all players lined up in numerical order for the playing of the National Anthem.

SNAPSHOTS

The final NFL-AFL game before the merger took effect in 1971 was Super Bowl IV in New Orleans (a game I attended) in which the Kansas City Chiefs, the first AFL team, owned by Lamar Hunt the founder of the league defeated the heavily favored Minnesota Vikings, 23-7.

The week of the game Lamar Hunt who all described as a quiet dignified man was presiding over a team meal at the storied New Orleans restaurant Antoine's. All of a sudden, Lamar Hunt beat his hand on the table and yelled, "Kill! Kill! Kill!"

It had been almost eleven years since the "Foolish Club" as the original owners called themselves had started on the journey to this place and this time.

The game was important to the people who had built the AFL. The players, the fans, the owners.

Hunt wanted this win. It was against the Minnesota Vikings and Max Winter who was an original AFL owner of the proposed Minnesota franchise that never was because Winter defected to the NFL when the NFL dangled a franchise league in his face. Hunt felt a sense of betrayal that he still harbored even a decade later.

Later, before the game, Hunt and his wife got on an elevator at the Royal Sonesta Hotel in the French Quarter and there were only two other people in the elevator till they got to the next floor. Those two people were Max Winter and his wife.

Awkward!

Nothing was said.

ART

Thomas Hart Benton, the famous American artist of American Art Regionalism and teacher of Jackson Pollock, became a bit of a Kansas City Chiefs fan in his 80s and contemplated painting scenes of the Chiefs in action.

Coach Hank Stram learned about Benton's fandom and invited the eighty-year-old artist down to the sideline for a closer look. Here the artist loved the motion and immediacy of the game.

The Chiefs, however, were worried that the players would run over Benton and maul him. He scoffed, "80 or not," he said.

"But, hell, I can move out of the way."

Benton believed that one of the missions of his art, influenced by Depression era America, was to "remind the American people of their strengths."

Indeed, in the 1969 Super Bowl season, Benton sketched along the Chiefs sidelines and created a lithograph, "Forward Pass." It depicts a Kansas City Chief quarterback in the process of throwing a pass surrounded by the other players in a skirmish-like atmosphere, a sketch that is now in the Canton Museum of Art.

PURCHASED BY THE CANTON MUSEUM OF ART

SAY CHEESE

Life magazine made a deal with the Kansas City Chiefs to have photographers take photos of the team during Super Bowl I. The understanding was that the photos would only be released if the Chiefs won.

Photographer Bill Ray and Art Rickerby embedded with the team but the photos, per the agreement, did not see the light of day until 2019.

The pictures include a jarring shot of quarterback Len Dawson at halftime sitting on a folding chair in his number 16 jersey smoking a cigarette. A rare shot indeed.

Another shows members of the team resting at halftime, like the backstage scene in a theatrical production, wearing Mickey Mouse ears.

Green Bay and the NFL fans had referred to the AFL as a Mickey Mouse league in the run-up to the game and the Chiefs decided they would wear Mickey Mouse ears and, when they won, the pictures would come out and they would have a last laugh. But they lost.

TAX

Rarely does the public get a glimpse of NFL business documents but, due to a court case—Kansas City V. Missouri State Revenue Department and *The Kansas City Star*—a brief window was opened and the Kansas City Chiefs' 2008 tax returns were made available to the public.

The case came about because of a dispute about the renovation of Arrowhead Stadium and tax obligations. If the planet known as NFL were to be destroyed in an explosion, the remnants of its stadiums would end up kind of like Kryptonite. Stadium issues pop up as paramount in the NFL time after time.

The tax returns showed that, unlike the early years of the NFL when pro football was not so lucrative an enterprise and even a money loser, today's NFL, mainly because of TV revenue and merchandising, is a cash generator extraordinaire for its owners.

A breakdown of the team's finances on the documents showed a $40-million-dollar gross revenue of which the owners of Chiefs plowed back about half into the team.

To give an idea of how money is generated, it broke down to $2.8M in concessions, $4.7M in parking revenue, and $51.8M in ticket sales.

The lessons in the revenue numbers as they correlate to performance on the field are interesting from a fan perspective. According to experts, on-field performance and revenue streams are irrelevant to the bottom line. Because of TV contracts and other shared league revenues, it doesn't matter whether you win or lose for the financial success of the modern NFL franchise.

WELL DRESSED GHOST

Kansas City Chiefs fans took it upon themselves to see if they could do something about a curse that might have kept the Chiefs from winning in the playoffs.

They hired a lady psychic medium from Kansas Paranormal Investigations (headquartered in...Kansas), an organization with a track record in these matters.

Checking the KPI website, one will find 140 different sites that KPI has checked out for spirits. Only seven were found to have measurable activity. Sounds good.

The psychic medium that came to Arrowhead to see if it was haunted (or whatever the proper term is) is quoted as saying she can't even go inside a fake haunted house at Halloween but nonetheless has a "gift." And I ain't saying she don't.

Two fans hired her or summoned her. (I'm not clear as to whether she was paid. The website says it will check out your site for free.)

Anyway, she toured a mostly empty Arrowhead before the AFC Championship with Patriots in 2018.

What did she find?

Indeed, she ran across what she described as a well-dressed man in a suit from the early 1970s, a time when Hank Stram was fired by the Chiefs.

Cue the sinister organ music:

Stram is not happy with his dismissal but he is a Chiefs fan and is ready to let bygones be bygones, according to the psychic. She suggests that Chiefs fans show a little more appreciation for Coach Stram, the only head coach to bring them to a Super Bowl.

She also says that, by the by, he, coach Stram, is in a good place and is doing fine on the other side, or other plane, or Jakarta or wherever he is supposed to be.

One of the fans who summoned the psychic relates this other curious happening during the tour of Arrowhead.

When the psychic was touring the stands and they neared section 111, where the fan in question's season tickets are located, she felt a pain in her right leg and she said "1-12, or 1-11. No, 11-1 meant something."

Indeed, the fan, Frank Stratton, and his dad, Richard Stratton, attended games together, sitting in that section. Richard had died on November 1, or 11-1. And Richard Stratton was an amputee. His right leg.

The plot thickens.

Cue the organ.

COINCIDENCE

Deland McCullough is a running backs coach of the Kansas City Chiefs.

Growing up in Youngstown, Ohio, with a single mom, he heard his name on the PA while playing Pee Wee football and the light went on. He was hooked on being a football player.

Unlike most kids, Deland had the tools and the talent to make his football dream come true.

One day, when he was in class at his high school, a fancy red Mercedes Benz pulled up outside. Deland got a note from the office and waiting for him in the office was the owner of the red Mercedes, Sherman Smith, RB coach at Miami Of Ohio, who had come to offer Deland a college scholarship.

Smith was a role model, a man who had played pro ball and coached at a major college. He awed both Deland and his mom.

Smith was a mentor to Deland and many others and, over the years, as their lives and friendship grew and was cemented, people always joked about them being so alike. People said they walked alike, they talked alike. They moved alike.

Growing up, Deland was aware that he was adopted. It caused him anxiety and pain. But his mom made sure he had a positive upbringing encompassing school and faith.

Deland became a coach after his playing days in pro football never really materialized after a knee injury his rookie year in Cincinnati Bengals camp.

Deland got married and had a family of his own, but he had always longed to find his biological parents.

New laws in Ohio and Pennsylvania made it possible for Deland to finally get his birth records and after much searching he contacted Carol Briggs on Facebook. His birth mother was found.

He called from the hall of the USC football building. They had a pleasant conversation that belied the fears they both had considering the emotional nature of the topic at hand.

The question: "Who is my father?"

The answer: Sherman Smith, the running back's coach at Miami Of Ohio, a man who Deland had been coached by, mentored by, and befriended for the last twenty-eight years.

Wow.

2nd MOST SEXY MAN ON EARTH

In 1998 *People Magazine* chose Kansas City QB Rich Gannon as its "Sexiest Man Alive for 1998."

They sent a photographer to Kansas City to take photos of the Kansas City QB.

There was a QB battle in Kansas City that year and the photographer didn't know from football.

He took photos of the Kansas City quarterback he found: Elvis Grbac.

When the photographer got back to New York and they realized he had taken the photos of the wrong guy the folks at People did not have the heart to break the news to Grbac that there had been a mistake.

So, this is how Elvis Grbac became "the Sexiest Man on Earth."

WILT

Hank Stram was serious about signing Wilt Chamberlain as wide receiver for the Kansas City Chiefs.

Wilt was, it is said, frustrated by the fact that the greater world did not recognize the depth and scope of his athletic abilities and he was intrigued by dabbling in other sports to show what he could do.

Wilt supposedly ran a 4.6, 40-yard dash at close to 300 lbs.

Coach Stram had Wilt stand by the crossbar and he threw the ball to the bar and Wilt would jump up, flat footed, and catch it. Eventually, after a few pass attempts from Stram, Wilt started to catch the ball with one hand.

Stram thought that the 7'1" Wilt would be uncoverable by NFL DBs.

But we'll never know as the NBA had other ideas and that seemed to work out okay.

HELMET MAN: THE MOVIE

Ed, not his real name, walked up and down the aisle at Arrowhead Stadium during Chiefs games banging on a drum.

He was a businessman, many times over starting businesses in New Jersey, Arizona, Washington state and Kansas City.

He became a regular guest on Q104 a morning radio show to the point that he wore a Kansas City Chief jersey with a 104 on it when he was banging on his drum in front of 80,000 Chiefs fans.

He became Helmet Man.

All of this while Ed, not his real name, was in the Federal Witness Protection Program.

Yep.

Can you say, "Hide in plain sight?"

You might think you have an interesting life, I hope you do.

But Ed—not his real name—sure as hell has had an interesting life.

Let's take a look at Ed's life:

Born and raised in Cairo, Egypt. As a young man he joined the Egyptian Army where he fought against the Israelis.

He moved to Italy and learned to speak Italian fluently but longed for something undefinable.

Ed moved to New Jersey and got married and started a limousine business.

He also joined a mosque—oh, his real name is Wahed Moharam—and as providence would have it he joined the mosque of Sheikh Omar Abdel-Rahman "the blind sheikh," who was convicted of masterminding the bombing at the World Trade Center in 1993. Abdel-Rahman was considered by Osama Bin Laden as the spiritual leader of jihad in the United States and, for good measure, is thought to have been a principal in the assassination of Anwar Sadat.

Anyway, Wahed had a limo service that also had some vans. One of his employees wanted to borrow a van but Wahed wouldn't let him.

One day a rented Ryder van full of explosives blows up inside the parking garage of the World Trade Center. Mahmud, Wahed's employee shows up at Wahed's a little bit worse for wear and shaking. Wahed calls the FBI and eventually is a witness in the prosecution of Mahmud and Sheikh Omar "the blind sheikh" and both of them are now in prison.

Wahed gets a new name, and Ed, is moved to Phoenix then Seattle and finally Kansas City where he becomes "Helmet Man."

Chiefs get wind of his past at some point and revoke his season tickets as they deem him a threat to other patrons if somebody decided to retaliate against, Ed-Anthony-Wahed-Helmet Man, choose one.

Wahed once called up the FBI pre-World Trade Center to offer to go to Iraq and kill Saddam Hussein because Saddam's shenanigans had impacted Wahed's striving for the American dream. The FBI told him they couldn't do that. But they did call him six months later to have him tape Sheikh Omar, who they suspected of plotting to harm America. And guess what? The FBI got that one right.

Wahed has been thrown out of the witness protection program as he has blown his cover three times.

That evidently is a rule.

In recent years he was pulled over for a traffic stop. He popped up on a terrorist watch list and drug sniffing dogs detected explosives in his van. The dogs were mistaken. The dogs were fooled by chemicals Wahed had for his carpet cleaning business in the van that gave a false positive.

He was outraged.

I don't know what Wahed is up to these days but I'm sure it's interesting. Movie?

PITTSBURGH

FRANK SINATRA   PITTSBURGH   FB

SUPREME COURT,
A NAKED MAN, FRANK SINATRA

14

THE MOST INTERESTING LEAGUE IN THE WORLD

PITTSBURGH

SayBrah®

"Quarterbacks should wear dresses."
—Jack Lambert

The Pittsburgh Steelers entered the NFL in 1933 as the Pittsburgh Pirates and changed their name to the Steelers in 1940.

Art Rooney founded the Pirates and his family still owns the Steelers.

The team struggled to field a team during World War II and had to merge with the Eagles in 1943 becoming the "Steagles" and in 1944 merging with the Chicago Cardinals to become the "Carpets."

Super Bowl Appearances: 8
Super Bowl Record: 6-2
('74, '75, '78, '79, '05, '08)
Super Bowl Losses: 1995, 2010

Art Rooney was cut from the colorful cloth of the men who built pro football in the depths of the American century.

TIME magazine wrote an article that described Art Rooney as "looking a great deal like a football himself."

There ya go.

Maybe he was a football.

Mr. Rooney, as he is reverently referred to by Steelerkind, is rumored to have won a big bet at the track, Saratoga to be exact, and that he used the money to buy the Steelers. What makes it plausible is that it is a well known fact that Art Rooney was a successful punter as the British say that is to say he knew his way around a betting window at the track. He once had a legendary winning streak over a two day period when he won a reported $259, 000 at Empire Park and Saratoga but that was 1937 4 years after he bought the Steelers (Pirates) He did claim to be one of the best thoroughbred handicappers in the country and he probably was.

He was much more.

On his way to becoming a beloved figure in Pittsburgh, he was an Olympic caliber boxer but never got to go because his mother didn't want him to go. The guy who took his place won the gold medal. Art Rooney beat the guy who won the gold in the ring before the Olympics and beat him again after the Olympics.

Rooney was such a good fighter that, for a brief time, he made some nice money at carnivals where he would go into the ring with the carnival's fighter and get three dollars for every round he lasted.

The carnival people finally got wise that he was better than the house fighter and asked him to please leave. As a gentleman he did.

Knute Rockne recruited him to Notre Dame but he didn't go.

Mr. Rooney spent years running the Steelers and made them an institution in a hardworking town even though it took them forty years to win a playoff game.

That's right.

The Pittsburgh Steelers were losers on the field until the 70s. But Mr. Rooney still became one of the towering figures in Pro Football.

And beloved.

He bought the Steelers. He sold them. He moved to Philadelphia to work for the Eagles, got homesick and bought the Steelers back so he could come home.

Art Rooney ran his life in the old style with an office located on the first floor of a Pittsburgh landmark Fort Pitt Hotel. His running buddies and even just regular guys would drop by and it was the scene of many a card game.

When his guests would leave the office more often than not they would leave through the ten-foot window that left them standing on the sidewalk rather than walk out the office door.

One of the regular pinochle players at the Fort Pitt Hotel office of Art was Pittsburgh Pirate Hall oF Fame third baseman Pie Traynor,

After Rooney moved his office to a fourth floor space in another building Traynor refused to play in Rooney's card game.

Why?

Traynor reasoned that he was so conditioned to walking out the window onto the sidewalks that he was sure to one day forget himself and walk out of the fourth story window.

Rooney lived in a nice home in Pittsburgh but over the years the neighborhood changed but he and his family remained until his death.

He is one of the pioneers both owners and players who built the league for the love of the game.

Not the money.

His family still owns the team.

SUPREME

In 1938 Art Rooney made the other owners angry when he drafted Whizzer White in the first round of the NFL draft and signed him to a bank breaking contract of nearly $16,000, which made him the highest paid professional athlete in America. Whizzer, a star from Colorado, played one year for the Steelers and performed at a very high level.

The following year he did not play as he went to England as a Rhodes Scholar.

He played two more NFL seasons with the Detroit Lions but he had other fish to fry as he would eventually become a lawyer and be appointed to the Supreme Court of the United States by President John F. Kennedy and served on the highest court in the land for 31 years.

Kennedy met Byron White during World War II when White, a naval officer, wrote the official report on the PT 109 incident.

Proof enough for "some" that White and Kennedy were members of the Illuminati.

In an ironic twist of Fate that is almost too good to be true, White wrote the dissenting opinion in the 1976 case Runyon vs McCrary in which the Supreme Court ruled that a private school in Virginia could not deny entry to a student due to their race.

White argued that the logical conclusion of such a ruling would inhibit voluntary self segregation and prevent social and advocacy groups consisting of members of one race to be forbidden under law.

The irony of this is that Michael McCrary the plaintiff and name sake of the case later became a star DE with the Baltimore Ravens and in 2000 was the recipient of the prestigious Byron Whizzer White Man of the Year award given to an NFL player for outstanding public service.

Rocky Bleier, Steelers RB, had a TV movie made of his life, *Fighting Back*. Quite a life it has been.

High school football star, Notre Dame All-American, 417th pick in NFL draft, drafted into the U.S. Army after his 1968 rookie season, Vietnam soldier, wounded in action, lost part of a foot in war, and 1,000 yard rusher in the NFL after army physicians told him he would never play football again, and a Super Bowl ring here and there.

When Bleier was in a Tokyo hospital recovering from several operations from his battlefield wounds he received a postcard which read

"Rock, team not doing well. we need you." Signed Art Rooney.

Rock went back to Pittsburgh not quite in football shape after his Purple Heart and Bronze Star heroics in war. Yet four years later in 1974, he was the starting back for the Steelers.

He along with Pittsburgh Post Gazette sportswriter Gene Collier have written a one man show 'The Play" featuring Bleier himself.

It chronicles his life's journey from Appleton Wisconsin, to Notre Dame, to the NFL, then to Vietnam and finally back to the NFL and the Pittsburgh Steelers,

The play is set in three bars. First his family bar in Appleton Wisconsin, a bar in Pittsburgh and finally Rocky's own bar.

He explores life as seen through the lens of one remarkable journey.

One reviewer describes the play as explaining the role that Northern Wisconsin played in making Bleier the man he is today, it also touches on his experiences in Vietnam where he lost part of his foot that was a career threatening injury and the musings that come from an amazing life.

Bleier on Vietnam: "We have chosen amnesia over history"

And he laments: "Things don't really happen for a reason."

Rocky Bleier has his own art festival of sorts:

- *Fighting Back :The Rocky Bleier Story* a made for TV movie.
- *Project 22* a documentary that follows a couple of vets (one of them Bleier) on a motorcycle tour of the country to look at PTSD.
- A 30 by 30 documentary on ESPN *The Return* an emotional return to Vietnam by Bleier and now *The Play* a one man show starring Bleier himself.

REF

Lots of NFL referee angst lately.

Where, exactly, do these guys come from?

Sam Weiss' family came to America from Poland and settled in Pittsburgh.

Sam graduated from Duquesne and, for a brief time, played pro football as QB of the Glassport Odds.

Sam went to law school and became a football referee who was called up to be an official in the NFL during World War II. He served as an NFL referee until 1964.

The unusual thing about Sam in Pittsburgh, at the time when he was called to be an NFL referee, he was serving in the United States Congress as the representative from the 39th Congressional district of Pennsylvania.

Sam was so well thought of as an official and public figure that his was one of the names that was bandied about as a candidate to replace Bert Bell as Commissioner of the NFL in the election process that was finally decided by Pete Rozelle being named to the position.

Now maybe we know why they have so many committee meetings on the field.

He was elected to three terms in Congress and ended his public life as judge in Allegheny County.

GONE

In 2005 Chiodo's, a venerable bar that had stood at the foot of the Homestead Grays Bridge in Pittsburgh, was demolished to put up a Walgreens.

Chiodo's was one of those places where, among other things, Pittsburgh Steelers fans congregated to talk about Steelers football.

Surely in the 58 years it existed a myriad of other topics were discussed and argued no doubt while eating or not Chiodos' signature "Mystery Sandwich." The sandwich's recipe was sold for $450 at an auction of the place when Joe Chiodo retired.

Chiodo's is an example, as it pertains to the NFL, of many things. One is the debt owed to those who came before who nurtured this game so that it was born, existed, stumbled, and preserved so we can enjoy it and so today's players can reap the financial rewards while often giving short shrift or no thought at all to those players and fans who are long gone. The peeps who built this thing called the NFL.

Such a dude was Joe Chiodo.

Joe Chiodo traveled to Cleveland to visit his army buddy Tom Wencke and see the Steelers play the Browns. They bickered and came up with an idea. They bought a trophy and the cumulative score of the Browns-Steelers match-ups would determine who got the trophy till next year. Joe had a bar to display the trophy and a bar in Cleveland got in on the spirit. Coho's Tavern in Cleveland got the trophy when Cleveland won the wager.

The Steelers are now one of the NFL's iconic franchises, winner of 6 Super Bowls. It was not always so. Art Rooney's Steelers went their first 40 years before they won their first playoff game.

In the 1970's when the national media discovered the Pittsburgh fandom they came to western Pennsylvania and asked locals where they could find the true Steelers fans.

They were pointed to the base of Homestead Grays Bridge on Eighth Street, to Joe Chiodo's bar.

Joe had purchased thirty-six season tickets for the bar when he first opened and held them his entire life. In fact, Joe Chiodo was such a Steelers fan that on the 50th anniversary of the Steelers, his picture graced one of the tickets that season.

Fans live, they die. Seasons come, seasons go. Places hum, places fall silent.

They may be gone but, in another sense, they are always there. Invisible blocks upon which the history of collective community is built.

LOST IN SPACE

Everybody in America, especially panty-waist poet types, knows who Colin Kaepernick is, even if they don't know or give a crap about pro football.

Kaepernick is now the Werner von Braun of discount store activism.

The stir caused by the National Anthem kneeling has taken on a life of its own but it took an interesting turn when it got to Pittsburgh.

A majority of NFL players are African-Americans and issues of race are particularly important and applicable in the game.

The anthem controversy caused a lot of teeth gnashing and soul searching in the league as well as PR concerns. Each team tried to deal with the issues differently. Some kneeling together or holding hands or not.

In Pittsburgh the team decided to, as a team, not come out on the field until after the National Anthem.

Only problem here is that one of the players, Anthony Villanueva, is a veteran of the Army and served three deployments in the Middle East as well as being a graduate of West Point. He is also a recipient of a Bronze Star for valor.

Presumably he has friends who died on the battlefield.

So here we found him, standing at attention for the Star Spangled Banner by himself in a concourse while his teammates stayed behind in the locker room.

The camera caught Villanueva, the son of a Spanish Naval officer, born in Mississippi, standing alone and—of course—that became a story. His jersey shot to the top ranks of merchandise sold in the aftermath of the incident.

Villanueva later said he did not mean to throw his teammates under the bus by doing what he thought was the correct thing. He said he felt embarrassed by the whole thing.

It seems to me it could be considered a case of his teammates throwing him under the bus.

United we sit.

Divided we stand alone if need be.

LITTLE PINK HOUSES...

Terry Bradshaw was drafted Number One overall by the Pittsburgh Steelers.

From northern Louisiana, he was ridiculed for his intellect and compared to *Lil Abner*, a popular 20th century rube from what used to be called the funny papers.

He was from a small school, Louisiana Tech, where he excelled in a bit of obscurity.

If you saw Bradshaw play in college what you saw was a guy who had a cannon of an arm and was one strong dude. In high school Bradshaw held the national javelin record.

Well, Bradshaw led the Steelers from decades of failure to four, count 'em, FOUR Super Bowl wins. The first quarterback to achieve that has gone on to become a national figure on TV as a commentator on NFL games, a recording artist, appearing in films, and becoming an all-around American success story.

The number one pick in the NFL draft, however, went from second string quarterback at Louisiana Tech playing behind another American success story.

When Bradshaw got to Louisiana Tech he played behind the starter, Phil Robertson, he of *Duck Dynasty* fame.

In an interesting footnote to the American cultural landscape, this bit of info is coupled with the fact that Bradshaw actually lost his starting job with the Steelers, for a brief time early in his career, to the first African-American starting quarterback in NFL history—that would be Joe Gilliam.

Gilliam was the first African-American quarterback to start a regular season NFL game, after he was given the task by Coach Chuck Noll over Bradshaw.

Bradshaw is quoted as saying that Gilliam beat him out that preseason and certainly deserved the starting nod.

Bradshaw, of course, won back the job and went on to make NFL history.

But not before going into the Oakland Raider locker room after a game to beg the Raiders to trade for him.

Gilliam and Bradshaw were both awed by each others rifle arms. Gilliam, unfortunately, crapped out of the league primarily because of drug abuse issues.

First African-American NFL starting quarterback, a TV reality star and darling of the American Right, and good ole boy from Louisiana who became a household name after NFL stardom.

Ships passing closely in the American night.

Ain't that America, something to see, little pink houses for you and me.

LOVE FIELD

The Pittsburgh Steelers are one of the more popular NFL franchises in NFL fandom due to success on the field during the Super Bowl era.

But it was not always so.

From their beginnings as the Pittsburgh Pirates in 1933 until, say, the 70s, the Steelers were one of the worst teams ever.

They never won s#!t.

Why? Art Rooney and the Rooney family are NFL royalty. Right?

Right.

Yet the Steelers were failures on the field for almost all of their history until...

1966, Tex Schramm, GM of Dallas Cowboys, meets Lamar Hunt in front of the "One Riot One Ranger" Statue of a Texas Ranger at Love Field, Dallas.

They go to Schramm's Oldsmobile and sit inside and they negotiate the NFL-AFL merger.

They git-er-done.

Pittsburgh gets $3 million in 1966 money.

Why is this so significant?

Because according to Dan Rooney, this was the first time the Pittsburgh Steelers had any real money to spend on players.

They would only draft players they could sign because they didn't have the money to do otherwise.

They once sat on their number one pick in 1962 and didn't pick anyone until the 8th round.

They used the windfall to draft Mean Joe Greene and, a year later, Terry Bradshaw—and they went on a winning streak in their draft acquiring a lot of great players and, along with the hiring of Chuck Noll, becoming the Steelers we know today.

The statue was moved to the Dallas Frontiers of Flight Museum for a brief time but has since been moved back to the airport.

Just in case you want to go see it.

BIRTH CERTIFICATE OF PRO FOOTBALL

Pittsburgh, November 12th, 1892 at Recreation Park near present day Heinz Field home of the Steelers 3,000 spectators showed up to watch what is today recognized as the first professional football game.

A grudge match between Allegheny Athletic Association and the Pittsburgh Athletic Club featured three ringers played by the Allegheny Athletic Association who won the game 4-0—a touchdown was 4 points then (inflation?). The lone score by one of the ringers, the legendary Pudge Hefflefinger.

Fingers were pointed out that Heffelefinger, the first American football star, and other players were paid.

Amateurism was a big deal in those days. The game was supposed to be an amateur endeavor but players were compensated in creative ways. Expense money, hockable awards like watches and trophies were given to winners. The Amateur Athletic Association was formed to try and monitor the amateur status of the game but payment was widespread if not publicly acknowledged.

Not until eighty years later did an accounting ledger reveal that indeed a payment of $500 was paid to one W. Heffelfinger.

That would be about $14,000 in today's dollars.

The ledger account is in a sports museum in Pittsburgh and is referred to as the birth certificate of professional football.

CROON

On a recent episode of the show *Masked Singer*, someone dressed as a deer in one of those elaborate costumes sings a song. And rather well.

This marks the reemergence of Pittsburgh Hall of Famer and Super Bowl winning QB Terry Bradshaw onto the radar as a fine singer.

In 1976 after leading the Pittsburgh Steelers to their second Super Bowl victory, Bradshaw went to Nashville to record a country album on Mercury Records,

He auditioned for the gig by singing a song over the phone for the producer. The song was Hank Williams' "Your Cheatin Heart."

Bradshaw's single, a cover of Hank Williams' "I'm So Lonesome I Could Cry" hit #17 on the country charts.

Bradshaw had been singing since his youth when he sang in his church choirs.

A ROSE IS NOT A ROSE

The Steelers found themselves in a playoff game with the Ravens in 2009.

What did not go unnoticed by a lot of Pittsburgh radio stations was the happenstance of the name of the mayor of Pittsburgh at that time.

Luke Ravenstahl.

The mayor, reacting to the radio station observation, went down to the Allegheny County Department of Court Records to file papers to change his name temporarily to Luke Steelerstahl.

The papers were not officially filed. Just another political promise not fulfilled.

But kind of cool anyway.

SUPPORT YOUR LOCAL SHERIFF

Art Rooney had a belief that pro football would catch on, someday. He put his money where his mouth was and bought an NFL franchise for his hometown Pittsburgh for $2,500 in 1933.

He also knew that Pennsylvania was about to lift its blue laws and that would allow for football to be played on Sundays.

The Pirates as the new team was called was to play its first game on Sunday and Mr. Rooney got a call from a city official who informed him that the blue laws had not been eliminated as of yet and his team could not legally play their league game that coming Sunday.

Rooney started calling around and he found the official he needed, that man demurred and told Rooney he would be out of town that day and could therefore not help Rooney with his problem.

Rooney then found Police Superintendent McQuade,who told Rooney that he thought it was a crying shame about them trying to shut down the football game. McQuade told Rooney that Rooney should give McQuade two tickets to the game and he would attend and that the folks who would be after the Police Chief, McQuade, to shut down the game would not be able to find him because they would never think to look for him at the game.

McQuade got his tickets.

50 yard line seats is my guess.

The game was played and the blue laws were lifted presently after and the first game was safely in the books.

Pro football owes a lot to men like Arthur Rooney.

OLE BLUE EYES

Franco Harris, is a Pittsburgh Steeler legend of the highest order. There's the "Immaculate Reception" of course, and the beginning of the rise of the Steelers championships.

Harris was unique in that he was the son of an African-American soldier and an Italian lady.

This unique combination made Harris a cultural bridge between two ethnic communities in Pittsburgh the African-American and the Italian.

Tony Stagno, a baker and Al Vento, a pizzeria owner, started a booster group, Franco's Italian Army.

It caught on and people from around the country could sign up to be part of the Army. One who did was a gentleman of Italian extraction and who was also from New Jersey like Harris was Frank Sinatra.

The Steelers were on the way to the Super Bowl as we now know but at the end of the regular season they had a crucial game with the Chargers coming up and Chuck Noll, the Steelers coach decided that the Steelers would go out to California early and practice for the game with San Diego in Palm Springs.

Myron Cope was the radio announcer for the Steelers and Tony and Al, the generals of Franco's Italian Army. Tony had the rank of 5 star general and Al a 4 star general told Cope that Sinatra lived in Palm Springs and that it would be beyond fab if Cope could get Sinatra to come to Steelers practice.

Cope had a mission. Mission Impossible it might seem.

Cope was dining at an upscale restaurant when Sinatra came in with his entourage, a group that included the famous baseball manager Leo Durocher and PGA champion Ken Venturi.

Cope wrote a note on a cocktail napkin and persuaded a waiter to bring it to Sinatra. It was an invitation to come to the Steelers practice that week.

Sinatra's surprised Cope by ambling over to his table and accepting the invitation.

Sinatra also left several bottles of wine for Cope and his table as a gift.

Practice that week was full of anticipation for Cope as well as for Tony and Al who flew out after Cope gave them a heads up that Sinatra might show up at practice.

Just when they thought that Frank was a no show, a guy in an orange cardigan sweater and pork pie hat comes over to Cope and Noll.

They had to persuade Harris to come over. A New Jersey boy himself Harris seemed in awe of Frank.

Handshakes and cheek kisses were issued and all was well in the world of Franco's Italian Army.

Tony and Al made Frank a one-star General.

The Steelers won the game and Frank sent Franco a congratulatory telegram signed "Colonel Francis Sinatra."

Sinatra demoted himself.

As for the surprise entrance: Cope had doubts if he would show. Said Francis Albert: "When Sinatra says he'll show, he shows."

HANG 'EM HIGH

How many times have you heard a football coach complain about his team's execution?

In 1941 the Pittsburgh Steelers were on the cusp of bringing this element one step closer to the game.

Alfred Jarret was discovered by Bert Bell and the 23-year-old, 230 lb. barefooted kicker from Hawaii was given a tryout with the Steelers as a prospective offensive lineman.

Alfred was an executioner. A real one. He was officially an assistant hangman at the penal colony on Oahu where he was a guard and his father the warden.

Alfred never actually hung anyone as he pointed out that the first-string executioner never missed an execution. I guess if ya love ya job you always show up.

Alfred never executed anyone and he also didn't make the Steelers team.

SHOWER

As the Pittsburgh Steelers entered the locker room after winning their third Super Bowl in five years, Steve Sabol of NFL Films says he saw what he described as a pasty-white bald guy entering the Steelers locker room next to Mean Joe Greene and a cameraman. The cameraman later said he had asked Mean Joe, "Who is this guy?'

Mean Joe didn't know who he was.

The guy started taking off his clothes next to Joe Greene's locker and, when the press started asking the guy questions and he started to answer them, they realized he was nobody associated with the team.

Never did find out who the guy who came into the post-Super Bowl locker room and took a shower with the Pittsburgh Steelers was.

DENVER

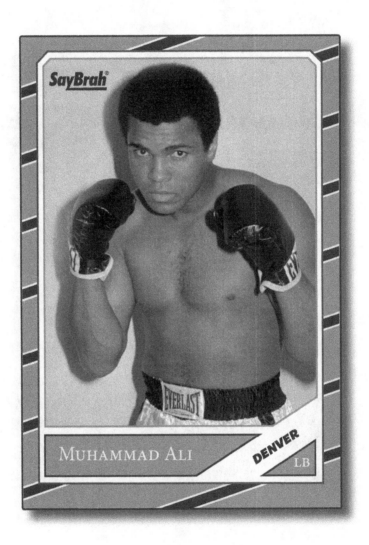

SayBrah®

MUHAMMAD ALI

DENVER

LB

MUHAMMAD ALI,
A DEVIL HORSE,
AND CARTMAN'S MOM

DENVER

SayBrah®

"I've been a Broncos junkie for a quarter century. I've tried every known cure, but nothing works."

—Leon Uris,
Author of *Exodus*

Denver Broncos are one of the eight original AFL franchises awarded in 1959 started play in 1960.

The team was almost relocated to Birmingham or Atlanta in 1965. It was saved by a civic effort to build a new stadium.

Super Bowl Appearances: 8
Super Bowl Record: 3-5 (1997, 1998, 2015)
Super Bowl Losses: '77, '86, '87, '89, '13

LOVE

Dan Klober and his wife started to paint their house blue. She was diagnosed with cancer and before they finished the paint job she passed away in 2013. The house painting was put on hold during her battle with the disease and, after the city sent him a citation to finish the job, he decided to paint the house the colors of her favorite team—the Denver Broncos.

The only thing is the house in question is in Sheboygan, Wisconsin. That would be Green Bay territory and the deep blue combined with the orange roof looked a bit too much like the colors of the dreaded Chicago Bears. So Dan fixed the problem by putting a huge Denver Bronco logo on the roof.

That is how Sheboygan, Wisconsin became home to the Denver Bronco House. Klober says he thinks of his wife every day and he knows she would have liked it.

Broncos fans have taken notice and drop by the place often to leave Bronco memorabilia for Dan.

And every year Dan hopes for a Denver-Green Bay Super Bowl.

THE GREATEST

Lyle Alzado is one of those stories you rarely hear anymore.

Played football on an obscure team in college. Discovered, by mere chance, by a scout. Signed by the NFL and became a star.

Alzado, like many players, had a difference of opinion with the Denver Broncos when his contract was up.

He had boxed in college so he came up with a scheme to fight a retired Muhammad Ali at Mile High Stadium.

It was an exhibition—Alzado hoped would get him some coin and some leverage in contract negotiations with the Broncos.

Ali played along.

60,000 tickets were available. The attendance was somewhere above 11,000.

Ali, in pre-fight hype said it would be a disgrace to lose to a "big fat football player."

The fight went the distance, eight rounds.

After the fight, Ali praised Alzado's skills.

It was a financial failure for Alzado but looking back, how many dudes got to go a few rounds with "The Greatest"?

⊕ Video on YouTube via Boxing Hall of Fame Las Vegas

ROMANCE

Little by little all the romance seems to be taken out of the human experience as time slogs on or time zooms on, depending upon your perspective.

Each NFL stadium comes with its lore, myths, moments seared into the fans' and players' minds, and with idiosyncratic touches that set it apart.

Sports Authority Field, the home of the Denver Broncos, has three quirks or unique touches that qualify on my romance meter:

The stadium itself is situated roughly upon the same real estate as the old Bears Stadium, the venerable minor league baseball park where the Denver Bears played, which opened in 1948.

If you find yourself in the right section of the present-day stadium parking lot, you may actually see the home plate of the old stadium, which is in the same spot as it has been since 1948 (only now just a random home plate sitting in a sea of cars in a parking lot). A nice touch.

You'll also see another relic from the original Bronco Stadium—Bucky Bronco, where it holds court above the scoreboard.

Bucky Bronco, in case you didn't know, is supposedly a replica of Trigger, Roy Rogers' iconic horse.

Still another special touch, only to be found at Sports Authority Field, is row 1 of the upper suite section. An entire row of seats that is a different color than the rest of the seats.

What's up with that?

Row 1 just happens to be exactly a mile high.

HISTORY

History is often not forgotten, it's simply misplaced.

Pro football history was made on October 6, 1968, when Marlin Briscoe was named the starting quarterback for the Denver Broncos making him the first African-American starting quarterback in AFL and modern pro football history.

He went on to lead the Broncos in five games that season and threw 14 TD passes. The 14 touchdowns are still a Denver Bronco record for a rookie.

Briscoe, known as "Miracle Marlin" from his days at Omaha University, went on to a nine-year pro football career.

In 1969, not getting a chance to start for the Broncos, he asked to be traded and ended up in Buffalo where he became a teammate of James Harris, an African-American QB from Grambling who went on to become the first black quarterback to win a playoff game.

Harris, Doug Williams (the first black quarterback to win a Super Bowl), and Warren Moon (a Hall of Famer) give Briscoe kudos and respect for his trailblazing. Moon said that just seeing Briscoe out on the field playing quarterback gave hope to other black athletes who had any doubts that there was an opportunity to play quarterback at the highest level.

Harris, who gives Briscoe credit for mentoring him as a rookie, used to go to the Grambling library to check out Briscoe's Broncos stats.

With Harris, Tom Flores and Jack Kemp in front of him on the QB depth chart in Buffalo, Briscoe was converted to wide receiver where he flourished—leading the Bills in receptions three years in a row and then being traded to Miami where he was part of the 1972 perfect season.

EXTRA: *It should also be noted that Gene Mingo of the Denver Broncos was the first black place-kicker in pro football.*

BRANDING THE BRONCO

Bakas Media calls itself brand builders, story tellers, and I'm not here to disagree.

In 1996 Pat Bowlen, owner of the Broncos, went to Nike and tasked them with creating a new logo for the Broncos helmets. Rick Bakas was the head of the Team Sports division of a Nike team that was given this task.

Bowlen wanted something specific, "I want a horse that looks like it is going to kick your ass."

So, the team embarked on the process that took months of research and ended up exploring team history archives at the Pro Football Hall Of Fame, forces of nature such as volcanoes, fire, lightning, ocean waves, and Native American lore of the "Ghost Horse"—a horse that was so spirited it could not be tamed.

Hundreds of design ideas were considered and whittled down to about twelve.

The design team came to the conclusion that the horse's power came from its neck and the unconquerable spirit of the horse is conveyed through its eyes.

The idea was to come up with a horse that was linked to the Nike swoosh.

Bowlen loved the final product and the logo now on the side of the helmets was born.

Not everyone agreed with the new logo at first. As soon as it was displayed at Bronco headquarters, a car sped by and shot it with paintballs.

Can't satisfy everybody.

BRONCO GANG RAP

Gary Andrew Young, like all too many young people, found himself spiraling downhill and in the grip of drug use. He says that he was consuming so much marijuana it caused him to have a mental breakdown. His habit was seven joints a day and a weed cookie.

The only thing that gave him joy was football.

Gary, at home in Connecticut in 2014, heard a Lil Wayne recording entitled, "Green and Yellow" (a remix of Whiz Khalifa's "Black and Yellow"), a tribute to the Green Bay Packers Super Bowl team of that year. So, being a huge Bronco fan he wrote a song, "Blue and Orange."

It revitalized his career as a songwriter and after he posted it on social media it ended up getting 30,000 hits. Even Broncos players hit him up on social media. It changed his life.

He was on the ropes. He had been prescribed drugs while in two different stays at psychiatric hospitals. The success of his Broncos songs led him to start Bronco Gang online.

Six albums of Bronco related songs later, the Bronco Gang now has 2,300 members in all fifty states and thirty foreign countries. His music can be obtained online and he even got a contract with CBS to perform his music before a *Thursday Night Football* broadcast.

He is a season ticket holder and tries to make as many Bronco home games as possible from his home in Connecticut. Pre-game performances of his tunes at Bronco games are now a widely anticipated event.

His rules to join Bronco Gang are simple: 1) No bandwagons 2) No fair weather 3) No violence.

NICE TOSS

As an NFL fan you've probably felt helpless when watching your favorite team at crunch-time of an important game and wished that you could do something to help.

Maybe it's a good thing you can't.

November 13, 1985 a Broncos fan actually helped determine the margin of victory from the stands.

Right before the end of the first half the visiting 49er are up 14-3. Ray Wersching is lining up to try a short FG to make the score 17-3 at the half.

A Denver Bronco fan and his pal throw snowballs toward the field just as the ball is about to be snapped.

One snowball hits an upright but the other snowball sails 35 yard on the fly and hits the field in front of holder Matt Kavanaugh just enough to distract Kavanaugh who muffs the snap and then throws an incomplete pass.

Kavanaugh later said he saw the snowball hit and it distracted him but he did not use it as an excuse he should have handled the snap.

Denver wins the game 17-16.

Jim Tunney, a long time NFL referee was the chief official in the game and he said there was nothing the officials could do in a case like that.

Security beefed up but no penalty on the home team.

In the press that week the chairman of the rules committee, Tex Schramm, said the officials should have stopped play when the snowball thrown from the stands disrupted the 49er FG attempt.

The *San Francisco Examiner* editor Dave Burgin offered a $500 payment if the fan would come forward to tell his side of the story providing he could also deliver two witnesses to the deed.

To his credit the perp came forward but would not divulge his name. He was embarrassed and sorry that he did it. He also refused the $500.

Nice throw though.

GENDER PIONEER?

Who was the first male cheerleader in the NFL?
A) J. Edgar Hoover
B) Ru Paul
C) Denis Rodman
D) Robin Williams

D) Robin Williams, one of the most brilliant comic minds and performers in human history, won many honors, portrayed many characters and did a lot of things for comic effect. That was his job.

In 1979, as part of a script on his hit show *Mork and Mindy*, he actually appeared on the field during a game as a member of the Pony Express, the Denver Broncos cheerleading squad, but of course, it was for comic effect.

Robin Williams, as far as I can tell, was the first male NFL cheerleader. All gussied up in sequins and hot pants, scarf, and vest, and white cowboy boots, Williams took the field in front of 74,000 fans during an actual game. (The footage was later used on *Mork and Mindy* to drive the story narrative.)

(You can find clips on YouTube)

WHO IS THAT MASKED MAN?

Once upon a time the mayor of Denver, Colorado, had an entry-position job. No telling where it might lead. In America, almost anywhere.

Michael Hancock's job, in his senior year of high school, was as the on-field mascot, "Huddles" of the Denver Broncos.

Years later Hancock said, in what could easily be the intro to a vintage radio show, "Huddles was his name, a horse on his hind legs, with a big helmet."

Now you call him *Hizzoner*.

That's right, the guy who pranced around on the field in a cartoonish animal costume was elected Mayor of Denver in 2011 and reelected in 2015.

As luck would have it, it was 1987 and a Super Bowl season so Hancock got to go with the team to Pasadena for Super Bowl XXI.

WRITER'S BLOCK

The NFL has a lot of famous fans.

In 1987, the *Times Mirror* was, by admission of its sports editor, spending a lot of money on product.

The Denver Broncos were in the Super Bowl playing the New York Giants in Los Angeles and the *Times Mirror* paid best-selling author Leon Uris $10,000 to do a few pieces about the Super Bowl from the perspective of a Broncos fan.

And Uris, the author of sprawling best-selling novels *Exodus*, *QB VII*, and *Topaz* was a huge Broncos fan.

He lived in Aspen and, back in the day when you had to do such things, he would rent a room at the Buttermilk, Colorado Holiday Inn so he could watch the Bronco games on cable television. He was a Broncos addict by his own admission. Going up to the game, he wrote that the Broncos had the edge with John Elway who, if healthy, would redesign the QB position.

However, after the New York Giants thumped the Broncos, Uris wrote as any good reporter the facts. Fact: Phil Simms threw for an 88% pass completion rate and Joe Morris ran roughshod through the Broncos. As Uris put it: "...and that is all she wrote."

Uris's wife was an accomplished photographer and came along to take photos to accompany his pieces.

The sports editor of the *LA Times* put Uris in the Super Bowl press box between Jack Smith and Jim Murray, two veteran sportswriting legends. Jim Murray was a wordsmith, his style poetic yet to the point. His Indy 500 column once began with this chilling phraseology: "Gentleman start your coffins." Uris knew who Murray and Smith were and was, of all things, intimidated by them as they sat next to him in the pressbox—their domain.

The sports editor of the *LA Times* said that the man who wrote the classic tomes listed above, each of which took years to write, was paralyzed as his deadline was upon him at the end of the Super Bowl and couldn't finish the piece. He told the editor as he looked at his typewriter, "I can't do this' ' so the editor had to write the last eighteen paragraphs.

COINCIDENCE?

Tim Tebow once toiled as quarterback of the Denver Broncos. They drafted him in the first round when no one else seemed to want to do that. Head coach Josh McDaniels had a vision.

And Tebow did have some success.

On January 8, 2012, he led the Broncos to an improbable playoff victory over the Pittsburgh Steelers.

This is probably the apex of his NFL career. That day, January 8, 2012.

Three years earlier to the day (January 8, 2009) Tim Tebow led the Florida Gators to the NCAA college championship. In that game, Tebow, a devout and *very* public Christian, decided to wear on his eye black, under his eyes, "John" and "3:16" from the gospel in the New Testament. The YouTube video was shared ninety-four million times. Or, so the figure that is thrown around is that figure, but either way it was an extremely popular action shared by millions upon millions on social media on January 8, 2009.

Then, January 8, 2012.

This is where it turns metaphysical.

On the a short-lived daytime talk show *Harry* Tebow told this story to host Harry Connick Jr.,: after the playoff game with Pittsburgh he came off the field and a member of the Bronco staff informed him that something interesting had happened.

Tebow really didn't know what the guy was referring to.

It was the third anniversary of the 3:16 thing.

That day, three years to the day, Tebow's stat line included these numbers: 316 total yards passing and 31.6 yds. per reception.

Tebow rattled off a few other stats on TV like a 31.6 rating—which I don't know if that's true—and that he, Tebow, ran for a 3.16 average rushing during the game—which is not true.

But the passing yardage of 316 is true, as is the 31.6 average yards per reception.

Tebow attributes it to God.

With a big G.

The TV comedy series *South Park* is set in Colorado so it would be natural for the Denver Broncos to be South Park's team and so it is.

No fewer than ten *South Park* episodes deal with the Broncos.

Church sermons, Osama bin Laden dream sequences, sacrifices to a statue of John Elway, and a lot more is associated with the Denver Broncos on the show.

The first appearance seems to be a storyline that crops up in the series: the paternity of Eric Cartman. At South Park's 12th Annual Drunken Barn Dance, Cartman's mother had "relations" with, among other regular characters of the show, the entire 1989 Denver Broncos.

Another episode deals with Scott Tenorman, one of Cartman's rivals, whose father was an offensive lineman on the Broncos. To exact revenge when Scott Tenorman cons Cartman out of money, Cartman hatches a plot to have Mr. and Mrs. Tenorman killed and turned into a chili which, because it's a comedy show, Cartman enthusiastically reveals once Scott has eaten them. But remember the Drunken Barn Dance? In a later episode, it comes out that Broncos lineman and chili ingredient Jack Tenorman was Cartman's biological father. The town covered up the paternity to protect the team from a scandal.

Suffice it to say that the Broncos are utilized for effect on many *South Park* episodes for many reasons.

The Dallas Cowboys are America's team but The Denver Broncos are South Park's team.

44

One morning when he was seven years old, police busted down Demaryius Thomas' door at 7am, pointed guns at him and told him to get down. Then they brought his mother and step dad out of their room in handcuffs.

His mother pleaded with the police to let her walk her children to the school bus one more time before taking her away. The police allowed it.

She eventually got life in prison for running a cocaine ring in Georgia. She got out twenty years later never having seen her famous son play football at any level in person.

White House visits for championship sports teams used to be one of the fun events of our culture and they still can be an honor but these days they have taken on, all-too-often, a political overtone of one kind or another.

Still, they are quite an honor for the players and teams generally and some time as Woody Allen said: "ninety percent of life is just showing up."

Demaryius Thomas was a star wide receiver on the Denver Bronco Super Bowl-winning team in 2016.

He, along with his teammates, met President Barack Obama, which I'm sure was an honor all of them cherish.

Thomas, however, had a bit more on his mind that day. He wanted to talk to "44" as President Obama is affectionately called in some circles, on a personal matter.

Thomas' mother and grandmother were in federal prison. And long story short, President Barack Obama, in an initiative he started to release and pardon non-violent drug offenders, pardoned both Thomas' mother and grandmother at different times.

Whether the Broncos visit had anything to do with this...?

BLUCIFER

A 32-foot-high, 9000 lbs. electric blue bronco greets visitors to Denver International Airport. Only it isn't a bronco exactly. Its official name is "Blue Mustang" but if you're an NFL fan you might assume it is a big Denver Bronco. Some do, saying that as soon as you see it you know you're in Broncos Country.

But it has nothing to do with the Denver Broncos.

Commissioned in 1993, it is the work of Luis Jimenez, a world-renowned artist, and is fashioned from fiberglass with red neon-like glaring eyes (the eyes a paean to Jimenez' father who ran a neon shop in Mexico). Those eyes have been giving the creeps to people ever since its installation at the airport in 2008.

It has many nicknames that speak to the controversial nature of the piece. You hear all kinds of descriptions, "awesome, hideous, scary, amazing, sick, horrible," and the nicknames attest to this, "Devil Horse, Blue Stallion of Death, Satan's Steed," and the most popular, "Blucifer." There was even a Facebook page set up to get rid of it.

Indeed, it now seems as if the statue which has weathered the outcry for its removal may remain as a Denver landmark.

There are a few circumstances and legends surrounding the piece of public art that add to its mystery. The Denver Airport itself is rumored to be the site of an underground chamber of the New World Order and strange alphabetical symbols in a concourse that turn out to be Native American symbols also lead to a bit of an Illuminati link in some people's minds, but the "curse" of the Blue Mustang was given impetus by an unfortunate circumstance that happened even before it was installed.

Jimenez, who has works all around the world including the Metropolitan Art Museum, was killed by the statue when its head fell on him and severed an artery in his leg.

The project was completed by his staff and family.

🌐 https://www.youtube.com/watch?v=dJKl38yfX4

🌐 https://www.youtube.com/watch?v=Ge5tMq_qGb8

INDIANAPOLIS

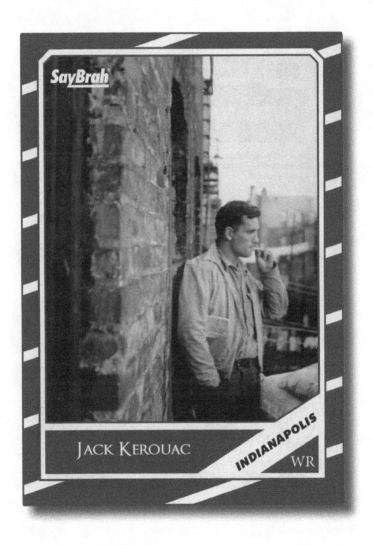

JACK KEROUAC, ORANGUTAN, ROULETTE

INDIANAPOLIS

"It's not your ball team or our ball team, it's my family's ball team. I paid for it and worked for it."

—Robert Irsay,
Colts owner

SayBrah

The Indianapolis Colts (originally Baltimore Colts) are one of the three teams that the NFL absorbed when the AAFC folded in 1949.

The Colts were moved literally in the middle of the night by owner Bob Irsay after stadium issues came to a head in Baltimore.

Irsay had acquired the Colts from Carol Rosenbloom in an unusual swap of teams in which Rosenbloom received the Los Angeles Rams in return.

Super Bowl Appearances: 4 (2 as BAL, 2 as IND)
Super Bowl Record: 2-2 (BAL, 1970; IND, 2006)
Super Bowl Losses: BAL, 1968; IND, 2009

Stick with me here.

The Indianapolis Colts franchise has an interesting and winding evolution and can be argued is one of only three NFL franchises that go back to the first meeting of the league at a Hupmobile dealership in Canton, Ohio, along with the Chicago Bears and the Arizona Cardinals.

The Dayton Triangles are the great-great-great-great franchise of the Indianapolis Colts.

Formed in 1913 in Dayton, the team was not only a charter member of the American Professional Football Association in 1920, but also played and won the very first game in the APFA, which became the NFL in 1922. They defeated the Columbus Panhandles in that game, 14-0.

Dayton, a team made up of workers from three local factories, soon found itself unable to compete with other, larger markets attendance-wise. Consequently, they became, from 1921 to 1929, what was known as a traveling team, rarely playing at home.

Losses mounted as the Triangles, relying on homegrown players, found it hard to compete on the field as pro football started to grow and the profession lured ever more talented players from far and wide.

In 1930, they were sold for the princely sum of $2,500 and moved to Brooklyn where they became the Brooklyn Tigers. The Tigers players were transferred to the Boston Yanks, the merger of teams due to, among other things, World War II. They played with little success and were moved back to Brooklyn as the Brooklyn Dodgers, from Boston to New York where they had played from 1930 until 1944. Meanwhile, former Tigers owner Dan Topping started a team in the new AAFC, the New York Bulldogs. This team later became the New York Yanks. There was a bit of cross pollination of players, leaving a tenuous link to Dayton.

In 1946 the new AAFC fielded a team in Miami, the Seahawks. On the field and on the ledger sheet they weren't much to crow about and were sold back to the NFL in 1951. They showed up in Baltimore as the Colts. They even wore the Seahawk jerseys (silver and green for the color aficionados).

Technically, the team was disbanded perhaps for tax reasons and only a handful of Seahawk players showed up in the new incarnation. The chain of the franchise is technically not recognized as the same franchise that became the Colts...but it kind of is, if only barely.

1952 saw them move to Dallas after a group of Texas businessmen bought the team. That team didn't last but one year and ended up being a road team by the second half of that season, playing all its final games as away games. They were then sold to a group that moved them to Baltimore where they kind of merged with the Baltimore Colts of the AAFC and were absorbed into the NFL.

Or something of the kind.

Whew!

1953 they became the Colts we now know. Sort of. I guess?

So, in what may be an exercise that physicians would prescribe to Alzheimer patients to sharpen the mind, let's recap:

Dayton begets Brooklyn Tigers, begets Boston Yanks, begets Brooklyn Dodgers, begets New York Bulldogs, begets New York Yanks, begets Baltimore Colts (after a winter in Miami as the Seahawks), begets Dallas Texans (and not the other Dallas Texans that became the Kansas City Chiefs but a different Dallas Texans), begets the Baltimore Colts, begets the Indianapolis Colts.

Of course, they moved to Indianapolis overnight, 26 years after winning what is called the greatest NFL game ever, the 1958 sudden death overtime game against the New York Giants.

That, at the time, was the TV broadcast with the largest audience in history. This storied franchise gave us, among others, Johnny Unitas, Raymond Berry, Lenny Moore, Big Daddy Lipscomb, Art Donovan, Jim Parker and other assorted NFL legends before they moved to Indianapolis overnight in 1984.

Quite a ride.

SNL

Peyton Manning is known as a workaholic. Ask any player who played with him. He is a perfectionist when it comes to his craft—QBing. He also brought this trait to his stint as guest host of *Saturday Night Live* in 2007 when it is reported he ran through the show's weekly budget half way through the week because he insisted in rehearsing and going over the script until they got it right.

His "United Way" sketch can be seen on YouTube and is considered one of the better skits from the show's history. Manning, in the sketch, pretty much abuses the kids and uses bleeped out profanity in faux mentoring. He throws footballs so hard that he knocks the kids down and makes one, who dropped a pass, take a timeout in a port-o-potty.

Manning later told the story of the sketch that almost didn't happen. Manning was uncomfortable with the sketch and thought it went too far over the line. He told the director that he couldn't do it, for among other reasons, he thought his mother would be very disappointed. The director agreed that, if Manning was uncomfortable, they wouldn't do it. Just at that moment a parent of one of the child actors in the sketch ran out and said, "I want you to hit my kid in the face."

Manning then agreed to go ahead with the sketch, which was done with Nerf footballs (which were described as light as a feather) and sound effects added to sound as if the kids were really getting it.

Manning still gets people coming up to him who remember the sketch.

One man told him that his son was one of the kids who Manning hit in the face. And the father said of his son, now twenty, who shows girls the video of him getting hit in the face by Peyton Manning on SNL: "It works for him."

THE COLLECTOR

Jim Irsay is described as different.

He is a poet, a philosopher, a guitar player and a collector of popular culture.

He has been described by the New York Times as collecting something to do with "our very plane of existence." He likes the things that make up our mosaic of being.

And he's got the scratch to afford to buy it.

Cool.

His collection of cool stuff was interesting enough to get its own gig, a museum exhibit at Indiana State University Museum in conjunction with the Super Bowl XLVI played in Indianapolis.

The exhibit was entitled "Chaos is a Friend of Mine," a Bob Dylan lyric.

The artifacts and things included letters from Thomas Jefferson, Abraham Lincoln and George Washington. The letter from Washington was about recruiting spies on the island of Manhattan during the Revolutionary War.

There were samples of Irsay's extensive guitar collection that includes a who's who of Rock 'n' Roll legends' personal guitars.

It includes Elvis' '75 Martin, Keith Richards guitar, John Lennon's guitar, and Jerry Garcia's legendary "Tiger," which Garcia used between '79-'89.

This is just a fraction of Irsay's guitar collection which runs to about 175 classic instruments.

The original script from Monty Python and the Holy Grail was also on display.

And perhaps Irsay's most famous piece, that original manuscript of Jack Kerouac's On The Road on one long piece of paper.

OMAHA

Peyton Manning is a man who demands attention.

During a telecast of live NFL play he was heard screaming "Omaha" while calling signals at the line of scrimmage and those who heard it, which could have been half of North America, it was on TV, wondering what it meant. Probably nothing. or just some trivial signal now of no importance to anyone. But when Peyton Manning speaks, people listen.

Pat McAfee, a rookie punter with the Colts, was invited to join a golf tournament by Peyton that was being held in French Lick, Indiana. McAfee didn't play golf but when the Colts demi-God invites, you accept.

The tournament was at a gambling casino and McAfee wandered over to the roulette table and bought $500 in chips. Manning entered the casino causing quite the buzz according to McAfee and signed autographs for a while. Manning walked up to McAfee and slapped him on the ass. People wondered who is this guy that Peyton Manning slapped on the ass? McAfee told them he was Mannings' caddy.

Manning stood behind McAfee for a brief time and as he left McAfee at the roulette table he said "How about the red 18?" Manning leaves the table with a wink and a smile.

McAfee moves all his chips to red 18. The other gamblers see this and they decide to do the same, this results in a pyramid of chips all on red 18. The little ball rolls and rolls and lands in red 18.

Olympus had spoken. The next morning McAfee sees Manning and asks him if he knew that red 18 hit.

Manning said, "Yes, I did." Stupid question?

GONZO LETTER

There is a copy of a letter that Hunter S. Thompson, he of the gonzo journalism fame, wrote to Jim Irsay in 1998 imploring him not to draft Peyton Manning but instead draft Ryan Leaf using the overall number one pick that Indianapolis possessed that year.

Dear James,

In response to your request for a quick $30 M loan to secure the services of the Manning kid—I have to say No, at this time.

But the Leaf boy is another matter. He looks strong. Manning doesn't—or at least not strong enough to handle that "Welcome to the NFL" business of two years without a world class offensive line.

How are you fixed at left OT for the next few years James? Think about it. You don't want a china doll back there when that freak Sapp comes crashing in.

Okay. Let me know if you need some money for Leaf. I expect to be very rich when that depp movie comes out.

Yr

faithful

consultant

HUNTER

It seems that Hunter and Jim became acquainted when Hunter implored Jim Irsay to purchase the scroll of the manuscript of Kerouac's On The Road which he did for a reported $2.43 million dollars.

Years later a fan at a Dodger game gave a copy of the letter to Ryan Leaf who became a huge draft bust. Leaf ended up in jail and has since turned his life around, helping substance abusers get back on track, among other things. Leaf, to his credit, thought the letter was a scream. As they used to say in Archie comics and other places.

A ROUGH GAME OF JACKS

My father had a saying about guys who never played the game mouthing off or putting their two cents in about football: "Here's a guy who never played a rough game of jacks in his life and he's an expert on football."

Cue up the 1998 NFL draft on ESPN. A youngish Mel Kiper, Jr., a draft guru, sporting a haircut he borrowed from 1965, the resident expert. He implores, for all to see, the Indianapolis Colts to draft a quarterback. His choice was Heath Shuler or Trent Dilfer. When the Colts GM Bill Tobin instead chose running back Marshall Faulk, Kiper panned the pick in no uncertain terms.

GM Bill Tobin then went on air with Chris Mortensen to return fire on Kiper.

Something to the effect of "who in the hell is Mel Kiper," and "I can assure you I don't give a shit what Mel Kiper thinks."

Kiper came back all chagrined and said that Tobin obviously has issues. It seems Kiper is also an expert mental health professional.

Faulk is in the Hall of Fame. Shuler not so much. In fact, Shuler went on to be elected to Congress. Talk about a fall from grace.

ORANGUTAN

At the Knoxville World's Fair in 1981 there was this new-fangled invention, a touch screen TV.

I am pretty sure one of the uses ballyhooed for the new technology so familiar to us now was not that an orangutan could announce draft choices for an NFL team during telecasts of the draft.

Nonetheless Rocky, an orangutan at the Indianapolis Zoo, was called upon in 2017 to announce the pick by touching the screen, and up pops the name Anthony Walker Jr. from Northwestern University.

Mike Mayock who, since that time, has become GM of the Oakland Raiders, didn't like it much. He threatened to walk off the set of his job as an NFL commentator—a high paid gig that doesn't require you to be correct about anything.

If one thing, this may finally turn off the NFL from repulsive sports announcers without the charm of a disinterested orangutan.

MAN OF LETTERS

The literary giant John Updike wrote a magazine piece describing Red Sox great Ted Williams' final game.

On Ted Williams last at bat in Fenway he homered. Williams was known throughout his career as somewhat of an aloof personality, not too touchy-feely was the man adoringly known as "The Splendid Splinter."

One of the things he was known for was never tipping his cap to the crowd after they acknowledged one of his heroic feats on the playing field.

As Williams rounded the bases on that dramatic final home run trot Updike and others no doubt considered if Ted would come out to give the crowd what they truly wanted after the deafening applause at such an ultimate moment.

Would he tip his cap? That one last chance.

The Thumper, Teddy Ballgame, The Splendid Splinter disappeared into the Red Sox dugout and did not reappear to doff his cap to an awaiting universe.

As Updike put it, "Gods do not answer letters."

Fast forward to another icon, this one a pro football player, Peyton Manning.

It turns out that Peyton not only answers an occasional letter but he writes a lot of them.

Petyon often writes handwritten letters to NFL players who have just retired.

He also writes to coaches, fans and people who have impacted his career or perhaps just crossed paths.

He wrote a letter to Patrick Mannelly, a long snapper for the Bears who was drafted in the same draft as Peyton on his retirement. An act that led Mannelly to talk about what a classy guy Peyton Manning is.

Many players and others who have received his letters would concur.

Manning gives credit to his letter writing habit to his mom Olivia, who insisted that Peyton and his brothers, Cooper and Eli, always acknowledge people with thank you notes.

Peyton has even written a series of letters to his children in the years after they were born even though of course they couldn't read, to be read at a later date.

The Colts, aware of Manning's letter writing, invited Colts fans or anyone else who wanted to write Manning letters on the occasion of the statue of Peyton Manning being unveiled in front of Lucas Oil Stadium.

Thousands sent a handwritten letter to Indianapolis.

And ya know what? John Updike, notwithstanding, sometimes...

THE MOVE: PART ONE

When Robert Irsay swapped the LA Rams for the Baltimore Colts in 1972, the Colts franchise had for years been in negotiations with Baltimore to improve or replace Memorial Stadium. In fact, Carroll Rosenbloom's failure to get traction on this issue was one of his reasons for swapping teams. Rosenbloom had even, at one point, offered to split a $62 million renovation of Memorial Stadium with his co-tenant the Baltimore Orioles but the Orioles turned him down.

Irsay, over his time as owner of the Baltimore Colts, used the time-proven tactic of threatening to move the franchise in order to leverage a better stadium deal.

Among other suitors for a new home of a vagabond Colts team were Phoenix, Memphis, Jacksonville, Indianapolis, and even New York City. In 1979 Irsay told Baltimore he was abandoning his attempts to move after receiving some assurances from the city. But the issue lingered.

This eventually ended up on the infamous overnight absconding of a whole NFL team, literally in the middle of the night, on March 28-29, 1984.

March 2 • As things heat up, NFL Commissioner Pete Rozelle announces the league will not contest a move of the Colts from Baltimore. This was influenced by the court case of Al Davis vs. NFL. With that announcement, the Colts had one foot out the door.

Indianapolis Mayor William Hudnut had at some point told Robert Irsay that Mayflower Transfer, headquartered in Indianapolis, had an offer on the table to move the Colts to Indianapolis pro bono. Hudnut's next door neighbor was James B. Smith, the CEO of Mayflower.

Irsay, in a little reported trip to Indianapolis to check out the facilities, had a cinematic moment. Walking into the interior of the Hoosier Dome, Irsay fell silent. His host asked him if anything was wrong. He answered that the white roof and thousands of blue seats perfectly mimicked the colors of the Baltimore Colts. Irsay then said, "Maybe it's fate that we move here." It's a moment.

March 25 • Colts expand the demands to Baltimore for them to remain.

March 26 • The Maryland legislature filed two bills that dealt with the Colts situation. One of those bills was a law to allow Baltimore to confiscate the Colts from Irsay under eminent domain.

March 27 • The eminent domain bill calling for the state to seize the Colts is passed.

March 28 • Rick Russel, a Mayflower executive, is having lunch at the Indianapolis Athletic Club. He gets a call from CEO Jimmy B. (as Smith was known around town) telling him we need to move fast, as the Colts need to be moved out of Baltimore. Like—now. Tonight.

Mayflower moved into action.

Fourteen, fifteen, or twenty-one empty trucks (thirty-year-old memories, even of closely documented events that hold the interest of a large modern city, morph in the human mind) were located from the Mayflower fleet, brought in from all over the country. After much searching, the trucks were dispatched without instructions to Owings Mills, Maryland, home of the Colts.

This, of course, is a day of infamy in Baltimore but counsel for Irsay, Michael Chernoff, said later, "They pointed a gun at our head and cocked it. And wanted us to wait to see if they would pull the trigger. We couldn't wait."

In a sense Irsay's hand was forced by political moves of the state legislature.

Mayor Schaefer of Baltimore later said he would have never used the eminent domain option. And he also lamented that, as he said, "My old friend Bob never called." Referring to the fact that as soon as the move was afoot, Mr. Irsay never answered the phone calls of the Baltimore political establishment.

However, a state senator, Thomas Bromwell, the bill's sponsor, was prescient and was quoted at the time, commenting on the sensitive nature of the eminent domain move and being careful as to not to spook Irsay. Which is just what happened.

The trucks were loaded with the entire team's stuff, lock, stock and barrel. The first truck was filled with business records of the team, which supports the often-used bromide by NFL players in contract negotiations, "This is a business." This pro football thing.

Drivers were sent on different routes so as not to form an easily spotted caravan. The first truck took the shortest route out of the state.

Hudnut and Jimmy B., the next-door neighbors, were together awaiting word of the movers' progress. Later Smith said it was like D-Day. The plan was set, put into motion and now all they could do was wait for the result.

When the trucks arrived on Indiana soil they were met by Indiana State Police escorts that brought them into Indianapolis.

The next morning there was a photo of the mayor of Baltimore on the front page of the Baltimore Sun in tears.

THE MOVE: PART TWO

Irsay moved the team overnight.

The other story of the move pertains to the logistics of the move.

If you decide to move a whole organization, you need someone to physically move it. At least one version of who moved the Colts claims it was the Hell's Angels. Sexy. But not true.

The night of the move the phone rang at Sigma Chi house on the University of Maryland campus. Joe Ponzo answers.

Members of the frat house had worked in the past for Mayflower Transit. The urgent call asked for workers for that night. Murky circumstance. "We'll send a bus for you at 11pm."

First offered $10 an hour, there were no takers. When the price was upped to $20 or $21 an hour (reports vary) Mayflower scored twelve or twenty frat boys for the "deed."

The boys were intrigued by the mystery of the unknown caper but, when the bus turned off to Owings Mill, they knew. They were there to move the Colts.

Once inside the facility they found equipment of all kinds laying around and, being young college fellows, they started taking Colts souvenirs. Mostly layering Colts jerseys under their garments.

At one point they, according to one of the participants, all looked like the Michelin Man. Mayflower officials stopped the proceedings and told them that they would be left alone for ten minutes to return all the contraband or there would be legal ramifications.

They eventually left with very little swag.

Now many of the movers, a radio talk show host, executives of many stripes, even a well-known presidential scholar, some of which had second thoughts but nevertheless all completed the assignment, have not much remorse.

One of the movers now working in Cleveland after that city lost its team to Baltimore, found himself taking a whiz in a Cleveland bar onto a picture of Art Modell incorporated into the urinal.

Aiming at the owner of the Browns visage in an act covered, no doubt, by the First Amendment and the long ago move presented a vivid reminder of the emotion inherent in the business of sports as it pertains to identity and place.

THE MOVE: PART THREE

Lingering feelings of abandonment and betrayal led to lawsuits that, once settled, called for, among other things, the return of Johnny Unitas memorabilia to Baltimore and the return of the Super Bowl V trophy that was dutifully bubble wrapped that infamous night by either Mayflower employees or University of Maryland frat boys.

But even here we have a twist. That trophy wasn't the real trophy. It turned out to be a replica.

Carroll Rosenbloom, yes here he is again. Living his life. Going down swinging, asked Bob Irsay in 1979 to let him borrow the Super Bowl V trophy to show it off at a Hollywood party after Rosenbloom became owner of the Rams.

Irsay obliged and lent the trophy to Rosenbloom.

Rosenbloom kept it.

Irsay demanded the NFL make him another. So they did.

The first trophy had omitted offensive line coach George Young's name and Ernie Accorsi, Colt GM, asked the NFL to engrave Young's name onto the second trophy. They did and that is how you tell the difference.

THE MOVE: PART FOUR

Irsay is a pariah in Baltimore.

There have been some who have, as time ages old wounds, if not heal them, come forward with an alternative view.

As Mayor Hudnut of Indianapolis said, "Indianapolis didn't steal the Colts. Baltimore lost the Colts." A very good case can be made for this argument.

To be sure Robert Irsay, from most accounts, was not a touchy-feely kind of guy but he did at one time have a more conciliatory attitude to the one issue that broke the camel's back: a new stadium.

A city councilman named Hyman Pressman in 1974 put a proposition on the ballot in Baltimore dubbed Question P. It would prevent public funds being spent on any new municipal stadium in the city. It passed with 56% of the vote. Clearly, Baltimoreans did not want to build a new stadium.

BAD GUY

Robert Irsay is the quintessential NFL villain. He stole the Colts in the dark of night. His mother is quoted as saying of him, "He's the Devil on Earth, that one."

His mother. His real mother.

In former player and big time NFL agent Ralph Cindrich's book, *NFL Brawler*, you'll find a chapter devoted to an inside look at his negotiations with Bob Irsay. The chapter is titled, "The Villain."

Cindrich describes how he, after a contentious bunch of phone calls, was going to meet Irsay face to face to negotiate the contract of Scott Ericson, a QB out of Miami University.

Cindrich researched Irsay and scheduled their meeting at Irsay's office for 7:30 in the morning, before Irsay could have his first drink.

The morning became the afternoon as both men were at loggerheads.

Cindrich contemplated combat during the negotiations, going over in his mind how he would do it, just like in a Jack Reacher novel.

Then Irsay asked him if he wanted a drink.

Irsay broke out the Coca Cola cups and poured the vodka.

Cindrich mentions that, at some point, logic and reason had left the room. They started sampling vodkas from all over the world. They got drunk.

Then they went to a barn party. A literary fundraiser, as it turned out.

The next day they met for bagels and coffee in the liquor-less morning and Cindrich got what he wanted contract-wise.

SEE *NFL Brawler* by Ralph Cindrich, page 194

CHICAGO

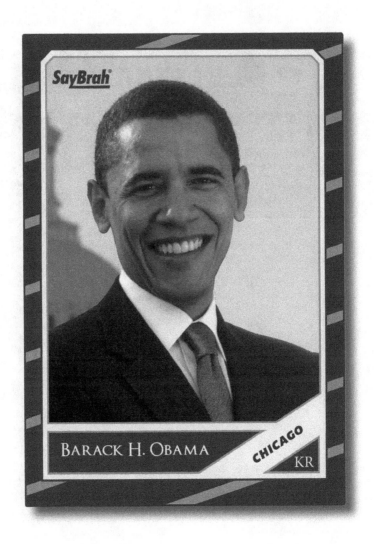

SNL, PRIMO CARNERA, AND OBAMA

CHICAGO

"If God had meant man to play soccer
he wouldn't have given us arms."
—Mike Ditka,
Bears TE (1961–1966)
Bears Head Coach (1982–1992)

SayBrah®

Founded in 1920 as the Decatur Staleys by George
Halas at the behest of the Staley Flour Company
and one of two original NFL franchises still in existence.

Moved to Chicago in 1921 and ownership acquired
by George Halas. The Halas family still owns the
team.

The Bears have won eight NFL championships.

Super Bowl Appearances: 2
Super Bowl Record: 1-1 (1985)
Super Bowl Loss: 2006

Chicago Stadium, the world's largest indoor sporting arena, was the site of the NFL's first championship game.

In fact, before this game the NFL had a rule passed in 1924 that forbade championship games.

The league, in those days, had a casual scheduling method. You could schedule non-members, you could schedule as many games as you wanted.

The champion was decided by winning percentage, ties didn't count. So when the dust settled on the 1932 season, the Chicago Bears, with a record of 6-1-6 and the Portsmouth Spartans with a record of 6-1-2 were tied.

The tie breaker?

Well, the two teams had played twice in the regular season with games ending 13-13 and 7-7. So we had a bona fide super tie.

The game was scheduled for Chicago to get a better crowd since Portsmouth was a small city of only 40,000.

The weather, as it does often in Chicago in winter, did not cooperate and a snow storm had left huge drifts in Wrigley Field, the site of the game. With frigid temperatures predicted, George Halas decided that if they wanted to have any crowd at all they should play indoors at Chicago Stadium. This was not without precedent as the Bears and Cardinals had played a charity game at Chicago Stadium in 1930.

The first NFL championship game was a hit with fans. Varying sources set the crowds at 11,000, 12,000 or 13,000 but, whatever the amount, it was packed.

It was a game with many differences from your usual football game.

Sportswriter Oliver Kueuchle, writing in the Milwaukee Journal, even went so far as to say it wasn't a football game. He didn't know what it was.

The field was only 60 yards with 20 yards extra for end zones. The field went up to the stand walls like in hockey, the goal posts nailed to the back of the end zones, and the end zones were half moon shaped, not being ten yards long at the sides. No field goals were allowed as no one wanted to knock out a window, punts and kicks indeed went into the stands, even hitting the organist. The field was on a concrete floor with 400 pounds of dirt, 6 inches deep, covered in tanbark. Footing was horrible. The night before, a circus had been in the building and some Chicago Bears players vomited from the elephant dung residue.

The Bears won 9-0, scoring all in the 4th quarter after a titanic struggle.

A pass from Nagurski to Red Grange provided the winning score.

It was noted or lamented or whined about by Portsmouth fans and sportswriters that the Spartans were at a disadvantage because their star, Earl 'Dutch" Clark, didn't play that day. Why? He couldn't get off work. He was coach of the Colorado College basketball team and they were playing Wyoming that day and the head of the university would not let him off to go to Chicago.

The game was one of the most influential in history.

The concept of a championship game became a regular thing. The dimensions of the field caused officials to move the ball back toward the field after each play as to not be up against the wall giving birth to the hash mark, which was adopted by the league at their next rules meeting, along with the change spurred by the controversial pass from Nagurski to Grange inducing the league to change the rule on forward passes. It allowed any player to pass from anywhere behind the line of scrimmage—the same rule we use today. Previously, a player needed to be at least 5 yards behind the line of scrimmage for a pass to be legal.

It basically introduced the forward pass as we now know it to pro football.

MITT 1.0

Mitt Romney, the former Governor of Massachusetts and Republican nominee for President in 2012 was named after his cousin Milton "Mitt" Romney, the starting quarterback of the 1926 Chicago Bears.

Milton "Mitt" Romney, was a first cousin once removed from Mitt Romney's father George Romney the former Governor of Michigan.

Mitt, the future Senator from Utah was named Willard Milton Romney. The Willard is for the founder of the Marriott Hotel chain, Willard Marriott and the Milton comes from the first name of the 1926 Chicago Bear.

Mitt, the senator, was called Billy in his earliest years but prefered the nickname Mitt, which is what the greater world knows him by.

Mitt, the quarterback, led University of Chicago Maroons to a Big Ten Title in 1922 and then went on to play in the NFL for the Racine Legion and then for the Chicago Bears from 1925 to 1929.

Mitt Romney, The Original, was the starting quarterback of all sixteen games the Bears played in 1926 a season that would see them go 12-1-3 and finish second to the Frankford Yellow Jackets.

The Bears played the Yellow Jackets late in the season and lost 7-6, which gave the NFL title to the Yellow Jackets.

Mitt Romney, the QB, was the starting quarterback on a team that had future Hall of Famers. George Trafton, George Halas, Ed Healy and Paddy Driscoll.

So it seems that Milton "Mitt" Romney as a pro football player definitely had game.

CRIME

Aristotle died over two millennia ago. This means we can't count on Aristotle for any new insights into human behaviour

No, we must turn to Ray Lewis, Hall of Fame LB late of the Baltimore Ravens.

Ray Lewis, may not be the Oracle of Delphi. Ok, he's not the Oracle of Delphi. Nonetheless his claims were the impetus for the University of California at Berkeley researchers to conduct a study on crime as it pertains to NFL football.

Lewis in 2011 as an NFL strike was looming said that if the NFL players struck and there was no NFL football then we as a society should be steeled for the consequences as it would cause a spike in the evil we call crime.

Cal Berkely released a study of crime in Chicago in 2014. The study was to measure crime activity during major sporting events that were televised.

Results? The data showed that during Chicago Bears Monday Night Football broadcasts crime in Chicago fell by 15%.

We're talking about violent crime, drug arrests, property crime.

The results were similar on days when MLB and NBA teams played although the percentages were decidedly lower.

The researchers speculate the reason that crime falls during Bears games is that fewer potential criminals are on the streets during the games.

Researchers also opined that the result of their study seemed to indicate that some crime may be recreational.

Which reminds me of a favorite Calvin and Hobbes cartoon.

The bully in the strip is in the act of thumping Calvin who asks him" Why are you doing this? What is there to be gained?"

The bully tells him "I just do it for fun."

The bully leaves, Calvin remains and says, "Just my luck, he's a sportsman."

Thanks for the heads up Ray.

DA CATCH

Monday Night Football, 1995: an extra point kick goes through the uprights at Soldier Field.

Out of the night a fan, Mike Pantazis, gets ready for the kick. He jumps out into time and space and makes perhaps the greatest catch in Chicago Bears history.

He's just a fan, a guy in the stands.

He's interviewed by Lynn Swann on the telecast. He's acknowledged with replays with Al Michaels and John Madden making the call. Madden even remarks that the guy is going to make the All-Madden Team.

Years later he is still a part of Bears history.

He was awarded ESPN's Outrageous Play of the Year in 1995.

And he got his own documentary. Ok, it's a mini-documentary.

You got ya own documentary?

 https://vimeo.com/3009114

DYCZKO—MIKE DITKA

Mike Ditka, nee Mike Dyczko—looks close to disco to me—is the definition of a larger than life guy. A demi-God in Chicago, not so much in New Orleans, yet he casts a wide shadow over the NFL zeitgeist.

Here in this Deadspin article, you'll find a flavor of Ditka in his popular habitat, testosterone land. WARNING! Segment is a tad graphic...

About 80% into the article you'll find a video that is no longer on YouTube. It shows a behind the scenes post game interview with Da Coach.

Hang on 'til the very end for a surprise ending.

You're welcome.

🌐 https://deadspin.com/he-reeked-of-jim-beam-and-slim-jims-your-best-mike-d-1655614740

CHEW CHEW

Two days after the 49ers creamed the Bears 41-0 in San Francisco the San Francisco police displayed an artifact of criminal activity to the press and public.

The police had displayed in the past guns, knives and other weapons or evidence of alleged crimes in the City by the Bay.

The "weapon" on display this day at the Hall of Justice was a green wad of gum.

The crime?

Terry Ornelas, a woman in attendance during the game two days earlier was hit in the head by a wad of gum. Ditka, head coach of the Bears, was less than pleased with the crowd pelting him with beer and ice and screaming invectives as he left the field at halftime allegedly threw said gum. He had gestured to the crowd and let loose with the big wad of gum he had been chewing.

That gum hit Ms. Ornelas in the head. Some reports said that it not only hit her but actually stuck to the back of her head.

She retained a lawyer. Ms. Ornelas' attorney was asked if he had ever had a case similar to the chewing gum affair.

He answered, "Yes, it is very much like a case I once handled in which someone was hit by a motorcycle and suffered brain damage." Okay?

The San Francisco D. A. Arlo Smith, after Ms. Ornelas refused to press charges, issued this official statement.

"We reviewed the instant replay and found a personal foul unsportsmanlike conduct. We declined the penalty. "

The incident was front page news in San Francisco. Someone in the San Francisco press reached out to Mike Royko, the celebrated columnist, of The Chicago Tribune to ask him if the gum assault was a big story in Chicago.

Royko, more of a Chicago guy than Mike Ditka will ever be, responded, "No."

Royko had a few thoughts on the gum "assault."

He asked this question and answered it in a column he wrote about the caper.

"Who runs to a lawyer if they are hit with a piece of gum? Californians do."

Royko went on to say that if a Bear fan had been hit by a piece of gum thrown by Mike Ditka they would probably take it home, stick it on a piece of canvas, frame it and hang it in their living room.

DA BEARS!

Robert Smigel is a comedy writer of some note. You've seen his stuff most notably on *SNL* or on Conan O'Brien's late night show. He is the voice of Triumph the Insult Dog.

In 1986, just starting out on his comedy adventure, he went to Wrigley Field, the cheap seats, and he did what comedy writers do. I know, I am one. He observed.

What you do is look at reality.

What he saw was a group of men who were wearing what he calls a Ditka uniform. He saw a fashion statement by the men in Chicago who idolized Mike Ditka: a certain swagger, thought Smigel, that was not earned.

Smigel thought the swagger was an illusion.

"You're a fat guy sitting in the third row. You can barely make it to the bathroom with all the beers you've drunk. You didn't do anything."

He made a mental note that this could be used as a comedy sketch idea in Chicago.

Smigel landed on the SNL writing team and he kept a phrase in his comedy quiver: Da Bears!—which would be delivered in what is called the Inland North Dialect or Chicagospeak.

Smigel believed the idea had potential but felt it was too localized to Chicago for SNL.

There was a writer's strike in 1987 and Smigel and others decided to use the time to do a live show until the strike was over.

That show was the *Happy Happy Good Show*. O'Brien and Smigel decided to try the Bears sketch and it went over well. He got a suggestion from a friend from Chicago to add a long S on the end of Da Bears!—something Chicagoans would recognize as more authentic.

Still, no matter that the sketch seemed to be a winner, Smigel still felt it was too tied to Chicago for a national audience.

After the strike, Joe Mantegna, a Chicago guy, was hosting *SNL* and the sketch was pitched at a meeting and Mantegna liked it. It was patterned after a local sportswriter forum held around a table in a bar setting.

Bill Swerski's Sportswriters was born.

It all came together and became a very popular recurring bit on *SNL*.

National commercials followed and the sketch can boast an all-star cast of *SNL*ers who have appeared on Bill Swerski, including Chris Farley, Smigel, Kevin Nealon, and Dan Ackroyd among others, and even a live appearance at a Bears playoff game, at which Farley and Smigel crashed a punt pass and kick competition at Soldier Field where Farley face-planted and Smigel nailed a 20 yard FG.

NFL meets SNL by way of writers' strike

This is how comedy legend is made.

Inspiration, timing, notes, opportunity, platform, and happenstance.

⊕ https://www.youtube.com/watch?v=kBnnon_iZOM

⊕ https://youtube.com/way=tch?v=f4eva_VN6_w

FRONT ROW SEATS

George Halas was known for among other things his frugality.

Halas used to sell spots at the end of the opposition bench to fans at games played at Wrigley Field.

That's right, at the end of his opponents bench.

So if you were an opposing player you would have rabid Bears fans on your bench giving you s#!t all game long.

Once against the Vikings, Head Coach Norm Van Brockln saw his QB Fran Tarkenton sitting on his helmet because there was no room left to sit on the bench.

The Dutchman asked the strange dudes sitting on his bench. "Who the f%^k are you guys?"

Vikings complained to Pete Rozelle.

Halas denied it but Rozelle had proof from footage he was sent from *NFL Films*.

The practice stopped.

Gotcha!

THE SWEET SCIENCE

Pro football players are often tempted to enter the boxing ring.

Steve Hamas, played briefly for a quasi pro team the Orange Tornados and with the New York Giants, he actually was a contender for the heavyweight title having defeated Max Schmeling. Schmeling destroyed Hamas in a rematch. Then Schmeling went on to defeat Joe Louis and, famously, be beaten by Louis.

Hamas was no hamburger. He had a record of 35-4-2 against top flight competition.

Hall of Famer George Halas compadre and former Notre Dame star George Trafton had a brief fling in the pro ring. His first fight was against Chicago White Sox first baseman Art Shires. Trafton won and then he won 3 more bouts which led to him going into the ring with a guy who was once described as a man who ate for breakfast, "a quart of orange juice, two quarts of milk, nineteen pieces of toast (not 20 pieces of toast), fourteen eggs (not 13 eggs, that would be bad luck), a loaf of bread, and a half a pound of ham."

That guy was Primo Carnera, who would become the heavyweight champ and who defeated a boxer named Ernie Schaaf on his way to winning the heavyweight crown by knocking out Jack Sharkey. Schaaf died from injuries after his fight with Carnera. Known as "the Ambling Alp," Carnera was a giant at 6'8". He also lost to Joe Louis and Max Baer.

Trafton lost in 54 seconds in the ring with Carnera and was suspended by the boxing commission after the fight for not putting up much of a fight. Trafton went on to induction into the NFL Hall of Fame as a center and to be an NFL coach with the Bears, Packers and Rams. He was my dad's line coach for awhile with the Rams.

In divorce proceedings with wife-number-two, Trafton claimed that his 110-pound wife (he weighing in at about 235, by the way) had hit him in the head with a ginger ale bottle, threw a chair at him, tried to kill him with a carving knife, kicked him in the stomach and more. She, in turn, said he was a gigolo at a local Chicago hotel and had broken her nose.

George had a raucous life there.

When coaching the Rams line Trafton would curse a blue streak which bothered Head Coach Clark Shaughnessy to no end. Shaughnessy, who did not curse, told Trafton, "George, every time you use that word I will fine you $50." Trafton answered, "Well coach, you might as well take my f#$@%g check now because I ain't gonna stop."

Quite a guy that George.

DAS BOOT

Five years before the founding of the NFL by George Halas and others the SS Eastland—an excursion ship docked in the Chicago River—capsized killing 844 people.

One of the passengers listed in the *Chicago Tribune* the next day as missing and possibly dead was one G.S. Halas, Papa Bear to be, himself.

Luckily for Halas, he was late to the dock and only arrived for the company picnic, which was the destination of the Eastland, right after the ship had already capsized.

Two of his best friends had boarded the vessel after waiting for the tardy Halas and were saved when they were pulled to safety through portholes by strangers.

Halas was late because his brother had insisted he get back on the scale to recheck his weight as George was trying to gain needed pounds so he could play football at the University of Illinois. A few seconds or minutes delay saved his life.

The SS Eastland disaster was the largest loss of life in one day in Chicago history. More souls perished that day in the twenty-foot waters of the Chicago River than during the Great Chicago Fire.

The Eastland had a rocky history. Years earlier it severely hit and sunk a tugboat. It was the site of a small mutiny, when six fire stokers refused to work because they were denied potatoes at their meal,they were arrested once back on shore and charged with mutiny. The vessel had also been the subject on three different occasions of serious listing problems between 1904 and 1914. The boat had problems.

Ironically one of the contributing factors to the disaster was the addition of lifeboats on the deck which added to the instability and top heavy situation on the Eastland. The extra lifeboats were a mandated provision of the federal law that was enacted after the Titanic sinking.

Fraternity pals of Halas who saw his name on the *Tribune's* list of missing and dead went to his home that day to give their condolences to his family only to be greeted by Halas himself.

Halas at his mother's suggestion said an extra rosary that night as thanks for his dodging a bullet.

Halas went on to serve in the U.S. Navy in World War I and II, play for the New York Yankees in the majors and found the NFL.

And let's not forget an interesting bit of trivia from George S. Halas' life. He has one IMDB listing: he appeared in the Elvis Presly movie *Blue Hawaii* as an extra.

Bet ya didn't know that?

MY (BEARS) PRECIOUS!!

1996. Walter Payton, in retirement, is helping out by coaching a high school basketball team in suburban Chicago. As a sign of trust he lends his Super Bowl ring to one of the young players, Nick Abruzzo, to keep for a few days to emphasize the importance of trust.

The kids pass the ring around to touch it for luck. It gets misplaced, lost or stolen. It never shows up.

It's gone.

Five years later Phil Hong is a student at Purdue in West Lafayette, Indiana. He is looking for a dog toy he lost under his sofa. He finds Walter Payton's ring on the floor under the sofa.

He bought the sofa from a friend, Joey Abruzzo, Nick's younger brother.

Hong thinks the ring fell out of the sofa.

Great news!

Except for one thing.

Water Payton died in 1999.

Hong returned the ring to the Payton family.

LUCK

Sid Luckman grew up in New York City and flourished on the football field in high school and at Columbia University. He ended up worthy of being on an overcrowded Mount Rushmore of T formation pro quarterbacks of the NFL's Golden Years along with Baugh, Layne, Waterfield, Van Brocklin, and Graham. He had a charmed life.

But in what will seem like an incredibly bizarre turn of events that could never happen now in this supercharged information age, Sid Luckman, golden boy quarterback, had a secret.

It seems impossible to believe that a man of Luckman's stature, known in every corner of the country, a star quarterback of the juggernaut Chicago Bears, had a father who died in Sing Sing, convicted of murder, and the American consciousness outside of the New York City area, was mostly unaware of this news.

Meyer Luckman, Sid's father, was put on trial twice for the murder of Sid's uncle, who had evidently crossed Meyer, his employer, in the trucking business in New York City. The first trial ended in a hung jury but after a new DA was elected, the case was resurrected and a sensational trial, with Sid sitting in the courtroom every day with his family, was splashed all over the papers in New York. In those days Sid was only an up and coming quarterback prospect in high school. He sat behind Meyer with his family during the trial in the spectator section.

After his father's conviction, such was the social atmosphere of the time that the family scandal was pretty much hidden. The press, for the rest of Luckman's life, ignored the fact, even going to great lengths to protect Luckman. In biographies of the famous sports figure the murder is never mentioned, something all but unthinkable in our own time.

Meyer died in Sing Sing with Sid never having ever visited him after the conviction.

THE GREATEST PASSER

Fact may not be always stranger than fiction but often it is more fun and amazing,

Forty years on into the NFL career of George Halas the man who started the NFL along with others and became a "The Matrix" visual presences in the league due to his stature and bespectacled spectre on many Sunday afternoons was asked to reminisce about some of the most memorable Bears in history.

This again was circa 1960 so Gale Sayers and Dick Butkus were still over the horizon.

Papa Bear named first Ed Healy (HOF) a tough guy from an era of tough guys, Automatic Jack Manders a legendary kicker in a game that was more kick dependent than today's, George McAfee a dandy runner without peer according to Halas for his dipsy doo like serpentine way of running through the opposition,Danny Fortman OG (HOF),Bill Hewitt a two way E (HOF), and of course the two giants of the early Bears Red Grange (HOF) and Bronko Nagurski (HOF). Everyone of those players a star.

And there was another name. Halas named John Doehring, a member of the undefeated 1933 Bears and a 6 year NFL vet with the Bears and Pittsburgh Pirates. But Doehring was not a star.

Why Doehring?

Because John Doehring was perhaps the most incredible or at least unusual talent ever to play in the NFL.

Halas once said of Doehring's skill set: "I saw it, But I don't believe it."

Doehring was a Milwaukee schoolboy star who never made it to college except for a brief stint at Kentucky Military Institute where he played football and baseball.

He was a stout lad throwing the javelin, putting the shot, and throwing the hammer in track and field and would later in life become a professional wrestler.

Being a Milwaukee boy he wanted to play for the Packers. He got a letter of introduction to Curly Lambeau the Packer potentate and coach from a local Milwaukee sports writer.

Lambeau, not up to date on his Wisconsin schoolboy gridiron, asked if Doehring was a lineman. The Packers needed lineman but not a back. Doehring although stout was a back. Lambeau was not even interested in taking a look.

Doehring was then encouraged to try to hook up with the Bears. Again an intermediary spoke to Halas on his behalf. Halas decided to give the boy a looksee.

Doehring had a bit of confidence as the story goes and upon meeting Halas, Doehring asked Papa Bear. "Do you want the greatest passer in football on your team?" To which Halas, perhaps taken aback by the cocksure lad replied. " I want the best of everything."

Doehring went out onto the practice field and in a few moments impressed Halas enough that Halas hired him as they said in those days to a Bears contract.

What did Doehring do in such a short audition to impress the head Bear?

He threw consistent sixty, seventy, and eighty yard spiral passses with accuracy. Doehring could throw the ball up to ninety yards in the air.

One Bear player years later said that Doehring threw the ball so hard that All Pro WR Luke Johnsos had such trouble dealing with the velocity of the ball that he had a severely bruised chest as the passes would zip through his hand uncaught.

Alas, Doehring, was a gimmick that just didn't translate to consistent success.

Early on in a game the Bears lost to Portsmouth a key rival at the time,they put Doehring in and he threw a long pass that resulted in a score. The play was sufficiently long that it took everyone by surprise.

After that, Doehring only threw 7 TD passes in a six-year NFL career. Doehring was however a useful part of the team as you will often see his name in the press reports of the games during those years as an important contributor. Yet his awesome talent never really flourished as Halas had surely originally envisioned after first seeing him throw the ball out of sight.

For instance, to utilize this awesome striking power you have to be deep in your own territory. A sixty yard toss from your opponents 35 would end up in the upper deck.

Nonetheless Doehring on one occasion had the ball lateraled to him and as he fended off the rushing lineman Luke Johnsos was told to run toward the goal and keep running. Johnsos kept running while looking over his shoulder for the ball. He said he didn't see it but kept running. As Johnsos approached the end zone he looked up and he saw the ball upon him. That would be 90 yards from where Doehring's left handed paw had released it. Johnsos jumped at the last minute but could only tip it. So he kind of dropped a 90 yard pass at the goal line.

Papa Bear was a businessman and he did use Doehring as a drawing card by having him put on pre game exhibitions for the fans during warm ups or sometime send him out to throw his unorthodox and soaring passes as a halftime entertainment. The pre-game shows would send receivers who would line up on either side of the field running out for long tosses and Doehring would simulate a snap from center and throw the ball as far as he could to the running Bears receivers none of whom could ever run fast enough to get to the balls. If they ran 65 he threw it 70 and so on. But it was a spectacle that got the fans juices flowing,

There's more.

In 1938 Doehring traveled to spring training to see what he could do as a baseball player. He had excelled in baseball in high school and in his brief stint at KMI.

Bill McKechnie, the venerable manager of the lowly Cincinnati Reds found himself with Doehring asking for a tryout. McKechnie, a veteran of the Major Leagues, gave him the horsehide and assigned vetertan catcher Virgil "Spud" Davis to catch Doehring. After a few fast balls Davis excused himself to get a sponge for his mitt.

McKechnie did not believe his eyes so he asked the veteran Davis if he saw the same thing as McKeckhnie.

Yes he did and what they saw was that they had never seen anyone throw a baseball that hard.

They signed him to a minor league contract but he never made it. By the way he was a very good hitter as well.

In fact, Doehring could hit and McKechnie said later he had never seen a better prospect in his life.

One of the drawbacks to Doehrings lack of success in football may have been a lackadaisical attitude. He would often miss practice.

Finally after missing practice one day Halas asked him where he had been. The movies and Pittsburgh he said.

Not that there weren't early warning signs.

'After the Bears signed him he didn't show up for the first game. He watched it from the stands later explaining to Halas he wasn't sure his mother wanted him to play pro football.

I saved the best for last.

When Halas or others would say they couldn't believe their eyes they were not only referring to Doehring tossing the pigskin sixty yards in the air with minimal effort.

No, more likely it was his incredible ability to throw an almost perfect spiral, with a 1930's unaerodynamic football, sixty yards behind his back, with accuracy.

Yes! You read that right. sixty yard behind his back.

He never threw a TD pass in a regular season game behind his back but on a barnstorming tour in a game played in New Orleans he did throw a 25 yard TD pass behind his back.

If you don't believe it, refer to YouTube: Southpaw Sensation 1934, and you will see Doehring not only throw a very long pass to Red Grange but also a 60 yard perfect spiral behind his back.

No, this is not a joke, or a Sacha Baron Cohen hoax.

Mike Ditka is a sports deity in Chicago.

But?

What does Mike Ditka claim to be the worst decision of his life?

According to press reports in American and even International press, Ditka claims that his worst decision ever could have prevented Barack Obama from being elected President of the United States.

It's 2004, Barack Obama is a failed candidate for Congress losing in Chicago to former Black Panther Congressman Bobby Rush. Still Obama is an up and comer.

Obama wins the democratic primary for the U.S. Senate after incumbent Patrick Fitzgerald, a Republican, does not run for reelection.

Jack Ryan wins the Republican nomination. Ryan was formerly married to TV star Jeri Ryan known for her role as the Borg character "Seven of Nine" on Star Trek. Their divorce in 1999 had papers sealed at the request of both Ryans, citing information that might be embarrassing to their children.

As the race heats up, the sealed documents are unsealed, revealing info about sex clubs and requests to Mrs. Ryan for certain activities by Mr. Ryan. Ryan drops out of the race at the last minute.

Republicans scramble for a candidate.

Did I mention that Mike Ditka is a sports deity in Illinois? I did. Didn't I?

Those of you with institutional memory may believe this is akin to a story describing how Mel Blanc, the voice of Bugs Bunny and Daffy Duck, announces sometime in the summer of 1944, "I could have beaten Roosevelt like a drum. But only if I ran as Bugs Bunny."

Put this in your pipe and smoke it.

Then Democratic candidate Barack Obama is quoted in the Daily Mail commenting on a Ditka candidacy. "He (Ditka) is insanely popular. I think if he gets into the race, he immediately becomes a favorite."

So there, all you haters. Mount Rushmore is safer as Ditka did not run, even though he said, "Not that I would have won, but I probably would have and he (Obama) wouldn't be in the White House."

Ditka spurned his chance for political immortality because his wife said no and because of business obligations. We owe the saving of the Republic in no small measure to Mike Ditka's Steakhouse.

And sex clubs.

SEATTLE

SayBrah®

FIGHTING ROOSTER

SEATTLE

LT

THE TONIGHT SHOW, FREDERIC REMINGTON, AND CHICKENS

18

THE MOST INTERESTING LEAGUE IN THE WORLD

SEATTLE

"The NBA is intense, but the NFL is a whole 'nother level of intensity."
—Paul Allen

SayBrah

Seattle Seahawks started play in the NFL in 1976.

They are the only team to have played in both AFC and NFC championship games.

They were the first NFL team with a 7-9 record to make the playoffs.

Super Bowl Appearances: 3
Super Bowl Record: Won 1-2 (2013)
Super Bowl Losses: 2005, 2014

DEAF PLAYER

When Derrick Coleman made the roster of the Seattle Seahawks, the undrafted player out of UCLA became the first NFL offensive player in history who was legally deaf.

Coleman, who played on the Seattle Super Bowl team of 2014, has been deaf since he was 3 yrs old due to genetic reasons.

It didn't let it stop him from success in life.

Taunted as "Four Ears" as a kid, he overcame his disability, and made it in the NFL.

When he found football he says it basically gave him a sense of where he stood in the world.

There is a lot of negativity in our society about many of the transgressions of football stars and ancillary elevation of importance in our society and rightfully so, on many occasions, but there are also as many stories of young men who didn't fit in or were socially inept, came out of poverty or a bad childhood situation to the game of football, its discipline and opportunity, to get an education.

Coleman excelled with loving help from his parents who didn't want him to play initially over worries it would harm him physically. He had to beg them to let him play.

He now has a foundation, "No Excuses Foundation," that helps kids with disabilities, telling them to just be who you are.

Coleman said he copes with the audible aspect of the game by lip reading, a skill he developed over the years, even behind face masks, and by moving at the snap when the ball moves, "If the ball doesn't move I don't move."

Elemental my dear Watson?

EARTHQUAKE

January 8, 2011, Marshawn Lynch, after a 67-yard TD run in a playoff game against the New Orleans Saints caused quite a stir.

The run was so great and on such an important stage, an NFL playoff game, that the 12s, as Seattle fandom is nicknamed, outdid themselves. With the help, no doubt, of Seattle residents throughout the region they erupted in a paroxysm of sports fan glee and frenzy to the point that nearby seismographic equipment registered the equivalent of a magnitude 1 earthquake.

CONFESSION

Fifteen-year veteran NFL referee Bill Leavy was about to brief Seattle media about NFL rule changes when he did the unexpected. He confessed that four years earlier as a referee in Super Bowl XL, a game the Seahawks lost to the Steelers, he had made more than one mistake. Mistakes that had been argued ad infinitum in Seattle. "I kicked two plays and it impacted the game."

The officiating of this game had long been a sore spot with Seattle fans.

The day after the game Seattle coach Mike Holmgren said this, "I knew it was going to be tough going against the Pittsburgh Steelers, I didn't know we were going to have to play the guys in the striped shirts as well."

Holmgren, for the record, has made peace with the result. Not so much Leavy, who says he will regret it to his grave and that he thinks of it often and has had many a sleepless night as a result.

Most Seattle Seahawks players I could find quoted on the issue seem to appreciate Leavy's apology and have reconciled to the result.

Hasselback, the Seattle QB that day, after meeting and talking with Leavy about the game, said, "All the guys who are referees in the league are stand up guys and Leavy is no different."

The Steelers, on the other hand, not so much. "He should go ahead and retire if he feels so bad about it. Just do us all a favor and not referee anymore," Max Starks, OL Pittsburgh Steelers.

Ed Hochuli, he of the famous "guns" said about the game after the revelation by Leavy, "The league felt, actually, that the game was well officiated."

As a New Orleans Saints fan, I say, "Ain't that reassuring, brah?"

SWEET TOOTH

Man smells freshly made maple bars that are somewhere in the same building in which he lives.

He finds an easy way into the doughnut shop that is closed and unattended at three in the morning.

He cannot resist. It is after all an age old biological drive of olfactory temptation.

Caught, by the doughnut maker as he comes back from a restroom break. Police are called.

The culprit as reported by *TMZ* is Seattle Seahawks rookie wide receiver Golden Tate.

He is apologetic in the presser the next day.

This is Seattle. The Cops told him to just not do it again.

He says no problem, but he does endorse the fare. "If you do want maple bars, Top Pot is the place to go."

Head coach Pete Carroll says of his rookie WR: "I do understand the allure of maple bars."

Four years later, Top Pot tweets an appreciative farewell to Golden Tate after he signs a free agent contract with the Detroit Lions, with an invitation to come back. But not at 3am.

LOGO

The distinctively Northwest Native inspired Seahawk logo, a stylized Eagle, is not only reminiscent of Pacific Northwest tribes from Washington all the way along the Pacific Coast to Alaska, but is thought to be taken from a specific Kwakwaka transformational mask that once belonged to the Fred Harvey Company and was once owned by 20th century artist Max Ernst, a contemporary of Picasso.

The image on the Seattle Seahawk helmet is similar to images western people first saw from steamships, images that appeared on totem poles or story poles and other native adornments in the Pacific Northwest. The Surrealists painters of the early 20th century, such as Ernst and Picasso, were especially taken with these images and took inspiration from them.

When the NFL commissioned logo graphic designer Marvin Oliver, he seems to have taken as inspiration the Kwakkawaka'wakw wooden mask that once belonged to Ernst and was purchased by a local art aficionado, brought back to Seattle and displayed at the Burke Museum on the University of Washington campus.

A photo of the mask can be found in Robert Bruce Inverarity's book *Art of the Northwest Coast Indians* (University of California Press, 1950).

BEAST MODE 2.0

There is a marijuana strain named after Marshawn Lynch.

Beast Mode and Beast Mode 2.0, which is advertised as being good for medicinal purposes. You're on your own from here on this story.

YOU CAN BET ME

The traditional city to city bet usually thrown down by the mayor of the cities playing in the Super Bowl usually are made up of culinary wagers, New England vs. New York, for instance, was Dunkin Donuts wagered against pastrami sandwiches.

But in 2015 the most cultured bet of all was inaugurated by Seattle and Denver. The Seattle Museum of Art and the Denver Art Museum put their masterpieces where their mouths are.

Denver put up the Bronco Buster, an iconic American piece of art by Frederick Remington. Seattle countered with a Nuxalk First Nations wooden mask that closely resembles the Seahawk logo. The idea was the loser would lend its art treasure to the winning city's art museum for 3 months.

The bet was changed because the Nuxalk tribe asked that their art not be part of a wager as it is more than simply a piece of art, but considered a sacred ceremonial item. Seattle was able to substitute and replace the mask with a 1900 Japanese painted panel called "Sound of Waves " by Tsuji Kakie which portrayed an eagle on the seashore. Kind of like a sea hawk.

The next year the Seattle art museum did another deal with the Clark Museum of Art in Western New England. The prizes this time were an American classics, "Puget Sound on the Pacific Coast" by Albert Bierstadt, and the Clark Museum bet Winslow Homer's "West Point Prout's Neck." Described as a bet of an Atlantic Ocean seascape vs. a Pacific Ocean landscape.

EXTRA: *It took Frederic Remington awhile but he finally made it into the Super Bowl conversation with this 2015 artistic bet, Remington played football at Yale in 1879. Remington played on the same team as Walter Camp, known as the Father of American football. Camp invented the line of scrimmage, the downs system, and the safety position—all innovations that helped evolve rugby into American football. Remington, one of the most famous American artists in history's first published sketch was of a football game.*

PUPPY HATE

Michael Bennett is an outspoken NFL player on a variety of issues and was said to have once read a book while Seattle coach Pete Carroll was addressing the team about the week's game plan because he, Bennett, said he had heard Carroll's spiel before.

Ok. Then there's this.

Bennett, who played in Tampa Bay before signing a contract with Seattle that guaranteed him $16 million, and his wife purchased a boxer puppy.

It seems they abandoned the puppy when they moved to Seattle.

A Tampa Bay kennel sued the Bennetts after calls and emails about the puppy, who had been left at the kennel for 4 months, and the Bennetts did not respond to court orders pertaining to the case.

The Bennetts settled the lawsuit for $15,000 but not until after a court ordered judgment that they ignored and the kennel owners had to find a new owner for the abandoned puppy which they say had caused the puppy to have an emotional breakdown.

SCORIGAMI

Scorigami is denoting an NFL final score combination that has never occurred before in NFL history.

Jim Bois came up with this little gem of trivial reckoning that gives a small bit of flavor to being an NFL fan, if you're a numbers sort.

And as it turns out, his invention or brainstorm applies especially to the Seattle Seahawks. Under Pete Carroll the Seahawks have achieved a scorigami every season. Nine times.

When they won a 43-16 game in 2018 against the San Francisco 49ers, it was the 1046th uniquely different score in NFL history.

Numbers and American sports are married in a special way.

When I was in college I had a history professor who was not a sports fan but pointed out that baseball would always be the American sport of choice because of numbers, batting averages, earned run average, runs batted in.

He did not foresee Fantasy Football or the NBA fascination with triple doubles. But he was right essentially on the American need for quantification.

American sports fans love our numbers.

PERFECT

Joe Vitt is a longtime NFL assistant coach. He was LB coach for the Saints when they won the Super Bowl and he was the interim Saints Head Coach when Sean Payton sat a year out at the behest of the league because of the so called Bountygate scandal.

He was also, early in his career, a special teams coach with the Seattle Seahawks.

Vitt was described as a high motor guy in those days—a coach who would ride his players in practice.

The story goes like this—a day of hounding future Hall of Famer Ken Easley didn't end once they were off the field. Vitt continued on Easley's case into the parking lot.

Easley had enough and knocked Vitt out.

The other players, as they went out to their cars, found Vitt laid out cold.

So, what to do? They went inside, got some chalk and drew a body outline around Vitt and left him there.

LATE NIGHT

Jimmy Fallon, the affable host of the latest incarnation of the *Tonight Show*, has a bit called "Superlatives." He shows photos of football cards of NFL players and his witty writers write humorous "Most Likely To:" fill-in-the-blank.

For some reason, the Seahawks were the subject of "Superlatives" quite a bit, to the point that the Seahawks, who were the butt of the jokes, took some umbrage.

Players Jon Ryan, Michael Bennett, J.R. Sweezey, Russell Wilson and Marshawn Lynch made a video of their own version of "Superlatives." They sent it to Fallon and he played it on his show.

Google "Jimmy Fallon Seahawks Superlatives" to watch.

CHICKENS COME HOME TO ROOST

Steve Largent was the first great Seattle Seahawk. He was the first into the Hall of Fame When he retired he held records for most passes caught, yards and touchdowns in NFL history. The Seahawks retired his number 80, the first Seahawk so honored. The Steve Largent Award is given in his honor to a member of the Seahawks for spirit, dedication and integrity.

After his playing days, he returned to his native Oklahoma and ran for Congress, winning four elections decisively as a conservative Republican.

In 2002 he ran for Governor of Oklahoma. He won the Republican primary and was poised to win the governorship. Up until a week before the election a poll had him up by 10 points.

Then, a contentious issue on the Oklahoma ballot got him.

He lost by less than seven-thousand votes out of a million cast. Close. What was the issue?

Cockfighting. Largent called cockfighting barbaric. The cockfighting ban, State Question 687, passed and cockfighting was outlawed. State Question 687 lost however in 57 out of 77 Oklahoma counties.

A reporter doing a story right after the election asked the owner of a cockfighting venue in rural Oklahoma if the cockfighting issue had defeated Steve Largent?

His answer: "You don't have to ask that." he said, "You know we beat that SOB."

It doesn't pay to count your chickens. He fought the chickens and the chickens won.

HOUSTON

SayBrah

BRUNHILD

HOUSTON

C

A PISTOL, OPERA, AND A RIVERDANCE

19

HOUSTON

SayBrah®

On RB Earl Campbell's inability to finish
the 1-mile run: "When its first and a mile,
I won't give it to him."
—Bum Phillips,
Oilers Head Coach (1975–1980)

Houston Texans entered the NFL in 1999 playing
their first game in 2002.

They are the newest franchise in the league.

After Cleveland left for Baltimore, and the league
made an agreement to award a new team to Cleveland, they decided to add another team to even out
the number of franchises.

Houston entrepreneur Robert McNair was awarded
that team.

The Texans have never been to the Super Bowl.

FOOTBALL PLAYER STEALS OWN TRUCK

DJ Swearingen had a 2013 Ford F-250 truck and wanted to trick it out, as most young men with nice wheels and a good job are wont to do.

He went to a place called Espi Motors, which had a very good reputation if you are to believe the kudos on the internet.

The makeover of the truck included a Batman logo, a custom grill, a lot of other basics and a train horn. When DJ went to pick up the new ride there was a "misunderstanding" and he drove ` off without paying the 20K bill. Espi tried to contact him about the bill. DJ was not to be found in a timely fashion.

A police report was filed and DJ was a star on TMZ. Headline, "Man Steals Own Truck."

The issue was resolved by full payment.

THE HEAD

The prevention of head injuries tops the agenda for the NFL.

The answer may be found by American ingenuity and free enterprise.

A start up company in Seattle, Vicsis, started by neurosurgeon Dr. Sam Browd in 2017, has created a helmet that scored the best in the latest NFL helmet testing.

The Vicsis helmets are called soft helmets and are multi layered. The outer layer is pliable as opposed to the hard helmet of yore, with a second layer of a series of vertical columns that bend on impact and absorb the brunt of the blow. The helmets can be adjusted to each individual player's head.

The Houston Texans were the first team to have players wear the new Vicsis helmets in a game.

In January 2020 after a promising start with its product, a safer football helmet, that was used by 180 colleges and at least one player on 70% of NFL teams during the 2019 season, Vicsis announced that its board had placed the company into receivership.

This was a harsh reversal for a company that had exuded so much optimism and buzz in the number one issue facing football, player safety as it pertains to the head.

The NFL even gave a $1.1 million grant to Vicsis and it had received investment from prominent NFL players Russell Wilson, Doug Baldwin, Aaron Rodgers and Roger Staubach as well as signed contracts with the U.S. Army for its products.

The company's executives and investors tried to raise more money to keep the venture afloat but came up short.

Principals in the company still hold out hope of resurrecting the enterprise

Sports lends itself to bigger than life heroes.

O.A. "Bum" Phillips, the legendary coach of the Houston Oilers, is both larger than life and a textbook American character with a perfect Texas ethos for good measure. Bum is just an ordinary guy who brought talent and everyday genius, for lack of a better word, of being a Texan.

In a 1991 readers of the Houston Chronicle, in a poll to choose the Top Ten Texans of All Time, picked Bum as number 6.

Sam Houston was first. George Bush came right before Bum.

Bum finished higher than LBJ and Willie Nelson.

Bum became a radio commentator covering the Oilers after his coaching days.

Here is but a small example of why Bum was both a legend and a regular guy.

Here is the concise quote. Describing a player with the Oakland Raiders, "He has that perfect Raider mentality, none."

PREMEDITATED DANCING

Billy Johnson was a smallish receiver who played at Division III Widener College in Pennsylvania.

He was watching the TV show *Soul Train* and saw Rufus Thomas, who had a hit with "Do The Funky Chicken" do the Funky Chicken.

He then told his teammates that he might want to do the dance next time he got into the endzone.

He scored in the very next game and felt obligated to do the Funky Chicken to save face with his teammates.

So he danced.

He was drafted in the 15th round of the NFL draft by the Houston Oilers and he brought the Funky Chicken TD celebration with him.

He had another signature: he had painted his football cleats white and that's how he became Billy 'White Shoes" Johnson. The name which he was known by in the football world ever since.

In 1965 Homer Jones of the New York Giants spiked the football after scoring a long TD. Some cite this as the beginning of the TD celebration.

But most trace the NFL TD celebration as it is today to Billy "White Shoes" Johnson.

In 1984 the NFL tried to rein the celebrations in and "White Shoes" started to get flagged for his dancing in the endzone.

As NFL ref Red Cashion put it: "He did a premeditated celebration wriggling his knees in a fashion of a premeditated celebration."

And so he did.

Curiously enough in 2016 in an interview about the state of dancing in the modern NFL game, the original, Billy, had a few interesting things to say:

"I don't know if I would do anything when it comes to dancing or anything like that in the endzone."

"I also wouldn't rehearse things and do all of the crazy stuff you see now."

"White Shoes" himself said that when he first did it he thought he would be called a hot dog.

He went back to the Oiler sideline and there he found Defensive Coach and dancing critic, Bum Phillips.

Johnson kind of apologized but Bum told him: "Shoot, If that's what it's going to take, I want to see more of the same from ya."

Johnson pointed out that he didn't dance after every TD as he felt it was important not to show up or embarrass his opponent especially if the game was too lopsided.

AUTOGRAPH WATT? WHAT!?

A pregnant woman asked J.J. Watt to autograph her pregnant belly.
He did.
A year later he met the child.
That is all.

CRAZY

George Henderson is known as Crazy George and, once upon a time, he was a big part of the NFL landscape and a big-time sports stadium entertainer.

Crazy George also claims responsibility for creating the WAVE.

The first wave is documented at a Yankees-Royals game in 1981 although George claims its roots are in a soccer game he was working years before.

So successful was Crazy that the Oilers out bid the Kansas City Chiefs for his services and, in his first appearance at the Astrodome, Crazy George had quite an impact on the game.

Franco Harris, the star running back of the Steelers, said that the volume of the frenzy George inspired in the crowd was really an unfair advantage. Chuck Noll, the coach of those legendary Steelers teams, said, "Every time we got the ball, the drummer (that would be George) started in on us, that's about as illegal as anything I've seen."

It led to the Steelers being shut out for the first time in 173 games.

Crazy George got a letter after that game from the NFL to try and stop him. Eventually it also led the NFL to ban George in 1989.

Crazy George was one of those throwback phenomena that surround the game.

George, who was a member of a National Championship judo team at San Jose State, plied his trade, crowd rabble rouser, in many sporting venues.

One interesting story George tells is of working a pro soccer game and asking to share the spotlight with a lion.

The lion and his trainer showed up a day early and they met Crazy George. The lion trainer told him they should do some promotion for the game by taking the lion to a bar. The trainer told George that the lion was an indoor lion. Sure enough,the lion was calm as could be in the bar.

The next day, the game was held outdoors. Before the game before a large crowd the lion who didn't much like drumming as it turned out and freaked. He mauled his trainer and a second lion trainer had to save the first trainer from his indoor lion.

BABYGATE

Babygate was big in 1993. It goes to show you how times and attitudes change.

David Williams was a starting offensive lineman for the Houston Oilers, who were in the middle of a winning streak they hoped would bring them to their first Super Bowl.

Williams' wife was expecting their son to be born at any minute, the week of the game with the Patriots. A game that would be played in Boston.

The timing seemed propitious as the doctors were scheduled to perform a Caesarean in time for David to see his child born and get to the plane in plenty of time.

It didn't quite work out that way. The baby had other ideas and David was at the birth but missed the plane.

David thought there was a possibility that he would lose his job and it was a good job. It turned out he didn't lose his job but he was fined $111,000.

In the delivery room David was on the phone with his coaches who were screaming at him and his wife and doctor could hear him getting reamed out.

The doctor yanked the phone out of David's hand and told him no more calls.

The plane left without David. Members of the Oilers organization tried to get him a private plane after his son Scott was successfully shepherded into the world. There was no promise that the plane could get him to Boston on time for the game. David finally canceled the private plane. The story went viral, even ending up on the Today show.

Some players were pissed at him, others took his side, but he said when he returned to practice that next week no one said a word to him.

Family and Medical Leave Act passed in 1993.

TEXAS FOOTBALL

According to Charlie Hennigan, in the early 60's the Oilers were playing the Dallas Texans and an unnamed Texas state representative's wife spent the night before the game going from room to room of the Oilers players.

They won the game.

Coach Lou Rhymkus in his post game speech told the players. "The team that lays together plays together?"

SNAKE

Kenny Stabler spent two seasons late in his career with the Oilers but it is a mostly forgotten fact that Stabler had a chance at one time to be a pro athlete in Houston but for the Astros.

Weeks before he was drafted by the Raiders in the NFL draft as the 52nd player chosen overall he had been selected as the 24th overall pick in the Major League Baseball Draft by the Astros,

Stabler was chosen as a Left Handed Pitcher. In fact he had been previously chosen by the New York Mets and the New York Yankees but instead went on to star as a QB on Bear Bryant's Alabama teams.

Stabler, an all around athlete, had also averaged 29 points a game as a high school basketball player and of course went on to a Hall of Fame career in the NFL.

Looking back Tal Smith the Astros GM when Snake was drafted remembers that the Astros were not all that keen on signing Stabler but that memory seems to be all wet as he was taken 24th overall in a baseball draft with hundreds of players many of which went on to play Major league ball taken after him.

THE PUNCH

"The Punch," which is arguably an attempted punch, is one of the sexier Oilers legendary moments, although the actual "punch" is somewhat of a letdown when you see it. The fact of when and why it happened at all is the story. In a nutshell, it's the wussiest punch since Cassius Clay knocked out Sonny Liston in their second fight with a phantom "punch."

The Oilers were riding high in 1993 in the midst of an 11-game winning streak, the longest winning streak in the regular NFL season of any team in 12 years. They had secured home field advantage, had overcome the adversity of a teammate's sudden death during the season and were in the waning moments of the first half in a season-ending win, Oilers 24 Jets 0.

However, defensive coach Buddy Ryan and offensive coach Kevin Gilbride did not get along. The defense had lost two starters in the last two games to injuries incurred in the later moments of the first half. Gilbride decided to air it out in a game they were dominating with only seconds remaining. Ryan wanted to run out the clock. Cody Carlson fumbled, the Jets recovered and the defense had to return to the field.

Ryan started bad mouthing Gilbride. Gilbride heard him, moved toward him and Ryan then delivered "The Punch." They were separated and the story was then not a successful regular season but "The Punch."

Jack Pardee was a low key old school leader. There seemed to be no discipline involved. Some players were cognizant that leadership on those issues seemed to be none.

Gilbride and Ryan never did get along. Ryan, the architect of the famous Chicago Bears 46 defense, and Gilbride, the creator of the Run and Shoot, seemed like a dream team of coordinators.

Ryan called the "Run and shoot" offence the "Chuck and duck."

Buddy Ryan was one of those guys with a big personality who it appears was created for the media age.

There are quotes from the time of the incident that give us a window into the personalities involved and a clue as to what, possibly, could have led to this event.

"Buddy was always an idiot." —Jack Pardee.

"The rapport I had with the father (Buddy Ryan, father of Rex and Rob Ryan) was non-existent from the beginning." —Kevin Gilbride.

A football coach going to the word "rapport" is interesting in and of itself.

"QBs are overpaid, overrated pompous bastards and must be punished." —Buddy Ryan.

After The Punch, another Ryan quote is instructive...

"Kevin Gilbride will be selling insurance in two years."

Gilbride went on to coach two Super Bowl winning teams as offensive coordinator of the New York Giants.

New York Times headline after "The Punch" game: "Oilers Coaches Exhibit More Punch than Jets"

🌐 https://www.youtube.com/watch?v=PRy9SOpBi78

2ND AMENDMENT

1968 GM Don Klosterman decides to cut Charles Lockhart.

Seems like a simple transaction you might find in the small print of a sports page. And so you might.

Only thing is...

Lockhart was a star at Texas State and the brother of the NFL player Spider Lockhart.

Charles, like so many players, injured his shoulder and it required surgery, eventually leading to the end of his football career before he made it into the NFL.

The surgery was successful as far as it went, according to the doctors and the Oilers. Lockhart did not agree.

His contract stipulated, as NFL contracts do, that the player should be paid his salary if he is injured and cannot be cut until he is healthy.

Oilers claim Lockhart is healthy, Lockhart disagrees.

This is where lawyers usually get involved.

Lockhart went another route. He confronts Klosterman at the Oilers offices and pulls a gun on him when it was clear Klosterman was not going to pay him.

Tom Williams, a scout, intervened and took the gun away from Lockhart.

OPERA

"Bum Phillips and the word opera don't belong in the same sentence," said Dan Pastorini.

Yes, they do.

Now.

Luke Leonard, theater director, and Peter Stopschinki, composer working in New York City, but both with Texas backgrounds, conceived, produced and composed "Bum Phillips All-American Opera" that had its premiere at The Ellen Stewart Theatre at La MaMa Experimental Theatre Club in New York in 1993 with Pastorini, Wade Phillips and Lawrence Harris, a former Olier, in attendance.

The opera is based on Phillips book 'Bum Phillips: Coach, Cowboy, Christian."

Pastorini, who paid to have the opera performed in Texas, later said of the first performance, "I sat there and watched this thing unfold for two hours, and at the end of it I had tears coming down my cheeks."

Notable lyrics from the work:

The singer portraying Pastorini: "My groin!" and a line from the opera sung by a Texas girl,

"Hell, in Texas we eat football for breakfast and shit a field goal at lunch."

La Scala here we come:

🌐 www.sportsonearth.com/article/69231956/both-sports-bum-phillips-aa-american-opera-not-your-typical-hi3

WORST RIVERDANCE EVER

The genesis of this book was to search each NFL team's history for off happenings related to that team. I called it a pro football subjective. That way I could decide what were the most interesting stories to include and what qualified. The story did not even have to be related to the franchise but in a small way to be included. That rule is rewarded by this unique tale that puts the fun in the National Fun League.

The story is included in the Houston Texans chapter because the event, although not concerning the Texans franchise, occurred in the Houston Texans

Stadium during Super Bowl XXXII in 2004. No Houston Texans franchise, no Super Bowl in this stadium. So, the Texans get the honor.

Second half kickoff is ready to start. Teams are lined up for the kickoff. Suddenly a gentleman in an NFL referee uniform moves toward the ball. So far so good. Then it turns quickly. What was about to happen was not seen by the billion or so TV viewers of the game.

The guy in the referee uniform closest to the teed-up ball, rips off his uniform, and, voila, we have a streaker.

This is only part of the story. This was no mere streaker. No. Mark Roberts, this streaker, may be the Babe Ruth of streakers. He has reportedly streaked over 500 events. But this is considered his crowning achievement because of the magnitude of the event and worldwide audience of the Super Bowl even though most people didn't see it when it happened. No telling how many have seen it since on YouTube.

As Roberts tells it, he was sponsored to pull off this streak. That's right. He had a sponsorship, Golden Palace online betting concern in the United Kingdom paid him to do it. Roberts is from Liverpool. I guess if you can't be the fifth Beatle, becoming the world's greatest streaker is a good option.

Roberts planned his Super Bowl stunt. He had the words Golden Palace. com written on his body in black markings when he did the deed and he had asked the NFL to send him an official NFL referee uniform, which, for some reason, they did. He used the uniform as a ruse to get close enough to the field to run out at the beginning of the second half.

He had a seamstress alter the ref outfit so he could easily pull it off. Like he was Gypsy Rose Lee. It all worked like a charm. He ran out toward the ball set up for the kickoff, he interacted verbally with at least one player, pulled off his clothes, then started to Riverdance.

That is the standard practice of streakers.

No?

Roberts says that his motivation is to "create something visual for people to laugh at." Why didn't you say so? He's a performance artist. He should apply for an NEA grant.

You can Google the performance of a lifetime and I must say he delivers on his goal to make you laugh.

See here:

⊕ www.youtube.com/watch?v=WBnCuzzf5JI

Read and see here:

⊕ www.theguardian.com/sports/jan/30/id-been-paid-1m-how-to-streak-at-the-superbowl

WASHINGTON

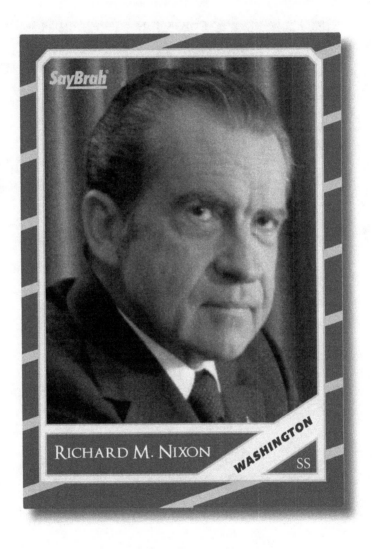

SayBrah

RICHARD M. NIXON

WASHINGTON

SS

A GIANT, SEGREGATION, AND NIXON

20

WASHINGTON

"He would hit you hard as hell but always in a Christian way."

—Sammy Baugh
[Redacted] QB (1937–1952)

SayBrah®

Washington [Redacted] were founded in 1932 as the Boston Braves moving to Washington in 1937 rechristened the [Redacted].

The name [Redacted] had been a lightning rod of controversy. Since 1940, when a Native American group tried to get the team to address this issue, the team has steadfastly clung to the name.

On July 13th, 2020, the team announced it would change its name.

Super Bowl Appearances: 5
Super Bowl Record: 3-2 (1982, 1987, 1991)
Super Bowl Losses: 1972, 1983

GIANT

Pro football is played by big guys.

In 1973 George Allen, the innovative head coach of the Washington Redskins, was said to be looking for something different to shake things up for his team.

There was at that time a big guy circulating in America who did not as of yet play football, at least not the American kind. This big guy was born in France.

Yet at 7'4" and 460 lbs (a conservative estimate), Andre The Giant, nee Andre Rousimoff, was an intriguing prospect.

7' 4" and 460 lbs? That's a lot of cheese.

Rumors flew and as with such things all kinds of stories circulated.

Andre did indeed not try out for the Redskins. It may have crossed their minds but it was never a serious possibility.

It was more of a publicity stunt than anything.

It created great photo ops, like Andre holding Redskins quarterback Joe Thiesman in his arms like a child. If ya can get a load of the picture it shows the size of Andre.

The overwhelming reason it was nothing more than a glorious pipe dream is that the Redskins could not compete financially with wrestling at the time. Andre was pulling down in excess of $256,000, while Sonny Jurgenson, the star quarterback of the Redskins, was making only $125,000.

It was another time, another financial paradigm.

LOONEY TUNES

From sea to shining sea and all across the fruited plain America is awash in splendid athletes.

However, it takes more than being the most gifted among them to become a star on the biggest stages that are provided.

It takes talent, it takes health, family circumstance, opportunity and attitude, among many variables.

In other words, history is strewn with great, gifted athletes who don't make the jump from here to there.

Joe Don Looney is one such man.

Gifted, in a football sense, compared to Jim Brown and Herschel Walker by NFL coaches on the field, drafted number one by the New York Giants even though he had been thrown off the team at Oklahoma after only three games. He was quite a specimen.

He was with the Giants for 28 days. Traded to the Colts, he just didn't fit in.

He would run plays wrong on purpose to make them more challenging.

He was traded to Detroit, where he had his most productive NFL years. But when he was asked by head coach Harry Gilmer to bring in a play to the quarterback during a game he told Gilmer, "If you want a messenger boy, call Western Union."

He was traded again, this time to the Redskins, the team he would spend the most time with in his NFL career, 14 games over two seasons.

The highlight of his stint in Washington seemed to be as a blocking back for Sonny Jurgenson when Looney, instead of blocking his man, just decked him with a right cross to the jaw.

He was called up with his National Guard regiment in 1968 to serve in Vietnam but not until he sued—along with others—President Lyndon Johnson, claiming that as a National Guard unit they could not be called up to fight in an undeclared war. They lost the case. And Looney served in Vietnam.

After Viet Nam he played three games with the Saints to become vested in the NFL pension system.

Then he got into drugs as a mule and as a user. It is believed he was an early user of steroids which were not illegal then.

He ended up converting to Hinduism and became a devout follower of Swami Muktananda, a famous guru, and was, among other things, in charge of taking care of the Swami's elephant as well as serving as the Swami's enforcer by using strong arm tactics to keep the 'followers' in line.

He was also known to give talks on the virtues of drinking your own urine.

He eventually came back to the U.S. and settled in rural Texas. When he was 45, Looney's motorcycle went off the road north of Terlingua and hit a fence. He did not survive the accident

He had. what lets' call, an Allen Iverson moment, as it applies to practice. He was known for not showing up for practice when he was an NFL player.

He had this to say about practice: "If practice makes perfect and perfection is impossible, then why practice?"

Socrates could have been Joe Don Looney's de facto agent.

EXTRA: *His father, Don Looney, was also a professional football player with Philadelphia and Pittsburgh and served as an NFL official from 1956 to 1962. When Don Looney died in 2015 he held the distinction of being the oldest living ex-NFL player.*

NIXON

Nixon got blamed for everything.

There is a lot of mythology around Nixon and his calling a play for the Redskins in an important playoff game with San Francisco in 1971.

Nixon and George Allen were good friends from Allen's days as Head Football Coach at Whittier College, Nixon's alma mater.

When Allen went to Washington, Nixon predicted the Redskins would be champions by 1972.

Allen invited Nixon to practice, Nixon called a play, a reverse, that went well in practice.

Fast forward to the playoffs in 1971.

Allen was talking to Nixon on the phone with QB Billy Kilmer in the room. Allen gave the phone to Kilmer and the reverse call was discussed among the three.

The reverse, called at a key time in the Redskins eventual loss to the 49ers, was a failure. It lost 13 yards and forced a FG attempt that was missed and some think this led to the demise of the Redskins. Even Allen in his post game press conference called the play a key to the game.

The rumor got around that Nixon called the play and Allen went along with it.

Allen never denied it but Allen's son George, a former U.S. Senator, and Bruce, an NFL GM, both deny the veracity of the story.

Enter Marv Levy, an assistant coach with the Redskins at the time.

Levy says George Allen gave the reverse play to Nixon and told him to suggest it to the team so it would seem like Nixon was calling a play. So Allen called the play.

And as Tricky Dick would tell ya if he could, "They blame everything on Nixon."

EXTRA: *Nixon was a big football fan. He played at Whittier College but was nothing more than a camp body. One teammate said that Nixon was not a good player but he practiced with everyone and he took such a beating and the guy admired him for his stick-to-it-ness.*

This odd tidbit I find interesting: Nixon spent the night of his election to the Senate in a legendary hard fought contest against Democrat Helen Gahagan Douglas at UCLA at former Ram Kenny Washington's home listening to music. Washington had always voted Republican up to that point but ended up supporting John F Kennedy when he ran for the presidency against Nixon.

THE NEWS OF THE DAY

December 7, 1941 the Redskins were playing the Philadelphia Eagles in Washington.

The reports of the Japanese bombing of Pearl Harbor were coming in but the 20,000 plus fans at the game were not informed.

During the game there were tell tale signs that something might be up.

PA announced calls such as

"Admiral Witt Bland is asked to report to his office"

or "Joseph Umglumph of the Federal Bureau of Investigation is requested to report to his office at once."

As the crowd left the stadium Shirley Povich the well known sportswriter said that the news hit the spectators leaving the game like a thunderclap.

The Redskins reasoned they did not want to cause mass hysteria and a stampede.

Robert Duvall, the great American actor is known for quite a few incredible performances. One of these memorable performances was as Augustus Mc-Crae in *Lonesome Dove.*

Duvall, as a part of his craft, has tricks and tools he uses to shape his characters.

As his star turn as Augustus McCrae was in the offing, Duvall was told that Sammy Baugh, the Washington Redskins great, lived nearby.

Duvall said he had always wanted to meet Baugh, who he had seen play during Baugh's NFL days.

Baugh was in his seventies at the time of the visit and was, as it turned out, a friendly sort.

Baugh is one of the truly iconic NFL players. Baugh played in a day when players had to play offense and defense and he is the only pro football player to ever lead the league in touchdown passes, punting, and interceptions in the same season.

Besides being a great football player, Baugh was also a cowboy.

Duvall visited for two hours with Slingin' Sammy Baugh and he took away some of Baugh's mannerisms.

In fact, the gestures Baugh used during the visit, the way he told a story with his hands, was the way that Duvall envisioned Augustus would.

Duvall said, "In two hours Sammy Baugh gave me the finishing touches to Augustus McCrae."

The way Duvall would point his long finger toward the horizon as Augustus was all Sammy Baugh.

The same hand that cradled and threw the football like no one before him and changed the passing game in the NFL lives on in Duvall's performance in *Lonesome Dove.*

Baugh himself had some experience as a Texas Ranger on the silver screen. Back in the day he appeared as Tom King, the star of *King of the Texas Rangers,* a serial that appeared in movie houses all throughout the country.

Baugh's sidekick in that serial?

Duncan Renaldo, whom some of you may remember as TV's *Cisco Kid.*

Baugh didn't care much for city life and would retire to his Texas spread as soon as his obligation to the team was over.

In fact Sammy had this to say about his star turn in Hollywood as Tom King: "I never did know what the damn thing was about." And: "I still to this day don't know what I was supposed to be doing in that picture."

🌐 *King of the Texas Rangers-Episode 1*
https://www.youtube.com/watch?v=p745kWbPW90&t=1302s

THE NAME

The Redskins management have argued the new name Boston Redskins (changed from Boston Braves) was initially given to the team to honor Lone Star Dietz, a Native American, and the head coach of the team at the time of the name change and other Native American players but there is a newspaper clipping that puts that assertion into doubt,

On July 5, 1933 in the Hartford Courant. George Preston Marshall is quoted as saying.

"so much confusion has been caused by our football team wearing the same name as the Boston National League baseball club " he said" that a change appeared to be absolutely necessary, the fact that we have in our head coach, Lone Star Dietz, an Indian,together with several Indian players,has not, as may be expected, inspired me to select the name Redskins."

In a strange twist to this story, a historian, Linda M.Waggoner, did extensive research into the life of Lone Star Dietz and her findings claim to prove that Lone Star Dietz, who indeed did play at Carlisle Indian School with Jim Thorpe, was almost certainly NOT a Native American.

Dietz was nevertheless known to play up his Native American links by dressing in full headdress at games and carrying on as a caricature.

Dietz had been put on trial in federal court on the charge that he had fraudulently claimed to be Native American as a ploy to get out of the military draft during World War I. Dietz demurred from service in World War I by declaring he was involved in an essential industry.

MORE NAME

The Redskins mascot controversy continued to be one of the most enduring sore spots in American sports until Daniel Snyder announced the name would be changed in July 2020. Snyder was responding to pressure from sponsors and co-owners as well as to the surge in protests around the country heavily based around racial issues.

The move had seemed inevitable.

Yet, just when you might think that you've heard it all, the root of the trend of naming sports teams after Native Americans you find can be traced all the way back to a guy born in 1625.

Tamanend, Chief of Chiefs and Chief of the Turtle Clan of the Lenni-Lenape Tribe to be exact.

It appears that the owner of the Boston Braves baseball team way back in the day in 1912, James Gaffney, was a member of Tammany Hall in New York and the American Indian was a symbol of Tammany Societies which were benevolent social organizations around the United States.

Tammany Hall in New York, of course, had other connotations in American civic culture as a corrupt political machine.

The early NFL teams often took mascots from established major league baseball clubs and this is how it was in Boston.

In Pre-Revolutionary War times the Indian statesman Tammaned was a figure of reverence and admiration that is the source of the name St. Tammany as Tammaned was held in such high esteem in the public consciousness of his time he was often referred to in print as St. Tammany.

George Washington's troops at Valley forge celebrated King Tammany's Day as a holiday and tribute to the peacemaking efforts of St. Tammany.

During the latter part of the 19th century and early 20th century many sporting organizations named themselves after Native Americans as a tribute to what they deemed the Native American spirit.

Nonetheless the appropriation of Native American symbols and attitudes were controversial even in the 1790's.

A play written about Chief Tamanend appeared on Broadway and the lead actress, one Charlotte Melmoth—described as the *grande dame* of the American Theater, refused to read the epilogue because of its jingoistic slant.

Be that as it may, it is possible that the name had some positive connotations shrouded in the mists of time.

It then follows that the Braves begat the Redskins and as we have seen the real reason that the name endured all that time is branding. It was a business decision.

GIVING LBJ THE BIRD

Robert F. Kennedy was assassinated in 1968 while running for president of the United States.

In January of 1969 a Washington lawyer named William Geohegan who had worked in the Kennedy Administration under Attorney General Robert Kennedy was having dinner with a friend Stewart Udall the Secretary of the Interior and one of the holdovers from the cabinet kept by Lyndon Johnson from the Kennedy Administration. Geohegan suggested that Udall could name the sports stadium in Washington after Rober F. Kennedy without any input from the President.

It was pointed out to Udall that he as Secretary of The Interior had jurisdiction over the stadium.

In fact under the Kennedy administration John and Robert Kennedy had brought pressure down on George Preston Marshall the owner of the Redskins to integrate the Redskins or lose the lease for what was then called District Of Columbia Stadium as it was a facility under the control of the federal government. By doing so the Kennedys had prodded Marshall into integrating the Redskins.

President Kennedy also refused to go to a Redskin game until Marshall integrated the team.

Udall knew that LBJ would not like the idea as LBJ hated Robert F. Kennedy and to add spice to the tale it was thought by some that LBJ wanted to name the stadium LBJ stadium.

Udall however went ahead and renamed it for RFK but kept it a secret.

Forty-eight hours before LBJ left office and Richard Nixon was sworn in Udall signed the papers and when a committee of three at the Department of the Interior voted unanimously to accept Udall's suggestion it was a done deal.

The stadium was then renamed Robert F. Kennedy Stadium.

When LBJ found out when it came across the wire service ticker he was pissed just as Udall knew he would be.

LBJ called Udall and "ate his ass out" as they used to say.

But it was done.

Monday before LBJ left office there were a few matters he had to take care of. One of them was to sign off on the designation of new park land that would be put aside for preservation by the National Park Service. LBJ signed off on most of the minor land additions to the national park service but he turned down most of the major land additions that Secretary Udall requested including millions in acres in Udall's home state of Arizona.

Payback?

LBJ seems to have done it for spite.

SNYDER FOOD

Among other ingestible issues pertaining to Dan Snyder as owner of the Washington Redskins...He twice left melting vanilla ice cream in defensive coordinator Mike Nolan's office, once with a note that read "I do not like vanilla." Hint, Hint....

1. In 2002 there was a partnership with Diageo, the world's largest liquor company, whereby they strategically placed liquor ads in FedEx stadium so network cameras would pick them up, a violation of a voluntary agreement of the NFL not to show hard liquor ads on TV. Anti-drinking advocates called it an attempt to end-run the policy.
2. A YouTube video showed Redskins beer vendors selling beer in bathrooms during games, a practice, some allege, that was going on for a while before video surfaced.
3. Five ounce royal blue and white bags of shelled peanuts with the logo of Independence Air on them were sold at Redskins games. A year after the airline ceased to exist. The company that distributes the peanuts in question said it had stopped delivering these peanuts to Independence Airline even before they went out of business. Experts on peanuts in sealed foil bags recommend that to avoid rancidity of the product they should be kept for only three months.
4. Weasel Chow—name of a menu item at the Princess Restaurant, Frostburg, Md., after Dan Snyder broke a contract to have Redskins training camp in Maryland to raise tourist revenue. An agreement he inherited from Jack Kent Cook.

Tony Robinson was a starting quarterback on a good Tennessee University football team and was a Heisman contender but, as things often happen in athletics, he was injured and his dreams of playing pro football were severely diminished.

Robinson got into cocaine and he was eventually arrested.

He was offered an opportunity in the Continental International Football League but he was incarcerated at the time. It was Tennessee, SEC country. A judge let him out to play football.

The year was 1987, the year NFL players went on strike and the owners decided to play the season with replacement players.

Robinson got the call and, as he later said in a piece on NPR, "They let me out of prison so I could play football." Indeed, as a backup quarterback for the replacement Redskins he got on the field when starter Ed Ruppert was injured. Robinson led this version of the Redskins to a huge upset over the Redskins rival Dallas Cowboys on Monday Night Football, no less, and helped the replacement Redskins to complete a 3- 0 run before the strike was settled. This upset over a Dallas team that had some of its key players on the field such as Tony Dorsett, Ed "Too Tall" Jones and Randy White helped the Skins get to Super Bowl XXII where they pummeled the Broncos 42-10.

In 2000, *The Replacements*, a major motion picture starring Keanu Reeves as a character based on Tony Robinson, came out.

Robinson, for his part, returned to Tennessee after he was cut from the Redskins, turning himself in to serve out the rest of his prison sentence and to watch Super Bowl XXII from inside a prison as an inmate.

In 2018 ESPN released *Year of the Scab*, a part of its acclaimed "30 for 30" documentary series dealing with the story of the replacement players in 1987.

Robinson says he did not receive a Super Bowl ring and at the time it hurt a bit knowing he had contributed to the team's record that year.

The ESPN documentary caught the eye of the Virginia State Legislature and a resolution to get replacements like Tony Robinson a Super Bowl ring was successful. The Washington Redskins, thirty-one years after the fact, awarded Robinson and each of his teammates a Super Bowl ring.

BLACK

George Preston Marshall's Redskins were the last team in the NFL to integrate in 1964.

John F. Kennedy and his brother Robert, the Attorney General, are given credit for pushing this along once John was in the White House and, as the Redskins were playing in a federally funded facility. However, in 1952 the Redskins were surreptitiously integrated by a subversive Washington sports writer, Mo Siegel.

In those days the NFL draft had beaucoup rounds. As the 30th round came along Mr. Marshall told Mr. Siegel, who had been hounding him all day to let him make a pick, that Siegel could make the Redskins 30th round pick.

Mo Siegel started to get advice on who to pick. He found a promising record-breaking receiver at Tennessee Tech by the name of Flavious "Nig" Smith. Siegel picked Smith for the Redskins and then informed Marshall, "Congratulations, you just integrated the Washington Redskins."

Marshall is said to have fumed over this turn of events and indeed had the pick stricken from the record.

However, there is more to the story of Flavious "Nig" Smith.

WHITE

Smith was the first athlete at Tennessee Tech to be named all conference on both football and basketball. He was said to be jet fast, book smart and a record-breaking receiver.

Marshall traded him to the Steelers after other teams passed on a trade.

When my Dad, Ed, lined up for his first play in practice after joining the Rams, he was at DT. Woody Strode, he of Spartacus gladiator and Hollywood fame, was at DE. Strode, along with Kenny Washington, were the first African-Americans to play for the Rams and the first to play in the NFL in over twelve years.

Pittsburgh traded Smith to LA but LA had Tom Fears and Elroy Hirsch, two Hall of Fame receivers, and the rosters in those days were only 37 players.

Smith was shipped back to Pittsburgh and again they didn't need a TE.

Lost in the personnel shuffle, Flavious Smith was drafted into the United States Army, and that is where his NFL dreams ended for all practical purposes.

He went to Europe with the Army, where he helped develop a physical fitness program for U.S. tank forces in Europe.

After his service he got his PhD on the GI Bill and went on to a distinguished career as one of the top professors in his field of Health and Physical Fitness at Tennessee Tech, where every year the Dr. Flavious Smith Distinguished Alumni Award is given to an outstanding graduate of Tennessee Tech in that field.

Smith said he had thought 100 times about what might have been. He said the Redskins receivers were not that good at that time and all he wanted was a chance. A chance he never got.

Mo Siegel, years later, called Flavious Smith to talk about the incident for a book he was writing and specifically about that draft pick. Seigel introduced himself on the phone as the guy who integrated the Redskins, if ever so briefly, by drafting Smith.

Smith at some point in the conversation asked Seigel, "You know that I'm white?"

Indeed, Dr. Flavious Smith is and was white. His nickname,"Nig," bestowed by a friend in high school, may have misled those supposedly in the know. Like the whole NFL.

And as the late, great Paul Harvey would say, "Now you know the rest of the story."

THE MARSHALL PLAN

When George Preston Marshall moved the Redskins to Washington the people of Boston weren't big Marshall fans.

In fact Marshall had the 1936 NFL championship game with the Redskins scheduled to play the Green Bay Packers moved to New York because he said that he was worried that the weather in Boston would be bad. But he was so unpopular that he feared the attendance would be embarrassingly low.

Then he moved the team to Washington in 1937.

He is also the chief villain in the "gentleman's agreement " that the NFL adopted to keep African-Americans out of the NFL for 13 years from 1933- 1946. He lobbied the other owners and got them to agree to ban African-American players.

The Redskins did not integrate until 15 years after Jackie Robinson broke the color line in baseball.

The pressure from the federal government and stadium lease forced Marshall's hand.

It was however a bone of contention with many that this policy was still in place with the Redskins into the 60's.

Shirley Povich, the Hall oF Fame sportswriter of the Washington Post, kept a steady drumbeat of criticism aimed at Marshall for not integrating the Redskins.

Povich had this almost perfect line in his account of one game

"Jim Brown, ineligible by birth to play for the Redskins, integrated their endzone three times yesterday."

WHAT'S THAT SMELL?

Tress Way, a punter for the Washington Redskins, has a creative streak off the field.

Tress and his wife, Brianna, invented what they hope will be the best trivia game of all time.

'What's Your Bid" came out in 2017 after a successful Kickstarter campaign.

But Tress couldn't stop there.

He has gone on to invent a card game because he says he "loves it when people get together and have fun."

"My wife will be really embarrassed with this," he explains while describing his new invention.

The card game, "Who Farted?"

Yes.

Fun. Fun. Fun,
Now that daddy's taken the inhibitions away.
As it turns out no actual farts are necessary.

THROWING GRANDMA UNDER THE BUS

NFL teams like to talk about "we" when talking about the team and their community and fans.

That is until they're not.

One thing you can count on from NFL teams and their players, they are on their side.

Anyone who doubts that the NFL is a business need look no further than the case of Pat Hill and other Redskin season ticket holders who were sued by the team for non-payment of season ticket agreements.

The team spokesperson says it ain't so cut and dried and perhaps, as with most things, there are two sides to this story.

Grandmother Pat Hill, a season ticket holder since 1962 whose daughter once danced in the Redskin field in a halftime show, had a home chock-a-block with Redskins merchandise and stuff like a burgundy and gold hook rug she made herself.

The Washington Post reported on Pat Hill's plight vis-à-vis the Redskins tickets and reported she was in tears sitting on her Redskins sofa lamenting that she believes that people are obligated to pay their debts. It says so in the Bible.

As a real estate agent when the economy went south, she could no longer afford her $5,300 season tickets bill. She had signed a 10-year contract to buy the seats in an exclusive section of the Redskins stadium.

The Redskins got a $66,000 judgment against her because she did not show up in court to fight it.

The Redskins, meanwhile, who claim to have a 10,000-person waiting list to buy season tickets, claim they only sue as a last resort. They also claim that all NFL teams sue their season ticket holders. Which, according to at least 9 NFL teams, is untrue.

The stories of the 125 people the Redskins sued are interesting due to the complexity of each case. The Redskins claim they settle 6 times as many of these cases as they end up litigating. Perhaps that is true, but the cases cited by an article in the Washington Post offers these tales.

One ticket holder who couldn't pay his tickets actually had his tickets sold by the team and they still sued him for the tickets.

One guy was in jail for embezzlement and he also had Washington Nationals tickets. He wrote a letter to each team explaining that he couldn't pay because he was in jail. Ok, not your most sympathetic character. Yet the Redskins sued and the Nationals, well, they sent the guy free tickets.

Still another guy was given a Pro Bono public defender and it was determined he was a paranoid schizophrenic. His lawyer asked that he not be named because of his mental illness and that the team should not pursue the case as judgment would be unrecoverable.

The Redskins sued him anyway.

The case was dismissed eventually.

Pat Hill's case was also dropped after they had hounded her.

When times were hard Ms. Hill, according to her friend Muhammad Khan, a loan officer who worked with her and went to games with her, she advanced people money, thousands of dollars, to help them save their homes. "She's like an angel," said Khan.

The Redskins also sell blocks of tickets to ticket brokers, according to an article in *Deadspin*, even though they have a 10,000 person waiting list for tickets.

Pat Hill, at the end of the *Washington Post* article is quoted as saying (and this was before the suit was dropped)—"I just love the Redskins."

It's a complicated issue.

You be the judge.

⊕ www.washingtonpost.com/wp-dyn/content/article/2009/09/02AR2009090203887_5.html/?sid=ST200909043219

NEW YORK (A)

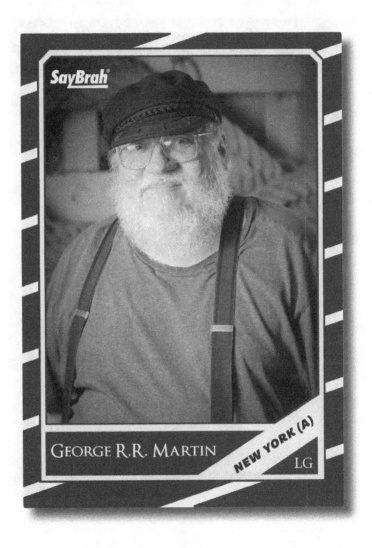

SayBrah®

GEORGE R.R. MARTIN

NEW YORK (A)

LG

MING THE MERCILESS, A LAWNMOWER, AND GAME OF THRONES

21 THE MOST INTERESTING LEAGUE IN THE WORLD

NEW YORK (A)

SayBrah®

"I got just one fan letter from an NFL fullback named Darian Barnes. NFL players might not have enough time to read my books."

—George R. R. Martin

Jets came into the AFL in 1959 as a charter member named the New York Titans and owned by announcer Harry Wismer.

Sold for $1 million in 1963 to MCA executive Sonny Werblin who changed name to Jets and colors to green and white. Werblin signed Joe Namath to a large contract coming out of college and, in doing so, changed the financial landscape of the league.

In Super Bowl III, the heavy underdog Jets defeated the Baltimore Colts 16-7 serving notice that AFL could compete with NFL teams.

They have not appeared in a Super Bowl since.

Super Bowl Appearances: 1
Super Bowl Record: 1-0 (1968)

1969, The New York Jets shocked the pro football world by upsetting the NFL's Baltimore Colts, who were a 17 ½ point favorite, the team was led by the brash QB Joe Namath and the win heralded a coming of age for the upstart AFL.

Along with victory, the winning team gets some personal hardware, a Super Bowl Ring, or as Golem might say, "My Precious."

And so it is, precious, that is—the Super Bowl ring.

And the stories that these rings, the 1969 Jets Super Bowl Rings, will echo through this chapter about the New York Jets, fifty years after the fact of the game. The emotion of these rings, and oh, the places they've been.

Don Maynard, the great receiver, holds his Super Bowl ring dear. "Nobody gets the ring unless they take a finger with it," says Maynard's wife. He keeps it in a refrigerator to protect it from fire and other things in the night.

Earl Christy sold his because he says he had a penchant for losing it. Fell off his finger in the snow, his kid dropped it into a toilet but it was, luckily, too heavy to be flushed. He had a replica made and put the real one in a safe deposit box. Then figured why not just sell it once and for all. He was never going to wear it again.

Larry Grantham was a tough, proud man from Mississippi who cherished his ring and what it stood for. His health was failing, he needed medical treatment he could not afford. He put his ring up for auction to save his life.

Friends found out, including those he had helped with addiction and other problems at Freedom House (a New Jersey drug and alcohol treatment clinic where Larry helped many and shared his Super Bowl ring). They put up an online fundraiser to buy it. The president of the auction house found about it and took the ring off the auction site and returned it to Grantham, and the $18,000 raised from the fundraiser was used to pay his medical expenses.

When Larry was surprised with the return of his ring, the proud, tough man from the hardscrabble land of Mississippi cried.

OWNER

Harry Wismer was the first owner of the New York Titans. Wismer was a well known radio announcer and kind of a peculiar personality. He would upon meeting anyone immediately tell them "Congratulations!" on the theory that everyone had accomplished something noteworthy in their lives. Wismer was renowned as a radio announcer for dropping names during the broadcasts of people who were not at the game pretending as if they were. Example: "There's General Eisenhower sitting at midfield enjoying the game." Even though Eisenhower was not there.

Example of Wismer call that did *not* happen:

"First down for the Detroit Lions, 3:45 left in the third quarter, Oh, look over there, Julius Caesar working on his third hot dog. How ya doing, Julie?"

Wismer is given credit for advising the AFL owners to split TV revenues evenly which is one of the financial pillars upon which today's NFL rests and as the owner of the biggest market team in the AFL this was of no little note.

The Titans struggled attendance-wise and financially and the league tried to take the team from Wismer. In fact Commissioner Joe Foss sold the team to Sonny Werblin, an executive at MCA, an entertainment powerhouse. On hearing the team was for sale, he wrote a personal check for $1,350,000 to buy it.

Wismer balked and took the league and Werblin to court.

At a birthday party that predated the sale, for AFL Commissioner Joe Foss at Club 21, Wismer and Werblin got into a fist fight after a drunken Wismer called Werblin an ethnic slur and Werblin told Wismer that night that one day he would own the Titans.

Wismer, not to be undone by the league's move however, filed Chapter 11 bankruptcy papers to stop the sale.

Wismer lost the case and the team was then sold to Werblin for $1 million. Wismer lost over $350,000 in the case.

Wismer some time later fell down the stairs at a New York Club and died from his injuries in another bizarre turn of events.

Werblin, known at one time as "Mr. Show Biz" and a TV executive at MCA was responsible for making the TV deal that kept the AFL afloat and he made the sports world stand up and notice the AFL with his blockbuster signing of Joe Namath for the newly christened New York Jets and the AFL at the then astronomical contract for the time of $400,000.

Namath was an instant star and Werblin as it turns out knew something about star power.

He had been at MCA the personal representative of a number of show business luminaries Jack Benny, Gene Kelly, Don Ameche, Joan Crawford, Harry James, Abbot and Costello, Alfred Hitchcock, Jackie Gleason, Ozzie and Harriet, Dean Martin, and Johnny Carson to name a few in the constellation of the rich and famous he personally represented.

Namath of course led the Jets to the upset of the heavily favored Baltimore Colts in Super Bowl III still the only Jets Super Bowl victory and appearance.

Werblin had sold the team before 1968 to one of his partners Leon Hess, CEO of Amerada-Hess.

The scuttlebutt at the time of Werblins sale of the Jets was that Werblin had stayed out till 7 am on game day with Joe Namath, in a game in which Namath do not perform well and the Jet lost and that his partners demanded Werblin buy them out or sell. Werblin could not make a deal to retain ownership that satisfied him so he sold.

As of 2019 Woody Johnson, the scion of the Johnson and Johnson family fortune and Jets owner and CEO was named the United States Ambassador to the United Kingdom by President Donald Trump.

One thing I learned from this book is that the most interesting people in the league are not the players but the owners.

JOSEPH CONRAD

Late 90's Rich Cimino is the beat writer covering the Jets. The *New York Daily News* his employer has a feature each game day Sunday to have the Jets opponents best play diagrammed in the Sunday paper.

Had to get the play from somewhere? The defensive coordinator of the Jets agreed to provide the play each week.

His name—Bill Belichick.

Yep, that's what Cimino said in a *Sports Illustrated* interview.

It was against the Jets—or more importantly head coach Bill Parcelll's—rules to do this but this is how it worked.

Wednesday night Cimino would call Belichick's office phone and let it ring once then hang up. This was Belichick's signal to come down to the press room which on Wednesday night was empty save Cimino.

Belichick would appear with a 3 x 5 index card and diagram the play for Cimino then Belichick would explain it to Cimino. Sometimes Belichick would stay and chat for a while.

Again all of this was against Parcell's rules.

It was a popular feature. People would ask Cimino where he got the info and he would say Belichick.

MANTLE MEN AND NAMATH GIRLS

In 1969 you'd be hard pressed to find two guys more famous in New York than Joe Namath and Mickey Mantle.

George Lois, a very successful ad man at Lois Holland Callaway in New York, decided to get into the employment agency business.

He signed Mickey Mantle and Joe Namath to be the face of his new jobs agency and this strategy of putting these two marquee sports celebrities out in front of his product in TV commercials, print ads and other advertising vehicles was considered cutting edge in 1969.

At first it worked, after one year in business the new agency named "Mantle Men and Namath Girls" became the second biggest employment agency in the world grossing $2 million dollars that first year.

Alas five years later the company filed for bankruptcy due to the economic turndown in the recession of 1969 the biggest recession in the United States since the Korean War and the resulting paucity of jobs.

NEW YORK STATE OF MIND

Boomer Esiason is from New York and he got to be quaterback of the hometown New York Jets.

That's a special kind of pressure being an NFL QB in your hometown.

Boomer and his fellow Jets found themselves in a close game one Sunday at home against the Miami Dolphins.

Dan Marino pulled off a fake spike at the end of the game and fooled the Jet defense and it led to a close loss. But QB's don't play defense.

After a tough loss at home Jets players had the prospect of a long commute due to traffic patterns and the nature of New York's geography.

Esiason that day chose the route that would take him through the Lincoln Tunnel and back to Long Island.

He was alone in his car with tinted windows and for whatever reason as he sat in traffic he listened to New York sports talk radio. Which meant he had to listen to fans rant and vent about him and how much he sucked.

While sitting in bumper to bumper traffic listening to himself being castigated the car next to him was rear ended and by Esiason's account it was a pretty hard collision.

Now he had to decide if he would emerge from his car to see if he could help. Thereby, of course exposing his well-known kisser to the angry mobs in their cars coming home from the Jets game.

He gets out to check on the inhabitant of the smushed in car and sees a woman slumped over the wheel with a lit cigarette in her hand. It appears that she may have been knocked out.

Boomer beats on the window and calls to the woman to see if she is alright.

He cannot open the door because the collision had bent the door frame and it wouldn't open. He continues to thump hard on the window.

He calls out to her: "Ma'am, you've gotta wake up."

She snaps out of her groggy state.

She looks out her window and who does she see?

Boomer Esiason, QB of the New York Jets.

She says, "Boomer, you guys suck!"

Welcome to New York City.

TERPSICHORE

George R. R. Martin, the author of *Game of Thrones*, is a big New York Jets fan.

In his blog Not A Blog, he often opines on the Jets and on the New York Football Giants, as well as he also roots for the Giants.

Martin had been a fan since his youth but some of the fans of his writing and literary creations are not on the same page with George as it comes to football.

George has some advice for those who read his blog but do not care for his football musings.

"Here is a suggestion for all those complaining about my football postings. Don't read them."

George has some suggestions for the NFL hierarchy as well as it pertains to the dancing and choreography added by players when they score TD's.

"I really wish the NFL had the guts to put a stop to all this goddamn dancing and celebrations and other nonsense" says he.

COSLET

Cerebral coaches can be problematic. Truly cerebral coaches I'm talking.

Coslet, then head coach of the Jets, in what was an off the record remark presumably trying to build up some good will with the press, throws his starting quarterback under the bus.

"My QB sucks. I know my QB sucks. You know my QB sucks. Everybody knows my QB sucks."

I guess that covers it.

This of course verifies what generations of football fans, most of whom know little about the game, have suspected must be true.

Sometimes, their QB does suck.

EXPOSURE

Gate D of Met Life Stadium has a ritual that occurs at Jets games and has received a bit of press in 2007 in the *New York Times*.

Rowdy, low class fans gather on the spiral that brings them to and from their seating area at halftime. Drunken, obnoxious losers, they scream to the women below to bare their breasts.

Some women do. In 2007 the stadium security claimed to have thrown seven women out of the games for indecent exposure.

When the women fail to comply with the loud intimidating requests, the unruly Jets fans sometimes boo loudly, spit downward or throw beer bottles.

Isn't that special?

Law enforcement, security and the NFL spokesperson kind of pass the buck. They cite 1st amendment rights and chain of command excuses.

It was a regular enough ritual that fans would line up at halftime and comment on the quality of the "show" as it compared to previous games.

Stadium authorities claim the problem is a Jets phenomena, as the Giants also play in the stadium but the ritual seems to be isolated to Jets games.

FOOT

Videos appeared on the internet that appeared to be Rex Ryan's wife with her feet sticking out of an SUV and another that suspiciously looked like her displaying her feet surfaced.

There is also a picture of Ryan's desk with a framed picture of his wife's feet. The New York media asked copious questions of its football coach about it.

He danced around the question a bit and said it was a personal matter.

Players later said that he addressed the issue with them and that he was embarrassed by the incident.

Ryan's quote was, "It's a personal matter and I'm really not going to discuss it. Ok?"

He also is quoted as saying of his wife, "She's awesome."

And, Ryan also said, "I'm the only person to ever get into a sex scandal with my own wife."

🌐 https://www.youtube.com/9osyCkDzpjA

FLASH GORDON

Little known anecdote: The quarterback of the New York Jets saved the Earth.

Well, not really.

In the 1980 film *Flash Gordon* produced by Dino De Laurentiis, Flash is the QB of the New York Jets.

On a flight the plane is hit by a meteor and Flash flies it to safety. Well, it was a jet.

Next thing ya know Flash, played by Sam J. Jones, is gallivanting all over the planet Mongo, matching wits with Ming The Merciless, played by Max Von Sydow.

Sam J. Jones received a Raspberry Award nomination as the worst actor of 1980 for his star turn as Flash. The film was a hit in the UK, not so much in the USA, although Roger Ebert gave it a good review and it got 82% on Rotten Tomatoes. it has become a cult classic of sorts.

De Laurentiis wanted Federico Fellini to direct, but he didn't do it. George Lucas tried to option it, but failed. Lucas then decided to create *Star Wars*.

MY (JETS) PRECIOUS!! #2

Randy Rasmussen, offensive guard on the 1969 team, went golfing with his buddies.

He went inside to change into shorts and he realized he didn't have his Super Bowl ring on his hand.

He went home later, searched, as he said, everywhere five times. No ring.

Almost four years later, he gets a call from a stranger. Lots of strangers get their paws on Super Bowl rings, it seems.

The stranger found the ring at the golf course four years later, encrusted with so much mud it took two days to wash it off to read it.

The stranger refused a reward and Rasmussen now has his ring and one helluva story.

TICKET SCORING

1991, one of those Reeses's Peanut Butter Cup moments is about to happen when Marvel Comics and the NFL sign a licensing agreement to do an NFL themed superhero.

Fabian Nicienza, a writer later known for his work on *X-Men*, *Deadpool*, and *Thunderbolts* among other titles, is asked to join the project after the project got off to a rocky start.

So, as a favor, he says, he did.

Fabien wrote the scripts of the first four issues of Superpro, a Marvel hero with the NFL logo on his leotard.

Even though remembrance of this title is negative in the world of comic aficionados, Fabien says the issue sold well because he got a nice royalty check.

Despite it having lasted twelve issues, *Superpro* is considered by some to be the worst comic book of all time.

That might be a bit of a stretch but let's just say the collaboration of two superbrands, the NFL and Marvel didn't work out too well.

Here's the skinny:

Superpro's alter ego was Phil Grayfield, a former NFL player turned sports reporter.

Phil goes to visit a rich collector of NFL memorabilia in the origin tale and ends up in the middle of a home invasion in which he is tied up with NFL football game film.

A vat of chemicals is released during the violent crime and a super football uniform that was designed and built by the millionaire collector is in the room. The chemicals burn Phil and he dons the uniform which is made from a fiberglass and plastic alloy that repels bullets and fits like a skin. The mixing of chemicals, heat and old football game films and...Voila!

Instant superhero complete with super powers is born!

In a kooky connection, Phil's super powers come in part from the chemicals on the football game films.

A superhero who gets his super chops from NFL films?

Why the hell not? Say I.

They tried valiantly, did Marvel.

Spiderman makes a guest appearance in issue #1.

And what's a successful superhero without bitchin' villains? Villains in the series include:

1. Quick Kick a former field goal kicker turned evil ninja
2. Instant Replay, an assassin who is a time traveler
3. Sanction, a crime boss who shoots at policeman with a concussion mortar (in 1991)
4. Head Hunters (still 1991), a group who dig holes in the football field to kidnap players

And one issue where the Hopi tribe appearing as themselves are the villains. (The Hopi filed a legal complaint and that issue of Superpro was taken off the market.)

Fabien, for his part, said the reason he did it in the first place was to score Jets tickets. Which was a success. He got Jet tickets. Sweet sidelines tix.

And...Marvel execs and his editor scored tickets to the1994 Super Bowl in Atlanta.

LAWNMOWER?

Bizarre almost doesn't begin to describe this story.

December 9, 1979, at the Jets-Patriots game at Shea Stadium, the halftime show was a demonstration of radio controlled airplanes under the auspices of the Electronic Eagles Radio Control Association of Greater New York.

Various model airplanes flew around the field doing stunts and maneuvers. One plane crashed into the field. Some eyewitnesses said the planes flew a little too close over the spectators for their comfort.

A model plane made mostly of metal, it is reported, built to look just like a lawnmower, went out of control and fell into the stands at a high speed and hit two fans in the head.

Both were injured significantly. One survived. One died four days later.

If you go on Wikipedia and look at unusual deaths in history, you may find the names of Aeschylus, the famous playwright, who died when a seagull, mistaking his head for a rock, dropped a tortoise on his bald head, and John Nowen, a twenty-year-old man who went to a Jets game on December 9, 1979 only to be killed by a flying lawnmower.

John Schmitt, the starting center on the 1969 team, was swimming in the surf at Waikiki in 1971.

Upon reaching the shore refreshed, tired, or exhilarated, he realized his 1969 Super Bowl ring had come off his finger and was now somewhere at the bottom of the Pacific Ocean.

He went back in and nearly drowned trying in vain to find it.

Heartbroken, he had it replaced but still the original was always in his mind when he thought about it in Davy Jones Locker.

2011 the phone rings.

On the other end is Bob Parento of the New York Jets.

"You sitting down? He asked Schmitt. He was.

His 1969 Super Bowl ring had been found.

And the story becomes even more incredible.

A lifeguard picked it off the ocean floor and, not realizing what it was, put it into a box he kept in a closet.

When the lifeguard died one of his relatives was cleaning out the closet and the box fell on the floor and the ring bounced out.

The family brought the ring to a jeweler and had it verified as the genuine article.

The family contacted the Jets.

The family then flew to New York and refused the $3000 reward.

They did inform Schmitt that in island custom they were now family and they talk on the telephone once a week.

NEW YORK (N)

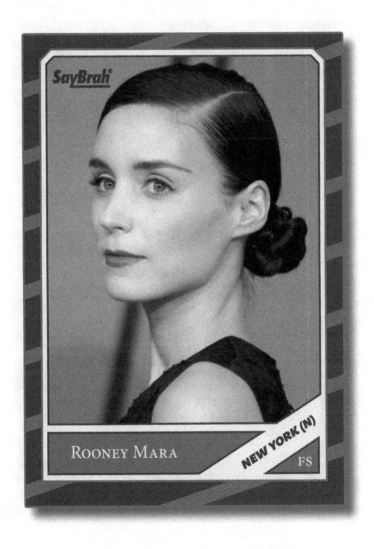

SayBrah®

Rooney Mara

NEW YORK (N)

FS

THE GIRL WITH THE DRAGON TATTOO, SING SING, AND JOHNNY CARSON

NEW YORK (N)

*"Pro football is like nuclear warfare:
There are no winners, only survivors."*
—Frank Gifford

SayBrah®

New York Giants entered the NFL in 1925 owned by bookmaker Tim Mara. The Mara family has remained in control of the franchise since its inception.

They changed their name in 1937 to the New York Football Giants because the New York MLB baseball team was also called the Giants.

On December 28, 1958, the Giants lost to the Baltimore Colts 23-17 in the first NFL playoff game to go into sudden death (overtime). Referred to as "The Greatest Game Ever Played," it is often credited as the game that heralded the rise of pro football to surpass baseball as America's past-time.

Super Bowl Appearances: 5
Super Bowl Record: 4-1 ('86, '90, '07, '11)
Super Bowl Loss: 2000

TV

The 1958 NFL championship game is known now as the "Greatest Game Ever Played." Although participants on both sides, including prominent players Frank Gifford and Art Donovan, pooh-poohed the notion of the greatness of this game, it was nonetheless a watershed game in league history.

It was the first game ever to end in overtime and was the most widely watched game to date, bringing a ton of publicity to the NFL.

NBC had the telecast rights and when the game went into overtime, no doubt NBC execs were excited that this live event had turned so dramatic.

However, as these things often do, fate interjected.

Right as Johnny Unitas was driving his team down the field and into immortality on the Giants 8 yd line, someone or something at that very moment disconnected the cable sending the signal out across America. All of a sudden—no picture. At this crucial time.

The cable was disconnected just before Unitas called a timeout. NBC sent out a business manager (who did stats during game telecasts, Stan Rotkiewicz) to delay the game to buy time to fix the technical difficulty. Rotkiewicz, acting like a drunken fan, ran the length of the field chased by police and others. He was caught and only one play was missed on the TV feed. The picture was restored just in time for Alan Ameche to barrel over for the win.

FIX

Gambling has always been a part of the landscape of football, the importance of the point spread is indicative of this...plus, the number of NFL owners in its history known to be big time gamblers is impressive.

The NFL, nevertheless, tries to keep its image as squeaky clean as possible in this regard. But if there is money to be made, well, that is the American Way, making money.

There have been few rumors of the fix being in during recent decades. The money the players earn makes it hard to bribe them.

In the 1946 NFL championship game, Giants vs. Bears, the defending champion Bears were 10 point favorites.

The night before the game a meeting was held in the office of the Mayor of New York. At the meeting were the mayor, the NFL commissioner, the Police Commissioner of New York and Tim Mara, owner of the NY Giants. (Mara, by the way, made his money as a bookmaker before he owned the Giants.)

Frank Filchok, quarterback for the Giants, and Merle Hapes, a star running back, were accused of taking a bribe to fix the game. Hapes admitted being approached but said he didn't take the money. Filchok denied it all together.

Hapes was suspended for the game. Filchok was allowed to play.

Bears win by 10, a push, in betting parlance. No one wins the bet. No one loses the bet.

Filchok subsequently admitted he had been approached by gamblers and was eventually, along with Hapes, suspended for life. Filchok went on to star in Canadian pro football although, ironically enough, he had to be paid under the table in Canada because there was a facade in Canada that the game was amateur.

Most people know about Shoeless Joe and the Black Sox scandal and the suspensions that still keep Jackson out of the Hall of Fame. Most football fans nowadays are little aware of the star QB for the NY Giants who was banned for life.

GATORADE

How do these things start?

The dumping of Gatorade or another watery thing by football players after the Super Bowl or significant victory is now a tradition.

October 28, 1984, is when it started.

Jim Burt, a DL for the Giants, came up with the idea as revenge for what he termed bad treatment by his head coach, Bill Parcells, during the week of practice coming up to the game.

Burt said that he had LB Harry Carson do the deed because Harry was a Parcells favorite and he wouldn't get into trouble.

It became a tradition and one of the reasons is that the Giants went to the Super Bowl that year.

It is solidly set in modern football and almost de rigueur for championship teams.

George Allen was coach of the Long Beach State college team when his players doused him with Gatorade. He died 6 weeks later. They say it wasn't related. George Allen was 72 years old. Sometimes, maybe, they are incorrect.

HOFFA

The Giants played in the Meadowlands Complex starting in the mid 70s.

Jimmy Hoffa disappeared in the mid 70s.

Mob informant Donald "Tony the Greek" Frankos, in an article in Playboy magazine, said he was told that two wise guys whacked Hoffa and buried him in concrete in the end zone in the stadium.

Sexy.

Investigations of the allegation seem to point to it not being true, although Hoffa did disappear while the stadium was being constructed.

COLLEGE VS. PRO, Part 1

In the 1920s college football was way more popular than the pro game. Most felt the college game was better and that college men played a more vigorous, superior game.

The Depression was on and Notre Dame, a juggernaut on the gridiron under Knute Rockne, went to New York to raise money for charity. Something named the Committee on Unemployed.

55,000 people showed up to see a team of Notre Dame All-Stars play the New York Football Giants. The game raised $100,000 for the unemployed.

Notre Dame assembled a team of its stars, present and past, to play in the game including the Four Horseman, Layden, Stulderher, Miller and Crowley.

Many expected the Notre Dame All Stars to prevail but the New York Giants, led by QB Bernie Friedman, beat the crap out of the college players, 22-0.

After the game Rockne said, "That was the greatest football machine I ever saw. I am glad none of you were hurt."

The pro game got a shot in the arm from the publicity of the thrashing.

Sadly, it was the last game that Knute Rockne would coach as he died in an airplane crash the next spring.

COLLEGE VS. PRO, Part 2

The premise of this book led me to this ancillary gem. The game against the NFL Football Giants at the end of 1930 was the last game that Knute Rockne coached because on March 31, 1931 he died in a plane crash near Bazaar, Kansas.

At the time Rockne was a superstar in America mentioned in the same breath with Babe Ruth as a sports icon. His sudden tragic death was a shock that reverberated across America.

There are several interesting historical facts that surround his death and the lasting impact it had on America, and for the salacious conspiracy theories that linger in the mind of those who subscribe to such notions.

An eyewitness to the crash that took Rockne and 7 other lives, a Kansas farm boy, describes hearing something akin to a bomb blast before the plane plummeted to the ground killing all aboard.

Later a Chicago newspaper headline on January 6, 1933 blared of a bomb blast and the reasons why a bomb might have been the culprit.

Most deeper dives into the bomb theory, a bomb, by the way, planted by none other than Al Caopne, have been discounted as flights of overactive imaginations. Members of Rockne's family and a key biographer of Rockne's in fact believe these claims of mob conspiracy to be hogwash.

However in a book by James Bacon a prominent Hollywood insider there is this curious story of how a mob bomb connection got some traction in the minds of some.

Bacon was a Notre Dame man and as such was well acquainted with Father John Reynolds, himself a Notre Dame athlete, coach and professor and the key to any conspiracy theory.

Father Reynolds as it turns out a drinking buddy of Bacon's in his matriculation years, related this tale to Bacon.

Father Reynolds was in Chicago waiting for the train to take him back to South Bend when one Jake Lingle, a low level *Chicago Tribune* crime reporter was gunned down in a mob hit.

Father Reynolds witnessed the murder and gave Lingle the last rites.

Lingle as it turns out unbeknownst to the average Tribune reader was a Capone bagman. He is alleged to have delivered money to the mob to Cicero, Capone's headquarters.

Lingle became a *cause celebre* to the newspaper business with up to $55,000 in rewards offered by the Tribune and other newspapers for information on the killers. As time went on Lingle's life became a bit more illuminated.

Lingle worked for $65 a week as a crime reporter for the Tribune yet he had two houses, one a $16,000 home on Lake Michigan and he had a fancy suite at a ritzy hotel. He was driven around town by a chauffeur in a Lincoln limousine. He also had $9000 in his pocket when he was gunned down. He soon became known as the richest newspaper reporter in the world at the time of his death.

Father Reynolds immediately became the focus of mob pressure. They wanted to know what Lingle told the priest as he was dying.

The mob harassment continued at a heavy pace until the trial in which Father Reynolds testified.

Father Reynolds returned to South Bend as soon as he finished testifying. He soon ran into Rockne while walking across campus. Rockne told the priest that he was trying to get to Los Angeles where he was offered $50,000 to be an expert advisor on the making of *The Spirit of Notre Dame*, a movie being filmed in LA.

He was having a hard time getting a plane ticket.

Father Reynolds related to Bacon that he had booked a flight to Los Angeles as a way to get away from the threats and hub bub of the murder trial.

He had the plane ticket in his pocket when he ran into Rockne. He gave his ticket to Rockne.

Rockne traveled to Kansas City by train where the TWA flight was to take him to California.

Reynolds later said, "My name was on Rockne's ticket reservation. He wouldn't have had time to change them and all these threats on my life. Did people plant a bomb on that airplane? I don't know. I know if I didn't give him that ticket he would be alive."

The result of Rockne's death was one of those moments in American history, like the murder of John F. Kennedy or 9/11, when everyone would remember where they were when they heard the news.

CBS, the network only four years old at the time, broadcast the funeral nationwide, an almost unheard of occurrence. 10,000 people greeted Rockne's body at the Chicago train station when it was returned from Kansas in transit back to South Bend. It was said that 100,000 people lined the streets to watch Rockne's body leave the funeral. The King of Norway, King Haakon VI sent a personal emissary to the funeral. It was a big deal.

The federal authorities investigated the crash finding that the airplane a Fokker design made of wood was at fault.

As a result of the crash and subsequent federal investigation the Rockne crash and the aftermath were responsible for the end of wooden airplane construction and a federal law that led to the federal government requiring all air crashes to be investigated and a report issued to the public. In this way the death of Rockne had a lasting effect on the safety of the flying public and modern aviation rules.

BACKSEAT QUARTERBACK

Charlie Conerly was the starting QB for the New York Giants throughout the 1950's.

Perian Conerly,his college sweetheart and wife followed him to New York and became the first woman sportswriter in the National Sportswriters of America.

Perian wrote a syndicated column that appeared in newspapers around the country in the 60's entitled "Backseat Quarterback."

She later compiled her columns and other observations from an NFL player's wives perspective into a well received book of the same title *Backseat Quarterback*.

Perian revealed inside info such as how many tickets were allocated to each player, two with option to buy six total, sideline decorum, wives were not to criticize other players during the heat of the game (all the players wives sat in the same section at home games) and wives were not to discuss players salaries. The most stringent written in stone rule, no babysitter stealing.

Most of the families lived in the same Bronx Hotel near Yankee Stadium and according to the Perian's column most of them got along swimmingly.

After the games in New York the husbands and wives would decompress and gather in groups at various restaurants to have a post game meal and discuss the game and other matters.

Being New York, Perian discusses the celebrity spotting aspect of life in the fast lane.

Often accompanied by luminaries as Toots Shor and his wife, the likes of Stan Musail, Eddie Arcaro and other sports figures (not to mention the celebrities in their own midst, Perians husband Charlie who was the original Marlboro Man in print and TV ads, Madison Avenue proximity don't ya know). Still the highlight for many of the wives was the occasional movie stars who were spotted in the same establishments as the New York Football Giants.

Perian, who was the only female member of the pro football writers association to show up at the convention in 1963, mentioned two of the more memorable celeb sightings, one Elizabeth Taylor at an Italian restaurant in New York. Liz was sitting near the women's bathroom so a lot of traffic went that way to take a close look at the megastar.

But the sighting that Perian Conerly voted number one was meeting Rock Hudson who she described as "nine feet tall and all of him gorgeous."

CALL OF DUTY

The Giants were playing against the Brooklyn Dodgers at Polo Grounds Dec 7, 1941.

An announcement on the loudspeakers interrupts the game: the Japanese have attacked Pearl Harbor.

Al Blozis (#32) was on the Giant squad that day.

Even though he was considered too big for combat service at 6'6", Blozis insisted they take him off his desk job once he was in the military. Blozis died at the Battle of The Bulge in the Vosges Mountains.

Think about that for just a minute.

On December 7, 1941 Jack Lummus also a member of the New York Giants who lost the game to the Brooklyn Dodgers 21-7 that day.

Those Giants went on to play in the NFL Championship game that year and lose to the Bears.

Lummus, who had previously washed out as a military airman in the summer of 1941 before he joined the Giants as an end, enlisted in the Marines in January 1942 to answer the call of his country.

Lummus served as a First Lieutenant in the Marines and was in the first wave to hit the beach at Iwo Jima on February 19,1945.

On March 6th, as the battle for the strategic island raged on, Lt. Lummus was given command of the 3rd Rifle Platoon.

He led his men during a two-day assault of heavily fortified enemy positions from the front and took out three enemy positions that were one of the last impediments to the advance of U.S. forces.

After he destroyed the third enemy position, he stepped on a landmine and his legs were blown off.

He was taken from the battlefield while still barking out commands for his men to advance.

He died from his wounds shortly after but not before he told the doctors "Well, Doc, the New York Giants lost a mighty good end today."

He received the Medal Of Honor for his effort, one of only two pro football players to ever receive that award.

In the Presidential citation of the award it read in part: "In the face of over-whelming odds First Lieutenant Lummus inspired his stouthearted Marines to continue the relentless drive on thereby contributing materially to success of his regimental mission."

In 2015 the New York Giants honored Lummus by including him in its Ring Of Honor.

The U.S. Navy honored Lummus' sacrifice by commissioning the USNS 1st LT Jack Lummus {T-AK_3011) class cruiser.

BERMUDA

Rocky Thompson is the only NFL player to ever come from Bermuda. Rocky was an Olympic caliber sprinter who played college ball in Texas with future NFL star Duane Thomas.

Rocky was drafted in the first round in 1971 by the New York Giants and Deadpsin ranked Rocky as the 7th worst draft pick of all time.

Rocky played three seasons in the NFL primarily as a kick returner.

Rocky went home to Bermuda after the 1971 season ended determined to hone his receiving skills. He caught 16 passes in his rookie campaign.

Rocky had an unusual training regimen.

He would stand on a cliff 15 feet above the Atlantic Ocean, toss the football out into the air and then jump after it, catch it and then plummet into the ocean. He said that it improved his concentration and helped with ball security as when he hit the water it was like an NFL player hitting him.

Rocky according to the New York Times was listed in British track records as Ralph Gary Symonds. So maybe Rocky was an impostor? Maybe Rocky is not who we thought he was.

After his Bermuda training sessions, Rocky went on to play two more NFL seasons with the Giants in which he caught as many NFL passes as I, Chris Champagne

That would be none.

CLANG

Night before the game in Dallas, Giants are having a team meeting. Lawrence Taylor is late but shows up in a sweater with his hands underneath the sweater.

The Giants watch the film in the dark.

The other players hear a metal noise, a clanging or clanking.

What's that?

Turns out it was handcuffs. LT was handcuffed.

They asked him.

"I'm handcuffed, from, you know?"

The man who is purported to have used strawberry flavored penicillin to fight off STDs had to have a Dallas State Trooper come in to cut the handcuffs off of him.

SPY IN THE SKY

In the late 50's if you went to a Giants home game you might see an unusual sight of a man in the front row of an upper deck seat with a camera taking pictures of the action on the field.

This guy was part of the Giants game plan.

He was using a new fangled quick developing film, created by Polaroid, and tossing the photos down to the field where Vince Lombardi, yes, that Vince Lombardi an assistant coach with the Giants, would take a gander and adjust his strategies accordingly.

"It's a tremendous help to us." said Lombardi at the time.

"I have great faith in its value."

The cameraman was none other than Wellington Mara who was accompanied by former player Ken Kavanaugh who, phone in hand, would call down to the Giants bench to alert them to developments that might lead the Giants to alter their strategies against their opponents.

The photo was developed in a hurry and the quality of the image suffered but Mara said they were in a hurry.

The photo quality also suffered from being stuffed into a sock to be thrown down to the field in a timely fashion.

SAVED BY THE BUCK

Jack Buck, Ray Scott, Tom Brookshier, Frank Gifford and Pat Summerall were the TV crew for the Ice Bowl, the NFL championship game in 1967 between the Packers and Cowboys that was played in Green Bay in 14 below zero weather.

Gifford's ad lib asking someone for a bite of his frozen coffee is one of the best in my memory of watching sports on TV. (it did freeze after he put it down)

CBS had a plane chartered, a twin engine plane to fly them to Chicago after the game.

As they took off the front door on Gifford's side didn't close properly.

Gifford said he would open it and shut it fully. Buck advised not to do so. Gifford opened the door anyway and with a strong yank in an attempt to close it the armrest flew off.

The door then was fully open and flapping in the wind. Buck, sitting behind Gifford, grabbed hold of his shoulders to prevent him from falling out of the plane.

The pilot made an emergency landing in New Holstein, Wisconsin.

According to Buck's story, Brooskshier, meanwhile, was feeding Gifford scotch out of a rubber flask with the door completely open and blowing in the freezing wind.

They finally made it to Chicago.

Yikes!

MY (GIANTS) PRECIOUS!!

The question, who has the most Super Bowl rings?

Answer: Lisbeth Salander's mother.

That would be Katherine Rooney Mara, wife of Giants President Chris Mara.

She also is a member of the Rooney family of Pittsburgh.

She has 6 Pittsburgh rings and 4 Giants rings.

Her daughters are also Hollywood stars: Kate and Rooney Mara. Rooney Mara played Lisbeth Salander in *The Girl with The Dragon Tattoo*.

So, that makes Katherine Mara the mother of Lisbeth Salander, kind of.

THE HIT

Frank Gifford was a star, in high school, in college, in the NFL.

The famous episode of the time was the pass that the Giants threw to Gifford over the middle and the stupendous hit that Chuck Bednarik of the Eagles laid on Gifford. He laid there still.

Knocked out Gifford, cold.

His injury was so bad that he became a pass catcher in the NFL after that game with a lengthy time out of action. He had been a running back prior to the injury.

Carted off the field on a stretcher and out cold, motionless, his teammates did not know his fate.

Pat Summeral told this story that, as the players trooped off the field at the end of the game, medical workers rolled what appeared to be a man on a gurney with a sheet covering his entire body. You've seen the movies, somebody was dead.

The thought that it was Gifford went through some players' minds.

During the game there was no way for the players to know that a fan in the stands had a heart attack and died.

They brought the body of the fan to the Giants dressing room and that, not Gifford, was who the medical workers were wheeling out of the locker room, as the stunned Giants later learned.

Circa 1962, Johnny Carson, the host of the *Tonight Show*, hires a young attorney, Henry Bushkin.

He was known for years in Carson's monologues and from his desk as Bombastic Bushkin.

Bushkin was Carson's personal lawyer for years but they had a falling out at some point and Bushkin wrote a book released in 2013, "Johnny Carson."

In it you'll find this tale.

Bushkin is called by Carson to accompany him, Carson, and a hired private detective to an apartment in New York City that Carson suspects his wife, Joanne, is using to have an affair. Carson claims he, Carson, is paying for the apartment and reasons he can therefore break in. So, Carson decided to break into the apartment against Bushkin's advice as his lawyer. Johnny was going in.

What they found was an altar like tribute of several photographs of the guy Joanne was allegedly shagging. It was Frank Gifford.

Carson leaned against the wall and wept. Bushkin said it was one of the only times he ever saw Carson cry. As Carson leaned against the wall in pain, his raincoat opened up and Bushkin saw a .38 revolver stuck in Johnny's pants.

Joanne, when the book came out, denied the affair.

Kathie Lee asked her hubby Frank about it.

His answer...

He did not remember if it was true or not.

Later that night of the break-in Bushkin says he was called by Johnny to join him at a bar downtown where he was drowning his sorrows.

Ed McMahon was also at the bar.

Johnny quipped,

"What does that A-hole have that I don't? He plays three positions, I could never get her to do more than two."

FORGOTTEN GAME

Red Grange, the football great, who is given credit for putting pro football on the sporting map with his white hot celebrity status in the Roaring Twenties said that the 1927 New York Football Giants champions of the NFL in 1927 were the best team of their time.

The Giants won the NFL title, which had no championship game at that time, with a 11-1-1 regular season record.

After the season the Giants, as was the habit of many professional teams in those days, went on a barnstorming tour of the country. The tour was to travel across the country all the way to California. The barnstorming Giants even had a few ringers from other teams on the tour but were also without some members of the championship team. Barnstorming was how players could make a few extra bucks in this time way before lucrative contracts were available to pro football players.

One of the stops on the tour on the way to California was in Pawhuska Oklahoma to play an all Native American squad called the Hominy Indians. The Hominy Indians domiciled in Osage country had members of 22 different tribes and even one Eskimo.

The game was played on December 26th, 1927.

The Hominy Indians were a team that also traveled the country including many games on the East coast against other professional and semi professional teams and were a well known commodity in pro football circles of the time and a good draw at the box office.

The Hominy Indians had a 26 game winning streak when the Giants came to Oklahoma.

The Hominy Indians were financed by a couple of Osage brothers who played on the team and had struck it rich in oil. In fact the Osage land of Oklahoma supplied a large income for many of its residents said to be as much as $165,000 average a year in present day money.

The Hominy Indians are said to have come to the game with the Giants that day after Christmas in an array of automobiles including Pierce Arrows and the footage of the game that survives does show a football field surrounded by copious amounts of fancy wheels.

The Hominy Indians, the pride of the Osage, defeated the New York Football Giants, 1927 NFL Champions, 13-6, only three weeks after the Giants had been crowned NFL champs.

Hominy Indian Games were often lively affairs with a lot of money bet on the outcome. It is estimated that one game against a team from Kansas City, the Cowboys,that as much as $2,000,000 was bet on the side in present day money.

The Kansas City Cowboys were an interesting team in their own right as they were a traveling team and in the New York stop they rode down Broadway on horseback in full cowboy regalia to drum up business for their game with the Giants. The crowd was 38.000, not too shabby.

There is a documentary film called *Playground of the Native Sons* that chronicles the Hominy Indians victory which holds a legendary status in Oklahoma but has been all but forgotten in the wider world.

UP THE RIVER

Sing Sing, the infamous penitentiary in New York state, gave us the term 'up the river,' as it is situated up river from New York City.

It was a brutal place, opened in 1826 and known for its cramped, suffocating cells and corrupt administration.

In 1931 New York instituted prison reform and one of the things new Warden Lewis Lawes did was start sports teams.

Tim Mara, owner of the New York Football Giants, donated equipment and uniforms, along with players and coaches of the Giants to coach the prisoners.

Tim Mara himself was the coach for the team its first season. The team was known as the Black Sheep.

From press reports the enterprise seems to have been a big success.

Money collected from attendance was given to a fund that, among other things, helped families of those who had been executed in Sing Sing's electric chair.

Newspapers began to send reporters to cover the games. Westbrook Pegler, the famous New York scribe, even expressed disappointment at the lack of mayhem on the field at Sing Sing. Players and spectators alike behaved themselves, as it was a privilege to play and a respite from the brutal nature of prison life.

The practice flourished, the team made a profit, and they had a winning record. 39-10-2 lifetime. Of course, they had a home field advantage as only home games were allowed for the Black Sheep.

There were hiccups along the way. Once, the day before the game, the star quarterback and two other starters on the team escaped.

In 1934 a new prison commissioner came into office and he forbid the collecting of admission for events at the prison. This ended the football team as there were no longer funds to support it.

One player, Alabama Pitts, (in for stealing about $75 worth of stuff in the 1920s, mind you) was the star of the team. He was given early release because of his skills. He was so good that he signed a baseball contract (Sing Sing also had a baseball team) with a minor league team and actually appeared in two games in the NFL with the Philadelphia Eagles before he was cut.

See the team in action here:

🌐 https://www.youtube.com/watch?v=fOjrFtV-Ybc

CARDINALS

SayBrah®

AL CAPONE

THE FOOTBALL
CARDINALS

DE

AL CAPONE, WHITE DEVILS,
A CURSE

THE FOOTBALL CARDINALS

"Anytime the Arizona Cardinals play football, I scream at the top of my lungs at the television and I have certain dances that I do."
—Blake Shelton

SayBrah®

The Arizona Cardinals are one of the two original NFL franchises still in existence. They moved from Chicago to St. Louis in 1960 and from St. Louis to Arizona in 1988.

The Cardinals are an extension of a team formed by the Morgan Athletic Club in 1898 on the south side of Chicago and thereby thought to be the oldest pro football franchise extant.

Super Bowl Appearances: 1
Super Bowl Record: 0-1
Super Bowl Loss: 2008

CAPONE

The Cardinals are the oldest pro football franchise in the NFL, founded in 1898 on the south side of Chicago at the Morgan Athletic Club. Eventually they were linked to the mob and Al Capone just by proximity on the south side, if nothing else. The south side was Capone territory, and it appears the Capone crowd were Cardinals fans.

The story is that there was actually a schism at the club and two teams emerged. One team went with the Capone element the other became the Chicago Cardinals. The Cardinals eventually joined the new NFL and retained their mob fans.

Charlie Bidwill, a politician and gambler, was a rumored associate of Capone and he bought the team in 1932. His family still owns the Arizona Cardinals.

Here is a story I found on Facebook about the Chicago Cardinals and the "boys."

Cardinals and Bears playing on the South Side one wintry day.

Paddy Driscoll, the star of the Cards, is roughly tackled by none other than George Halas and a guy named Jerry Sternaman. Driscoll takes exception and starts to pummel Sternaman. Fans, other players, even cops with night sticks enter the fray.

Then the Capone guys, fans mind you of the Cardinals, come to Paddy's aid and defense—he was the star of their team after all.

Ed Healy, a player for the Bears and eyewitness and participant said this:

"All of a sudden, they came out of the stand with their rods."—that's guns.

Healy continued, "I'm playing for a hundred dollars and these guys want to kill me!"

Halas saw it differently.

Said Papa Bear, the opposition to the rod guys, of that long ago day:

"We lost 6-0. But everyone had a good time."

SUPERGIRL

If you found yourself at the Arizona Cardinals-LA Rams game in 2017 before the game, you may have thought you were seeing a new addition to the Arizona Cardinals, Kara Zor-El or Supergirl.

It was Arizona Cardinal QB Drew Stanton, who had lost the weekly quarterback challenge that week.

What's up?

The weekly quarterback challenge competition between Cardinals QBs was started by Carson Palmer when he joined the Cards. Palmer brought the skills competition and penalty phase, the costumes, with him from Cincinnati where he and John Kitna started the practice.

The competition consists of things such as throwing a football into a garbage can in the end zone.

The loser must pay up by wearing an unusual costume either on the plane going to a road game or during pre-game warm-ups.

Patrick Peterson, Cardinals All Pro cornerback, thinks of himself as a pretty good passer and has participated in the competition and lost, resulting in his donning an elf costume once and a T-Rex get-up another time.

TOMBSTONE

Conrad Dobler was billed as the dirtiest player in the league.

He played against Merlin Olsen the Hall of Fame defensive tackle of the LA Rams and there was no love lost.

Dobler said, "I hated that son of a bitch."

They played tough and they played for keeps to hear Dobler tell it.

Olsen of course went on to a successful acting career on *Little House on The Prairie* and as the lead character in his own TV show *Father Murphy*.

Dobler, years after his retirement, was watching *Father Murphy* and he said there was a tombstone in the graveyard on the show that said: "Conrad Dobler, Gone But Not Forgiven"

Dobler might add: "And Not Forgotten"

CHEEKY

During the time that Jimmy Conzelman was leading the Chicago Cardinals to the NFL championship in 1947, his young son Jimmy Jr. used to hang around the team. A dream situation one would imagine for a kid.

It was the last championship for the Cardinals and they didn't get a championship ring.

So, fifty years later when the Cards had a ceremony in Chicago to bestow rings on surviving members of the team, Jimmy Conzelman Jr., at the age of seventy-one, was there—along with the other remaining members of the 1947 Championship team.

Jimmy went one step further and got the Cardinals logo tattooed on his ass.

He said that if the Cardinals were to defeat the Pittsburgh Steelers in Super Bowl XXXI he'd get one on the other cheek.

Alas.

HIT PARADE

At some point in every NFL player's career they begin to seriously think about life after football.

They need a new job or they need a place to invest their money.

Times have changed as to player compensation but you still need something to do, maybe just a neat hobby. The NFL and its connections to the limelight and to the community in which you play or reside provide a lot of opportunity in a variety of fields.

No names need to be used in this story but one former DL for the Chicago and St. Louis Cardinals is purported to have found a unique position after his playing days were over.

This former Card was referred to in newspaper clippings and in Dan Moldea's book "Interference'" How Organized Crime Influences Professional Football, as a pro football player turned syndicate enforcer or sometime more crudely as just "hitman ``.

The player was described as a constant companion of another guy who was the chief enforcer for the head of the Chicago Mob.

In the 60's and 70's if ya saw this ex-Card's name in the papers it might describe him as being suspecetd in a car bombing that killed a mistaken victim(he was cleared in that case) or being indicted for highjacking a shipment of electroncs or a suspect in an underworld murder.

There ya go.

THE COST

Times were tough in 1944. The Eagles and Steelers merged rosters becoming the "Steagles" and then a year later the Cardinals and Steelers merged and were referred to as the "Carpets." This was because of a player shortage due to World War II.

In 1944 the Cardinals had a star running back, Joe Grikas. In an interesting, if not unusual, turn of events at the end of the season, Grikas, leading rusher in the league, failed to show up for the final game of the season which caused eyebrows to raise, as if he had bailed on the team

But this was a different world. The pay was not that much, plus players needed regular jobs, as they are called, to make a living. Grikas worked in a steel mill where he had to stand up all day, then they practiced at night, then he had to play 60 minutes every game. Talk about an iron man.

Grikas wrote a letter to the team and his teammates...

"I tried to run and worked hard, but the workhorse, as I was termed by the newspapers, is almost ready for the stud farm. The human mind is the faculty of the soul which is influenced by the human body. When your mind is changed because of physical beating, week in and week out, your soul isn't in the game."

Philosophers need not apply.

ECCENTRIC

Bill Bidwell's parents bequeathed him the Football Cardinals. He moved them to St. Louis in 1960 during the days when the AFL was being born and there was a lot of maneuvering over territory between the leagues.

There was eventually as there always seems to be in the NFL a stadium issue in St. Louis and a struggle between the city and the suburbs as to where the stadium should go. So it looked as if Bidwell was not going to get his stadium.

A reporter for *The St. Louis Post -Dispatch* Bill McClellan reported Bidwell was kind of socially awkward and a bit eccentric.

Jim Hart, the star QB for the Cards in St. Louis, said that one year he was called into Bidwell's office to discuss his contract only to have Bidwell place a 3 minute egg timer on the desk and tell Hart, "Talk." Hart asked if he was serious and Bidwell said, "As a heart attack."

During the stadium issue Bidwell wore a necktie that had a message on it. It was one of those things that you don't see at first because of the pattern but when you do see it you can't unsee it.

The message?

F@¢^ You.

MAN OF GOD

Mark Arneson was a LB with the Cardinals when they played in St. Louis.

Arneson is a very religious guy and very public about it.

Billy Graham Evangelical Associates was coming to St. Louis and Arneson's Bible study leader asked Arneson if he would like to address the gathering.

Arneson was reluctant because he was not used to addressing large groups of people but he agreed.

That Sunday the Cards were playing the Denver Broncos and Arneson was scheduled to speak to the Evangelical group that week following the game with Denver.

During the game Arneson's assignment was to block a certain cornerback on special teams. Arneson was much bigger than the corner and repeatedly pushed him down on kick returns.

As the game progressed Arneson was about to tackle the ball carrier when the corner that he had been dominating hit Arneson from the blind side and punched Arneson in the throat,

Arneson abandoned the ball carrier and threw the corner onto the ground and started beating the Bejesus out of him.

Referees threw Arneson out of the game.

On the bench Roger Wehrli, the Cardinals star DB and Arneson's room-mate asked Arneson if he was going to be giving testimony about Christ's meaning in his life to a religious group.

Arneson, embarrassed, called to cancel his speech.

The organizer of the event said I have one question before we cancel.

He asked Arneson, "Were you going to share that you're perfect and you're a goody two shoes and never make mistakes or are you going to share that being a Christian, that even though you did that your sins are forgiven?"

He made the appearance.

FRENCH BACK

Jimmy Conzelman was a Renaissance Man. Not only is he in the NFL Hall Of Fame as a player and coach, he also ran a newspaper, was an assistant to the team president of the St. Louis Browns in the only year they won the pennant, wrote speeches that became required reading at West Point, was a song and dance man, a musical theatre leading man in shows like, *Good News* and *Damn Yankees* in local productions, and was an after-dinner speaker said to have rivaled the best in America. Pat O'Brien the movie actor and well known speaker once followed Conzelaman to the dais by saying, "Following Conzelman is like following *Gone With The Wind* with a magic lantern."

One of Conzelman's most interesting roles was as a model for sculptor Charle McMonnies.

McMonnies was perhaps the most famous American sculptor of his time. He studied under Augustus St. Gaudens and as a student at L'Ecole de Beaux Arts in Paris he was awarded the honor of best foreign student more than once and eventually set up his studio in Giverny the artist colony made famous by Claude Monet.

McMonnies moved back to his native New York at the outbreak of World War I.

McMonnies' big break had been a commission to create a piece for the 1893 Columbian Exposition in Chicago.

His "Columbia in her Grand Barge of State" became a focal point of the World's Fair and cemented his reputation among the top sculptors of his time.

His most recognizable piece is probably the life size statue of Nathan Hale that is in the City Hall Park of New York.

McMonnies was commissioned to create a statue to be given as a gift to the French people in return for the Statue of Liberty that would honor those who died in the First Battle of The Marne in World War I.

This is where Jimmy Conzelman, NFL Hall of Famer, comes back into the story.

The statue, called "The Tearful Liberty in France" where it is located in the city of Meaux is seven-stories tall and at the time of its unveiling in 1932 was the largest stone sculpture in the world.

Jimmy Conzelman, who dabbled in sculpting himself in Greenwich Village for a time was the model for the fallen soldier in the piece.

A nine-foot tall bronze copy of the statues stands in Atlantic City.

Cecil Burns had played for the Providence Steamrollers the previous year. The Steamrollers had dropped out of the NFL so the Steamrollers that Cecil played on competed at a lower level than the NFL. Still he was a big strong boy.

He went home to Dallas and a friend of his came up with an idea that at the very least got Cecil mentioned twice in *TIME* magazine in the depths of the Great Depression.

The idea was for Cecil whose goal was to play that year for the Chicago Cardinals in the NFL to garner publicity and make a few bucks along the way by walking from Dallas to Chicago, where there was a World's Fair going on in 1933, all the while carrying a cotton bale on his back.

Come again?

Yes, they changed his name to Cecil "Red Hot" Burns and he walked to Chicago from Dallas through Oklahoma, Missouri and Illinois with a cotton bale on his back.

He also went by the "Texas Atlas" as he tried to drum up interest along the way.

He did garner a lot of press as his arrival was heralded in the local papers of most of the towns he walked through. It was reported on his eating habits along the way that he drank a lot of milk, a little beer and spinach. Popeye the Sailor must have been a dietary consultant.

In case you're wondering, a cotton bale weighs in at about 500 lbs. The PR guy hollowed the bale out to make it doable.

The press did find out that the bale he carried was actually about 123 pounds. Still.

Cecil made it all the way to Chicago, after he learned how to walk so as to not destroy his feet,yet the escapade was not as financially rewarding as they had hoped. They sold pieces of cotton and other souvenirs of the walk. But Cecil was in shape at the end of the journey... And Cecil contended all would be fine if he could just make the Cardinals team.

He didn't make the team.

SHORT BUT NOT SWEET

Pat Tillman was named Pac-10 Defensive player of the year in 1997.

He also received a raft of academic All-American awards in recognition of him as one of the country's premier scholar athletes.

He excelled as a safety for the Arizona Cardinals as a rookie.

At the height of his career in the NFL he was offered a $3.6 million contract by the Cards but he turned them down and instead, inspired by the events of 9/11, enlisted in the U.S. Army and became an Army Ranger.

He was deployed in Iraq and Afghanistan for several tours. He was killed in action in 2004.

After his memorial it was revealed that Tillman succumbed to friendly fire, a fact that higher-ups in the Army knew full well but tried to spin differently for public relations reasons.

This new knowledge of the events leading to Tillman's death led his family, among others, to castigate the Army for fraudulently exploiting Tillman's death for propaganda reasons.

It has become known since then that Tillman had arranged a meeting with anti-war activist Noam Chomsky to take place after Tillman was discharged from the Army. It is believed that Tillman had expressed reservations over the legality of the wars he participated in.

Nonetheless, Tillman gave up his lucrative life to serve his country.

More on Pat Tillman and his life can be found at pattillmanfoundation.org.

AIRPORT

Edward O'Hare was a prominent attorney in Chicago. He was also an associate of Al Capone. He was a member of the Board of the Chicago Cardinals.

His son, Edward "Butch" O'Hare Jr., was a fighter pilot in World War II.

On February 20, 1942, Butch found himself separated from his squadron, alone in his fighter and confronted with nine Japanese bombers headed for the USS Lexington. Butch, between the Lexington and the Japanese bombers, engaged the enemy.

On April 21, 1942, President Franklin Roosevelt awarded O'Hare the Medal of Honor.

Here is some of the description of Lt. Butch O'Hare's actions on that day, from the Presidential citation:

> "Having lost the assistance of his teammates, Lieutenant O'Hare interposed his fighter between his ship and advancing twin-engine heavy bombers. Without hesitation, alone, and unaided, he repeatedly attacked this enemy formation, at close range, in the face of intense continued machine gun and cannon fire."

He shot down five of the Japanese bombers and decisively damaged a sixth.

He saved the Lexington.

His act was called at the time perhaps the most daring and intrepid act in aviation history.

O'Hare returned to service in his plane and was lost on November 26, 1943, in the Pacific theater fighting the Japanese.

The city of Chicago named the airport after him.

Jimmy Conzelman is an all-time football great. He is in the NFL Hall of Fame and was named quarterback on the All-Time NFL 1920s team.

He coached many teams in the NFL and played for numerous teams with names that are now all but forgotten: Providence Steamrollers, Milwaukee Badgers, Decatur Staleys,... Rock Island Independents, Detroit Panthers, and he coached the Chicago Cardinals twice. He was also the Cardinals coach when they won the NFL championship in Chicago in 1947.

He once owned the NFL franchise in Detroit, the Panthers, a team that predates the Detroit Lions. He paid $50 for the team.

He was also a stage performer and had a contract with the Four Horsemen of Notre Dame fame to play for the Panthers which would require them to clog dance on stage while Conzelman played the piano. But the Horseman had a change of heart on that one.

He sold the franchise back to the NFL after two seasons.

In 1942, the United States was at war. Conzelman, a World War I veteran, gave a commencement speech to graduates at Dayton University. The title of the speech, "Young Men's Mental and Physical Approach to War" became a thing. The speech was printed to the tune of 3 million copies and given to other collegians, and copies were given to all the football coaches at Texas high schools.

Conzelman was also a noted musical comedy performer and knew his way around a stage and, presumably, an audience—which may have added to the effect of the speech. The speech also became, most notably, required reading at West Point for generations of Army officers.

WHITE DEVILS

Robert Rozier was drafted by the St. Louis Cardinals in 1979, in the 9th round, a DE out of Cal Berkeley, he lasted 6 games. Most say it was because of a drug problem. He went on to Canada and played Canadian football.

He then returned to the USA and the Oakland Raiders for whom he played just two games before they gave him the heave-ho.

Rozier then found himself in the after-football years. A scary place for successful athletes once the cheering stops.

He traveled the country looking for something and trying to stay one step ahead of the Canadian authorities who were after him for passing a reported $50,0000 in bad checks.

Rozier found "The Temple of Love," a Miami based group that is considered a cult. The Temple of Love was founded and run by Yahweh ben Yahweh and Rozier, when he joined the cult, changed his name to Neariah Israel (Child of God).

Rozier wanted to fit in with his new-found home and there was a group of insiders in the Temple known as the "Brotherhood," but you had to go through an initiation or fulfill a requirement to be accepted as a member of "The Brotherhood."

You had to kill a white person. Or as they were called, a white devil. Could be anybody, man, woman, child. Just had to be white.

Robert was in luck. There are a lot of white people in America.

So, Robert went looking. He found a sleeping drunk and stabbed him to death. Cut off his right ear as another requirement was a body part as proof, but in his excitement he dropped the ear.

Nature supplies most of us with two ears. This helped Robert out.

He cut off the left ear. He was in.

Went to the movies the next day.

Rozier later admitted to murdering seven white devils. After one of the killings police nabbed Robert. He sang like a canary.

Turned state's evidence and made a deal to save his own skin.

He got twenty-two years for cooperating despite murdering seven innocent people.

Put in the witness protection program, Robert supposedly turned his life around except for one thing, he still liked to pass bad paper. A $66 bounced check brought him to the attention of California authorities and he got 25 to life on the three strikes statutes.

Meanwhile, Yahweh ben Yahweh who was once given the honor by the Miami Chamber of Commerce of "Yahweh ben Yahweh Day" by Miami Mayor Xavier Suarez was soon after arrested for his murdering ways.

He was found not guilty of muder but Yahweh ben Yahweh was sentenced to prison on other charges and released in 2001 and died still on probation in 2007.

FATE

Jeff Burkett played his college ball at LSU where he was a teammate of my dad, Ed.

Jeff was a great punter who had the unusual skill of kicking a football in a spiral, just like a finely passed football, for 50 or 60 yards. My dad said it was a thing to behold. My dad played for the LA Rams, Jeff for the Chicago Cardinals.

The year was 1948.

Burkett had an attack of appendicitis when the Cardinals were in LA to play the Rams. Because of the medical situation he stayed behind when the Cardinals team flew back to Chicago. The Rams were soon to fly to Philadelphia and Burkett asked my dad if he would ask the Rams if he, Burkett, could hitch a ride back east with them.

My dad asked. The Rams, citing league rules, said no. The reason stated was because the league had a non-fraternization rule and they didn't want different teams commingling on official team business like on flights.

No harm. no foul. It would seem.

This was, of course, still considered the early days of commercial aviation and the Packers were the first NFL team to fly to a game in 1940. Even as late as 1948 flights would rarely fly nonstop from LA to Philadelphia. The Rams flight stopped in Denver on the way to Philly. Once on the ground, the team learned of a terrible accident. The United Airlines flight from LA had crashed killing all fifty-two passengers including Jeff Burkett.

The Rams were spooked.

They, as a team, insisted they return to LA after the game by train.

WANDERING CURSE

The Chicago Cardinals are the official NFL Champions of 1925.

However, not everyone agrees.

In 1925 the champion of the league was determined by a number of victories during the year and not with a championship game.

In 1925 Chicago and Pottsville, Pa., were tied.

Another peculiar quirk in the league back then was that a team could schedule extra games even in late December to gain extra wins. The Cardinals scheduled two such games in December against weak opponents. In fact, both of the late opponents scheduled by the Cardinals had already disbanded for the year and had to be reassembled to play the Cardinals.

After Chicago defeated both teams it was discovered by the league that one Cardinal player, a guy named Art Folz, had recruited players from his former high school to give the Milwaukee Badgers enough players to field a team against the Cardinals, a game the Chicago Cardinals won 59-0.

The league suspended Folz for life. It later lifted the ban but he never played in the NFL again.

The wins were disallowed. Meanwhile Pottsville, the team tied with Chicago for most wins, played again in Philadelphia against a team of Notre Dame players and won. Unofficial opponents were leniently given status for purposes of padding teams' record. But the league disallowed this victory after a protest from the Frankford Yellow Jackets who claimed that the Pottsville team had violated the territorial rights of Frankford whose territory was Philadelphia. The game according to the NFL didn't count.

The league then awarded the Championship to the Chicago Cardinals.

After the dust cleared, Chris O'Brien, owner of the Chicago Cardinals, denounced his team's championship because he felt it was achieved in an underhanded way.

Yet, when the Bidwills purchased the team in 1933, they started claiming the 1925 championship.

So, the good people of Pottsville put a curse on the Cardinals that they would not lift unless the NFL gave Pottsville the 1925 championship they rightfully deserved, according to the Pottsville fans.

Who knew the NFL was such a voodoo friendly league? Curses come to play in Chicago, Detroit, Miami and New Orleans.

The NFL did revisit the issue with a special commission in 1963. The league voted 12-2 to keep the championship officially in the hands of the Cardinals

In 1964 the surviving members of the Pottsville Maroons had a championship trophy made to honor the championship they feel is rightly theirs and the place they represented Pottsville in the heart of coal country.

A football made out of anthracite coal to commemorate the purloined Pottstown championship is today displayed at the Pro Football Hall of Fame.

The curse has been pretty successful as the Cardinals have only won one championship since 1925 and the curse has legs, having followed the team to St. Louis and Arizona.

The league was asked to revisit the issue in 2003, but only two teams took Pottsville's side—Pittsburgh and Philadelphia.

"58"

Mario Tonelli was an All-American at Notre Dame.

He scored the winning TD in the 1937 Notre Dame-Southern California game. It was a memorable game in Notre Dame's rivalry with Southern Cal. Tonelli then went on to play for his hometown team the Chicago Cardinals in 1940 and at the end of the season he enlisted in the U.S. Army.

Tonelli had been burned on 80% of his body when he was 6 years old and told that he may never walk again. His father had other ideas and helped Mario regain his strength and of course go on to excel in high school at Depauw in Chicago and then to become an All American and pro football player.

Tonelli had planned to return to the Cardinals in 1942 but a little thing called World War II intervened.

Tonelli was a sergeant in December 1941 stationed in the Philippines when the Japanese attacked Pearl Harbor. On December 8th the Japanese attacked the Philippines.

Tonelli soon found himself along with the rest of the Americans in the Philippines fighting the Japanese on the Bataan Peninsula. After five months of intense fighting the Americans Forces surrendered.

Tonelli then became part of history as a participant in the Bataan Death March, one of the most infamous incidents in World War II. The Bataan Death March was a brutal forced march in which the POW's were denied food,water and medical treatment along with killings and beating all along the way for good measure.

Early in the march Tonelli was confronted by a Japanese Officer who demanded his Notre Dame class ring. Tonelli resisted but when it was clear that the Japanese officer might just kill him and just take it another soldier implored Mario to give up the ring. He gave the ring to the officer.

Moments later another Japanese officer came over to Tonelli and in perfect English asked if anyone had taken anything from him. Tonelli answered that his Notre Dame ring had been taken.

The Japanese officer handed Tonelli back his ring and told him to hide it because next time he might not get it back.

The Japanese officer explained to Tonelli that he had been educated at the University of Southern California and he had seen Tonelli score the winning touchdown in 1937.

Tonlelli spent forty-two months in Japanese captivity.

Late in his years of captivity at a Japanese POW camp he was assigned a number that he was required to sew onto his prison uniform. The number "58."

Tonelli could hardly believe it.

58 had been his number as a football star at DePauw High, Notre Dame and with the Chicago Cardinals.

When he saw the number 58 he took it as an omen and he told himself that he would make it home.

Liberated in 1945, Tonelli who at one point weighed only 90 lbs during his captivity, once back in the United States soon got up to 183 and was signed to a contract by the Chicago Cardinals and actually suited up for one game in the NFL in 1945.

He then retired and started a career as an elected official in Chicago that would last forty-five years.

GREEN BAY

SayBrah®

Bob Dylan

GREEN BAY

FS

MILK SHAKES, LIBERACE, AND BRRRRRR!

GREEN BAY

"If there was a contest with 97 prizes the 98th would be a trip to Green Bay."

—John McKay

SayBrah®

Green Bay Packers were founded in 1919 by Curly Lambeau and sponsored by the Indian Packing Company (hence the name Packers) and later joined the NFL.

After several restructures the Packers are the only team that is owned by a non-profit community corporation and as such the only major professional team of its kind in the United States.

Super Bowl Appearances: 5
Super Bowl Record: 4-1 ('66, '67, '96, '10)
Super Bowl Loss: 1997

MY (PACKERS) PRECIOUS #1

In 1987, an ad appeared in want ads around the country with a PO Box in Fort Collins, Colorado, signed Bill. "Super Bowl I ring for sale. Best offer."

Bob Greene, well known columnist for The Chicago Tribune, answers the ad.

Bill said he had purchased the ring from someone who found it on a bar floor in Green Bay for $75. Bill said the best offer was $18,000.

Greene contacted Tommy Joe Crutcher, a backup LB for the Packers that year, because the name engraved inside the ring was Crutcher's.

Crutcher told Greene that he had invited three ladies back to his hotel room years ago and one of them stole the ring. Crutcher also told Greene, "I'm nostalgic, but I'm not $18,000 worth. Tell him I'm not a buyer but good luck selling it."

Like most players who lose their Super Bowl rings, Tommy Joe had had a replica of the ring made for $700.

NO SWEAT

Rikki and Sean McAvoy of Knoxville, Tennessee, sell vintage clothing online.

On one expedition to the Goodwill in Asheville, North Carolina, they purchased an old West Point sweater.

Sean was, some days later, watching a documentary and he saw Vince Lombardi wearing a sweater a lot like, if not just like, the one he and Rikki had purchased for 58 cents.

The McAvoy's checked with the Hall of Fame who wanted them to donate it.

They called an auction house in Dallas that specializes in sports memorabilia and drove the sweater to Dallas for a look-see. Eventually, Mears, an authentication company, confirmed it was indeed Vince Lombardi's sweater.

It was sold at auction for $43,020 in 2015.

Turns out they found who donated it to Goodwill. A gentleman named Wannamaker who coached with Lombardi at West Point.

His wife and he asked the McAvoys to donate some of the proceeds to Goodwill and they did and the auction house donated their fee which was about $4000.

As a comparison, at the same auction that day a Brooklyn Dodger rookie uniform of Sandy Koufax went for $573,600.

FIRE!

Curly Lambeau was with the Green Bay Packers for a long while.

He was also an egomaniac, womanizer and self-promoter but, then again, no one is perfect.

The Field at Green Bay is named after him and it would seem rightly so for all his contributions to making sure that the Packers were born and survived.

The frozen tundra of Lambeau Field, baby!

In 1937 Lambeau bought a Norbertine Order property called Rockwood Lodge north of Green Bay overlooking the bay.

Lambeau plowed a big chunk of Packer money into the property to turn the Rockwood Lodge into the unified Green Bay Packer training facility, even wanting it to be the home of the Packers players and their families during the season.

Over time, Rockwood Lodge, for all its good points, was despised by the fans and most everyone associated with the Packers. It required fans to travel 17 miles to watch Packer practice. The players hated being confined under Lambeau's dictatorial nose and many thought the hard practice field caused injury. It was felt by the board of directors to be a money pit for a struggling small market team.

Yes, in the late 40s the iconic Green Bay Packers, a mythological sports franchise in the American firmament, was in jeopardy of being sold or maybe even moved out of Green Bay.

In 1950 Rockwood Lodge caught fire and burned. Its location in a rural area prevented fire fighting forces from getting to the blaze in a timely fashion. The lodge that was the headquarters of the team burned to the ground and some live-in employees barely got out with their lives.

A week later Lambeau resigned and went to Chicago to become head coach of the Cardinals.

The $75,000 insurance settlement, no questions asked, saved the Packers' financial bacon and kept them in Green Bay.

LOCKED OUT

1938 the Packers are in New York to play the New York Giants in the NFL Championship Game.

Losing 16-14 to the Giants at the half the Packers moved toward the locker room.

Somehow Lambeau takes a wrong turn and becomes disoriented, opens a door and finds himself outside of the Polo Grounds standing on a sidewalk on the streets of New York. The door closes behind him. It's locked and he can't get back into the stadium.

Lambeau is now in a Twilight Zone/Seinfeld sitcom plot twist.

He pounds on the door. Nothing,

He runs to a stadium entrance and tries to convince the hardboiled ticket taker that he is the coach of the Green Bay Packers. They weren't having it.

One reportedly rather predictably in New York, tells Lambeau, "And I'm the King of England."

Lambeau goes nuts.

Still no dice.

Finally he puts up such a fuss including colorful language that he gains the attention of a few members of the press who recognize him and he gets in.

Unfortunately by that time halftime is over and his players are wondering what the hell happened to the coach?

Not much halftime prep for the second half.
Giants 23, Packers 17.

HIS TWO CENTS

Emmet Platten was a successful butcher and rabid Green Bay Packer fan as proved by his letters to the editor complaining about Curly Lambeau and personnel matters as well as a 15 minute radio show that Emmet paid for and was broadcast before every Packer game.

Don Hutson said that the Green Bay players listened to Emmet's radio show before the home games even though Emmet complained and criticized them.

In fact, Hutson was introduced to Emmet's kvetching when Platten complained that Hutson was too small and would most likely be killed and be of little use to the Packers.

Hutson heard this on the radio right before his first game as a pro in a Packer uniform.

Hutson caught a pass for 80 yards for a touchdown on the first Packer play from scrimmage in that game. And oh, went on to be considered one the greatest ends in the history of the league.

That gives a pretty good window into Emmet's football expertise.

Emmet though saved his best work for when it counted—on the field. There was the 1936 shellacking the Packers took from the rival Bears for example.

With the score an embarrassing 30-3 in favor of the Bears the Packers scored a touchdown only to see the refs call the play back for offsides.

Emmet had enough, he ran onto the playing field at that point and took a punch at the referee, Gunner Elliot, only to hit Ted Rosequist, a 6'4" 222 lb. Bear lineman who was trying to protect the referee.

Emmet popped Ted right in the kisser.

Emmet by the way weighed in at 6'4" 235 lbs.

Emmet in a letter to *The Green Bay Press Gazette* on the Tuesday following the game explained his actions.

He said that he is a Packer stockholder and that he keeps a close eye on the situation and was suspect of official Gunner Elliot even before the game. Platten believed that Elliott was a closet Bears fan. It was Elliot who had called the offsides that nullified the Packers touchdown.

Platten goes on to say in his letter that he went onto the field,during the game now, to have a word with Elliot. Elliot for his part decided to hide behind several Bears players. One of those players, presumably Rosequist, came at Platten. According to Platten he had no choice but to "tag" Rosequist.

George Halas in a post game utterance asked if there wasn't something to be done about Platten.

Platten went on to say in his letter that in the future he was going to give up on Elliott as a fair arbiter.

Take notice, Emmett was escorted off the field and not arrested.

It seems he got away with it.

Emmet was a well known presence in Packer fandom, eliciting other letters to the editor of the Press Gazette to answer his opinions.

Emmet as a stockholder considered himself a kind of watchdog of Packer dealings and not limited to things on the field.

In one letter Platten penned to the Press Gazette he questioned Curly Lambeau's purchase of Rockwood Lodge, Platten asserted that Lambeau's claim that the property was worth $100,000 whereas Platten said he had it appraised by a knowledgeable local real estate agent as being worth only $25,000.

That Emmet was "the dickens."

TIE

Vince Lombardi, as most coaches back in the day (we're talking the 1960s, the TV age) wore coats and ties on the sideline.

This is a story told by Steve Sabol, of NFL films about the necktie Vince Lombardi wore during Super Bowl I.

The Packers were big favorites and the whole world expected the NFL team to win the very first Super Bowl played between the AFL and NFL champions. The game, by the way, was not called the Super Bowl at this point but the NFL-AFL World Championship Game.

Lombardi knew a lot was at stake. The entire reputation of the NFL. There was precedent as when the Cleveland Browns entered the NFL, after the AAFC folded, they won the NFL championship their first year in the NFL. Lombardi was a thoughtful man. He was nervous.

In the story Sabol says that in the pre-game interview with Frank Gifford, Lombardi had held Gifford's arm tightly and Gifford's arm was soaking wet after the interview from Lombardi's perspiration.

All week Lombardi had been bombarded with phone calls from NFL owners to remind him that the honor and reputation of the league was at stake.

Lombardi had tied his necktie so tightly that its knot was the size of a dot or a pebble.

After the win, Lombardi tried to loosen his tie. It was tied too tightly. The trainer, a guy named Dan Brazier, helped the coach cut it by using the device they use to cut tape off players' legs and ankles.

A month later the scene moved to Lombardi's basement bar where Sabol had flown to show the NFL film of the historic game.

Lombardi would make a drink he called the White Cadillac, which was described as basically all vodka.

The film was shown and when it ended the film strip continued to flap and make that sound.

Sabol noticed a discussion between Lombardi and his wife, Marie, who had been drinking as well.

She was pissed. She had bought the tie for Lombardi in New York City as a Christmas gift. It was at a Hermes store.

She exploded, "How could you do that?" she screamed. "How could you be so stupid? Did you know that cost $40!?"

Sabol says the night went downhill from there.

GOT MILK?

Oliver Greise owned an ice cream parlor in Green Bay and at the age of over 100 Oliver, the proprietor of Oliver's Ice Cream Parlor, told this charming anecdote about Lambeau and the Packers.

Lambeau had some peculiar dietary rules for his Packers. He would feed them all 14 ounce steaks on game day. But he would not allow them to have ketchup or milk.

They would, according to Oliver, sneak to his ice cream parlor after practice to pig out on malted milks.

Griese remembered that, when Curly walked by the ice cream parlor, players would hold their malted milk under the counter until he passed.

Whoa! Pro football players with contraband milk shakes.

FLIGHT

On November 14, 1940, the Green Bay Packers became the first NFL team to fly to a road game, sort of.

They traveled by train to Chicago and, after a photo op, they got on two chartered DC-3s painted with 'Green Bay Packers' special for the occasion thanks to United Airlines.

They landed in Cleveland and found out that New York City was under a heavy fog. Curly Lambeau decided the best action from that point was to continue by train, which they did.

Arriving in New York City the next day they practiced in Central Park. Played the game against the New York Giants which the Packers lost 7-3 and then went back to Chicago via United and the DC 3s without incident.

It is of some interest that they chartered two planes. The NFL was worried about the efficacy of air travel and their valuable asset, the players. So they divided up into two squads, like Noah's Ark, just in case one of the planes went down. That way they would still have a team.

THE WORD

The year 1993 was the beginning of unrestricted free agency in the NFL the result of a landmark court ruling.

Conventional wisdom was that Green Bay, as the smallest market team by far, would be at a disadvantage, luring high priced modern athletes to the frozen tundra and, besides, the Packers had not been winning on the field.

Mike Holmgren was the head coach and the organization and GM Ron Wolf put on a full court press to get Reggie White, who was a perennial All Pro and the marquee free agent that year.

White finished his tenure with the Eagles by having recorded more than one sack a game. This is a dominant performance over eight years.

White was impressed with the Packers because, even though they actively pursued him, they were low key in a way, bringing him to Red Lobster instead of a fancy restaurant on the first meeting.

It was also well known that White's Christian faith was very, very important to him and he made it clear he wanted his new team to afford him the opportunity to do Christian ministry and outreach to the inner city.

Holmgren kept in touch with White during the process and once, when Holmgren called White on the phone, he got White's answering machine.

He left a message, "Reggie, this is God. Come to Green Bay." I guess Reggie White had a sense of humor. He signed with Green Bay and they won Super Bowl XXXI.

MY (PACKERS) PRECIOUS #2

Jerry Kramer threw the famous block that led Bart Starr into the end zone in the Ice Bowl that sent the Green Bay Packers into Super Bowl I, which of course they won.

Kramer eventually made it into the Hall of Fame and, as with many or most pro football players, the Super Bowl rings they receive for being World Champs is an emotional touch stone of their youth, or their greatest personal triumphs, their greatest identifiers that they carry through life.

Kramer was on a flight from Chicago to New York and he went to the restroom. As he washed his hands he took his ring off and when he got back to his seat he realized he had left his Super Bowl ring on the sink counter. He went back but it was gone. Stolen.

Numerous announcements by the pilot and attendant got no response. It was gone.

One passenger who claimed to be a psychic told him she was seeing the ring in an old lady's purse wrapped in tissue. Kramer looked but could find no one who fit that description.

The ring was gone.

Fourteen years later Kramer received two phone calls. The first was from an anonymous person calling from Canada who asked him if his Super Bowl ring was missing and that Kramer would soon hear something about that.

Soon after, John Nitschke, Ray's son, called Kramer and asked him if he was selling his Super Bowl ring. Kramer said no. That, in fact, someone had stolen it 14 years ago.

It was on sale at Mastro's Auction.

Kramer went into action, calling Mastro's and informing his lawyer to look into the matter.

Mastro's removed the item from auction and said the collector who was selling it was well known to Mastro's, and had purchased it from a third party years prior.

The collector offered to give it to Kramer if Kramer would give the collector the replacement Super Bowl ring Kramer had made when his ring was stolen.

Kramer said, "Hell no!"

Kramer got his ring back with full cooperation of Mastro's and later sold the ring, 11 years later, at auction for over $125,000 to raise money for his grandchildren's college fund.

William Afflis was born into a relatively prominent Indiana family; his mother was active in Democratic Party politics at a high level.

Then life intervened. His father died when William was young and he ended up living his junior and senior years in a YMCA in Delphi, Indiana where he excelled in football.

William went to Purdue, and in a foreshadowing of the field of endeavor he would become nationally famous, he hit one of the Purdue coaches in the head with a helmet.

He was thrown off the Purdue team and then went to Miami U. and was tossed there for allegedly running a hand book. He was a bookie. Then a brief stay in Notre Dame where he never played and he passed through Alabama until he landed at Nevada Reno where he not only played college football but also earned a degree in engineering,

William was drafted by the Green Bay Packers in 1951 and played with the Packers for 4 years in which he played in all 48 Packers games. He started 34 out of 48 games while a member of the Packers. So he wasn't great but he was pretty good on a mediocre team.

In his last season with the Packers he was hit in the throat and his larynx was badly damaged which led to him having a gravely and sometimes menacing voice for the rest of his life. This voice would come in handy and help him to reach the heights of his new profession.

The injury led to a theatrical presence.

William became a professional wrestler. But not just any professional wrestler. No, he became Dick the Bruiser billed as "The World's Most Dangerous Wrestler."

If you were a child in the late 50's or early 60's and had access to a TV set and you were a sports fan you knew Dick the Bruiser. He was the number one bad guy in pro wrestling. In fact he is given credit for bringing a lot of the schtick that pro wrestling is famous for in bad guy antics many that he poineered.

His image was burnished along the way by a few notable public acts of mayhem.

He got into a fight after a tag team event at Madison Square Garden and dozens of police were injured after the fans got involved and Dick the Bruiser was banned from wrestling for life in New York state.

But of course luckily there are forty-nine other other states and he became a top draw—if not the top draw, for some years.

His base was Indiana and David Letterman, an Indianapolis native, named the house band on his *Late Night with David Letterman* the World's Most Dangerous Band as an homage to Dick the Bruiser, a hometown hero.

Another famous bout from Dick the Bruiser's career included another NFL player, Alex Karras the Detroit Lions star who had also been a pro wrestler during his football career had been suspended by NFL commissioner Pete Rozelle for gambling on NFL games. Karras could not play during the 1962 NFL season.

Karras with his wrestling background having also wrestled as a college student at University of Iowa was scheduled to wrestle Dick the Bruiser in Detroit.

The Bruiser met Karras in a Detroit bar a couple of days before the match to do some promotion and the meeting went south when the Bruiser lost his temper and got into a fight that took 8 cops to quell and subdue him. One of the cops broke his wrist. Karras was a peacemaker but the press ran the story as a confrontation between the two future combatants who were about to meet in the ring.

On April 27, 1963 Karras was dispatched by the Bruiser in 11:21 at Olympic Stadium in Detroit and Karras went back to the NFL in 1963 season and onto a successful showbiz career including a memorable appearance as Mongo in the Mel Brooks film *Blazing Saddles*.

The Bruiser suggested that football players should stick to playing football.

Dick the Bruiser with his gravely football injured voice, menacing presence and bulking physique—52" chest and 30" waist in his prime, was a tough guy who joked that he had so many stitches in his head that it looked like a baseball.

And he often put his money where his mouth was. In Baltimore while still toiling in the NFL for Green Bay he once assisted teammate Bob Mann, the first African-American Packer player, who was refused a ride in a taxi. Willim Afflis at the time, pulled the cab driver out of his cab and threw him onto the sidewalk. The cabbie changed his mind and Mann got his ride.

After leaving the NFL and into wrestling stardom, Dick the Bruiser and his wife at the time were invited to sit on the Packer bench during a Bears-Packers game at Wrigley Field.

The Packers scored a TD and Mrs. Bruiser was so excited she ran from the bench and followed the Packers player into the endzone.

Security intervened, The Bruiser objected, and the couple were tossed out of Wrigley.

Dick the Bruiser, former Packer, one time schoolboy hero, "The World's Most Dangerous Wrestler" is a member in the Wrestling Hall of Fame

HARDWARE

A most unusual device.

Cecil Isbell is a name that harkens to those who are steeped in Green Bay Packer lore and NFL history as the guy who threw to Don Hutson if nothing else, but Isbell was a remarkable player.

Isbell joined the team that already had a star tailback or quarterback if you prefer in Arnie Herber, a true star.

Isbell, out of Purdue, was a runner, kicker, defensive player, blocker and passer—an all-around player as many were in those days of playing on both sides of the ball.

George Halas said that Isbell brought another dimension to the Packers that even a player as great as Herber couldn't.

Indeed in his short NFL career, 1938-42, Isbell became the first NFL quarterback to throw for over 1200 yards in a season. He held the consecutive game record of throwing at least one TD pass in 24 straight games until Johnny Unitas broke it in 1958.

Isbell was picked on the all time Packer backfield by Curly Lambeau in 1948. And he ought to know.

Isbell had what I would guess was an unprecedented, ah, contraption, with which he conducted his football business while on the playing field.

In his first game at Purdue he dislocated his shoulder and he had trouble with that shoulder, luckily his non-throwing shoulder, ever after.

He devised his contraption, a six inch chain that was strung to his non-throwing arm and attached to his body to prevent him from raising his arm too high and injuring it again. He played every game in the NFL with a chain tied around his arm.

HARD NAME GONNA FALL

Bob Dylan, an American icon if ever there was one.

Dylan's name change has been the subject of some speculation and never really pinned down to a definitive story.

Dylan has said he changed it when he went to college at the University of Minnesota when someone asked him his name in 1959 on the streets of Minneapolis and he answered "Bob Dylan."

Ramblin Jack Elliot says that Woody Guthrie told Dylan, nee Zimmerman to change his name and Dylan Thomas name came up and Guthrie said "That's it, Bob Dylan."

As it turns out Dylan is on record as saying that he changed it to Bob Dillon, a name with which he is said to have performed under and then saw Dylan Thomas name and decided that it was better with a Y.

He never comes out and says which theory is correct and then stick to it.

Other theories are that his uncle was named Dillon, there is a Dillon street in Hibbing MN, where he grew up, Marshall Dillon was a TV character of great fame on *Gunsmoke*, and of course the one most people believe is the Dylan Thomas connection.

In a *Playboy* interview in 1978 Bob Dylan says, "I just changed my name and it stuck."

"Not so fast, my friend," as Lee Corso might say.

There's one more theory.

Bob Dylan, nee Robert Zimmerman grew up in Hibbing Minnesota from 7th grade to high school, in 1952 -1959.

At that time there was a famous guy named Bobby Dan Dillion, playing DB for the Green Bay Packers,

Before 1961, Minnesotans were mostly Green Bay Packers fans and the Packers played an exhibition game in Hibbing in 1953.

Now no one had linked Bob Dylan to being a huge NFL fan but as a young boy in Hibbing, it is highly plausible that Bobby Dan Dillon, who by the way was named All-Pro four times in his career as a DB playing for the Packers when the team was pretty awful was well-known to most kids in little Robert Zimmerman's neck of the woods. Bobby Dan still owns the Packers career interception mark. In 2020 he was named as an inductee to the Pro Football Hall Of Fame.

Did Bob Dylan, a few letters rearranged, got his name from a Green Bay Packer DB?

SERIAL KILLER

"With the 428th pick of the 1974 NFL draft, the Green Bay Packers pick serial killer Randall Woodfield."

I mean, wide receiver Randall Woodfield.

Woodfield played at Portland State, caught a few passes in Packer training camp.

The Packers cut him after a dozen indecent exposure incidents.

Picky. Picky!

Randall went back to the west coast, to Oregon, where he grew up north of Freeport on the Pacific Coast, as the member of a well thought of family unit. His sisters became a doctor and an attorney respectively.

He was eventually arrested as the I-5 Killer and, although he was only convicted of one murder on further review and DNA tests, he has been linked to perhaps 44 murders and numerous rapes and assaults.

He denies it all.

His Wikipedia page will make you sick to your stomach.

CANDELABRA

Scott Thurson, who claims to be Liberace's ex-lover, wrote a tell-all book entitled Behind The Candelabra. In it Thurson reveals that Liberace told him that he, Liberace, lost his virginity to a member of the Green Bay Packers who was also a lounge singer.

In Liberace's book, *The Wonderful Private World of Liberace*, Liberace says he lost his virginity to a lusty older lounge singer at the age of 16.

Well, Liberace was touring on a Wisconsin circuit at that time and, according to Thurson, the Green Bay Packer took a shine to Liberace, followed him to nightclubs where Liberace was performing and took him home one night. The Packer was described by Liberace as being "as big as a door."

A place called the Wunderbar in Wausau, Wisconsin, where Liberace played in those days, pops up in the chasing down of this story.

So, who knows?

DALLAS

**A Song, Wolf Hunter,
Prince Bandar of the Kingdom
of Saudi Arabia**

DALLAS

SayBrah®

During 1982 NFL players strike:
"[Football players] are the cattle and
we're the ranchers. And ranchers can
always get more cattle."

Tex Schramm,
Cowboys GM ('60-89)

Dallas Cowboys entered the NFL as an expansion
team in 1960 and didn't win a game its inaugural
season.

In 2015, *Forbes* estimated that the Cowboys were
worth $4B (that's with a 'B') and as such were the
most valuable sports team in the world.

The Cowboys are referred to as "America's Team."

Super Bowl Appearances: 8
Super Bowl Record: 5-3 ('71, '77, '92, '93, '95)
Super Bowl Losses: 1970, 1975, 1978

WOLF HUNTER

Leighton Vander Esch hails from Idaho and was a walk-on at Boise State. Nonetheless, even though Vander Esch was told by his own reckoning thousands of times he would never make it to the NFL, he was drafted in the 1st round by the Cowboys and became a key contributor.

During NFL combine interviews Vander Esch says the coaches of the Cowboys talked more about hunting than football.

He talked about how he had hunted wolves back home and soon the Cowboys coaches started calling him Wolf Hunter. Then the players and fans started calling him Wolf Hunter and he added a wolf howl after he made a play on the field.

Leighton Vander Esch, overachiever, NFL 1st round draft choice and Wolf Hunter.

DOGNAPPED

Lucky Whitehead, a Cowboys wide receiver, went off with his teammates on a road trip to play a game in the NFL.

On his return, he found his pet pit-bull, Blitz, had been dognapped after someone broke into his house. Lucky soon received a ransom demand to the tune of $20,000 for the safe return of his pooch.

Lucky posted this info on Instagram.

He got a Twitter missive from a local rapper, who goes by the name Boogotti Kasino, that claimed he had Blitz, with photographic proof and a story that he, Boogotti Kasino, had not dognapped Blitz, but had indeed paid the dognappers the $20,000 in question to get the dog back safely and that he, Boogotti Kasino, expected Lucky to reimburse him for the return of Blitz.

After a few social media posts filled with copious amounts of "urban language," Boogotti returned Blitz without payment.

SPIDERMAN

In 1981 Sanger Harris department store sponsored a five-part comic series revolving around the Cowboys as an advertising vehicle to appeal to kids so they and their parents might frequent the store.

The series starred Spiderman, with various appearances by other Marvel heroes like the Incredible Hulk.

The comics, designed to turn on children to "enjoy the lowest prices with the highest quality" at Sanger Harris, are now collector's items.

Other comics featuring the Cowboys were an *X-Men* comic and a Christian comic in 1971 (with text from Tom Landry on how God helped the Cowboys succeed). This comic was illustrated by Al Hartley, the illustrator of the popular *Archie* comics.

THE K BALL

Many fans remember the wild card playoff game when the Cowboys were trailing the Seahawks 21-20 late in the game. Tony Romo botched a hold on a chip shot field goal and the Dallas Cowboys lost the game. The culprit?
The K Ball.

Every NFL game has twelve special footballs named K Balls, supplied by the league that are used exclusively for place kicking and are guarded by a special designated ball boy, to keep them away from the Russians and others who mean our game harm. They are right out of the box and since they are new they tend to be slick and slippery.

The kickers are said to hate the K balls.

CITIZENS UNITED

On page 14 of *The Dallas Morning News* on November 22,1963 you will find a full page ad paid for by prominent Dallas citizens that was addressed to President John F. Kennedy welcoming him to Dallas.

The letter basically calls Kennedy an aider and abettor of Communist regimes and other anti-American subversive leanings.

Bum Bright, who would purchase the Dallas Cowboys from Clint Murchison, was the main financier of the ad along with Nelson Bunker Hunt, the brother of Lamar Hunt who founded the AFL and was the owner of the Dallas Texans, (now Kansas City Chiefs).

The NFL seems to be connected to everything.

WE HAVE MET THE ENEMY AND HE IS US

In 1960 pro football wars came to Dallas, in the guise of the Dallas Cowboys in the NFL and the Texans in the AFL.

The main combatants were the owners of these franchises, both well known Texas oil men, Clint Murchison and Lamar Hunt.

It was a game to the death in a way and the Texans eventually left town to become the Kansas City Chiefs.

This anecdote tells a story of rivalry and civility for better or worse.

Murchison's friends wheeled out a huge birthday gift, a box with a ribbon around it, the sheer size of the gift piqued the interest of all.

Murchison pulled the ribbon and the box fell apart to reveal the "gift." Candy Barr, a Dallas stripper and one of the most famous strippers in the country.

Ms Barr who was tied to Jack Ruby and Mickey Cohen as love interests and a celebrity in the exotic dancing firmament had among other things as a young woman been in an underground film XXX that is considered the first widely distributed pornographic film.

The following year at Mr. Murchison's birthday party his friends wheeled out another huge box with a ribbon on it. Those in attendance who had been at the previous birthday or who had heard of the previous years "gift" were wondering, "How could they possibly top last year?"

The ribbon pulled, the box fell open. The "gift"?

Lamar Hunt, owner of the hated rival Dallas Texans.

Mr. Murchison is said to have laughed so hard that people thought he would never stop.

NEON DEION

Deion Sanders, NFL hero, MLB player, media star, seemed to have the world by a string swinging from a rainbow, or some other lofty feel good phrase.

However, by his own admission, at the height of his professional sport careers, Deion Sanders drove his car off of a cliff on purpose, going 65 to 70 mph in an attempt, it appears, at suicide.

The cliff in question was a 30 to 40-foot drop. Deion says that the car landed and neither he nor the car suffered as much as a scratch. I guess he fell onto a rubber street.

You do what you will with this information.

FRIDAY NIGHT LIGHTS GIRL

In 1966 the Dallas Cowboys, only seven years old, were knocking at the door to compete for the NFL championship.

Their quarterback was the destined-to-be-TV-star Don Meredith, he of not too distant in his future Monday Night Football fame. His wife Cynthia was driving to the Cotton Bowl on game day but running a bit late.

The game was between the Green Bay Packers and Dallas Cowboys, who would later meet in the famous Ice Bowl game. But this was now.

Cynthia Meredith was caught in traffic and afraid she would miss kickoff.

She flagged down a Dallas policeman and told him her predicament with the added info that she was the wife of the QB of the Dallas Cowboys and could she please park in a restricted area just this once.

He said no. She asked again. He still declined.

She got out of the car and left it there.

"Just impound it," she told him. "I'll get it after the game."

She made the kickoff. She retrieved her car later at the auto pound. It cost her $4.

LOTTO

Hollywood Henderson was a star linebacker for the Dallas Cowboys. He was eventually released from the Cowboys by Tom Landry because of Hollywood's drug abusing ways.

Henderson admits he had a cocaine cocktail hidden in his pants in a nasal spray during Super Bowl XIII, and that he used it pre-game and during the third quarter of the game. The Cowboys lost to Pittsburgh.

He was sent to prison for drug fueled crimes that included two teenagers as victims. He then turned his life around for the better.

He has been sober for over 20 years and serves as a motivational speaker. He's made several instructional videos about the dangers of drug addiction that are shown in state and federal prison as well as treatment centers.

Mr. Henderson, who no longer wants to be called Hollywood, also contributes his time and money to helping others through drug rehab clinics and sports activities for young people.

He has a bit of coin to spread around because Thomas Henderson, formerly Hollywood Henderson of the Dallas Cowboys, has won the lottery, not once, but twice.

Once it was for a modest amount, $20,000, but the other time it was for, drum roll, $28 million smackers.

POWER

Prince Bandar, the Saudi Arabian Ambassador to the U.S. from 1983-2005, is a big Dallas Cowboys fan. How big?

So big that it is rumored he helped bankroll Jerry Jones' purchase of the team and therefore was part of the ownership group of the team.

His A340 Airbus, his personal plane, is painted Dallas Cowboy silver and blue.

Bandar is no Johnny-come-lately Cowboy fan. As a fighter pilot instructor in North Texas in 1971 he found the Cowboys and became a fan.

Over the years Bandar has been Jerry Jones guest many times in the owners' suite and, if you believe some reports, his own suite to the tune of $500,000 yearly at the new AT&T Stadium when it opened.

So chummy is Bandar with Jerry Jones that he accompanied him on to the field at the end of a Cowboy victory and into the Cowboy locker room after the game to celebrate. (A fact that did not sit too well with Coach Jimmy Johnson at the time.)

Cowboy players became so used to having Bandar in the locker room that they just call him the Prince.

Prince Bandar took Nelson Mandela to a Cowboy-Redskin game, introducing the South African icon to American football. Prince Bandar is such a friend of the Bush family that he is referred to as Bandar Bush.

His Airbus A340 with the Dallas Cowboy paint job is the source of some speculation in an investigation in the UK dealing with payoffs in a large arms and plane deal with the Kingdom of Saudi Arabia. The investigation was said to have been quashed by Tony Blair, the Prime Minister of England.

If you need a ticket fixed (or just a Cowboys ticket) it would be good to be Bandar's friend. Or so it would appear.

DEATH DO US PART

Hypothetically speaking, or at least I hope so, you find yourself walking into a courtroom after being convicted of two first degree murders. The jury is about to go off and deliberate on sentencing you to the death penalty. You might want to look your best or put your best foot forward that day for your court appearance. Think?

What would be your fashion choice for this very important occasion?

How about a Tony Romo Cowboys jersey? No?

Well, Thomas Henderson walked into a Las Vegas courtroom under just such a scary circumstance and that is what he wore.

Henderson was convicted of killing his sixth wife and the guy he had asked to kill her.

Henderson was in line to receive $36,000 in insurance money from his wife's death—and, by the way, his second wife's death had landed him an insurance payoff of $500,000. He was also tried for that murder but acquitted.

Mr. Henderson told reporters before his sentencing that wearing the Cowboy jersey comforted him.

"I've been a Cowboys fan since I was 12 years old," he said.

His attorney told the jury they could consider the fact that he was a Cowboy fan when deciding whether or not to give him the death penalty.

He was sentenced to death by the jury.

He said he would do one appeal but that he had had a blessed life and if that appeal failed he would take the lethal shot.

After the verdict was announced he walked out of the courtroom escorted by police and gave thumbs up to reporters.

A SONG IN YOUR POCKET

George Preston Marshall owned the Washington Redskins.

The Redskins were the southernmost team in the NFL and Marshall considered the South, including Texas, as part of his proprietary territory. Consequently, he tried to prevent the NFL from expanding south and that included Clint Murchison's attempt to bring NFL football to Dallas. Marshall tried to stop Murchison's attempts as many ways as he could.

Marshall was an innovative owner. He had a song written that is still played today at Redskins games, "Hail to The Redskins." He loved his song. Only thing, he didn't write it and the guy who did write it had a feud with Marshall about something. And the songwriter owned the rights to the song.

Murchison got wind of the feud and purchased the rights to "Hail to The Redskins." One of the reasons the Cowboys were finally awarded the franchise in Dallas was a deal to turn over the song rights to Marshall.

One song for one franchise.

Tom Landry has said of Murchison, "He was as crazy as anything."

Murchison once let dozens of chickens loose on the field before a Redskin-Cowboy game. So I guess Tom might have been on to something.

MICHAEL SCISSORHAND

NFL Players in the modern age of scrutiny get into a lot of trouble with the law. Sometimes they are guilty. Sometimes they are not.

So, who knows?

Michael Irvin, said to be the guy at the center of the infamous White House shenanigans, a suburban home where the Cowboys players are alleged to have used as a sex playground, had a reputation for "partying" back in the day.

After his playing days, this story, that the Cowboys went to lengths to quash, surfaced.

There was a barber who would be at Cowboy training camp to cut the hair of the players. One day a rookie OL, a 335 lb guy, is in the barber chair.

Irvin comes in and demands that the rookie get out of the chair, like now, so he, Irvin, can get his haircut because he was a veteran and more important or had seniority or some other macho crap.

Another Cowboy player, a veteran offensive lineman, tells the rookie to stay in the chair.

Irvin, allegedly, grabbed a pair of scissors and cut the rookie's neck. Blood gushes. Ambulance called. Stitches ensue. Just another day in pampered, up-on-a-pedestal, pro athlete land.

No one heard about the incident at the time because the Cowboys brokered a deal to pay off the rookie for his silence to the tune of a reported six figure settlement. The rookie did not miss any playing time due to the injuries, and the rookie, to this day, will not comment on the incident.

And oh yeah, Irvin was on probation for other transgressions with the law at the time of the incident and, if the cops had intervened, would have faced up to 20 years in the slammer. Just a minor detail.

Mothers, don't raise your sons to be Cowboys.

IRON EYES ROBERT

Robert Murchison's dad, Clint Murchison Jr., was the owner of the Dallas Cowboys. Robert was a student at Dartmouth when they changed their school mascot from the Indians to the Go Green. Dartmouth was a prestigious eastern college that also educated Native Americans as part of its mission since the 19th century so I would imagine that is why they chose that team name. Nonetheless, they changed the mascot to the Go Green when Robert was there, which gave him an idea to stick it to the Cowboys' rival, the Washington Redskins.

Robert knew his father's barber back in Dallas was a full-blooded Cherokee and was related to Russell Means, the leader of the American Indian Movement and a prime mover at Wounded Knee. So Robert thought it would be a great idea to have Means hold a protest at Washington's stadium, RFK, to embarrass the Redskins for the racial insensitivity of the team's name.

Dad put the bee in the barber's bonnet, so to speak, and he contacted Russell Means with the idea.

The scheme fizzles at this point. It turns out Russell Means was a rabid football fan and I'll give you one guess who his favorite team was?

The Washington Redskins.

MINNESOTA

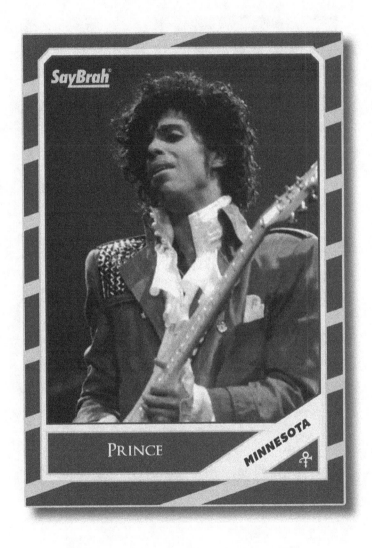

SayBrah®

PRINCE

MINNESOTA

A GOAT, A SNOWSTORM, AND PRINCE

MINNESOTA

SayBrah

"A good football coach needs a patient wife, a loyal dog, and a great quarterback— but not necessarily in that order."
—Bud Grant,
Vikings Head Coach
('67–83,85)

The Minnesota Vikings were awarded an expansion franchise in 1960 by the NFL to prevent the city from entering the rival upstart AFL. Max Winter, a Minneapolis businessman, was to become owner of the AFL franchise in the Twin Cities but when the more-established NFL offered him a franchise, he defected.

This left the AFL one franchise short and that franchise was then given to Oakland.

Super Bowl Appearances: 4
Super Bowl Record: 0-4
Super Bowl Losses: 1969, 1973, 1974, 1976

ONE DOLLAR

The early years of the NFL were a real seat of your pants kind of operation.

The New York Giants were purchased for $500. Jimmy Conzelman, a Hall of Famer, is quoted as saying, "In 1931 I lost my mind and I bought the Detroit NFL franchise for $50."

In 1926 there was a team called the Duluth Kelleys which were a semi-pro team in Minnesota sponsored by a hardware store. These were tenuous times financially for professional football and in the case of the Kelleys they were sold (including debts, it might be noted) to business manager Ole Haugsrud for 1 American dollar.

Ole had a plan. He was friends with Ernie Nevers who was the best football player coming out of college that year. He signed Nevers to a personal services contract and promised him a hefty amount of cash and a nice cut of the gate.

In order to make this a profitable endeavor Ole scheduled as many games as possible which meant traveling a lot. He also cut corners by making a deal with the other players to take modest pay days. $50 a player if the game was lost, $60 if the game ended in a tie and a whopping $75 to each player if the game was won.

By 1927, with Nevers surely one of the greatest football players of all time in the fold (he still holds the record for most points scored in a single game, 40) the rechristened Duluth Eskimos were a financial success. Nevers himself played 1714 minutes of the 1740 the Eskimos played that season and the team barnstormed from coast to coast, logging some 17,000 miles in 1926. This arrangement didn't last and the team sat out 1928 with Nevers pitching for MLB St. Louis Browns in the American League that season.

Haugsrud had his personal service contract with Nevers and he eventually sold him to the NFL with a promise from George Halas that if the NFL ever expanded into Minnesota, Ole would get first crack at the new franchise.

In 1960, 32 years later, the NFL expanded into the Twin Cities and Ole took them up on the offer and bought 10 percent of the team for $60,000, remaining a partial owner of the Vikings until his death in 1975.

Ole still has a connection to the team as the purple and gold Vikings colors were chosen because they were the colors of the high school from which Ole Haugsrud graduated.

Ole, his contract with Nevers in hand, attended the NFL owners meeting in an attempt to get his Duluth Eskimo team into the league.

Joe Carr the commissioner of the league surprised the teams owners by announcing the Nevers get for the league and according to Ole a celebration ensues with one attendee screaming "You saved the league!"

These were indeed lean times for the NFL and it might be close to the truth that Nevers and Ole who were old classmates and cemented the deal with a handshake had quite a bit to do with the NFL surviving.

The $1 that Ole bought the franchise with was reportedly spent immediately on nickel beer. So, the team was sold for 20 beers. That is no doubt reason enough to call them the Good Ole Days.

SOUTH DAKOTA'S TEAM

A new NFL team in town is cause for not only excitement in the city lucky enough to get the team, but it creates and sustains a regional buzz, eventually leading to growing pains as in:

"What do we do now?"

The Vikings were coming to town but had not played a game yet. As it happens, one of the regional movers and shakers of Sioux City South Dakota was in town on a recruiting trip.

He overheard Max Winter, owner of the Vikings, talking about needing a place to play the Vikings first preseason game. He was head coach at Augustana and he had a football stadium and a city with civic pride. The chance meeting was in a barroom setting and the coach got to talking with Winter and he proposed playing that first game in Sioux City. He was told it would take $40,000 to secure the game. He raised it in less than a day and the game was set.

The Dallas Cowboys, only one-year-old themselves, were the opponent. The game was not well attended and the investors lost money. But not before the coach and erstwhile promoter made an impression on the city slickers both for good and bad. Dallas sports writers called the instigator Coach Bob Burns the funniest son of a bitch in the world. In a good way.

The Cowboys, when they arrived, found out they had to use their hotel rooms as a locker room. Tom Landry is said to have been pissed.

It remains the only NFL game ever played in South Dakota and on the field that day were Hall of Famers Hugh McIhenny, Fran Tarkenton (his first appearance in an NFL game) and Don Meredith.

GROWING PAINS

Max Winter was to be the owner of the Minnesota AFL franchise in 1959. But George Halas cut the AFL off at the pass so to speak by getting an NFL franchise awarded to Winter.

There was a bit of palace intrigue involved in the Twin Cities. All of this was happening while the AFL was having its first big owners meeting in Minneapolis, with Max Winter as the host to the AFL owners there to hold their inaugural college player draft.

The NFL's Chicago Cardinals were playing an exhibition game in Minneapolis and Winter took most the AFL owners in his car to the game.

On the way to the stadium Winter says he informed Lamar Hunt, Bud Adams and Bob Howsam (Denver ownership) that he Winter had a deal in place with Halas to get four NFL franchises.

By Winter's account his car mates were ecstatic.

Winter would get Minnesota and take Howsam as a partner. Hunt would, along with Clint Murchison, be awarded the Dallas franchise. Bud Adams said he would get Barron Hilton (Los Angeles AFL owner) to join him as a partner in Houston and Wismer and Ralph Wilson it was proposed would partner in the New York franchise.

All of this would mean no AFL.

Meanwhile, Charley Johnson of the *Minneapolis Tribune* ran a huge headline about the deal in the Tribune.

After the Cardinals game at the meeting to have the first scheduled AFL draft, Wismer burst in with an armful of *Tribunes* and called Winter everything but "a Child of God."

Winter says it almost came to blows and Winter just left to let things cool down leaving a guy named Skoglund, one of Winters partners, to speak for Minnesota.

Wismer made everyone vow to stay the course in the AFL. Skoglund agreed to that deal. The next day Winter took Halas' offer saying Skoglund had no authority to speak for him.

This left seven AFL franchises.

The AFL draft which picked college players out of a hat was held that night and Oakland eventually became the 8th AFL franchise.

So, I guess you can say that...

Harry Wismer saved the AFL and Max Winter was the father of the Oakland Raiders.

MONKEY SHINE

Tommy Mason of Tulane University was the Vikings first number one pick. He went first overall. He had a promising career until he injured his knee.

His salary, which was only $12,000, was still a windfall as it was more money than his parents earned in a year.

Mason bought a guitar, a Cadillac, and a monkey.

Yes, a monkey.

He named the monkey Dutch, after his head coach Norm Van Brocklin.

After a newspaper article that featured the monkey, Van Brocklin was less than amused.

Masson and Van Brocklin must have had a certain kind of relationship because later in his career, Mason was in Central America, surrounded by pet iguanas, and he told a reporter he was going to crate one up and send it to "the Dutchman."

AFL DRAFT

In November of 1959 the AFL met in Minneapolis to have its first league draft of college players.

I once read a story in a sports magazine where Harry Wismar, owner of the New York Titans, claimed to have had just a Street and Smith's Pro Football magazine as his only scouting tool that first year.

As crazy as that may sound, it appears to be true, or very close to the truth.

None of the teams in the AFL had any front offices in November 1959 at the time of the draft.

The owners met to hold the draft in Minneapolis and they allowed each team a territorial pick to help kindle fan interest in the new league.

Houston got the Heisman Trophy winner Billy Cannon from LSU and neighboring Louisiana. The Titans got George Izo of Notre Dame, the Dallas Texans got Don Meredith of SMU and so on.

The rest of the draft consisted of a list of eight best players at each position chosen, probably by a magazine consensus, or some other shallow scouting criteria. The eight player's names were put into a hat and each team picked names out of the hat. This would give each team a player at each position.

Maybe it was a box not a hat.

There are some present-day NFL teams that might want to lobby for this system as it might work much better in picking future talent than what they do now, and it would save a lot of the money they spend on scouting

PILLOW FIGHT

Huge football stadiums aside, the facilities can be and are used for other purposes enriching the community that helps to bring them into being.

One such event took place in the Minnesota Vikings U.S. Bank football palace, on May 18, 2018, when upwards of 60,000 people came downtown to participate in a fight.

A pillow fight.

Yes, 50,000 free pillows were donated by My Pillow, a company headquartered in Chaska, Minnesota, for an attempt to break the Guinness Book Of World Records for a pillow fight. The event was sponsored by a Christian group called Pulse and also featured a rap concert and other attractions.

The event was attended by at least four players on the Vikings roster and featured a video message on the big stadium screen from Vikings new free agent quarterback Kirk Cousins.

The record under the keen eyes of judges from the Guinness Book was broken with an official number of 7,681. There were strict parameters as to who counted. Something about only those on the floor wailing away at each other for ten straight minutes. The old record was beaten by a bit over a thousand.

The video of the event shows thousands more in the stands fighting it out and is quite a sight. The first 50,000 people got free pillows.

🌐 www.youtube.com/watch?v=CNouUYZ186A

BARTER

There was a meat shortage in America in 1974.

Alan Sachs was the president of a sausage company located in Golden Valley, Minnesota.

He put a want ad in the newspaper offering to swap a hindquarter of beef for two Vikings season tickets between the 30 yard lines.

He said his phone rang off the hook for two days.

He received fifteen offers.

PRINCE

Prince went to his first Viking game in years and watched the Vikings destroy the Cowboys to get to the NFC Championship game against the Saints in 2010.

He said: "I saw the future."

He went home and wrote a fight song for the Vikes entitled "Purple and Gold."

It's awful.

🌐 https://youtu.be/Fq3SfauwzgQ

Prince did not see the future very clearly as it pertained to Vikings. They lost on a stupid play by Bret Favre. I know it was a stupid play because I was in the Superdome watching it.

Listen to play by play call of Vikes radio of the stupid play:

🌐 https://www.youtube.com/H2TZQlVPvjk

WRONG WAY

Jim Marshall was a stud defensive end for the Vikings.

However, he will be remembered by most people and history for one thing,

Recovering a fumble in a regular season game in 1964 against the 49ers and running the wrong way toward his own goal, 60 yds.

He did not score a touchdown for the opposition, but a safety.

He won an award and accepted in good humor.

He was to receive the Bonehead of the Year Award in Dallas.

He was running late to catch the flight to Dallas and his award. He got off at the wrong exit. He rushed into the airport and he did, indeed, catch his plane. Or I should say he caught a plane. Not his.

The plane he got on was not going to Dallas, it was going to Chicago.

NUMBER ONE

Technology and innovation are hallmarks of human history.

The Minnesota Vikings are associated with one of the more unseemly applications of human ingenuity.

Onterrio Smith, the leading rusher of the Vikings at the time of this incident, was stopped at Minneapolis-St. Paul Airport in 2005 after a suspicious contraption was found in his luggage.

It turned out to be something called the Whizzanator, a fake penis ensemble that comes in a variety of colors, one being Latino.

The modern device is designed to help one fake a urine test and comes with a fake bladder, fake penis and dried urine.

Smith, who had twice been cited for failing league drug tests, and with a third offense would be banned from the league for a year, claimed he was transporting the fake member for his cousin.

Close family?

He was not disciplined by the league because they said it was not a violation to have the Whizzanator in possession, only illegal to use it.

Smith subsequently failed another drug test and his NFL career came to an end.

Sometimes fact just blows away fiction.

RICO

Zygmunt Wilf is the owner of the Minnesota Vikings, buying the team in 2005.

The NFL is very image conscious as are most huge American corporations. It's an exclusive club and they won't just let anybody in. Donald Trump, for instance, shouldn't hold his breath, to drop one name.

So it was somewhat peculiar to read reports of a New Jersey judge finding that Wilf and his brother defrauded their business partners in a real estate deal to the tune of multi-millions.

This happened just as the new Minnesota Vikings stadium was to be built using state revenues, along with the signing of contracts and start of construction after the usual "build us a stadium or we are out of here" talk.

The judge in 2013 awarded upward of $84 million to the plaintiffs and the judge is quoted in multiple press reports claiming the Wilfs acted in bad faith and evil motives while committing fraud, breach of contract and breach of fiduciary duty, among other things, on the way to being found guilty of violating the state of New Jersey's RICO statutes. Yes, the type of laws often used in organized crime cases.

The judge found that the Wilfs had not acted with gross negligence. No, the judge found they had acted with gross willfulness. That's different by the way. Kind of like the difference between black and white.

The Gov. of Minnesota, Mark Dayton, had come out backing the Wilfs in the stadium deal and he had a pause in his Wilf enthusiasm after the verdicts. The Wilfs appealed the verdict, claiming through lawyers something about anti-wealth bias as a factor in the court's findings.

The stadium was built.

NERF

Fred Cox was the longtime placekicker for the Minnesota Vikings.

In 1972 a guy named John Mattox came to Cox with an idea that would allow kids to set up portable kicking goal posts to practice kicking. Mattox wanted to use a heavy ball so that the kids wouldn't constantly be kicking the balls over fences.

But Cox told him he should use a lighter ball so that the kids wouldn't get sore legs from repeated kicking, perhaps a foam ball.

In 1970 Hasbro had come out with round Nerf balls made of foam. Cox and Mattox got a fabrication machine to make a full-sized foam football. Hasbro bought the idea and in 1972 the Nerf football was born.

Cox and Mattox had a meeting with Hasbro, the game company. In the meeting the Hasbro executive made a phone call. A large box was brought in with failed versions of a Nerf football. Parker Brothers had been trying to develop just what Cox and Mattox had brought them. They signed an agreement almost immediately.

When he was eighty, Cox is quoted as saying he was very proud that he invented the Nerf football.

Cox says he has received a lot of money from royalties since that time. No specific figure. But he says, a lot. They sell millions of these things a year and have come out with souped-up Nerf footballs of different designs over the years. So, I think Fred's assessment of the money made is spot on.

In an interesting twist, the U.S. Army once charged the Land Warfare Laboratory to come up with a prototype of the Nerf football as an anti-tank weapon to fight the Soviet Army in Europe. The weapon, which for one reason or another never made the cut, was a lightweight football hollowed out and packed with explosives, a charge, and detonator.

GET YA GOAT

Woman pulls her car into a car mechanic shop to get a fan belt changed the weekend in 2009 that Brett Favre is to debut wearing the Purple and Gold of the Minnesota Vikings.

The lady casually tells the mechanic that she has a live goat in the trunk.

He asks if he heard right?

"Yes, I have a live goat in the trunk and I'm going to slaughter him later," she tells him.

She leaves. The mechanics go about their business of replacing the fan belt and they hear the goat cries.

They crack the trunk open and sure enough—a goat. Big horns too.

No ordinary goat here, as this goat was painted Minnesota Viking purple and had the number 4, Brett Favre's number, shaved into its side.

Long story short, animal control is called. Goat is rescued.

It's not clear what happened to the woman.

JERRY BURNS PRESSER

Post-game coaches' press conferences can be almost rote events depending upon the circumstances, but sometimes they provide high entertainment value. One such occasion was this gem of a presser in 1989 by Jerry Burns or, as the press calls him, BURNSIE.

WARNING -XXX Rated

🌐 www.youtube.com/watch?v=SNcBFZ26lcl

Jim Marshall is one of the all-time great Vikings. His 247 game streak, a record at that time, speaks to his toughness.

For better or worse, Marshall will always be remembered as the guy who recovered a fumble and ran the wrong way, thereby scoring a safety for the opposition. But that is not the most interesting odd-ball story about Marshall.

Marshall and other Minneapolis and Minnesota notables, along with wilderness guides, went on a snowmobiling expedition in 1971.

The weather turned sour and they were caught in a blizzard.

The severity of the situation can be understood by the fact that one of the members of the expedition, Hugh Galusha, 51 and president of the Federal Reserve Bank in Minneapolis, died from exposure.

Marshall was known for always carrying a lot of cash on him.

Some people are like that.

Marshall and his group, separated from other members of the expedition, stayed alive with the help of a lighter and heat from the burning of Marshall's cash money.

But even before the $20 bills went up in flames Marshall's snowmobile had gone off of a cliff and over Marshall throwing him down a slope about 30 feet where he dug his fingers into what is described as loose rocks and was saved from falling two-thousand feet to the bottom of a canyon. He was pulled up by his companions.

By the way, one of the other notable participants in this ill fated expedition was one Jim Klobuchar, a sports writer for the Minneapolis Star Tribune and father of U.S. Senator and presidential candidate Amy Klobuchar.

LOS ANGELES

SayBrah®

HARRY S TRUMAN

LOS ANGELES (N)
ST. LOUIS

LS

HOLLYWOOD, HARRY TRUMAN, AND THE KING OF ETHIOPIA

27   THE MOST INTERESTING LEAGUE IN THE WORLD

LOS ANGELES (N)

About Head Coach Clark Shaugnessy:
"Never get me another warm up game
against a team coached by that guy."
—Knute Rockne

SayBrah®

The Rams were started in Cleveland in 1936 as the Cleveland Rams. They won the NFL championship in 1945 then moved to Los Angeles in 1946.

Robert Irsay bought the Rams in 1979. Then, in a tax saving maneuver, Irsay swapped his Rams for Carroll Rosenbloom's Baltimore Colts in a transaction that is still studied in law schools.

After Rosenbloom's death in 1995, his widow moved the Rams to St. Louis where they played until 2016 when they moved back to Los Angeles.

They have never won a Super Bowl playing as the Los Angeles Rams.

Super Bowls Appearances (STL/LA): 4 (2/2)
Super Bowl Record: 1-3 (STL, 1999)
Super Bowl Losses: STL, 2001; LA, 1979 & 2018

ART

Ideas have consequences. In fact, the human imagination, a weightless entity, can move mountains.

Not all ideas work out but some do.

Fred Gehrke, running back for the Los Angeles Rams, was an art major in his college days at the University of Utah and he worked as a commercial artist in the off season.

One day in the off season, Fred took a plain brown leather Rams helmet and painted it a bright blue. Then he put his imprimatur on it by painting a bright pair of spiraling horns onto the helmet. He brought his idea to Rams owner Dan Reeves, who loved it. Fred painted 75 Rams helmets that summer at $1 apiece. When the Rams entered the LA Coliseum for a pre-season game wearing the new helmets, the crowd gave the team a standing ovation.

Now, of course, all the teams save the Browns have distinctive headgear.

Riddell started to make plastic NFL helmets in 1949 and they baked the colors in so Fred lost his painting gig, but certainly his efforts are a big part of NFL history. Fred, a very good running back in his day, entered the NFL Hall of Fame because of his paintbrush by way of the Daniel F. Reeves Pioneer Award.

AUTHOR'S NOTE: *My dad Ed was one of the guys wearing those helmets that day in 1948, by the way.*

HORNS APLENTY

Pretty sure there are no actual lions roaming free in Detroit, Or bears in mid-town Chicago. Zoos don't count.

When the LA Rams moved from Cleveland where they won the NFL championship in 1945 and were named, by the way, after the Fordham Rams, they might have been surprised to realize that they were not the first LA Rams.

Indeed, Los Angeles is home to a thriving wild ram population. The population has dwindled since 1945, with the rams even showing up on the Endangered Species List in 1998. They live mostly in the San Gabriel Mountains and after a conservationist assisted existence, now have rebounded to number about 400. They have been known to wander onto La Quinta golf course in search of grass and water.

Rams, the big horn kind, are in fact indigenous to the LA area.

Interestingly enough, the ram butts its head using what can be up to 30 lb. horns in mating rituals that last for hours and scientists have observed that this headbutting that consists of collisions of the skull at high velocity seems to cause no serious brain damage to the rams. The rams skull is built a lot like a football helmet, to absorb blows to the head. In fact, some scientists study the ram and its physiology, with an eye to addressing the concussive effect of head butting and how nature copes something known as bio-mimicry, as a way to address the concussion problem currently in the news as it pertains to the NFL.

Woodpeckers anyone?

THE MAN

Clark Shaughnessy is not in the Pro Football Hall of Fame.

This is the thing about Halls of Fame, they are akin to popularity contests in high school.

Political.

Arguments about who invented the T formation or who made it popular are probably not truly knowable.

They say Stagg invented it back in the day. Maybe so.

But Clark Shaughnessy is the father of the modern T formation that is still the basis of what's used today.

Shaughnessy could be listed in a number of team's chapters: the Bears, where Halas gave Shaughnessy the laboratory he needed; the Packers; and the Redskins, where he nurtured Sammy Baugh. All can claim him. But we need to put him somewhere for the purposes of this format, so we will place him here in the LA Rams chapter where he was successful in creating a team framework that led them to greatness in 1949-1952—or maybe for no other reason than the fact that he was my dad Ed's coach when my father played for the Rams.

Shaughnessy is described as eccentric. He was definitely that. He got so many traffic tickets while coaching in LA he asked the cops if he could just pre-pay the fines he was sure to get. Ya see, he would write down football plays while he was driving as the inspiration hit him. Sometimes diagramming them on his windshield.

He was also described as a Mr. Clean; he didn't drink, he didn't smoke, he didn't use profane language.

But he loved him some football.

For his work with the T formation he was called by Halas, "The greatest play designer in the game."

He is often referred to as a genius.

Stan Jones, Hall of Fame tackle for the Bears, put it this way: "It was like having Albert Einstein work with first year algebra students."

My dad told me that one week during the middle of the season Coach Shaughnessy came in and made everyone turn in the playbook. He gave out a whole new playbook with new plays, 1,000 of them, in the middle of the season. They had a week to learn the new plays.

He told them, "You're all college boys, you should have no problem."

He coached all over the place because he was said to be hard to get along with, yet in high demand. He had integrity. He didn't put up with BS.

He left the U of Chicago when they abolished football.

He then went to Stanford. He implemented the T formation and the Stanford team that went 1-7-1 (the year before went 10-0) and won the Rose Bowl.

Word spread rapidly. Coaches all over America started studying Stanford's game film. Halas implemented it with the Bears.

Frank Leahy at Notre Dame and Red Blaik at Army, with Lombardi and Sid Gillman on the Army staff, they learned it. Paul Brown, as a young coach, came to Chicago to study the Bears' use of it. Later Shaughnessy would mentor George Allen on defense and set up the Bears' 1963 Championship. Allen mentored Maxie Baughn, in turn Baughn mentored Bill Belichick. A lot of football was born in the fertile imagination of Mr. Shaughnessy.

Halas called him to Chicago after Stanford's Rose Bowl season and he implemented his T formation with the Bears who were to play the Washington Redskins in the Championship game and defeated the Redskins 73-0. The Redskins had defeated the pre-T formation Bears that season (14-7) in their previous meeting.

Shaughnessy could also coach defense.

Red Hickey put in the Shotgun Formation in the early 60s. It was running roughshod through the NFL. The 49ers won games 49-0, 35-0 and 38-24. The Bears were next.

Which meant they would face a Shaughnessy plan to stop them.

Shaughnessy and the unpredictable Bear defense thumped them 31-0. He did, however, tell Hickey after the game that he was onto something with his new formation and it would work eventually.

Smithsonian Magazine printed an article about the genius of Shaughnessy and in it reveals that Shaughnessy retooled, reinvented, and perfected the modern T formation by studying the tank warfare tactics of German General Heinz Guderian. One of Shaughnessy's other passions was military tactics.

Put that in your pipe and smoke it, Hall of Fame voters.

Still another curious but lesser known aspect of Shaughnessy was detailed in a newspaper article in the 1931 *States-Item* when Shaugnessy was the head football coach at Loyola of The South.

As a young boy of six Clark learned to play the piano and well. He stopped at the age of ten after his piano was damaged in a fire at his home.

The newspaper article contends that Shaughnessy's musical talent may give some insight into his football success as it describes the way he diagrammed plays on a blackboard as the same way a music teacher would use a metronome.

Indeed the "Shaughnessy Shift" as his offense was known then was based on perfect split second timing that allowed for deception and speed of his often smaller players to out maneuver the bigger opponents and to great success.

A music professor in the article says that he sees the same rhythm in Shaughnessy's plays as he puts into playing the piano.

Then not so curious that music may have been passed down in his family.

That would be in the person of none other than Bill Kreutzman, the drummer for the Grateful Dead, and Clark Shaughnessy's grandson.

So I guess Clark's DNA is in The Rock 'N' Roll Hall of Fame.

RAP

1987, the year of the NFL players strike and the replacement players, saw Suge Knight, the notorious rap mogul, take the field for the replacement Rams.

Before he was a rap music producer and other colorful things, Suge had been a star football player at UNLV, leading them in sacks in 1986 and being named to the All-Mountain West defensive team. He was not drafted by the NFL but was invited to LA Ram camp where he was cut.

The strike gave him an opportunity to play for the Rams. He appeared in two games and played sparingly.

In his last NFL play he jumped offsides for a 5-yard penalty and was taken out and that was that.

Knight was better known, of course, for his colorful reputation and music career. It consisted of, among other things and depending upon who you listen to, threatening Vanilla Ice by hanging him out of a hotel balcony to get him to relinquish rights to his song "Ice Ice Baby," allegedly, and threatening a rap producer with a pipe and baseball bat to release Dr. Dre, and paying Tupac's $1.4 million bail if Tupac would sign with Suge's record label (Death Row Records) which Tupac did. He is also associated with Snoop Dogg and other top line rappers.

He has had a lot of legal entanglements and has had numerous run ins with the law and been sentenced to prison more than once and, as of 2019, was serving a twenty-eight-year term in prison.

Synopsis of Suge Knight's football career:

 www.youtube.com/watch?v=KTfaQmF7_9g

A NAME

In the December 3rd, 1973 edition of *Sports Illustrated* you'll find it is noted:

A twenty-year-old lady became a naturalized citizen of the United States at Lancaster, Pa. courthouse.

She came to the United States from her native Cuba in 1966.

Her name, Maria de los Angeles Rams.

In case you're wondering she said that she was a Baltimore Colts fan.

MANLY THINGS

Rosey Grier, all 6'5" 300 lbs of him, was kind of a Renaissance guy.

After his fame as a ferocious defensive lineman with the NY Giants and as a member of the LA Rams Fearsome Foursome, he became a movie star, recording artist and the guy who wrestled the gun away from Sirhan Sirhan the night of the assassination of Robert Kennedy.

In 1973 he did an unexpected thing, at least for a pro football player—by authoring a book about one of his hobbies, needlepoint.

Yes, an original copy of *Needlepoint for Men* by Rosey Grier is still available on Amazon at a hefty price somewhere in the vicinity well above $100.

At the time of its publication he said that he started doing it after hanging around a craft store where a female friend of his worked and to help him calm his fear of flying. He would embroider on flights.

The reaction he got besides curiosity was not always positive and challenged male stereotypes of that time.

Some objected. Grier said he got a message from an unnamed teammate—"cut that crap, Ro, you'll have everyone who thought football players were rough and tough looking at us like we are sissies or something else."

Grier admits as he got into needlepoint that he wanted to challenge gender possibilities and he said that eventually he had a lot of his football brothers joining him in a sewing circle.

There are reviews of the book on Amazon that praise Grier for writing the book and even one that extols the virtue of needlepoint as a way her husband dealt with pain.

HOORAY FOR HOLLYWOOD

The move of the Rams to LA made it inevitable that the team and its players would be linked to Hollywood and its glamour.

Woody Strode, who my dad Ed lined up next to on his first play from scrimmage in the NFL, went on to a long Hollywood career, appearing in many John Wayne films and, most notably, as the Gladiator who fought Kirk Douglas in Spartacus.

Many Rams have gone onto film or TV careers like Fred Dryer, star of TV's *Hunter*; Rosey Grier; Merlin Olsen on *Little House on the Prairie* and *Father Murphy*; Rams LB Mike Henry starred in a trilogy of *Tarzan* films and played the son of Buford T. Justice in *Smokey and The Bandit*—to name a few of the more notable.

There was also the relationship of the Rams with Hollywood stars.

Bob Hope and Bing Crosby owned part of the Rams when my dad played on the team and family lore has me as a newborn fouling Hope's dressing room couch during the filming of the *Lemon Drop Kid*.

When Dan Reeves moved the team to Los Angeles he took several high profile partners as a hedge against financial losses. The partners including Bob Hope and Edwin Pauley got a piece of the Rams for a reported investment of $1 each. They promised to share in the losses. The team however turned out to be a financial success.

The two most famous, I suppose, are from the days my dad was on the team.

QB Bob Waterfield was married to Jane Russell, a big sex symbol of the movies. In fact, Russell and Waterfield were high school sweethearts at Van Nuys High.

Glen Davis, a RB on the Rams, another California boy, dated and was engaged to Elizabeth Taylor, if only for a brief period. Davis did marry movie star Terry Moore. Moore later claimed that she secretly was married to Howard Hughes.

My mother, Elsie, told me that Jane Russell was a very nice, down to earth person who she, Elsie, met at various Rams social occasions in those years.

Russell once accompanied Waterfield on the road and attended the Eagles game in Philadelphia. I found this quite interesting account of that trip.

"Jane Russell was a regular person," said a man who knew her in those Rams years. "I remember after a game with the Eagles we were at the Washington Club on Market Street, Jane Russell sitting at a table with us drinking a couple of beers. One of the girls wrote on the wall of the ladies' room, "Jane Russell peed here."

My dad told me they were on the train going east to play a game and Ms. Russell had just gotten back from shooting a film in Europe and there was a lot of press about her and one of the leading men in the film. A particular blowhard in the Rams entourage made comments to Ms. Russell about the press rumors and she threw her drink in his face.

BIG BOY

Andy Reid, coach of the Kansas City Chiefs and Philadelphia Eagles, grew up in Los Angeles and, before he was a famous NFL coach, represented the Los Angeles Rams in the "Punt, Pass and Kick" competition.

The video still exists of thirteen-year-old Reid, dressed in a Rams uniform, throwing a pass at halftime of a Rams-Redskins game.

The thing is, Andy Reid at thirteen was about 6'2" 220lbs. A behemoth. Take a look at the eight-year-old behind him in line. Reid was so big that the organizers of the event had to borrow a jersey from Rams running back Les

Josephson to fit him. He played catch with Redskin quarterback Sonny Jurgenson before the game and he was bigger than Jurgenson who was only 5'11."

Reid, whose father was a set builder for TV movies and stage productions in Los Angeles, was so damn large as a kid that he was a legend among his friends for his athletic feats like long home runs and game winning placekicks.

🌐 https://www.youtube.com/B4gNFL2upZE

THE GOOD EARTH

Jason Brown signed a $37.5 million contract in 2009 that made him the highest paid center in the NFL. He was cut by the Rams in 2012 and other teams were interested in signing him because he still had a bit in the tank.

But Jason had other ideas. He took his $25 million or so of his contract that he had earned and went back to North Carolina to become a farmer.

Jason says he prayed on what to do at some point before leaving the NFL and that God answered his prayer by telling him what to do. He bought 1,000 acres about thirty miles from where he grew up and there he started a farm with the idea to feed the needy.

Now get this, he didn't have a clue how to be a farmer. So, what did he do? He tried to learn how to farm from YouTube. He went online and tried to learn how to farm.

Jason now supplies food to over 800 food pantries and other charitable organizations.

As for the YouTube farming tutorial? Jason's neighbor Les Wester is a commercial farmer. He said he watched Jason toiling away at his 1,000 acres and one day he called Jason up to meet him high on a hill on Jason's property. They looked down and Jason saw his land all tilled and ready for planting. Jason said he was too proud to ask for help.

With an assist from Les and the vision of Jason, the memory of his brother and a push from God, it seems Jason now supplies thousands of pounds of fresh produce to the needy every month and he's happy.

GENDER ISSUES

Dominic Frontiere, the husband of Rams owner Georgia Frontiere, once insisted that he was eligible to compete in the NFL owner's spouse tennis tournament even though he was the only male spouse.

He insisted.

He was allowed to compete.

He won the tournament.

Ruth Bader Ginsburg won a big bet on the tournament.

No she didn't.

I'm sure of it.

SLATER ON SAX

The Chicago Bears' "Super Bowl Shuffle" in 1986 got every pro football team's players wanting in on the entertainment game.

At least thinking about it.

The LA Rams were in Hollywood so it figures they would carry through.

The result, a music video shot in one day, "Let's Ram It."

To hear them tell it years later, it was a nightmare that ended up in living color and on film, therefore for eternity.

Their friends bring it up, their kids rib them about it and they always tease each other when they run into old teammates from that fateful day off.

Shooting lasted all day and all night, past midnight. They remember it got very cold at night.

Some others' remembrances of the group that included two Hall of Famers, Jackie Slater and Eric Dickerson—

"A wasted day off,"

"Probably one of the worst nights of my life,"

"We were half in the bag,"

"I thought I'd be the next Kirk Douglas," and

"We had fun making it."

There's always one in every crowd.

The NFL gave the sanction and head coach John Robinson gave his blessing with this caveat, "Go ahead and do it as long as you don't make a fool of yourself."

The title is "Let's Ram It" so the music video and lyrics are suggestive "much."

Check it out:

 www.youtube.com/watch?v=YZO8Zeye5KO

FAVORITE SON

Following a Rams victory over the Washington Redskins on December 11, 1949—a win that clinched the Western Division crown for the Rams and sent them into the NFL Championship game against the Philadelphia Eagles—this curious little item was in *The Los Angeles Times:*

"Captain Fred Naumetz, who played one of his greatest defensive games, joined with his mates in giving the game ball to Tackle Ed Champagne. Ed became a proud father at midnight Saturday, his wife presenting him with a son, Christian Champagne, at the Queen of Angels Hospital. Young Christian thus probably sets a world record for being the most youthful recipient of a pigskin prize."

In further news: My Mom's name was Elsie.

THE BUCK STOPS IN LA

Ownership of Bob Hope and Bing Crosby in the Los Angeles Rams was well known but the Rams had another famous part owner.

Harry S Truman, a president not usually associated with athletics, invested $65,000 in the Los Angeles Rams after he left office. This was a rather large sum in those days circa 1952-53.

How did this come to pass?

The Rams were a successful team in those years but the friendship or association with oil millionaire Edwin Pauley was the key to Truman's investment. Truman invested in the NFL team on Pauley's advice.

Pauley, the namesake of the UCLA basketball arena Pauley Pavilion, was a huge contributor and fundraiser to Democratic Party politics in pre war and wartime America and eventually became the Treasurer of the National Democratic Party. Pauley was a business partner with Geoge H. W. Bush in Zapata Oil and with Howard Hughes, among others.

Pauley was appointed by President Franklin Roosevelt as the coordinator of oil supplies to Russia and Britain right before the United States entered World War II at the urging of Senator Harry Truman.

Pauley was the chairman of the Demicratic National Convention in 1948 and is said to be the prime mover to dump Vice President Henry Wallace from the ticket in favor of Harry Truman, at the time a U. S. Senator from Missouri.

Truman is said to have made several thousand dollars in profits from his investment in the Los Angeles Rams over a ten-year period.

VIETNAM

Willie Miller graduated from high school and, although he was a good student and very fine athlete, he turned down college scholarships to join the Army. This was 1965 so that meant one thing—Vietnam.

Willie joined the special forces and served two tours in Vietnam.

While stationed in El Paso he caught the eye of football coaches at Colorado State University. So, after 5 and a half years in the U.S. Army and seeing combat in Vietnam, Willie entered the world of college football at the age of 24.

He excelled, he broke all Colorado State receiving records, is now in the school's Hall of Fame and was drafted into the NFL as a twenty-seven-year-old rookie.

He played with the Browns, briefly, but when he got to the LA Rams he flourished. The team went to the Super Bowl in those years and he led them in receiving in 1978.

Willie played seven years in the NFL and he didn't like to speak of his military service and experiences. He said he still had nightmares. When asked about Vietnam, he told his football teammates the truth but when the story got too gory, they dropped the subject.

Willie Miller's war was not like in the movies.

Sgt. Miller received the Silver Star for retrieving his wounded platoon Sergeant under heavy enemy fire.

There was a story about it written by Cleveland veteran journalist Hal Lebovitz in the Plain Dealer. Lebovitz did some digging and discovered Sgt. Miller retrieved his platoon leader after eliminating some of the opposition.

Willie Miller, late of the LA Rams, is a hero, but he doesn't like to talk about it.

MORMON AND BLUES

Check this out: The Fearsome Foursome on *Shindig*.

www.youtube.com/watch?v=Hg1C3VfbTKs

Shindig was a prime-time music show that, among other things, once featured an appearance by the Beatles that was shot in England and, in January of the same year, showed a live performance of "Satisfaction" by the Rolling Stones before the record was released.

The guests on *Shindig* the week before the Fearsome Foursome appearance and the week after gives you an idea of the significance of a *Shindig* appearance if you were a musician.

Let's see...

Petula Clark, Bobby Vee, Glen Campbell, Little Anthony and the Imperials, Freddie and the Dreamers before...Johnny Cash, Herman's Hermits, and the Righteous Brothers after.

Rosey Grier went on to have a weekly TV show in LA and, of course, appeared in many films.

The Fearsome Foursome signed a record deal with Capitol Records and had a single released called "Fly in the Buttermilk."

NIWRADISM

William Hayes, on the 2015 version of *Hard Knocks*, said, among other things, that he does not believe in dinosaurs. "I don't believe a T-Rexer walked this earth," says William, a defensive end for the LA Rams at the time.

Mr. Hayes does believe that mermaids could exist. In fact, he seemed to be excited about the team moving to LA, according to coach of the then St. Louis Rams, Jeff Fisher, because LA is closer to the Pacific where mermaids might hang out. You know? By the beach? No mermaids in the Mississippi River, brah.

He also believes that other life forms exist in the universe, like maybe but not necessarily space dudes with antennae and s@#t. But he doesn't believe we went to the moon.

How does Hayes explain the plethora of dinosaur bones we have found?

"I just think they just put those things there just so we can have something to talk about, you know what I mean?"

To explain I'll use what I call Niwradism, which is Darwin spelled backwards with an ism. This explanation comes from Chris Long, William's teammate with the Rams in 2015: "He thinks archaeologists place bones underground like parents would place Easter eggs. They planted them. It's a large conspiracy."

Okay.

There is no word whether or not William Hayes believes in David Attenborough.

LOS ANGELES FRONTIERE TICKETS

When Carroll Rosenbloom died suddenly by drowning his wife Georgia became the owner of the Los Angeles Rams.

Georgia, a former singer, media personality, and weather woman on *The Today Show with Dave Garroway* for about two weeks, met Rosenbloom at a party thrown by Joseph P. Kennedy who was said to be a fan of her TV work.

After her husband's death, she married Emmy Award-winning composer Dominic Frontiere, becoming Georgia Frontiere.

Dominic was a well known musical figure in Hollywood. He was at one time the musical director of 20th Century Fox and later head of the music department at Paramount Pictures.

He composed several well known TV theme songs among them the theme of *The Outer Limits, The Flying Nun, The Fugitive, Rat Patrol* and many others. His film work, which was extensive, included the Clint Eastwood film *Hang Em High* and *Number One,* a film starring Charlton Heston.

Georgia, upon her inheritance of the Rams, became the only woman to be in charge of an NFL franchise. At her first press conference as head of the Rams she said, "There are some people who feel there are two different kinds of people—humans and women."

The 1980 Super Bowl was to be played in Los Angeles and that made the Rams the host team and participant in the game the largest ticket holder.

The Rams received a 32,000 allotment of Super Bowl tickets.

Dominic Frontiere, who was at that time engaged to Georgia and lived with her in Bel Air, approached a friend Donald Whitman about a scheme to sell or scalp Super Bowl Tickets.

Whitman, who owned a restaurant on LA's Sunset Strip, found Roger Cohen a convicted counterfeiter to peddle the tickets to ticket buying agencies.

Georgia had sent a memo to the Rams office that no complimentary tickets were to be given away and indeed Tom Bradley, the Mayor of Los Angeles and even Georgia's brother actually ended up buying their own Super Bowls tickets.

However Georgia had all 32,000 plus tickets sent to the Bel Air home where they were kept in a bedroom.

The majority of the tickets were eventually returned to the Rams office to be sold to season ticket holders but a significant amount of them went unaccounted for.

Dominic was eventually charged with tax fraud due to his profit on the scalped Super Bowl tickets which the government claims was $500,000. Frontiere said that he only made $100,000 and most of that was extorted out of him by Cohen who threatened Dominic with mob ramifications.

Dominic was sentenced to a year in prison and fined. Georgia was never indicted in the scheme. They divorced a year after he got out of prison.

There is more to this story as Whitman and a guy named Robert Cohen—no relation to Ray Cohen—had come up with a plan to murder Raymond Cohen in order to prevent him from testifying about the scheme.

Dominic according to government prosecutors met with Raymond Cohen who he believed was going to give evidence to the feds and tried to convince him to tell the IRS agents fictitious, fraudulent and manufactured evidence.

Robert Cohen was at some point caught selling cocaine to an undercover FBI agent and told the authorities about the plan to murder Raymond Cohen.

The Federal Strike Force charged with rooting out corruption set up a wiretap to catch Whitmer confessing to the crimes.

In order to pull off the deception to get Whitmer the Strike Force informed Raymond Cohen of the murder plot and had him brought to a TV studio to have him made up by professional make up artist to make it look like he had been shot in the head and killed. They took pictures of the made up Raymond Cohen laying faux dead in a bush and also photographed him lying on a slab in the morgue.

The photos were shown to Whitmer who was pleased with the murder.

Whitmer went to prison.

Okay.

Remember Georgia was never implicated.

WEST COAST BIAS

The following information is gleaned from a paper by Dr. Raymond Stefani PhD, California State University, Long Beach.

In 1946 the LA Rams and Cleveland Browns reintegrated the NFL after African-Americans were banned from the league since 1934 by what was called a gentlemen's agreement among the owners.

A convergence of circumstances came together after World War II that facilitated this change.

A new league would give competition to the NFL led by Coach Paul Brown, who was pushing to integrate. With the move of Cleveland Rams to LA, the black press would be instrumental in making sure the LA Coliseum was not available to an NFL franchise that discriminated.

Dr. Stefani, in a well researched account, tells of what led to this landmark in American sport history that also involves the iconic debut of Jackie Robinson and breaking the color barrier in baseball, which of course is one of the singular moments in American history.

We will use Dr. Stefani's five-step approach to explain this fascinating tale.

Kenny Washington is the star of this story. It starts, though, a little earlier in an unsung part of pro football history.

The San Francisco 49ers are given credit for being the first pro team in California when they got an AAFC franchise in 1946. But...in 1936 the NFL, from a high of twenty-six teams at one time, had shrunk to nine teams. They were seeking a tenth.

To that end, the Los Angeles Bulldogs were founded by Harry Meyers and actually played six of the NFL teams in 1936. The Bulldogs defeated the Eagles, Pirates (Steelers), and Cardinals, lost to the Bears and Packers, and tied the Brooklyn Dodgers.

This establishes that the LA team could compete with teams in the NFL.

The league then decided among three prospective teams for the tenth franchise in 1937: Los Angeles, Cleveland, and Houston. The league chose the Cleveland Rams.

Speculation is that the distance to LA, most folks frequently traveled still by train, had a lot to do with it because the Bulldogs had averaged 10,250 a game when the NFL average that year was 15,000. The Bulldogs continued into 1937 but in something called the American Football League and went 16-0.

That league folded after the 1937 season.

In 1938 the Bulldogs—in an independent league—played against five NFL teams going 2-1-2.

So, the Bulldogs in three seasons were 5-4-3 against the top football competition on the planet, which, of course, proved that they belonged.

While all of this was going on Kenny Washington was tearing it up at UCLA as the single wing tailback, and he was throwing passes to his backfield mate Woody Strode.

They would be joined in the UCLA backfield in 1939 by Jackie Robinson.

Kenny Washington was awarded something called the Douglas Fairbanks Award as the best college football player in the land in 1939.

Pro football continued to be somewhat popular in California and, since Kenny Washington, who played in the 1939 College All Star game in Chicago, was banned from the NFL, George Halas tried to sign him but could not get agreement from the other teams. Washington returned to LA and commenced to star for a number of West Coast teams in the war years. Washington's knee surgeries kept him out of the draft.

Nonetheless he tore up the Pacific Coast Professional Football League.

An interesting bit of this is that Paul Schisler, who lured Washington from one team to another on the West Coast as there were two teams in LA in the league, paid his stars Washington and Strode very well.

Don Hutson, star of Green Bay, was getting $175 a game in the NFL at the same time Strode was getting $100 a game plus a cut of the gate. Surely the cut of the gate insured that he made a significant amount more than Hutson. Washington, meanwhile, was promised $200 a game and a cut of the gate. What this means is Washington sometimes made $500 a game. This made these two cats, Washington and Strode perhaps the highest paid players in professional football at the time.

Meanwhile, their UCLA teammate, Jackie Robinson, had tied his financial wagon not to baseball but to pro football, and spent the better part of 1941 playing for the Honolulu Bears. Luckily, the last game of the season for Honolulu was Dec 5, 1941. Jackie Robinson was two days at sea going back home to California when the Japanese bombed Pearl Harbor, having departed by ship on December 5.

Robinson served in the armed forces, resumed his football career in Los Angeles, injured his ankle which ended his football career and started his baseball career in earnest as he joined the Kansas City Monarchs of the Negro Major Leagues.

Branch Rickey, who had played pro football with a gentleman named Charles Follis, an African-American in pre-NFL days, remembered his teammate's attitude as to how he dealt with the taunting and unpleasantness of being treated as a second-class citizen. Rickey kept track of Robinson as a potential candidate to break baseball's color barrier. Before Rickey did that, the NFL had been doing the same, and Rickey related to some that the atmosphere he saw when Marion Motley came to play in Brooklyn for the Browns helped to convince Rickey that Robinson could be successful in the majors.

Ironically, the Cleveland Rams, who prevented the Los Angeles Bulldogs from entering the NFL, moved to LA after the 1945 season—a season in which they won the NFL championship behind rookie Bob Waterfield.

The Rams were entering, as is not always understood, a market that was used to pro football with the attendance success of the Bulldogs, The Hollywood Bears and the Hollywood Stars, as well as the star power of Kenny Washington in the market. The other essential to NFL success was the stadium issue. Here, though, it was a different problem.

Led by the black press in LA, it was pointed out that the LA Coliseum, where Washington, Strode and Robinson had starred for UCLA, was a public facility and by law could not be used by entities that discriminated against African-Americans.

Consequently, Rams owner Dan Reeves signed, or as they put it then, hired Kenny Washington who, by that time, was an aging but still effective football player. Washington insisted that Strode be hired as well.

You can read Dr. Stefani's full paper on www.thesportsjournal.org.

EXTRA: *Kenny Washington was the recipient of the Douglas Fairbanks Award as the outstanding player in college football in 1939.*

The Douglas Fairbanks Trophy was the Heisman Trophy before the Hesiman trophy. The Fairbanks was awarded from 1931 to 1941 and the Heisman then became the most prestigious award in college football after 1941.

Other winners of the Fairbanks Award were Jay Berwanger, also the 1st Heisman Winner in 1935, Whizzer White, Davey O'Brien 1940, Tom Harmon 1941.

Liberty Magazine *published the winner in its magazine and Liberty also announced the official All-American Team sanctioned by the NCAA at that time.*

There was a process, each player who played in college football in any given year was asked to vote on the best player at each position that they had faced in the season. They were also asked to vote for one outstanding player.

In 1939, it was unanimous, as all the players who filled in an outstanding player chose Kenny Washington as the winner.

One of the features of the Liberty team was that it was chosen by the players and not the "experts."

THE KING OF ETHIOPIA

Woody Strode is the Ram who had the most successful and extensive film career.

Strode is an icon as an African-American actor who blazed many trails.

You may not know him from his name but if you watched films in the 40s-90s you know who he is.

His first film role was in 1941 and his last in 1995.

In between he made over sixty films and appeared on many TV shows.

Strode often played African warriors as was apropos to his physical stature.

His two most famous roles were as Draba in *Spartacus* (1960), in which he is the Ethiopian gladiator who fights Spartacus, a role for which he was awarded a Golden Globe Nomination for Best Supporting Actor, and the title role in *Sergeant Rutledge* (1961) as a black soldier on the frontier.

Strode said the studio wanted a more bankable star to play Sergeant Rutledge, like Sidney Poitier or Harry Belafonte, but director John Ford insisted on Strode. Ford said he needed someone tougher than the studio favorites. Ford and Strode became very close friends.

Strode spent the last four weeks of Ford's life sleeping on Ford's floor as his caretaker in the director's waning days. He was with Ford at the moment of his death. Strode said that John Ford treated him as he would a son.

As Sergeant Rutledge, it can only be imagined what went through the minds of African-Americans in movie houses all over the United States as they watched Strode in the role.

This is the way Strode described a part of the film: "I had the greatest Glory Hallelujah ride across the Pecos River that any black man ever had on screen and I did it myself. I carried the whole black race across the river."

Strode grew up in Los Angeles and said he was insulated from the institutional racism of the rest of the country. He was introduced to the racist nature of American society only when he became an athlete and traveled around the country, being denied access to restaurants and hotels.

Strode had quite a life.

Football star, movie star, he married a Hawaiian princess and became an icon.

Woody in *Toy Story* is thought to be named after Woody Strode.

He was hired by Cecil B. DeMille to play a slave in *The Ten Commandments* for $500 a week. The actor who was to play the King of Ethiopia became unavailable.

DeMille auditioned Strode by asking, "Show me your legs." Strode said he dropped his pants and Demille then said, "Congratulations son, you have just become the King of Ethiopia"

PERSONAL NOTE:

When my father, Ed Champagne, went to LA, his first experience at training camp was to be asked to scrimmage right off the plane.

He put on his uniform and walked to the practice field. He told me he had to pass through a large room that was evidently the Rams scouting draft war room and he saw a list of players from that year's draft on the wall. At the top of one list he saw his name: Ed Champagne, LSU, best defensive tackle in America.

My dad was a big guy (for that time, anyway), almost 6'4" and about 245 lbs. but he was known for his quickness.

On the first play of his professional career he lined up at DT next to Woody Strode. Strode playfully called him "Wine." He asked my Dad who was going to get to the quarterback first. My father said, "I am." Strode then shook his head and said, "No, Wine, nobody gets to the QB in this league quicker than me."

The ball was snapped and my dad knocked the living crap out of Bob Waterfield, the highest paid player in the league.

My dad told me, "I thought I committed murder. Everyone was screaming and asking me what I was doing!"

"I just tackled the man with the ball."

He didn't know you didn't hit the highest-paid player in the league in practice.

Strode, as they got back into the defensive huddle, told him,

"You alright, Wine, you just like me. Quick and fast."

SAN FRANCISCO

SayBrah

SHORT-HAIR CAT

SAN FRANCISCO

DE

LIL WAYNE, LOUISIANA POLITICS, AND ORGANIZED CRIME

SAN FRANCISCO

"The NFL, like life, is full of idiots."
—Randy Cross
Niners OL ('76-88)

SayBrah®

The 49ers were formed in 1946 as a member of the AAFC becoming the first major professional franchise located on the West Coast. The 49ers were one of three teams absorbed into the NFL in 1950 when the AAFC folded.

In 1977, Edward DeBartolo, Jr. (HOF class of 2016) took ownership of the franchise. DeBartolo hired Bill Walsh as his head coach, and the 49ers organization flourished.

After an extortion plot by Louisiana governor Edwin Edwards, DeBartolo stepped down as CEO and the team has been operated by his sister's family since 2000.

Super Bowl Appearances: 7
Super Bowl Record: 5-2 ('81, '84, '88, '89, '94)
Super Bowl Loss: 2012, 2019

TRAGEDY

Tony Morabito was a San Francisco guy. Played football on empty lots in North Beach. Made his business a success in the middle of the American Century and had a dream. He believed that with the advent of easy air travel, San Francisco was ripe to join the world of professional sports.

He approached the NFL in 1942. They rejected him and his idea of a West Coast team.

He tried again and was again rebuffed.

This time however, the beautiful thing that is competition raised its head. In Chicago, where NFL Commissioner Elmer Layden pooh-poohed Tony's idea of a California franchise, there was a move afoot to start a new league that would become the All American Football Conference.

Tony got his San Francisco franchise in the AAFC.

The first game was September 8, 1946, in San Francisco.

The 49ers, the first major sports team on the West Coast, and was one of the three franchises that the NFL absorbed when the AAFC folded in 1949.

There was no love lost between Tony and the NFL. He was controversial for actions like chasing the owner of the LA franchise around in the locker room looking for a fight after one game.

In 1950 Tony Morabito's doctor told him that football was bad for his health. He had a heart attack in 1953 and was warned then that the excitement of the game was too much for his heart and that he should give up the team.

That wasn't Tony's style. In fact, he is quoted as saying if he was going to die it might as well be at a football game.

So it was on October 27, 1957, with his team the San Francisco 49ers playing the Chicago Bears at Kezar Stadium, trailing 14-7, that Tony had a heart attack in his 50-yard line seats in the lower press box.

He was given the last rights in the stadium and pronounced dead at the hospital as the game continued.

The 49ers, trailing 17-7, were told of Tony's death at the half.

They went out and defeated the Bears, 21-17 behind quarterback Y. A. Tittle.

In the locker room, the man, Tony Morabito, who never got along too well with the NFL brass, calling NFL Commissioner Bert Bell "the quintessence of nothing," brought his football players to tears.

His players loved him.

DNA

In 2016 the San Francisco 49ers had a partnership with a biologic startup named Orig3n to collect blood samples from fans attending 49ers home games to help with the LifeCapsule, the world's largest crowd sourced cell repository on human genome research, to allegedly assist with treatment for a rare genetically inherited disease.

The samples taken from fans would be used to generate pluripotent stem cells of livers and hearts.

Sure. Why not? It was only a matter of time before they wanted to harvest the fans' bodily fluids.

Orig3n claims it can measure your DNA to see if you are more likely to be linebacker or quarterback material.

Experts in the field are skeptical.

8,000 free DNA kits were to be given to all 49er fans in 2017 for use via cheek swabbing to measure three different genes.

The Baltimore Ravens had a similar promotion scheduled but before it happened, the Maryland Department of Health Commissioner stopped it over what was deemed privacy issues.

Booths were set up at Levi's stadium for 49er fans to avail themselves of the offer and the California Health Department started an investigation to look into the possible ramifications dealing with potential privacy issues,

Brother, this is not your Grandma's NFL.

NO FREE LUNCH

Tim Kawakami is a sports writer who covered the 49ers.

He had a bet with 49er CEO Jed York that Kawakami would spring for lunch in Napa Valley if the 49ers built a stadium in Santa Clara by September of 2014.

Stadiums almost never open on time.

Well, this one did. So York, the grandson of the guy who bought the 49ers from the Morabito family in 1977, took up Kawakami on his wager.

A bet's a bet, a deal is a deal and so on.

No problem, Kawakami was on board.

Only thing is, the bill for lunch turned out to be $2,100.

Kawakami revealed the details on a podcast some time later and said he doesn't think York was trying to stick it to him, but that York is just oblivious to what it means for a working stiff to cough up $2,100 for one lunch.

To hear Kawakami's version, York texted him before the meal to ask if his wife could come and that he, York, would pay for her, and Kawakami said sure.

Two others joined, they paid for theirs, and when the bill came, York didn't even pay for his wife or help with the $500 tip.

Later York, whose net worth is $100 million, issued a statement saying that if Tim wants to talk about it, we can, so we can move on.

FREE FOOD

If you want to spot a 49er player out and about you could do a lot worse than to try to get a burger and a beer at the Canyon Inn in Emerald Hills California. It's a good bet that every 49er from the glory years of 1981 to 1988 have all been there.

In 1972 Tim Harrsion spotted an empty 7-11 store and thought it would be a choice spot to open a bar and grill. He rented the property and with the help of his friends turned it into the Canyon Inn.

The Canyon Inn is less than a mile from the practice facility that the 49ers used from 1956-1986 so Tim thought it would be nice to maybe do a promotion to get the 49ers to come over and have a burger or a beer. It would be fun and good for business.

He met with 49er great R. C. Owens who worked in the 49er front office as a liaison to business and other groups. Owens gave Harris this advice.

"There was no way in hell he would get them to come by unless he offered free food,"

Harris then made an offer to the 49ers that anyone in the organization could come by for free food the day after a 49er victory.

The next Monday after a 49er win Harris came to the Canyon Inn to find a line of 49er employees and players waiting for the place to open.

An NFL organization has many employees. That translates into a lot of hamburgers. Harris had special cards printed for the 49ers that would make it easier for them to claim the free grub.

Harris said that the idea has been a rousing success for his business. 49er players still patronize the Inn and the place is kind of a 49er shrine with 49er memorabilia and player sightings as a draw.

The three years before the offer the 49ers won only a total of 10 games, The next eight years they won 80 games.

STRATEGY

On November 23, 1958 the San Francisco 49'ers went into Green Bay to play the Packers.

At some point an unidentified Green Bay Packer fan managed to spike the 49er water coolers with scotch.

The somewhat inebriated 49ers won the game 33-12.

CANADA

Right as the 49ers, led by Joe Montana, commenced their game winning drive in Super Bowl XXIII Montana went up to one of his offensive linemen, Harris Barton, and told him, "Hey, there's John Candy in the stands."

Then they went ahead and scored the winning touchdown.

Three years later John Candy, the comedian known for many film roles such as in *Stripes* and as a member of the *SCTV* cast, tried to sign Montana to a Canadian Football League contract.

Candy was a humongous CFL fan. He was part owner of the Toronto Argonauts until his death at forty-three in 1994.

Wayne Gretzky and Bruce McNall, two of the owners of the Argonauts, were all onboard to lure the aging Montana from the 49ers to Canada.

Montana did eventually change teams but he ended up in Kansas City, not Canada.

The Argonauts had lured Rocket Ismail, the Heisman Trophy runner-up, to sign out of college and they took a swing at a bigger prize in Montana but it didn't work out.

CUISINE

The San Francisco 49ers of 1970-72 issued a recipe book of the players favorite recipes.

One players' favorite recipe: "1 package of Stouffer's Frozen Lasagna. Open package, remove cover from lasagna. Prepare as per directions on the back of the package."

SAFE SPACE

In 2018 the San Francisco 49er were the first NFL team to have an official emotional support animal, a French Bulldog puppy, they named Zoe.

DL Solomon Thomas had lost a sister to suicide and was dealing with depression and Austin Moss the team director of player engagement then adopted Zoe to serve as a positive fun way to help the players with stress depression and anxiety in what is a high pressure business.

Zoe is a big hit with the players as she looms in the locker room at practice and other spots in the 49er facility serving as a soothing comforting presence to provide what can be called a safe space for the players to be themselves and relax.

Zoe doesn't travel with the team but she's always there to welcome them back.

Jack Kirby is an American icon for his work with a staggering number of comic book vehicles, many of which eventually leapt to the silver screen. His collaboration with Stan Lee helped Marvel get to the top of the comic book food chain.

Kirby was called upon by the NFL, in a little remembered enterprise, to create futuristic NFL player images and uniforms in 1973.

Kirby's time-traveling uniforms appeared in *Pro! Magazine*, the program that was sold at NFL games.

Among the teams Kirby created uniforms for were the 49ers, Browns, Giants, and Packers. Kirby created *Captain America*, the *X-Men*, *The Fantastic Four*, *The Incredible Hulk,* and too many others to mention.

Check out the images here:

🌐 www.grayflannelsuit.net/blog/jack-kirby-1973-NFL-artwork-fantastic-trippy-hell

EWE

Until Drew Brees and Sean Payton showed up in New Orleans, the Saints were one of the least successful franchises in NFL history.

The team was awarded to New Orleans in a celebrated political deal with the Louisiana Congressional delegation which had a lot of stick in 1966, headed by Senator Russell Long, Huey's son.

When the Saints became competitive under coach Jim Mora Sr., there was one team in their way. They were in the same conference as the San Francisco 49ers in the hey-day of Montana. The 49ers were in the midst of their Super Bowl winning years.

The Saints had a great defense but, alas, it was not to be.

Enter Louisiana politics.

In 1998 the federal government convicted former Louisiana Governor, Edwin W. Edwards, of extortion and other crimes that got him ten years in federal prison.

49ers owner Edward DeBartolo Jr. was also involved. He pled guilty, was fined $1 million and testified against Edwards.

The NFL suspended him and it was thought DeBartolo lost the 49ers due to this escapade, that dealt with the improper awarding of riverboat gambling licenses. DeBartolo, who was suspended only one year by the NFL, claims he voluntarily gave control of the 49ers to his sister and her family for personal wishes to spend more time with his family.

The 49ers won five Super Bowls under DeBartolo's leadership. They have a record of going 141-168 since he left.

EWE, as Edwards is known, theoretically did what the Saints couldn't.

NOTE: *In 2020, President Donald Trump pardoned Eddie DeBartolo.*

THE GREATEST?

Charlie Powell was a great athlete.

At San Diego High he won twelve varsity letters for baseball, football, track and basketball.

He was offered scholarships to Notre Dame and USC but instead signed a contract with the St. Louis Browns to play minor league baseball and later went right to the NFL as a nineteen-year-old, the youngest player ever to play in the NFL.

In his first game against the Detroit Lions he was credited with 10 sacks.

At 6'4" and 230 he was a DL who had run a 9.6 100 yd. dash in high school.

And, oh yeah, he was offered a contract with the Harlem Globetrotters coming out of high school.

There's more.

He played for the 49ers for five seasons but he also found time to become a professional boxer.

As a pre-teen, he would get up and go over to Archie Moore's house and train as a boxer. Moore lived in the neighborhood and was the longest reigning World Light Heavyweight champion of all time and considered pound for pound one of the greatest boxers ever.

In 1959, near the end of his NFL career, Powell knocked out Nino Vades, a Cuban heavyweight who was ranked #2 in the world. The Earth.

This led to a bout with the Heavyweight Champion of the World, then known as Cassius Clay.

Powell lost—knocked out in round three.

He got paid $12,000 for the fight, more than he ever made in one season of salary as an NFL player.

Resume?

"THE HATCHET"

Innovation is an American trait forged throughout our history.

It may take many forms.

Hardy Brown was a LB who was one such innovator and unfortunately not everyone was happy about it.

His innovation was a kind of personal Krav Maga technique, displayed on the football field. Brown was one of only two players who played in the AAFC, NFL and AFL and was known as the "The Hatchet."

His trademark "shoulder push" as he called it was LB Brown launching himself at the last second to hit the ball carrier with his shoulder usually aimed at the bridge of the nose for best effect.

He is pretty much considered the roughest player in NFL history. That's a mouthful.

However, it seems to fit pretty well as Brown by his own reckoning knocked about eighty opposing players unconscious on the field in his pro football career.

Y. A. Tittle, a teammate of Brown's, claims the count of twenty-three players that Brown knocked out in the 1951 season.

He was so feared and hated that the LA Rams put a $500 bounty on his head to anyone who could put him out of the game. This at a time when $500 could buy you a new automobile.

In a game against the Washington Redskins he knocked the entire backfield, but for quarterback Harry Gilmer, out of the game.

He was once searched by the officials at halftime to make sure he did not have a metal plate in his shoulder pads.

To give you an idea of what went on when Hardy Brown was on the loose, take the case of running back Joe Geri of the Pittsburgh Steelers. Geri said that he had heard of Brown but didn't believe the stories. During the game that Geri got to experience Hardy Brown for himself, Brown came in with his shoulder push and hit Geri right in the face, no facemasks, with his shoulder. Dazed, Geri asked a teammate if it was bad?"

The answer, "Well, your eye is out."

The eye was said to be hanging from a tendon.

Brown was so dangerous that his coach with the 49ers would ban him from practice to make sure he didn't hurt his own teammates.

Hardy Brown's story is an interesting study.

As a four-year-old he saw his father, a bootlegger, gunned down by several shots and murdered in front of him. Four months later he was in the room when one of the men who had murdered his father, a rival bootlegger, was also murdered.

At this point Brown's mother put him, at age five, and his other siblings into the Texas Masonic Home, an orphanage where he grew up and where he excelled for the Mighty Mites football team that went to the state playoffs three times during Browns' years at the school.

A book by Jim Dent, *Twelve Mighty Mites : The Inspiring True Story of the Mighty Mites Who Ruled Texas Football,* tells the story of the high school team that Brown played on.

1953 the 49ers were playing the Philadelphia Eagles. The Eagles are said to be pissed about one of Hardy's previous shots on one of their players. They go after Hardy. They go after Hardy's teammate Charlie Powell. Bad choice all around. Powell was a world-class boxer. The Eagles then go after Hugh McIlhenny, the HOF running back.

Next thing ya know all hell breaks loose, everyone the players, the benches, anyone on the field, even spectators swarmed onto the field according to some accounts were in the midst of a melee. Officials try to stem the fighting. No luck as the crowd pummels the refs as well.

Charlie Powell all 6'2", 230 pounds of him, a guy who was a professional boxer who would go on to knock out the #2 contender for the heavyweight crown and a guy who would fight Muhammad Ali for the heavyweight crown runs to join the fray.

Powell comes up to Bobby Walston, 6', 190lbs of tight end and the place-kicker of the Eagles.

Walston, who had fought collegiately at University of Georgia, lands his only punch, a left hook that connects and Powell goes down like a ton of bricks,according to Tom Brookshier, DB with the Eagle at the time. One punch.

Turns out Walston was a tough guy. Walston just said it was a lucky punch.

Walston was a deputy sheriff in Georgia in the off-season who chased moonshiners around the roads of Georgia in what was described as "a souped up Chevy."

As the fight continued for about fifteen minutes unabated, thinking quickly Joe McTigue leader of the 49ers band strikes up a rendition of the National Anthem and the crowd hearing the Star Spangled Banner is calmed. Game continues, 49ers win.

A quaint glimpse of 1950's NFL action in those halcyon days when Hardy Brown was the most feared dude in the forest.

Brown died in a nursing home from dementia. His infamous shoulder was so racked with arthritis he could not raise his arm to scratch his head.

 https://nfl.com/videos/nfl-network-top-ten/09000d8117b47/top-ten-feared-tacklers-hardy-brown

https://www.youtube.com/watch?v=TeJFEf7JfUA

MEOW

Jim Burt played at a high level in the NFL as a big DL. He spent his last years playing for the 49ers. When players are traded or leave in free agency their new team often asks them for scouting information when they play against their old team.

Burt was asked by the 49ers for some inside info on the Giants when they were about to meet his old team. Burt told the 49ers that there was a Giants OL who had a strong fear of cats.

When the teams lined up across the scrimmage line, the 49er players, on cue, started to meow and make other cat noises.

There was no reaction.

They ratcheted it up. Louder meows as the game went along.

There were a lot of perplexed Giants and some frustrated 49ers as things progressed.

Burt had pulled a fast one. There was no such player with a fear of cats.

NAME GAME

Kyle Shanahan, head coach of the San Francisco 49ers, is a big fan of Lil Wayne.

How big? He named his son Carter.

Lil Wayne's name is Carter. As in *Tha Carter I,II,III,IV,V*—titles of his CDs.

Shanahan's wife liked the name Carter and it came to pass.

Pierre Garcon, wide receiver for the 49ers, knew of Shanahan's love of Lil Wayne and is a friend of the hip hop artist.

Garcon arranged to get the news to Lil Wayne who sent Shanahan autographed copies of both *Tha Carter III* and *Tha Carter IV*.

He sent the radio version, no cuss words.

The players on the 49ers like hip hop in the locker room and some say it helps them relate to coach Shanahan.

TMC

Joey Bosa followed his brother Nick into the NFL as a first round draft choice in 2019.

Joey became the 7th member of his family to make it in the NFL.

A tough group, no doubt.

You ain't heard nothing yet.

In a *Sports Illustrated* article about the Bosas, who both came into the league after playing at Ohio State, it is revealed that Nick and Joey's great grandfather was Tony Accardo.

Who, you may ask?

Well, Tony Accardo is considered to be the most powerful organized crime figure of the 20th Century.

Kind of the Don Corleone of real life.

He started working the streets at 14. At some point he got a job as a bodyguard of Al Capone.

He once dove in front of Capone to save him from a barrage of machine gun fire.

Tony is thought to be involved in the Valentine's Day Massacre, but not proven.

In the movie, *The Untouchables*, there is a scene where a Capone underling takes a guy outside and beats him to death with a baseball bat. That was based on Tony Accardo in real life, for which Capone gave Tony one of his nicknames, "Joey Batters."

Accardo was also known for his brains. Although not educated in school, he was street smart and thought to have a photographic memory.

When Capone went to prison and Frank Nitti, Capone's successor, did as well, and still another mob boss died, Accardo eventually rose to be the MAN. He reigned, more or less, for 40 years as the guy in charge of the Outfit, as the Chicago Mob was called.

His business acumen led the group into new fields, changed some operations, and jettisoned others, basically modernizing the business model.

He died in his sleep, never having spent a night in jail even though he had 22 documented arrests.

Cinematic life.

The scene from *The Godfather* when the FBI takes down license plates at a mob party is based on true events at a July 4th party Accardo used to throw.

Here is a link to the *SI* article.

It includes vengeance and blow torching of faces.

🌐 https://www.si.com/nfl/2019/05/02/tony-accafrdo-mobster-great-grandfather-nick-joey-bosa

PHILADELPHIA

SayBrah®

DIANA, PRINCESS OF WALES   PHILADELPHIA   FS

PRINCESS DI,
GUANGDONG PROVINCE,
AND STAR WARS

PHILADELPHIA

"[NFL Hall-of Fame cornerback Deion Sanders] couldn't tackle my wife."
—Chuck Bednarik
Eagles C/LB (1949-62)

SayBrah

In 1898 the Frankford Athletic Association was formed and the Frankford Yellow Jackets entered the NFL in 1933.

Frankford's franchise was transferred to Bert Bell and moved to Philadelphia where they became the Eagles in 1934.

Super Bowl Appearances: 3
Super Bowl Record: 1-2 (2017)
Losses: 1980, 2004

CHRISTMAS in PHILADELPHIA

December 15, 1968. Though the Eagles have an abysmal record, 54,000 and more come out to cheer on the beloved "Iggles."

Management decided to hire a guy to be Santa Claus. Christmas was coming up and all. Santa for hire is a no show. A fan named Frank Olivo had worn his own homemade Santa costume to the game. Thinking on their feet, Eagles management recruit Frank. He agrees. The fans boo and for good measure pelt Frank with snowballs.

This incident is one of the defining symbolic moments of Philadelphia cultural lore. They will never live it down. Yet, Mr. Olivo, Santa for a day, had this to say about that day and the Philadelphia Eagles, "I'm a Philadelphia fan. I knew what's what. I thought it was funny."

He later added that he thought Philadelphia Eagles fans were the greatest fans in the world.

GMAN

Davey O'Brien entered TCU as the backup quarterback to the legendary Sammy Baugh. After Baugh graduated, "Little Davey," as he was called for his 5'7" 150lb stature, all he would do after succeeding Baugh at TCU was to break Slingin' Sammy's passing record and, in 1938, lead TCU to an undefeated season culminating in a Sugar Bowl victory against Carnegie Tech, giving the Horned Frogs the National Championship. O'Brien became the first college football player to win the Heisman Trophy, The Walter Camp Award and the Maxwell Trophy in the same season. His supporters from TCU actually hired a stage coach to bring O'Brien to the Downtown Athletic Club in New York City to receive his Heisman.

Drafted by the Philadelphia Eagles, he was named Rookie of the Year, All Pro, and broke the NFL passing yards record. He was rewarded by the Philadelphia Eagles with a contract that made him the highest paid player in the NFL. Yet, after the 1940 season at the height of his career, he quit to become an FBI agent. He served as an FBI agent until 1950 when he went into private business. In the FBI he, among other things, was a firearms instructor at Quantico, Va.

After his untimely death from cancer, the Dave O'Brien Award was named after him and is given to the most outstanding quarterback in college football every year.

GO GREEN

In 2003, the Philadelphia Eagles started recycling efforts in its administration offices in a continuing effort to Go Green and offset the team's carbon emission footprint. In 2007, the Eagle Forest in nearby Neshaminy State Park was established with the Eagles planting hundreds of trees.

Players and former players have chipped in to plant trees in the forest over the years since and there is an initiative to plant 10 trees for every field goal the Eagles kick every season. It is estimated that the tree planting has offset 7,500 tons of CO_2 in two years.

JAIL

At a *MNF* game in Philadelphia against the 49er's in 1998 there were sixty fist fights in the stands.

The Eagles decided that things like this were getting out of hand so the city of Philadelphia and the Eagles put a courtroom and jail in the stadium to be in session during Eagles' home games. The jail has since shut down and been moved to an off site on game days.

The first game it was in session twenty cases were heard.

Judge Seamus McCaffery, one of the presiding judges had this to say about the court and jail,

"Eagles Court was a lot of fun and it served its purpose. One of the interesting facts that came out of Eagles Court was that 95% of the people arrested were not from Philadelphia. But Philadelphia was getting broad brushed as the city with horrible fans."

The truth will set you free.

IT'S A SNAP

Jon Dorenbos was twelve-years-old when his dad bid him goodbye in the morning on his way to school and by mid day Jon got word that his father had shot and killed his mother.

In less than a day Jon was for all practical purposes an orphan.

He was put into a series of foster homes and eventually adopted by his aunt and uncle.

Life can take sharp hurtful turns quickly and the human spirit can be versatile and strong.

Also fragile.

Jon became an honor roll student and an outstanding athlete in high school, winning several letters in a variety of sports.

His football career led him to UTEP where he became a long snapper and, at the NFL combine, one veteran scout called him the best long snapping prospect he had ever seen.

Still he was not drafted. He signed with Buffalo and played 14 seasons with the Philadelphia Eagles. He was traded to New Orleans but a routine physical found he had an aneurysm and he was operated on and his career was over.

As a child, Jon found a way to cope with daily existence and his own personal baggage he had experienced with magic. He learned and performed tricks.

As an adult, he appeared on America's Got Talent and was a finalist for his skill as a magician.

Jon, now in retirement from the NFL, is a professional magician perform-ing in front of large crowds, and is a motivational speaker sharing his unique and inspirational journey with others.

🌐 https://www.youtube.com/watchv?=yeYvdijgK-M

CAPTIVE AUDIENCE

Meek Mill is a popular rapper from Philly. His music was played by players in the locker room during the season that they went to and won the Super Bowl. Alshon Jeffery played it in the Eagles' locker room after the Vikings win that sent the team to the Super Bowl. Jeffery posted the team celebrating with the song that night.

Fast forward slightly to the night of the Eagles' victory over Tom Brady and the New England Patriots. Meek Mill watched the Super Bowl that night from prison. The State Correctional Institution, Chester, Pennsylvania. He was there two to four years for a parole violation.

HIGH ROLLER

The NFL is proud of its charitable partnerships and indeed the NFL fran-chise in Philadelphia was at ground zero on creating one of the more visible charities of our time.

The first Ronald McDonald House built to give families with children be-ing treated for cancer a safe place to stay while going through the challenges of the deadly disease was built in Philadelphia and the Eagles were instrumental in building the first house as well as giving impetus to the concept.

Ronald McDonald House is now a well known institution with over 350 houses in forty countries.

An oncologist in Philadelphia, Dr. Audry Evans had the idea that such a facility was badly needed. At that same time a player on the Eagles, Ken Hill's daughter was diagnosed with childhood leukemia and the Eagles were raising funds to help Hill and his family.

One thing led to another and owner Leonard Tose, known as a very gener-ous man, wrote the check that bought the first house.

The project took off when Eagles GM Jim Murray approached the Elkman Ad Agency of Philadelphia with an idea to have McDonald's donate twen-ty-five cents from the sale of every Shamrock Shake at their fast food restau-rants in the Philadelphia area.

McDonald's regional manager Ed Rensi signed on with the agreement that McDonald's could name the house.

Tose wrote the check and the rest is history.

Tose was one of a hundred Philadelphia area residents who plunked down $3,000 each to buy the Eagles in 1949. They were called the Happy Hundred.

Tose eventually bought the Eagles himself in 1969 for a record at the time of $16,155,000.

He ended up selling the team in 1985 for $65 million.

Tose was a compulsive gambler and alcoholic by his own admission. The reason he sold the Eagles in 1985 was due to his heavy debt from his gambling losses.

When Tose sold the Eagles he had been in negotiation with buyers in Phoenix to move the team to Arizona. The league sued Tose and a day long meeting called by Commissioner Pete Rozelle resulted in Tose selling the team with a promise that the new buyer would keep the team in Philadelphia.

Tose lived an extravagant over the top life.

He flew to Eagles games in a helicopter. He and his wife had his and hers Rolls Royces.

Tose, by almost every account was a beloved man. His players loved him. Many visited him on his deathbed. He was generous, he constantly gave to charities and helped others financially. He lived his last days in a hotel after his mansion was foreclosed on, the hotel paid for by former Eagles GM Murray, a man Tose had once fired and other friends.

Tose's problems stemmed from his gambling. He was a legendary gambler. He was known to play 7 hands of black jack at a time betting up to $10,000 a hand. He lost 100's of thousands of dollars in one night of gambling on numerous occasions. Tose himself estimated he gambled away anywhere from $40 to 50 million in his lifetime.

Of special note is this, throughout his tumultuous life of drinking and gambling he was never accused of betting on the NFL.

EAGLES FILM FEST PART 1—MUMMER ANGRY

Jason Kelce, offensive lineman for the Philadelphia Eagles, gave what is described as an epic speech before a victory parade in 2018 after the Eagles won the Super Bowl. Kelce, bedecked in a colorful Philadelphia Mummer costume before the backdrop of the Philadelphia Art Museum (which is where the Rocky statue is), and before a throng of the Philadelphia faithful, lets it all hang out.

WARNING: vulgar language alert. It is Philadelphia.

⊕ www.youtube.com/watch?v+UqBnNxDkKSl

EAGLES FILM FEST PART 2—A KICK

Husband and wife bet on the game. She, Dallas fan. He, Eagles fan. Dallas wins. He loses. This is why they call them fans.

⊕ www.youtube.com/watch?time-continue=16&v=rVjRPLhCrc8

The Eagles win the Super Bowl over Patriots. Eagles fans celebrate. Do not read any further if you have a delicate stomach.

WARNING!!! No, I'm not kidding!

WARNING!!!! Ok, you've been warned.

Fan eats something that you would not eat with somebody else's face.

🌐 www.youtube.com/watch?=iXRL1-FV_98

EVE

The 1926 Frankford Yellow Jackets, the franchise that would morph into the Eagles, hired two teams of women to play football as halftime entertainment.

The history of football for women is spotty at best.

In 1896 a group of Princeton and Yale men had a party in New York City in which two teams of five women each played a version of tackle football wearing sailor suits and short dresses. This seems to have been more of an entertainment than a true attempt to play the game. Nonetheless the game was quite a sensation it seems with police having to intervene to keep the scene from getting out of hand.

The year before the Yellow Jackets halftime promotion Gladys Scherer of Upsala College had her photo appear all over the U.S. in the newspaper when she was selected captain of the women's 11 at Upsala. The only problem was that Upsala could not find another women's team to play.

In 1930 two teams in Toledo, in "the Tigris and Euphrates of Pro Football" as one scribe labeled Ohio, went on a barnstorming tour that was cut short when the First Lady of the United States Lou Hoover complained in a widely circulated letter that she felt as if the promoters of the tour were exploiting womanhood. This brought the enterprise to a halt.

In 1939 two women's softball teams in Los Angeles were formed into football teams.

Softball at that time was a big draw as a women's sport. The women's team soon gave up football because the softball gig was more appealing from an opportunity to travel abroad and to get movie roles and such.

One of the women softball players said at that time that the women would let the men play football and beat their brains out in what turned out to be a somewhat prophetic toss away line.

In the 1960's promoters started to attempt to have women's professional league and there have been many since then but it never seems to catch on.

In 1970 Patricia Palinkas became the first woman to appear in a men's professional football game as a holder for the Orlando Panthers,

She successfully held on two out of three kicks.

On her first try the snap was a bit high and off center and she dropped the ball only to be leveled by a large defensive player who afterward said he was trying to knock her brains out, because he felt she was making a mockery of a men's sport.

Nice.

This was not a universal sentiment among men as can be seen in a CBS report of the event, narrated by Walter Cronkite. In the short piece her teammates are observed as being incredibly supportive throughout.

CRIME OF THE CENTURY

Bert Bell was the guy who founded the Eagles and picked the name after Roosevelt's NRA Eagle symbol. He was also the Commissioner of the NFL.

If you doubt the scope and depth of NFL gravitas as it relates to our society chew on this little gem.

Bell was born into a very prominent Philadelphia family and played football at Penn. He was a sporting man of means acquainted in the roaring twenties with all sorts including gamblers and mobsters as they often traveled in the same circles.

As Commissioner of the NFL his son said Bell had a telephone line at his home that kept him in touch with gamblers as a means to keep him informed of any hanky-panky that might be going as to betting on NFL games.

When the Lindbergh baby was kidnapped the police spoke to Bert Bell and asked him to go to Sing Sing to ask Al Capone if the mob was involved. Bell knew Capone from back in the day.

Bell did go to Sing Sing to speak to Capone.

In twenty-four hours Capone through whatever communication was at his disposal assured Bell that the mob was not involved.

KLAATU BARADA NIKTO

When David Acord a sound designer and re recording mixer was tasked with making up a language for a reptile-like alien named Teedo, in 2015's *Star Wars: The Force Awakens*, he slipped in these words for Teedo to say: "Celek" and "Fletcher."

Brent Celek, TE for Philadelphia Eagles and Fletcher Cox DE for Philadelphia Eagles.

Acord, a graduate of Delaware University and an Eagles fan was planning a trip to Thailand so he slipped in a mixture of Thai with the Eagles players' names.

And get this.

Ya know when Cassian Andor and Jyn Erso are looking for Saw Gerrera in Jedha City in *Rogue One: A Star Wars Story*?

No? Well, even if ya don't, Mr. Acord made the prayer chant in that scene in the words from the Eagles fight song, "Fly, Eagles, Fly"—but in Esperanto.

Nice job.

BRAVE NEW WORLD

Leading up to the 2018 Super Bowl, if you went all high tech and asked Amazon's Alexa or Apple's Siri who would win the big game, you'd get a split decision. Alexa went with the Eagles, even chanting at the end of the answer, "E-A-G-L-E-S, Eagles!"

Siri, on the other hand, said, "Those in the know say the Patriots will defeat the Eagles by five points."

Alexa's reasoning was, "I'm flying high with the Eagles on this one because of their relentless defense and the momentum they've been riding. And their underdog status."

These are the answers you would get no matter what locale you were in.

In case you were wondering.

CAMELOT

In 1962, the Philadelphia Eagles were for sale for $6 million. John F. Kennedy was interested in buying them. Yes, he was President of the United States at the time. He called his brothers, Ted and Bobby, and asked them if they would go in for a third each. They agreed.

However, on second or third thought, the fact that Jack was President of the United States made the deal iffy. So, the purchase never came to pass.

Indeed conflict of interest came into play when John F. Kennedy as President of the United States signed into law the Sporting Broadcast Act Of 1961 which allowed the league to bundle franchises for the purpose of selling TV rights which opened up the gate for vast riches to NFL owners.

It can be argued that this legislation signed into law by JFK is the most important piece of legislation in NFL history.

It allowed sports teams to circumvent the Sherman Antitrust Act.

The man who sponsored the bill was U.S. Congressman Emmanuel Cellar D-NY. Maybe Mr. Cellar should be enshrined at Canton.

If JFK had owned the Eagles it would have been a blatant self serving act to sign the Sports Act into law.

PRINCESSES

People Magazine once had a cover photo of Princess Di wearing an Eagles jacket.

What? How?

Credit a Philadelphia radio network dude named Jack Edelstein, a man about town, who it is said once dated Marilyn Monroe. Once hung out with Don Rickles and Jerry Lewis. Back in the day, that was some highfalutin company.

Edelstein met Princess Di at the funeral of Princess Grace of Monaco. Edelstien was friends with Philadelphian Jack Kelly, whose sister just happened to be Grace Kelly, a Philadelphia girl.

So, Edelstien and Di chatted about sports teams among other things and as it turned out the Eagles colors green and silver were Princess Di's favorite colors, one thing leads to another, Jack Kelly sends Princess Di a nice Eagles jacket supplied by the team. She likes it. Supposedly wore it a lot.

Next thing ya know it's on *People Magazine's* cover.

Fashion decisions are made.

Etc, etc, etc...

GUANGDONG PROVINCE

Philadelphia Eagles defeat the Atlanta Falcons in the 2017-18 NFL playoffs. That morning in Guangdong Province, the People's Republic of China, Jason Lee checked his laptop.

On a usual day his company, CreepyParty, sold ten lifelike German Shepard masks.

Lee was astonished when he saw that overnight he had sold 230 German Shepard masks. His entire inventory, as it turns out. He was a bit perplexed until he figured it out.

After the Eagles had upset the Falcons, Eagles players Chris Long and Lance Johnson, miffed over being slight underdogs to the Falcons, donned German Shepard masks as they walked off the field to gloat over the fact that they, as underdogs, had won. The rest is dog mask history.

Lee and a friend had started CreepyParty in a rented house in a basement. The American dream is alive in places like China. They ran out of German Shepherd masks and started selling other breeds. When people started scurrying around Philadelphia looking for dog masks, they were disappointed when they could not find CreepyParty masks. Brand, don't ya know, matters in all things. So popular were the dog masks from China that the Philadelphia Eagles had to waive the rule that did not allow fans to wear masks to the stadium for the game against the Vikings.

People in dog masks were all over the stadium the day they defeated the Vikings for their ticket to the Super Bowl. Lee and his friends celebrated their good fortune and the money they made as they prepared a few days later to celebrate the Chinese New Year.

The Year of the Dog.

TERREL OWENS UNAPPRECIATION NIGHT

Teams often run promotions to attract fans. The NFL doesn't have to do this as a rule, but it, the NFL, is an inspiration to others. To wit: The Atlantic City Surfs, an independent minor league baseball team, ran a promotion rooted in the dislike of Eagles star wide receiver Terrell Owens.

Terrell Owens Unappreciation Night was born. Those in attendance received a free whoopee cushion with Terrell's face on it. Hot dogs were 81¢... Owens wore number 81 with the Eagles. If you brought Terrell Owens memorabilia you got two free seats. After the game, the Terrell Owens memorabilia was exploded.

He was still with the team when this promotion went down.

NEW ENGLAND

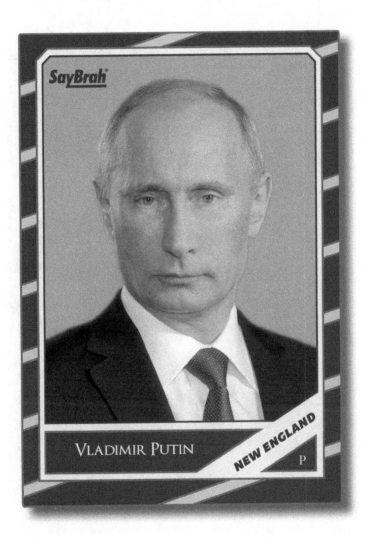

SayBrah®

VLADIMIR PUTIN

NEW ENGLAND

P.

A BIG FLUSH, NATURE CALLS, AND MICHAEL JACKSON

30 THE MOST INTERESTING LEAGUE IN THE WORLD

NEW ENGLAND

"I don't know. MyFace, YourFace, Insta-Face. Go talk to whoever you like that does that stuff, I don't know."
—Bill Belichick
Head Coach (2000-)

SayBrah®

In 1959, the AFL awarded Billy Sullivan their eighth and final AFL franchise. Christened Boston Patriots, the team began AFL play in 1960.

Throughout their years in the AFL, the Patriots were never able to claim a regular home. In 1979, two years after the Patriots' absorbtion into the NFL, the team moved to Schaefer Stadium in Foxboro, Massachusetts. In conjunction with the move, Sullivan changed the team from Boston Patriots to New England Patriots.

Robert Kraft took ownership of the franchise in 1994.

Super Bowl Appearances: 11
Super Bowl Record: 6-5 ('01, '03, '04, '14, '16, '18)
Losses: '85, '96, '07, '11, '17

HOLLYWOOD LUCK

The Farrelly Brothers film *There's Something About Mary* (1998) features Bret Favre as Mary's former boyfriend.

Ok? So, what does this have to do with the New England Patriots?

Bret was not the first choice of the Farrelly Bros. New England Patriot quarterback Drew Bledsoe was. Enter Rock N Roll.

The week before shooting of Drew's scenes in Florida, Drew and some of his teammates decided to attend an Everclear concert. Everclear, an alternative rock grunge band best known for its single "Wonderful," was performing in Boston, and Bledsoe, twenty-five at the time, and his friends, did what twenty-five-year olds do—they went to a rock concert. They were invited onstage.

Mosh pits were in session. Drew and the boys jumped off the stage and into the crowd. One of Drew's teammates that night was an offensive lineman. A woman in the crowd, according to press reports of the time, sustained neck, shoulder and arm injuries.

15 yards for unnecessary roughness? Not so much.

Very large American football players jumping on your head? Allegedly.

Lawsuits follow like night does day. Drew decided he can't make it to Florida for his close up. Which he later described as one of the biggest disappointments of his life.

The lady in the crowd was awarded a substantial settlement and Favre ended up in the movie.

But, Bret was not even the second choice.

That would be Steve Young. Young turned it down because of his Mormon faith, surmising that Mormon young people would go to see the movie and some of the content wouldn't be appropriate for Mormon youth. Good for Steve.

NEW FRONTIER

John F. Kennedy, when he was president, was known for his White House lawn and Hyannis Port touch football games with a passel of Kennedys and White House aides.

In the John F. Kennedy Presidential Library in Boston you'll find a curious letter on Boston Patriot stationery festooned with the old Minute Man in football pose logo in the upper left hand corner, that is addressed to John F. Kennedy the President of the United States.

The letter was sent in 1961 by Lou Saban, the head coach of the Patriots asking tongue in cheek no doubt if President Kennedy might lend his pass catching abilities to the Boston Patriots.

In the letter, Saban refers to JFK's prowess on the Harvard Touch football team.

However as it turns out according to *The Harvard Crimson* newspaper, John F. Kennedy, the future president of The United States played two years on the Harvard football team.

The coach at Harvard Henry Lamar is quoted as saying that John Kennedy is the most adept pass catcher on the Crimson 11 but that his lack of weight was a drawback. A photo of that Harvard team shows among his larger team-mates a small thin lad destined for great things.

EXTRA: *Senator Ted Kennedy also played end at Harvard. Ted caught TD passes against Yale in a 21-7 Harvard loss.*

GRAND THEFT JEWELRY

Sometimes networking backfires.

Robert Kraft, owner of the New England Patriots,was slumming through St Petersburg, Russia in 2005 and wrangled a meet up with the Fearless Leader of Russia, Vladimir Putin. Fake cordiality no doubt ensued. As Kraft was showing a friend, who was along for the schmoozing, his Super Bowl ring, the friend suggested Mr. Kraft show the ring to Putin.

Putin admired the ring. Vlad tried it on for size. At some point, according to Kraft, Valdimir Putin, fun guy that he is, told Kraft, "I could kill somebody with this ring." I don't know about you, but I believe him.

When Kraft asked for it back, Putin put it into his pocket and walked away with a KGB escort. What's a billionaire to do in a situation like that? Putin doesn't remember the incident or even meeting Kraft. Kraft at first claimed Putin stole the ring. Video seemed to back that up. Oh, that instant replay!

Kraft went to President George W. Bush who sent back word that Mr. Kraft, for international diplomatic reasons, should just admit it was a gift.

Kraft is a friend of Donald Trump. In fact, Kraft is said to have given a Super Bowl ring to President Trump in a visit to the White House. Trump doesn't get to keep it. The ring will be required to be given to a museum as its value is way over the accepted value of gifts that presidents may keep.

Even Senator John McCain asked Putin to give the ring back.

The Russians maintain it was a gift and that this story is weird, and mentioned that Mr. Kraft might need psychoanalysis.

It had been reported that Putin said he would have a replica made for Kraft. Kraft wants his ring back. Putin has nuclear weapons. Advantage Putin.

Meanwhile the ring—all $25,000, 124 diamonds, 49.4 carats of it—is said to be in the Kremlin Library. Putin, Trump, Super Bowl rings, George W. Bush, and Rupert Murdoch—who is in the photo of the ring theft.

Only Alex Jones can truly explain it.

The weather has always been a part of football history but never so much as the legendary "Snowplow Game" of December 12, 1982.

The story is simple enough yet had many interesting twists and turns.

A snowstorm had frozen the field in New England and snow covered the field at game time. Conditions were so frightful that the Patriots offered $10 and a free ticket to any fan who would help to get rid of the snow. 400 to 500 fans did just that. Officials talked over the conditions with both teams before the game and decided that snow-plowing or in reality tractors with sweeping equipment would be allowed to clear the yard lines during the game. Make note that the agreement was to clear yard lines, not make the footing or other conditions an advantage to players from either side.

The game went on well into the 4th quarter at 0-0 as both teams struggled with the elements.

At the 4:45 second mark of the quarter the Pats had a field goal opportunity. This is when Coach Ron Meyer is seen on video footage looking frantically for the tractor driver.

What followed made tractor driver Mark Henderson a folk hero in New England.

Henderson was a convicted burglar serving time in the New England penal system and was on work release for the game. He later said no one wanted to drive the tractor so he, as the newest member of the work release crew, volunteered. Henderson also said that Meyer, after calling timeout, found Henderson and was gesturing and shouting at him, pointing to the field, telling Henderson "Do something." He did.

Henderson knew what to do. He drove his tractor out toward the Patriots and Matt Cavanaugh, the back-up quarterback and holder on place kicks. Cavanaugh directed him to the spot that kicker John Smith needed cleared. Henderson later admitted to doing what he called a nonchalant swerve, as time is of the essence for the opposition to realize what is afoot and to protest in a timely fashion. The swerve is an added bit of subterfuge and a nice touch to the story, to get the tractor in position to sweep a swath of carpet clean for kicker John Smith to drill the 33-yard field goal that would ultimately win the game.

Dolphin coach Don Shula, a member of the NFL rules committee, protested strenuously as the event was unfolding and later said it was "the most unfair act ever perpetrated in the history of the league."

Shula subsequently protested, days later, to Commissioner Pete Rozelle to change the outcome of the game under the unfair acts clause of the NFL. (When obscure rules are rolled out in sporting event disputes it is usually an inch too far and most results after games are concluded are rarely if ever overturned.) Rozelle agreed with Shula but refused to overturn the outcome of the game because he had never done so before and presumably didn't want to set a precedent. The league changed its rules the following year to prevent anything like this happening again.

Henderson was told by Patrick Sullivan, (who may or may not have been wearing a trench coat), the owner of the Pats, not to speak to the press after the game, but Mother Nature intervened again. As Henderson tried to get away from the press, his tractor kept slipping on the frozen ramp. He finally was cornered by the reporters who asked him who put him up to it. Henderson of course knew the answer but, hey, he was a convict at the time, he told the over a dozen reporters surrounding him that he didn't know.

Henderson for his efforts was given a game ball that had the words "CLEAN SWEEP" and the score 3-0 written on it.

Today, the John Deere tractor used in this infamous game hangs suspended on metal cables from the ceiling at Patriot Place similar to how The Spirit of St. Louis (Charles Lindbergh's plane) does at the National Air and Space Museum in Washington, D.C.

Henderson, who served his time and has lived a lawful life since, is of course a hero in New England and at the twentieth anniversary of the event it was suggested he be brought back to attend the festivities. One problem Mark Henderson of Attleboro, Massachusetts had recently died. But it turned out there was another Mark Henderson of Attleboro, Massachusetts, who coincidentally also had a criminal record.

After the Pats front office found out that 'the' Mark Henderson, who grew up in North Attleboro, was indeed thought to be alive they contacted him and after an eyeball ID by Patriot equipment managers who had been at the original game, he was included in the anniversary celebration.

By the way, kicker John Smith contends he didn't need the help. In fact, Smith says Henderson sent more snow into Smith's preferred spot. Video of the kick shows Smith planting his foot on green turf plowed off by Henderson and video from earlier in the game of attempts of Smith to kick a field goal on the treacherous turf pretty much attest to Henderson's getting the assist.

Don Shula for his part missed a chance. He said, "I wanted to go out there and punch him out," and "I should have laid down in the front of the snowplow."

If only. Shula most definitely should have. Then we'd really have a helluva story.

ROCK 'N' ROLL

Every NFL team seems to have traditions that become part of the experience. Lambeau Leap in Green Bay and the Saints "Who Dat" chant come to mind.

A New England Patriot tradition is the player intro at home games. Music. A combination of *Carmina Burana* and "Crazy Train" by Ozzy Osbourne.

In the 2005 NFL opener the NFL built a huge Patriot Helmet. The crowd, ready for some football, watched as the helmet was raised like a car hood and Ozzy Osbourne was there to sing the song in person. At some point in the middle of the performance, Robert Kraft, mic in hand, introduces the Super

Bowl champions. Smoke bellows, the face mask of the big helmet opens like a gate and the Patriots come onto the field while Ozzy continues to belt out the tune.

Google "Ozzy Osbourne Crazy Train New England Patriots" to get to the YouTube video. Notice Tom Brady's nonchalance throughout the video.

Marketing man Lou Imbriano tells how it came about as he tried to find a new song to introduce the team in his second year on the job. He thought of "*Carmina Burana*: Introduction" from the movie *The Doors* right off for its build and crescendo, but the other song he wanted escaped him until he got a call from an associate who told him to check out a song on a Mitsubishi Montero commercial.

GOOD BELICHICK

The Patriots were the underdogs in the 2001 Super Bowl played in New Orleans against the St. Louis Rams.

A not-so-well-known Super Bowl ritual was started that day that may have escaped many fans even though it has been the "tradition" observed ever since.

NFL games are usually preceded by one of the home teams starting lineup either the offense or defense and sometimes the special team units.

Before Super Bowl XXXVI the NFL asked coach Belichick which squad he wanted introduced. He said neither. He wanted the team to be introduced as a unit and run onto the field as one. The NFL didn't like that idea as it ran counter to tradition.

Belichick insisted, against NFL brass pressure and with backing from players in the pre-game locker room, notably a speech by Lawyer Milloy, and the team was introduced together.

The image of Coach Belichick to most fans is one of a gruff almost anti-social presence at press conferences, but this gesture or decision gives insight into his meticulous view of the game and speaks to an understanding of the many players he has led to unprecedented success.

Since that time all teams do it this way.

Steve Young is quoted as saying that he remembers that moment and thinking at the time: "This might be the most important moment we've seen in football in the last twenty years."

Asked about the decision, players and coaches said it showed they were a team and that everyone was part of it.

In today's look-at-me sports world, this is indeed a significant statement.

GENESIS STORY

Like any superhero or mere mortal there is a background story.

Bill Belichick's starts with his father.

Steve Belichick, Bill's father, was a star player at Western Reserve University, playing on the school's first team to play in a bowl game, the 1941 Sun Bowl, in which he scored his team's first touchdown.

After college, he was thought not good enough to go pro but instead got a job as equipment manager of the Detroit Lions at, get this, NO SALARY. The players each chipped in a dollar a week to pay him. After 4 games the coach, who had previously coached him, decided that Steve Belichick might be better than the players he had. So they signed the equipment manager to a contract and it worked out pretty well. He later ran a punt back for 65 yards against the Giants and generally played better than the players he replaced.

Then a little diversion called World War II intervened and he fought at Normandy and Okinawa.

Football called again after the war and Steve Belichick became a coach most notably at the Naval Academy where his son Bill as early as 5 years old started soaking up all the football knowledge he could.

Steve Belichick wrote a book that came out in 1962 titled *Football Scouting Methods* which was reprinted after his death in 2011. It became, according to some sources, one of the top ten most sought out books out of print before its reprinting in 2011. It has been called by the L.A Times "The Bible of scouting techniques" and many consider it the best book ever on scouting

BOUNDARIES

Stadium issues seem to be almost a given in the NFL. Every team has a contentious stadium story in its lineage.

The Patriots had always had a tenuous stadium situation. The team was attracting offers to move from all over the country. E. M. Loew of the movie chain to the rescue. To keep the Patriots in Massachusetts, he gave owner Billy Sullivan a fifteen-acre site on which Schaefer Stadium was built in 1971 in record time.

So far so good.

Schaefer Stadium from day one was known for being built on the cheap and for monumental traffic snarls.

The stadium was built next to another Boston area sports venue, Bay State Raceway, a harness track. Enter Eddie Andelman, a Boston radio sports talk show host.

Andelman was a fixture on Boston radio for years and was known for his numerous charitable events, most notably something called "the Hot Dog Safari." He also once called up Buckingham Palace in London to ask them if they could spare any guard for the Patriots offensive line. This, of course, is pre- Belichick.

In a particularly ironic twist Andelman and some partners purchased Bay State Raceway and after a surveyor found that Sullivan had built part of Schaefer Stadium across their property line, sued.

It seems the south end zone was on Andelman's property.

This led to legal unpleasantness worthy of a *Fawlty Towers* episode.

The Patriots bought a fancy new scoreboard from Mitsubishi but Andelman would not allow it to be transported across his property, necessitating logistical "strategery" to install the huge modern scoreboard.

To drag the baby across the field would tear up the turf. They thought of flooding the field to float it across, not feasible. The solution was to break the scoreboard down to parts. And part by part reconfigure the electronic scoreboard. The Lego solution.

That is what they did. This, however, because of the weight and bulk of the thing, had to be put in the middle of the end zone as opposed to being attached to the border of the end zone.

The litigation almost prevented the Patriots from hosting a Monday Night Football game due to laws governing race tracks in Massachusetts. Only the intervention of Governor Edward King, who by the by was once a guard for the Baltimore Colts and had served as a "babysitter" for draft choices in the early AFL/NFL wars, did the game go on as scheduled. Much to Andelman's consternation as it turns out.

THE FLUSH

As is noted above, Schaefer Stadium was not a well liked venue.

Almost universally assailed as built on the cheap, it was located in Foxboro, approximately equidistant between Boston and Providence, Rhode Island. The move to Foxboro initiated the name change from Boston Patriots to New England Patriots, but only after Bay State Patriots was rejected because it was feared that the team would then be referred to as the BS Patriots.

As an example of the peculiar nature of the stadium, a case in point is the urinals in the players locker room. They were five feet above the floor. WR Randy Vataha, all 5'8" of him, had to stand on a box in order to take a pee. Don Nottingham, known as the human bowling ball for his compact stature, actually needed two of his teammates to hold him up to use the facility.

On opening day, a pre-season game, there was a massive traffic snarl on day one, and one other "minor" snafu, all the toilets overflowed.

The Board of Health would not allow the Patriots to open up the season until this problem was resolved.

Which led to what is called "The Flush" or "The Great Flush."

An array of team employees, stadium employees and even journalists was assembled at Schaefer Stadium and positioned in every restroom. At the signal, a blast of the stadium horn, all hands ran around and flushed every toilet and urinal at the same time.

The system worked. No problem. No overflow.

MICHAEL JACKSON SAVES THE PATRIOTS

Yes, that Michael Jackson, the King of Pop, can get a great measure of credit for, among other things, Bill Belichick and Tom Brady. Say what?

Robert Kraft had plotted to buy the Patriots. He purchased the land next to the stadium as a first move.

The Sullivans, founding family of the Patriots in 1960, had over time more than a few financial woes as pertaining to holding on to the franchise. At some point Ralph Wilson, owner of the Buffalo Bills, had lent money to Billy Sullivan to save the team.

In 1984 Chuck Sullivan, Billy's son, who ran the team, looked into booking the Jackson Family "Victory Tour" into Sullivan Stadium. Chuck ended up agreeing to partner with promoter Don King to front the tour and signed a contract to handle the merchandising.

It seemed like a good idea at the time as it was the first time the Jackson family had toured together in ten years and Michael, at the height of his superstardom, was coming off his wildly popular album, *Thriller*.

Long story short, Don King saw the Sullivans coming. King made a profit on the tour. The Sullivans lost $20 million.

The set of the tour was so huge it had to be built into the venues with extensive changes. Its size also limited the crowd capacity of the venues. Sullivan couldn't even get his home town of Foxboro to approve permits for his own stadium to host the concert.

They subsequently sold the stadium to Robert Kraft and the team to Victor Kiam who then in 1992 sold it to St. Louis businessman James Orthwein who wanted to move the team to St. Louis, but when a legal covenant that would not expire for another eight years in 2001 prevented the move to Missouri, Orthwein sold the team to Robert Kraft.

The rest is NFL history.

Kraft is said to have to this day a poster of the Jackson's "Victory Tour" hanging on his wall as a reminder of the huge assist that Michael Jackson gave to Kraft and by extension the Patriot dynasty.

NUMBER TWO

NOTE: THE AUTHOR'S APOLOGIZES.

Larry Izzo is the all time NFL special team tackler with an unofficial 298 special team tackles. He is the winner of three Super Bowl rings. He played fourteen years in the NFL but he makes it into this book of oddities and such for quite an unusual feat.

According to research and according to Wes Welker in an interview he gave to Dan Lebatard, Larry Izzo received a game ball from the New England Patriots because he took an undetected dump on the sidelines during an NFL game.

To quote Welker, "It's what Izzo does. I'm telling you the guy is phenomenal," or something like that.

Steve Miller is a rocker of some note, with #1 hits like "The Joker", "Abracadabra", "Space Cowboy", and "Rock'n Me."

The lyrics of "Rock'n Me" were recently mined for this gem that will appeal to conspiracy buffs and those who believe in fate.

"Phoenix, Arizona all the way to Tacoma, Atlanta, Philadelphia, LA, Northern California where ..."

Okay, now let's decipher the hieroglyph this information conveys:

Remember the song was a hit in 1971.

The Patriots played the Giants in the Super Bowl in Phoenix, Arizona. They next played a Super Bowl against the Seattle Seahawks. If you know your geography, Sea-Tac airport is the airport in Seattle-Tacoma metroplex.

Next Patriots Super Bowl vs. Atlanta, the big comeback game.

The next Super Bowl they played Philadelphia.

Hope you're keeping up.

The next time the Patriots played a Super Bowl? The hits keep coming-next Super Bowl opponent for the Pats was LA, the Rams, who by the way moved to St. Louis and back to LA in the interim from 1971 making Steve's prophecy even more interesting.

You can make the case that the first in the sequence was played in Phoenix not against the Cardinals. But then you would be a spoilsport. At least.

Plus, any conspiracy buff will tell you there is nuance in the unexplained. You see, Steve Miller was sneaking up on you.

Next up?

San Francisco or Oakland.

We shall see.

CRAZIEST PLAY IN NFL HISTORY

Nickerson Stadium, 1961: Boston Patriots vs. Dallas Texans. Boston 28 Dallas 21. Texans on Boston one yard line. Time for only one more play. The crowd rings the end zone at least five deep. The ball is snapped. Cotton Davidson, the Texan quarterback, fades back.

Meanwhile, a man in a trench coat, forever referred to in history as "the man in the trench coat," moves out from the crowd in a crouch and joins, more or less, the Boston linebackers. Davidson throws a pass aimed at Texan wide receiver Chris Burford. The man in the trench coats slaps the pass down and runs back into the crowd.

Game over. Patriots win!

What? Yep. How about that? No replay. It's 1961. During Monday's film session, defensive end Larry Eisenhauer of the Patriots says, "We saw the guy come out on the field and slap the pass down when we were watching the film."

Who was this guy? Nobody knows.

Owner of the Patriots at the time, a guy named Billy Sullivan was known to wear a trench coat. Hmmm? When asked if it might be him, Sullivan never denied it.

CLEVELAND

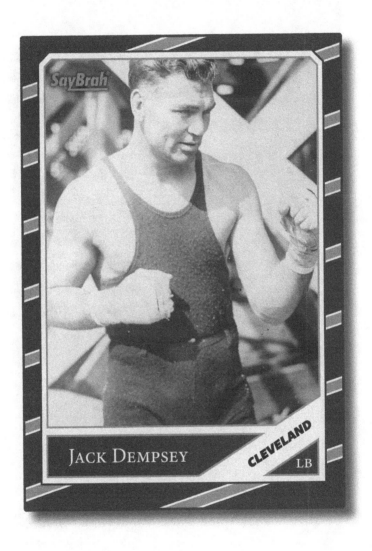

SayBrah

JACK DEMPSEY

CLEVELAND

LB

THE MURDER OF THE CENTURY

CLEVELAND

SayBrah

"The only way to stop Jim Brown was
to give him a movie contract."
—Spider Lockhart

Cleveland Browns entered the All-America Football
Conference (a rival league) in 1945 under the leadership of Coach Paul Brown. The Browns went 47-4-3
in the four-year history of the AAFC and were one of
three teams absorbed into the NFL in 1950.

Their first year in the NFL, the Browns won the NFL
Championship.

Brown was fired by Art Modell in 1963 two years after Modell bought the team.

Art Modell moved the team to Baltimore in 1996,
but Cleveland was awarded a new franchise with all
Browns history and name in 1999.

The Browns have never been to the Super Bowl.

"I feel for the Baltimore fans. I'm not sitting in judgment on whether Bob Irsay is right or wrong. What concerns me is where the league is going. This is the legacy of the Raiders move. Baltimore is paying for it now, and others might in the future."

—Art Modell

WHAT IS THE FREQUENCY KENNETH?

In 1956 an inventor or tinkerer named George Sarles came to present Paul Brown the head coach of the Browns, with a football helmet with a radio receiver in it. Brown liked the idea and Sarles and a GE engineer presented Brown with a system set up with a radio receiver in a Browns helmet. The idea was to have Paul Brown, who called all of the Browns plays by shuttling in guards, to be able to call the plays by radio frequency,

Brown, always the innovator, was intrigued. He obtained a frequency from the FCC to transmit radio signals.

They tried it out in an exhibition game in Chicago against the Cardinals. It worked, sort of.

The quarterback, George Ratterman, had the helmet with the receiver and kept getting taxi cab dispatches from Michigan Avenue.

Still a few bugs.

Brown at that point was undaunted and decided to use the helmet in a regular season game against the New York Giants. Brown told the Giants he was going to do it and he warned the Giants that to interfere with his signal would be a violation of law.

The Giants countered by bringing their own powerful radio receiver to their bench and hiring an ex-Brown player to monitor the signal and explain what the signal and play calls meant, a kind of "Spy vs. Spy" moment in NFL history.

The Browns only used the device for three series all of which failed so they abandoned the experiment.

The Giants later crowed to the press that they could hear Brown's instruction loud and clear and better than Ratterman could and claim it helped them to victory that day in Cleveland.

Paul Brown later that week told the press that the Giants were fibbing and the Browns only abandoned the system because of the crowd noise of the 60,000 Cleveland spectators.

There are some versions of this story that give this version.

At some point in the game Ratterman came off the field and told coach Brown, "Some guy just got stabbed on Fifth Avenue." Ratterman was picking up the police radio.

This sexy version of murder on New York's Fifth Avenue cannot be true as the game was played on the shore of Lake Erie in Cleveland.

Giants general manager Ray Walsh who boasted about his radio signal theft had this to say about the development of radio warfare in the NFL.

"If this trend continues the No. 1 draft choice of the Giants next year will be the valedictorian at MIT."

The NFL got around to radio transmission about forty years later.

OH MY!

One thing generally leads to another.

A large wall at Browns headquarters displayed images from social media platforms. A problem arose when one day an employee typed in #dp hashtag. The "dp" here was to stand for Dawg Pound, the fan group famous throughout the country as a signature of Browns fandom.

Only problem is that hashtags, keywords, and such often have more than one meaning in cyberspace.

Long story short, this #dp caused a giant wall projection, at Cleveland Browns headquarters, of porn. This lasted twenty minutes until someone pulled the plug.

Hope it wasn't "Bring Your Daughter to Work Day."

YOU CAN LOOK IT UP

Browns fans may wonder from time to time why their team can't get to the Super Bowl.

Houdini promised to try to contact the living after his death.

Crickets.

Yet, perhaps Sherlock Holmes, fictitious as he is, is sending clues to Browns fans.

To wit, in 2013 the Cleveland Browns opened up their new five million dollar training facility and showed it off to the local press.

Inspirational quotes are on many of the walls, which seems an appropriate use of walls in a competitive organization.

They say that success starts at the top with leadership. This doesn't make it true, but it does sound feasible.

Maybe not. Maybe failure starts at the bottom.

It was reported in the Cleveland press that most of the quotes are misattributed, incorrectly transcribed, or mostly fraudulent.

All in all—four correct, nine wrong, and one not sure.

Abraham Lincoln did not say, "Whatever you are, be a good one."

"The more I practice, the luckier I get," golfer Gary Player?

Nope. Jerry Barber, a golfer.

They at least got the sport right.

This is so awesome!

The NFL is a copycat league, which means that when one team does something that works on the field, other teams usually adopt it.

In the wake of the success of the "Super Bowl Shuffle" video, other NFL teams started daydreaming about the possibilities.

Mike Baab, the center for the Browns and his wife Lolis Garcia-Baab, a video producer, thought of maybe doing a music video to raise money for the United Way. MTV was popular and it seemed like a good idea. Teammates, though, decided that a music video was not the way to go because others had tried and the results were less than good. They feared it might turn out lame.

Garcia-Baab and Baab recruited a local comedy writer and they sat around with a couple of bottles of wine and they came up with an idea.

Baab had become a fan favorite in his tenure with the Browns and even had his own cheering section called the Baabarians, after the popularity of the film *Conan the Barbarian.*

Masters of the Gridiron was born, a medieval tale not unlike a campy *Game of Thrones.*

The NFL gave the green light to Garcia-Baab and the players took two days at an abandoned mansion, now under the auspices of Cleveland Metroparks, as a setting.

The seventeen-minute short film was a huge success as a fundraiser, selling out all 40,000 copies produced.

The cast included Baab, Ozzie Newsome (who has gone on to be one of the top GM's in the NFL), Earnest Byner, Clay Matthews, Hanford Dixon, Bob Golic, brother of radio personality Mike Golic, Tiny Tim (yeah that Tiny Tim), and a bear. Baab wrestled the bear.

They also put in a musical performance by a group called The Michael Stanley Band who had a few Top-40 hits in the early 80's. It was, after all, the MTV age, so it seemed like the thing to do, kind of like when the Marx Brothers used to stick an obligatory song into their films.

The Browns went on to a banner year, getting to the AFC Championship game against the Broncos and just losing on their trip to the Super Bowl because of "The Drive" courtesy of John Elway.

After the loss, Lolis Garcia-Baab was particularly distraught and her husband Mike tried to console her. What his wife had not told him was that she had secured an international agreement to release the film with a $250,000 advance but *only if* the Browns went to the Super Bowl.

It's still awesome!!!!

You can see it on YouTube.

STUTTER STEP

Otto Graham wasn't going to play forever. Graham quarterbacked the Browns to an unprecedented success in pro football history to a record of 57-13-1 in the NFL (104-17-2 if you factor in AAFC games) but football is a young man's game and father time is undefeated.

The Browns, planning ahead, drafted Stanford's star quarterback Bobby Garret with the #1 pick in 1954.

Garret had all the tools but there was one problem.

He had a very bad stutter. He couldn't get the signals out. Had an especially hard time with words that started with the letter "S."

The Browns traded him to Green Bay but they didn't tell them about his stutter. Teammates said he just couldn't communicate the signals. His very promising career never got off the ground.

BRAINS

The last time the Cleveland Browns won the NFL championship their starting quarterback was Dr. Frank Ryan.

Sports Illustrated wrote a beautiful article about Frank Ryan entitled "How Smart is Too Smart?"

Dr. Frank Ryan hails from Texas, his football career went through Rice University in Houston and then to the NFL where he eventually excelled as quarterback for the Browns.

Along the way he did a couple of other things like get a PhD in Mathematics and teaching higher math at Case Western Institute of Technology. He taught at Yale, becoming Yale Athletic Director for fourteen years, and created a computer program that streamlined how the U.S. Congress votes on legislation, a process allowing the body to vote on three times as many bills as before.

Maybe you've read his PhD thesis: *A Characterization of the Set of Asymptotic Values of a Function Holomorphic in the Unit Disc.*

Maybe not.

Dr. Frank Ryan once answered a sportswriter's question about the weather and its effect on the outcome of the game that day by referring to Bernoulli's Principle.

When he was traded to Washington his new coach was Vince Lombardi. Lombardi paid him $35,000 extra to do computer programming as it pertained to the game of football.

CHICKEN FIGHTING MAN

The Cleveland Browns drafted Johnny Manziel in the first round. Many said that he wouldn't make it in the pro game. It looks like many were correct.

Johnny Manziel became a household name in America because of his football derring-do at Texas A&M. Even garnered the nickname Johnny Football for his on the field heroics.

Like everyone Manziel had a family back-story but unlike most his family back-story is about as picturesque as it gets.

His great-great grandfather came to America from Lebanon settling in Louisiana and was involved in activities that ended him up in court which turned out to be a tradition in the making for the Manziel family as the American judicial system became kind of a natural habitat for the Manziels.

Members of Johnny Football's extended family—grandfathers, uncles, cousins—have had many success in chasing the American dream but have also been involved in all kinds of shenanigans or alleged shenanigans that tend to find them in a courtroom.

His great grandfather was a professional boxer who was a sparring partner of Jack Dempsey.

Manziel, the sparring partner was known as the "Syrian Kid "in his boxing days moved to East Texas with little money to get into the wildcatting business.

He wired Dempsey from Texas who staked him to $400 dollars to drill on the land of the Negro New Hope Baptist Church in Gladewater, Texas. The well was a gusher and Manziel was on his way to a fortune and a great deal of notoriety in East Texas.

The oil business was lucrative if you got lucky and Manziel did get lucky and he became rich. Dempsey said that the $400 bucks he fronted Manziel was the best investment he ever made.

The family over the years have become legendary in East Texas.

Involved in many alleged crimes they were involved in litigation pertaining to oil wells that became precedent in the oil and gas industry. The U.S. government spokesperson once said of a Manziel family victory in court that the case wrecked oil regulation in the country.

But was Johnny Manziel's great grandfather's passion was cockfighting. The older Manziel would make a name for himself in cockfighting circles.

There is a breed of fighting cock named the Manziel Grey which appeared as the cover bird on *The Cockfighter Magazine* in 1978 and Norman Paul, Johnny's grandfather, was the Cockfighting World Champion in 1983.

The family's wealth and success in the illicit game of cockfighting allowed them to fly on their own plane many of 1,200 fighting cocks they owned to cockfighting venues all over the United States.

For those not in the know, there was a time in the twentieth century that it was said that there were more cockfighting venues in Texas than there were movie theaters.

His great grandfather was a mover and shaker in East Texas when he died at the age of fifty-one. Two of his pallbearers were former World Heavyweight Champion Jack Dempsey and the Attorney General of Texas.

PUBLIC ENEMY

Mickey McBride was the founder of the Cleveland Browns and the guy who hired the legendary Paul Brown as his head coach.

McBride owned the largest cab company in Cleveland and as such he offered reserve members of the Browns jobs as taxi drivers while they awaited their chance to make the team. This is where the term taxi squad came. The players were on the taxi company payroll but did not actually drive cabs.

McBride's name was more famous in the American conciseness for more nefarious reasons.

In chapter six of author Dan Moldea's explosive book, *Interference: How Organized Crime Influences Professional Football*, Moldea asserts with copious footnotes that Mickey McBride who was the founder and owner of the Continental Wire Service which was considered by the Kefauver Committee to be "Public Enemy Number One," as it would pertain to racketeering and aiding and abetting corruption through gambling in the United States had some interesting friends.

Named for its chairman Senator Estes Kefauver (D-TN), The Kefauver Committee's official name was The Senate Special Committee to Investigate Crime in Interstate Commerce.

McBride had started the Continental Wire Service to fill a niche to replace the Nationwide News Service after Nationwide's owner Moses Annenberg went to prison for tax fraud.

Continental Wire Service provided every bookmaker in the country needed information and also was used by bettors of sports gambling particularly horse racing.

James Ragen was McBride's partner in Continental in fact Ragen had suggested McBride start Continental after Ragen also was indicted with Annenberg and plead guilty.

Ragen bought Continental from McBride two years later and kept McBride on as a one third partner.

The Chicago Mafia, again according to Moldea's book, run by Tony Accardo a one time Capone bodyguard and a guy who is considered the most powerful Mafia figure of the 20th century took an interest in Continental as a potential source of income. Accardo, Jake "Greasy Thumb" Guzik, and Murray "The Camel" Humphreys offered to buy Continental from Ragen.

Ragen balked and instead went to the FBI. The mob then opened its own wire service.

The mobs new service never got any real traction and on June 24, 1946, Ragen while sitting in his car in rush hour traffic in Chicago was ambushed and died seven weeks later from the wounds.

McBride, then bought Continental from Ragen's son and carried on with it appears the blessing of Tony Accardo.

The Kefauver Committee subpoenaed McBride and the subsequent pressure and notoriety from the hearings which were televised to a national audience, ended Continental.

The Kefauver Committee inspired Congress to pass laws dealing with gambling including requiring bookmakers to pay a $50 gambling stamp every year for income tax purposes. The laws passed at the committee's recommendation made such wire services as Continental unlawful.

McBride sold the Browns in 1953 for $600,000.

The Kefauver Committee was denied its more wide ranging recommendations and soon lost the headlines to the U.S. House Un-American Activities Committee and Senator Joe McCarthy's hearings.

Meanwhile it is important to remember in fairness that McBride was never arrested and maintained that he had no links to organized crime.

MARION MOTLEY

Marion Motley, along with Bill Willis, broke the color barrier in pro football when they were signed by Paul Brown for his new AAFC team in 1946. Or re-broke it, I should say, as there had been a "gentleman's agreement" to keep African-American players out of the league starting in 1933. Prior to that time, there was a smattering of black players. In 1946 the Browns and Rams in the NFL changed that by signing Motley and Willis (Browns) and Kenny Washington and Woody Strode (LA Rams).

Motley, one of the greatest backs in history, may never have made it through college much less to the pros but for the kindness of strangers and of course his ability on the football field.

Motley was just starting his college career at the University of Nevada in Reno but his play had already created a buzz of positive excitement. He was driving to San Francisco with a friend when he tried to pass another car and for some reason unknown to history the driver of the car he was trying to pass did not allow him to get back into his lane as another car came straight at him. A head-on collision occurred and one of the inhabitants of the other car died later.

Motley was charged with vehicular homicide and spent about 10 days in jail awaiting his fate. You can imagine that he didn't have much hope.

Supporters of Motley found there was a statute under California law that would allow the judge to hand down probation for someone found guilty of just such a crime under specific circumstances but it also involved a $1,000 fine. The fine was a bit out of almost every college student's means in the 1940's.

Students, faculty and friends of Motley in town and on campus, even school children and ordinary citizens started contributing to a fund to raise the money. On campus a thermometer chart was constructed and, as the money flowed in, the thermometer was colored in red until it hit the top at $1,000.

At his sentencing he had character witnesses, including law enforcement officials, speak positively about his character. He got probation and he went on to star at Nevada and eventually find his way to Cleveland and the Hall of Fame.

Motley in his own words: "I cannot tell you in words how grateful I am for what you have done for me. I shall try to show it by the quality of school work I do and the service I can render on behalf of the University of Nevada and the people of this state."

George Ratterman was the quarterback tapped to be Otto Graham's replacement when the all-time-great Brown retired. Ratterman played nine years of pro football after playing at Notre Dame and being called by Notre Dame coach Frank Leahy the greatest all around athlete in Notre Dame history. Ratterman was the last Notre Dame student athlete to letter in four sports. His pro career was mixed. He threw for 22 TD passes his rookie year in the AAFC for Buffalo, a rookie record that remained until Peyton Manning broke it fifty years later. Ratterman also was the first pro quarterback to wear a helmet with a radio receiver to get plays called from his coach.

Ratterman retired from pro football after a serious leg injury and became a lawyer.

He moved to Newport, Kentucky, across the Ohio River from Cincinnati after football to practice law. Newport was renowned for its vice and corruption in its political life.

Newport was nicknamed the "Sin City of the South" infamous for its casinos, prostitution, and underworld connections. Something that had been going on for over 100 years, starting during the Civil War.

Reformers got Ratterman to run for sheriff and it didn't take long for the powers-that-be in Newport to swing into action to defuse Ratterman's attempt at reforming the ways of Newport.

He was lured to a meeting with an executive at one of the gambling establishments, a guy he knew from his football years. At dinner he was drugged with chloral hydrate. He was transported to a hotel room connected to the casino, stripped of his clothes, and put into bed with a practically naked stripper. A photographer had been hired to take a compromising picture of Ratterman but the photographer smelled a rat and didn't show up.

The police were tipped off to Ratterman's so-called hijinks and burst into the room, found Ratterman in a compromising position, and took him and the stripper (dba April Flowers) to the police station where they were booked.

Ratterman went to trial and the charges were dismissed after testimony from the photographer revealed the framing plot.

At this point, the Governor of Kentucky got involved in the reform movement by cracking down heavily on Newport and the FBI, then under the leadership of Attorney General of the United States Robert F. Kennedy, who also took an interest in cleaning up Newport,

Ratterman won the election and Newport, a den of iniquity since the days of the Civil War, was cleaned up.

To those of you not in the know, it might seem that a small town in Kentucky with a population of about 30,000 being cleaned up was a great idea but not all that earth shattering in the big scheme of things. But consider the following:

Layoff bookmakers are an integral part of illegal gambling and a great source of revenue of organized crime. This is the process as to where bookmakers spread around the betting volume as to not lose their shirt. The bulk of these layoff bookmakers were believed by law enforcement at that time in the late 50's and early 60's to be run by the mob.

On any given weekend during football season, we're talking millions of dollars. In fact, gambling was the number one revenue source of the underworld at that time.

In 1961, it is believed that the underworld had two major centers that handled 90% of its layoff action in the United States: Biloxi, Mississippi and Newport, Kentucky.

Ratterman was rattling the cage of a large, lethal, well funded, and highly motivated enterprise.

OJ's OPENING ACT

1954: things were happening in Cleveland. The Indians were on their way to a record-breaking year in the World Series and events that would lead to the eventual placement of the Rock and Roll Hall of Fame were brewing in the mind of disc jockey Alan Freed. Meanwhile, the Browns, under the leadership of Paul Brown and Otto Graham, were in the midst of one of the most unprecedented successful runs in pro football history.

Then on July 4, 1954, Marilyn Shepard, wife of highly respected neurosurgeon Dr. Sam Shepard, was brutally murdered in their home. Dr. Shepard was eventually charged with the murder. Cleveland, the city on Lake Erie, became the focal point of America's latest murder trial of the century. How does this end up in a chapter dedicated to the Cleveland Browns?

Otto Graham was a close friend and neighbor of Dr. Shepard and his wife Marilyn.

The day after the murder, Graham, out for a drive to get a newspaper, saw police surrounding his friend's home—quite unusual in the upper class suburb. Graham stopped and, being that he was Otto Graham, the cops allowed him to go take a tour of the murder scene before it was secured.

Graham described the bedroom as if someone had splattered a can of red paint all over the walls. Graham at first believed in his friend's innocence. They had gone on a family outing with their kids to a stock car race just days earlier. It was unthinkable that this could happen here to people you socialized with.

Shepard claimed to be awakened by the sounds of his wife being murdered by a bushy headed man who knocked him out before he could discover his brutally murdered wife.

Graham was, for a brief time, considered a suspect because he had disappeared from a party the night before to go pick something up at his home, which was nearby the Shepard's. Also, Graham had bushy hair.

At first Graham believed in Shepard's innocence, but did admit that upon going home after perusing the murder scene and breaking the news to his wife, her first response was, "Do you think Sam did it?"

The trial was the sensation of the nation. Covered by national press including syndicated columnist Walter Winchell and others. The salacious press coverage eventually led to Shepard, who was found guilty of second degree murder, to get a new trial because of the circus-like nature of the first trial, which was deemed by a judge to be unfair. In a new trial, with the help of attorney F. Lee Bailey, Shepard was acquitted.

Shepard died at the age of forty-six from liver disease but not before he became a household name and a professional wrestler after his acquittal. The popular TV series *The Fugitive* starring David Janssen was based on the Sam Shepard case. For the TV series, the "bushy-haired man" was replaced with "the one armed man."

Otto Graham walking around the murder scene. Otto Graham, a suspect in the crime of the century.

So 1954.

THE LETTER

In 1974, the Cleveland Browns received a letter from a season ticket holder who complained about the practice of fans fashioning paper airplanes out of pages taken from the official program for the game and throwing them from the upper deck. He contends that this is dangerous, potentially causing injury to fans in the lower section of the stadium by hitting them in the eyes or ears.

The writer also threatened legal action if anyone in his party was injured.

It was couched as a friendly warning, but it was on the letterhead of a law firm.

The answer from the legal counsel of the Cleveland Browns is classic. In it, he writes, "Attached is the letter that we received on November 19, 1974. I feel that you should be aware that some asshole is signing your name to stupid letters." James Bailey, General Counsel.

The letter is on an official Cleveland Brown letterhead and is cc'd :Arthur Modell.

NEW ORLEANS

SayBrah®

RUTHERFORD B. HAYES

NEW ORLEANS

ST

VOODOO, A MUMMY, AND RUTHERFORD B. HAYES

32

NEW ORLEANS

SayBrah®

On being asked if he regretted never having a daughter: "Have you taken a good look at those boys?"
—Archie Manning, Saints QB (1971-82)

New Orleans Saints joined the NFL on All Saints' Day (November 1st) 1966, and were awarded a coveted NFL franchise after a deal was struck with powerful Congressional leaders from Louisiana and the league on tax legislation.

After the city was devastated by Hurricane Katrina it was feared the team may be moved to another city.

The NFL led by Commissioner Paul Tagliabue was instrumental in the Saints remaining in New Orleans.

Since Katrina, New Orleans, one of the smallest NFL markets with a population yet to recover to pre Storm numbers has sold out every home game.

Super Bowl Appearances: 1
Super Bowl Record: 1-0 (2009)

DAVE DIXON

Few men are more synonymous with the procurement of an NFL franchise for a city than Dave Dixon.

1. Dixon, a local entrepreneur and a visionary, spearheaded New Orleans' attempts to get an NFL franchise.
   As early as 1961 with the family then living in Paris, Dave would fly to New York every six weeks and wrote numerous letters to both Pete Rozelle and Joe Foss, the Commissioner of the NFL and AFL respectively, promoting New Orleans as a prime spot for a pro football team.
   In 1962, Dixon found out the Oakland Raiders were for sale. He flew from Austria, interrupting a family skiing trip to fly to Oakland and make a handshake deal to purchase the Raiders for $236,000.
   It was all but done. The New Orleans Raiders would start play in the "Crescent City" in 1963. Enter politics.
   The mayor of Oakland, John C. Houlihan, got wind of the deal and convinced F. Wayne Valley, owner of the team, to stay in Oakland. Oakland mayor Houlihan, by the way, was a convicted felon.

2. Dixon was also at the forefront of another almost. Lamar Hunt was ready to move the Dallas Texans to New Orleans but needed Tulane Stadium. The college was resistant to having the pro game played on its campus.
   Hunt called Dixon on the QT, and Dixon produced a secret weapon: Joseph Merrick Jones, a resident of Metairie and former President of Tulane University, who had influence with the Tulane board. Jones was ready to go to bat for bringing the Texans to New Orleans.
   Tragically, Jones' house caught on fire and, in an attempt to save his wife from the fire, he died.
   The Texans, without a stadium, went to Kansas City.

3. Dixon lined up civic leaders and promoted some of the most successful exhibition games in NFL history in New Orleans.
   He lined up support from African-American leaders in the city because the NFL would not tolerate segregation. This was a big deal in New Orleans in the early 60s.

Frank Dixon, Dave's son, tells this story about that exhibition doubleheader of 1963 held in the city:

On the Saturday morning the tickets went on sale, a black gentleman was first in line. He wanted tickets on the 50-yard line. No problem. He bought his tickets. He then, according to Frank Dixon's account, went to the street, sat down on the curb, looked at his tickets, and wept. Such was the significance of buying the best seats in the house for a public event circa 1963 New Orleans.

4. This item in *Sports Illustrated* in May of 1965:
   "Dixon has been struggling for five years to get some kind of pro football in New Orleans. He is even involved now in the possibility of a winter league, a six-team circuit comprised of major cities whose owners would bid against the NFL and AFL for talent."

5. Finally, the NFL was sniffing around New Orleans in 1966. By this time Dixon and the men in search of an NFL team had the full support of politicians in the area.
   The merger of the NFL and AFL was in the offing to bring peace and financial stability to pro football.
   This would require anti-trust legislation to be passed in Congress. Russell Long (chairman of the Senate Finance Committee) and Hale Boggs (House majority "whip") were movers and shakers in Washington and they promised Pete Rozelle they would pass the anti-trust legislation he needed.
   Cokie Roberts, Hale Boggs' daughter, writes this story: "As Rozelle and Boggs walk through the Capitol building, Rozelle seems to be having doubt that New Orleans might be in line for a team."
   "Boggs stopped walking. 'No team for New Orleans, no law.' New Orleans got its team."

Dave Dixon was honored with a banner hanging from the Superdome along with other Louisiana sports heroes like Pete Maravich and Archie Manning.

FAKE NEWS BUT IN A GOOD WAY

1987: the infamous NFL replacement players, the players' strike.
Football fans in the midst of football season with no pro football.
   Enter the imagination of Mike McGee, GM of WGSO radio. It was his idea. Radio dudes Tim Brando and Bill Wagy take it from there.

McGee's idea was to have WGSO, which had recently lost the play-by-play broadcasting rights for the Saints to local powerhouse WWL, just make up a Saints game broadcast every Sunday and have WGSO broadcast it to the football insane Saints fans. The Saints sucked but the fans in New Orleans didn't care. They just love them some football.

So, it would be a cousin to the radio reenactments of yesteryear when a radio guy would use wire service play-by-play to relay baseball games using sound effects. Only this was all made up.

The star of every game seemed to be the versatile Guido Merkens, jack-of-all-trades Saints wide receiver.

Wagy was given the task of writing the scripts and he and Brando, the play-by-play guy, would just play-act as if actually calling a game. Wagy was on color and the NFL referee that worked every game was voiced by McGee.

Wagy used down and distance stat sheets, replays from previous years, and referee voices calling penalties along with crowd noise and background from actual broadcasts.

Wagy would think of fantastic ways for the Saints to pull out every game.

Brando even had a fake post game call-in show.

HEAVEN

Crossover in a modern society can be surprising. Johnny Cash, the great country artist, dabbled in covering rock songs with great success.

The cross-pollination of our institutions is not as prevalent as in the music industry, yet on October 13, 2019 there was a melding of divergent institutions that was accidental.

Pope Francis, the leader of the Roman Catholic Church, went to Twitter to thank God for a group of new Saints, the canonized type, and by using the #Saints, set the Twitter algorithm into action and it automatically posted the New Orleans Saints logo at the end of the tweet.

The Saints (the NFL kind) were to take the field that day against the Jacksonville Jaguars and New Orleans, being a Catholic city, the Twitterverse noticed.

The New Orleans Saints prevailed 13-6 in a hard fought game.

The Saints covered as well so Pope Francis is 1-0 against the spread.

CLOSE

Losing an NFL team is a heartbreaking thing to fans and the community left behind. Just like a love affair.

In pro sports, you're all in this together: players, owners, fans, city. Except when you're not.

If you're a fan, the players, owners, and team are NOT on your side. They are on *their* side. Jacksonville lost out on the Colts, but they were a determined bunch and unbeknownst to most, including Jacksonville fans and New Orleans Saints fans, Jacksonville came *this close* to purloining the Saints.

John Mecom was having cash flow problems. The city of New Orleans had given the new USFL team, the Breakers, financial incentives and not given incentive to the Saints, which soured Mecom greatly on city leaders. And let's face it—losing and failure were not fun under the ownership of John Mecom.

Mecom traveled to Jacksonville to sign the papers. Jacksonville leaders later confirmed, "We had a handshake deal."

But upon arriving in Jacksonville, Mecom tried to change the deal. He wanted more. He wanted them to buy up some of his bad real estate deals.

It was a game breaker.

Eddie Jones, then president of the Saints, later said, "There was no doubt whatsoever that we were moving to Jacksonville. We were all set. All we were waiting for were the final signatures and the official word to start packing."

It is notable that Bum Phillips, coach of the Saints, was reportedly all gung-ho about taking the team out of New Orleans and moving it to Florida.

Something for Saints fans to chew on when thinking of Bum's legacy.

MVP

November 10, 1991: Saints fans got a little lagniappe for their price of admission.

The halftime show was an indoor display of fireworks that were shot off from high above the Superdome field approximately 280 feet up.

Fireworks went off fine.

Only problem: the burlap bag used to secure speakers for rock 'n' roll concerts usually taken down after was left by somebody. Sparks from the fireworks caught the bag on fire.

It wasn't a big fire but there were smoke and flames.

An employee of the fireworks company, Frank, was sent to put out the fire while the game went on. All while the players looked up at Frank.

He became a show and of in himself.

I was there that day, sitting in my seats right behind the Saints bench. It was awe inspiring to see that guy climb out on the scaffolding of the gondola. That is way the hell up there.

He finally did extinguish the flames but at the last moment a piece of the flaming bag fell to the field and was put out for good with Gatorade.

During the heroics, Pat Summerall and John Madden kept viewers abreast of what was going on high up in the Dome.

Madden named Frank his MVP of the 1991 All-Madden Team.

Frank says he wasn't nervous until he saw his escapades being beamed on the large screen in the stadium.

OSCAR?

In 1969, the Saints had already won an NFL championship. At least in the Hollywood film, starring Charlton Heston, *Number One*.

The film made almost no impact on cinema history or recollection.

It wasn't even released on DVD until 2015.

However, if you were to read Howard Thompson's review of *Number One* in the September 18, 1969 edition of The *New York Times*, you might be intrigued to give it a first or second look. One of Heston's more obscure films, you'll find these descriptions of Heston's performance:

> *"One of the most interesting and admirable performances of his (Heston)career."*

> *"It is a brooding scorching and beautifully disciplined tour de force for the actor."*

> *"If Heston could have been better, we don't know how"*

Hmmm?

The Saints players who had roles in the film received praise for their acting performances. The film gets a 5.7 rating on the IMBD page.

Quarterback Billy Kilmer was Heston's stunt double at about fifty pounds heftier than the movie icon. Kilmer had this to say about Heston's ball skills: "I know women who can throw a football better than him."

Saints center Joe Wendryhoski also said he had rarely seen a more unathletic man than Heston.

During a pivotal scene in the movie, aging star quarterback Cat Catlan (Heston) was to be sacked brutally.

The director and Heston told the real New Orleans Saints players, who were portraying the opposition defense in the scene, to be more realistic in the next take. The movie peeps wanted it to be more authentic.

The Saints obliged by knocking the living crap out of Heston and breaking three of his ribs.

Show Biz.

DOPE

The picture and video of a chain-smoking Saints head coach Dick Nolan, defeated, clueless, desperate at the failure of his 1979-80 team, are pitiful to see today.

Yet the blame for this does not fall to Nolan, who suffered from whatever was going on with his team. No, the shame belongs to his players, the ones who were wallowing in cocaine.

In 1982, defensive end Don Reese wrote an article that appeared in *Sports Illustrated* explaining in painful detail what was happening throughout the league in those days.

Reese is candid. Even though he assumed a great deal of responsibility and expressed shame for what he brought down on his family, he is a bit too easy on himself in parts of the article and assigns blame to others, including the league itself. The league should have saved this grown ass man from himself. And, indeed, he is right to some extent—the league should have done more.

Reese says the league sent a representative around each year to warn the players of the evils of drugs. He gave Reese his card. Reese said he called and left a message with his secretary. No call back.

Maybe.

Reese names names—Chuck Muncie not least among them. Reese claims that if Muncie had gotten off the coke he would have been "two Jim Browns" he was so talented.

He has interesting things to say about other teams such as the Pittsburgh Steelers: clean and successful. Or the Dolphins, who won the Super Bowl when they were clean and went downhill when they had a cocaine problem. The Chargers, where he landed after the Saints, he says were a den of free-basers.

Reese quoted Fred Dean, a defensive end for the Chargers, screaming in the locker room, "Why don't you freebasing bastards get out of here? You're killing us!" The Chargers got rid of Dean by trading him to the 49ers where he then earned a Super Bowl ring.

Reese says he had fifteen sources of cocaine in New Orleans. He says that during Dick Nolan's star-crossed tenure, New Orleans lost fourteen games in a row in 1980 when freebasing became popular in the NFL. Players snorted cocaine in the locker room before games and at halftime, and stayed up all night roaming the streets to "get more stuff."

He also says that at some point Mecom, the owner, knew, because he talked to Reese about it later. Yet Reese is also on record as saying that Mecom helped him by paying his drug debts and giving him moral support to get through his drug problems.

Reese tells of the pain it caused his family, and how he "did not come from a ghetto environment." No, no he came from a strong, loving, God-fearing family that taught him the responsibility and joy of hard work.

How is a fan supposed to feel about all this?

Selfishness beaucoup NFLPA.

RICKY WILLIAMS TRADE

Legendary.

Not in a good way.

Mike Ditka telegraphs that he will trade all of our magic beans for a bell-cow.

Okay, Ditka effuses to the press and lets it be known that the Saints will trade the entire draft for one player.

The story is even more strange as you hear Mike Detillier tell it. Detillier has been a staple of Saints drafts for two decades on WWL radio. The resident draft guru. And he was next to Ditka at Saints headquarters when the actual trade went down.

To hear Detillier tell it, the Saints were willing to give up *more* than they did to get Ricky Williams but teams were not biting.

Detillier, one night, relived the events of twenty years past for listeners of flagship radio station WWL 870 AM.

Detillier told of how Saints capologist Terry O'Neil had forewarned him that the Saints—at Ditka's behest—were all-in on trying to get Ricky Williams to the point of giving up the whole draft and more, future draft picks included. But the Saints were having trouble getting anyone to agree. No takers.

When the Colts took Edgerrin James, Detillier said he knew the Saints deal would go down. It did and the crowds erupted at Saints draft central. Detillier describes the reaction of Saints faithful as tumultuous—in a positive way.

Ditka, after addressing the crowd about the pick, raised his arms, sat next to Detillier and told him, "I think this is how Julius Caesar started."

It didn't work out as planned, but Williams turned out to be an interesting personality.

Hokie Gajan, former Saint and WWL broadcaster, told Detillier on draft day that he had met Williams and he described him as "a strange bird."

Hokie used to be a Saints scout and that scouting report was "on the money, honey."

GM Randy Mueller, whose dismissal by Tom Benson is still as big a mystery as the disappearance of Amelia Earhart, later traded Williams to Miami and got two number ones in return. It was one of the greatest trades in Saints history, considering all that went on before with Ditka and Williams.

JEDI KNIGHT

Terry O'Neil is a Jedi knight. No other explanation is as sexy or plausible:

Here is a link to the tale of Ricky Williams rookie contract negotiated by a firm headed by Master P and the Saints Jedi Knight, Terry O'Neil.

Master P has recently contended that the contract was Ricky Williams fault.

https://fivethirtyeight.com/features/ricky-williams-awful-nfl-contract-never-gave-him-a-chance/

BARROOM BRAWL

Billy Kilmer was the quarterback of the Saints in 1971. At that time he was dating owner John Mecom's secretary.

As the story was told to me, Kilmer and his lady were out on the town in a popular French Quarter bar sitting at a private table with a wall that put them out of view of the other customers.

John Mecom walks into the bar and is asked by the bartender how he was doing?

Mecom answers something to the affect of: "I'm okay but for my drunken quarterback who is dating my slut secretary."

Kilmer emerges from the shadows to demand an apology for the lady from the Saints owner.

The next day at Saints headquarters Mecom tells his general manager to trade Kilmer.

The Saints shop Kilmer. They receive four offers.

Mecom looks at the offers. He says trade him to Washington,

"Why Washington?" the general manager asks, as that is the worst offer.

Mecom's reasoning was that Washington had Sonny Jurgenson, one of the best passers in the league, Mecom said that if Kilmer found himself playing in Washington he would never see the light of day because he couldn't beat out Sonny Jurgenson.

Kilmer is traded to Washington.

In the 1971 season Jurgenson was injured. Kilmer takes over as quarterback and leads the Redskins to the Super Bowl in 1972.

Now you know the rest of the story that you didn't even know.

LEVITRA

Mike Ditka should be in the Shill Hall of Fame. The number of products Ditka hawked during his Saints tenure alone seemed inexhaustible.

Ditka is a deity in Chicago—not so much in New Orleans where I would venture to guess Ditka is at the top of the list of most disliked Saints of all time. Nonetheless, he is, over the years, all over the damn TV in America.

Madison Avenue evidently loved the lout.

Which brings us to Super Bowl XXXVIII in 2004.

USA Today publishes an "ad-meter" after every Super Bowl to rank the commercials which are a big part of the show on Super Bowl Sunday.

In the 2004 rankings, a commercial with Mike Ditka as the shill came in last. That's right, the worst commercial of 2004 Super Bowl featured Mike Ditka.

The product: Levitra.

Which is probably a good sign. The American people, it seemed, did not want any product that hints at making Mike Ditka a bigger dick than he already is.

Bam!

CURSE OF THE MUMMY

The New Orleans Saints were born, or at least the franchise was officially announced, on All Saints Day, a Catholic holiday, the day after Halloween.

The NFL is infested with curses; Detroit, Miami, Arizona bequeathed from the Chicago days, and more.

The Saints were one of the more unsuccessful franchises in NFL history, not winning their first playoff game for thirty-three years.

Enter voodoo, and the so-called curse.

It is contended that when the Superdome was being built, engineers discovered an old cemetery, the Girod Street Cemetery, and the remains were removed to another resting place.

Since this revelation, it is thought by some that the Saints are cursed. Voodoo is not that prevalent in the Big Easy, but there were and are people of "spiritual tendencies" lurking about New Orleans, Catholic city that it is— humans do believe in a lot of things that go bump in the night.

So, then the Saints found themselves in a playoff game, something they had never won before and we got voodoo hanging around in the crevasses of the city, so....

Enter Ava Kay Jones, voodoo and Yoruba Priest. (I guess Kay Ava Smith, voodoo priest and Harry Potter's first girlfriend, was not available.) At midfield, with a boa constrictor and artifacts, Ms. Jones exorcised the demons, and the Saints won their first playoff game 31-28.

They bring her in the following year and they somehow displease the gods by disrespecting Ms. Jones, according to her.

Okay.

Believe if you must.

But, let's look a little deeper.

The Saints played the first seven years in the NFL at Tulane Stadium, a big college stadium, home to the Sugar Bowl and located on Tulane University's campus.

As it turns out, at every game the Saints played in Tulane Stadium, there were two, er, people, or ex-people, in attendance.

Got Thothi Aunk and Nefer Atethu were languishing away under the stands but always there.

These two entities are Egyptian mummies that happened to be in residence at Tulane since 1852. Tulane Stadium was their home from 1955 to 1974. Every Saints game and every Green Wave game and three Super Bowls too.

The mummies were a gift to Tulane from one George Glidon, a one-time envoy to Egypt and well-known Egyptology lecturer of that time. He even shows up in a story, "Some Words with a Mummy," written in 1845 by Edgar Allen Poe.

So, it could possibly be that the Saints are suffering from some kind of Curse of The Mummy.

RUTHERFORD B. HAYES

If you Google Rutherford B. Hayes as a young man and the image comes on your screen of the photograph of the 18th President of the United States, you just may believe in reincarnation.

BLASPHEME

Mike Ditka found himself in 1997 coaching again in the NFL in New Orleans, still a very Catholic city.

Ditka is a practicing Catholic dude.

So, it seems he might pay attention to the Catholic press, and in New Orleans that would be *The Clarion Herald*, the newspaper of the New Orleans Archdiocese.

During Mike Ditka's tenure as head coach of the Saints, there was a column written by father William Maestri, a priest who wrote a regular column in *The Clarion Herald* pointing out how it was difficult for a working class family to afford to take their kids to an NFL game.

Ditka had recently been quoted about locals' reaction to a substantial ticket price hike by the Saints, "If everybody is going to complain, maybe New Orleans doesn't need a franchise."

This, on top of other disparaging remarks Ditka had strewn in the press about New Orleans since his arrival as head coach of the Saints.

Ditka somehow took umbrage at this and was moved to write a letter to the editors of *The Clarion Herald*.

In Ditka's defense, Maestri did refer to Ditka as being "beastly" in the column.

THE LETTER

Concerning Father William Maestri's article mentioning (The Beast) Coach Mike Ditka of the Saints.

It sickens me as a lifelong Catholic to read the ranting judgmental statements of a supposed-to-be Catholic priest.

The last I looked, the Bible tells us to judge not that we be not judged, But Father Maestri has taken on the role of God, who knows all and has blasphemed me because he has no concept or understanding of what was said.

Good writers as well as good priests should get their facts right before they condemn and judge others. Not only that, but to paint a picture of any person, for his audience to believe, before he has met or talked to that person is an act of cowardice.

I would have to believe that I'm a better Catholic than the holier than thou Father Maestri, because I choose not to play God concerning my fellow Christians.

If this letter seemed cutting, it was meant to be. I could have turned the other cheek, but that would have allowed Father Maestri to continue his yellow journalism.

I believe Father Maestri should ask for God's forgiveness, I know I'll ask God to forgive him.

MIKE DITKA
Head Coach,
New Orleans Saints

There ya go.

FEARS

I heard the late Buddy D, a radio icon in New Orleans, the guy responsible for the Bagheads among other things, relate this story over the airwaves one night:

Buddy said it was the first preseason game in Tulane Stadium of the Saints, a new franchise in the NFL, and as such it was a new experience for New Orleans sportswriters because they now had their very own pro team to cover.

It turned out that Buddy and the head coach, Tom Fears, were the last two guys in the locker room after the game and something occurred to Buddy. He asked Coach Fears about it. He and the other writers had noticed something they thought was peculiar during the game.

Often, when plays finished, Fears would run way down the field to argue with the refs, even on plays that didn't seem to warrant a coach's ire. It happened quite often. It included Fears running down all the way to the goal line, which was against the rules. Coaches are only allowed to run down so far.

Buddy asked the coach what was up?

Fears made Buddy D promise not to share the reason for the unusual running up and down the sideline.

Fears said strictly off the record...and I mean off the record. Buddy D agreed.

John Mecom owned the Saints. A young twenty-something, he was one of the first owners to habituate the sidelines. He stuck close to Fears.

Fears told Buddy D that before the game an FBI agent came to see him and told him they had a tip that a local physician who claimed Mecom was having an affair with his wife had told people he was going to shoot Mecom that night.

Fears said every time he looked around during the game he found Mecom right next to him. Fears was afraid that if the doctor made good on his threat, he, Fears, might get shot by mistake. So, he ran away from Mecom every chance he could.

OVERTIME

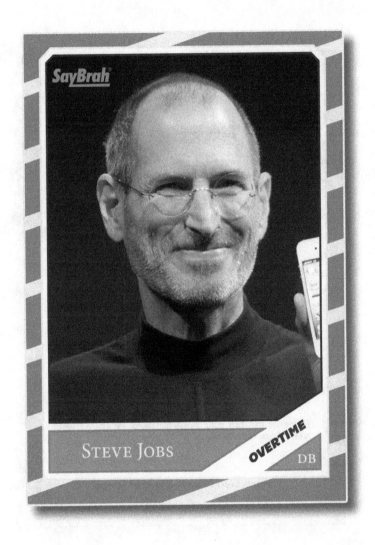

STEVE JOBS, BIRTH OF HALFTIME, AND TAKE THE POINTS

33

OVERTIME

"In football everything is complicated by the presence of the other team."
—Jean-Paul Sartre, French Philosopher

SayBrah®

The National Football League was founded on August 20th, 1920 in Canton, Ohio.

Twice as many people name pro football as their game of choice over the NBA and MLB combined.

In 2019, the 32 teams of the NFL generated revenue of $15.26 billion U.S. dollars.

Variety reports 102 million total viewers tuned in for Super Bowl LIV between the Kansas City Chiefs and the San Francisco 49ers.

Three of the top four most-watched TV shows were NFL telecasts in 2020.

Super Bowl LV will be held in Tampa.

PUDGE

Pudge Hefflefinger as we have seen in the Pittsburgh Steeler chapter is recognized as the first pro football player.

There are a couple of things of note about Pudge that I find quite interesting.

His father Chrtistopher Hefflefinger was one of the first Americans to volunteer to fight for the union at the beginning of the Civil War. Christopher reached the rank of captain and he fought at Gettysburg where he was shot in the chest but a book he had in his pocket caught the brunt of the bullet and his life was saved.

Pudge himself, after becoming an All-American at Yale on a team that outscored its opponents 698-0, went on to become the first pro and a celebrity for his prowess on the gridiron.

In 1922 at the age of fifty-three he was enticed to play in a charity game against a team of former Ohio State stars and he dislocated his shoulder early in the game, had it popped back in, and went on to play thirty-one more minutes of that game (which his team won 16-0). It was the first time he had ever worn a helmet and shoulder pads in a game.

Pudge wasn't finished. In Minnesota in 1933 there was a game to raise money for charity and the tickets were not selling well so Pudge was recruited to play one more game because of his celebrity, at the age of nearly sixty-one.

He did play for about nine minutes and his knee started to act up so at that point he demurred, ending quite an illustrious football career.

He was so large by that time they could not find a uniform to fit him so he stuffed his clothes with towels and stuff to serve as padding.

THE FINAL OPTION

The case with the nuclear codes for the President of the United States is called "The Football."

AND THERE'S THIS

In 2014 *New York Magazine* had a list of the most influential New York based Tweeters of the year. Second? Donald Trump.

First? Adam Schefter, NFL insider.

Priorities.

A few tidbits of early pro football:

1. In 1902, Tom O'Rourke, manager of Madison Square Garden, decided he needed an attraction for his slow time at the end of December. His idea was a World Series of Pro Football that would consist of a gauntlet-like schedule of five teams from New York and New Jersey. It was the first indoor pro football game in history.

    It was a financial flop and after the 1903 World Series it was discontinued. Yet it left a couple of colorful anecdotes.

    The referee in the series was said to be decked out in full evening dress. This attire consisted of a top hat, white gloves, and patent leather shoes. At the end of the last game the winning team decided to run over the fancy-pants-dressed ref and the team paid for his dry cleaning.

2. Fritz Pollard was the star of the Akron Pros, the first champions of the NFL. He was also the first African-American player and coach in the NFL.

    It is a curious point of interest that in the days when Fritz Pollard was the biggest star of the Akron Pros that Summit County, where Akron is located, had the largest KKK membership of any county in the United States.

3. November 1926: the Duluth Eskimos played five games in eight days. One of those games was against the Pottstown Maroons and as the Eskimo players remembered it years later as they approached the field for the game they were met with the sight of the Pottstown Fire Department firefighters hosing down the field to negate the Eskimos' speed.

    According to Ole Haugsrud, the rest of the game the referees were real "homers." Time after time Duluth, after gaining yards, were penalized to excess. It got so bad that even the good-natured players were getting riled up to the point that star player Ernie Nevers had to remind them to stay cool as they would surely be thrown out of the game if they retaliated to bad calls or rough play.

    Russ Method, described as one of those even keeled players, who had enough when the Eskimos ran down to the 5 yard line and were then penalized 50 yards. On the next play, Method ran over the referee.

The most colorful gambit of the day was turned in by Jimmy Manion who was described as "our midget guard." Manion had perfected a technique in which he would run toward the line of scrimmage toward the other team and leap feet first across the line. He did it on that day and caught the referee right in the mouth. The result was to knock out several of the referee's teeth.

4. Canton-Massillon game pre-NFL. The game would settle the championship and was very close to a blood feud between towns only fifteen miles apart. Serious amounts of money were bet on such games.

Massillon in the fourth quarter with the score standing at 6-0. Canton breaks away on a potential winning score. As the runner approached the goal line around the 2-yard line he was swallowed by the home crowd. No one can see if he scored because of the throng of surging fans. Just then the ball popped back into the field and Canton's 6'3" tackle Charles Smith jumps on it and recovers the "fumble."

The runner insists that a Canton fan kicked the ball out of his hand. He even describes the villain as a member of the Canton police force. He then describes the culprit in detail down to his shiny brass buttons and blue coat. Only problem is everyone in Canton knew that Canton at that time did not have a uniformed police force. All hell broke loose as the crowd, many of whom bet, waited for the referee to make a decision. The confusion and hubbub that was raised by the play caused the game to end there as the crowd was just too unruly.

The referee's momma didn't raise no fool. He agreed to rule but he would seal his decision not to be opened until after midnight the next morning so he could catch a train and get the hell out of Canton.

Midnight came. The sealed decision was opened at a local hotel at 12:30 a.m. It read: "No buttons, no policeman, no kicking, no touchdown. Canton wins."

Years later one of the players who had played on Massillon's side met a man who told him that it was he who had kicked the ball out of the runner's hand. He said that he had bet $30 on the game, which was his entire week's salary. He was very believable. The man was a streetcar conductor. He was wearing a blue uniform with brass buttons.

5. 1912, the famed Carlisle Indian School team was playing Army. The Carlisle Indian School's mission was to de-Indian the Indians. Pop Warner was the coach of the Carlisle team that of course featured the great Jim Thorpe.

Here is Pop Warner's pre-game speech: "Your fathers and your grandfathers, are the ones who fought their fathers. These men that are playing against you today are soldiers. They are the Long Knives. You are Indians. Tonight we will know if you are warriors."

Final: Carlisle 27, Army 6.

Jim Thorpe and his teammates prevailed. And oh, by the way, the middle linebacker for Army? Dwight David Eisenhower.

NO ROOM AT THE INN

New Orleans is the preferred destination for the Super Bowl by most of the members of the press who have covered the big game.

Everything is centrally located including a downtown stadium, the Superdome.

That is not to say that there aren't sometimes problems with the good times to be had in the "Big Easy."

Case in point: Super Bowl week in the 70's, *NFL Films* showed up at the Bienville House, an inn located in the French Quarter.

NFL Films had reservations for all of its people and a few rooms for equipment.

When they arrive they are informed that some of their rooms have been sold to a dry cleaning convention, who paid a higher price.

This leaves *NFL Films* a few rooms short on Super Bowl week when the entire city is booked.

Improvisation is called for in the "Birthplace of Jazz."

A local physician was going to work as one of *NFL Films* '"amateur" photographers for the game. The local doc has the photographers who were roomless admitted into a hospital as "non-confining observation" patients. This means they are staying in the hospital but they can come and go as they please.

Interesting solution. One photographer was put in a non-private room with a patient. This *actual* patient was hooked up to medical machines, IV's, tubes the usual hospital patient accouterments.

NFL film guy and roommate get chummy. They talk into the night about children, family, World War II, what have you.

Photographer nodded off. In the middle of the night there was a buzzing. The *real* patient is coding. Unfortunately the gentlemen died that night,

Next day at the Super Bowl, the NFL photographer was so shook up he had to be reassigned to a less stressful duty for the game.

Two audibles.

In 1956 a group of disgruntled Cleveland Browns players got a lawyer.

Their first meeting was at the Waldorf Astoria in New York and every team but the Chicago Bears had a representative.

Creighton Miller, the attorney and former Notre Dame football star, sent a letter to the league mapping out the demands of the players, such as a minimum salary of $5,000 and payment for injured players.

Crickets from the league. No response.

In 1957 Bill Radovich, an undrafted USC player who had entered the league in 1938 by signing and playing four years for the Detroit Lions (and at a Pro Bowl level) before leaving the league to serve in World War II, happened to meet attorney Joseph Alioto at the Brown Derby in Los Angeles where Radovich was working as a waiter. Radovich discussed his predicament with Alioto and Alioto wrote out a legal brief on a cocktail napkin.

Radovich's situation? Radovich had come back from World War II in 1945 to find his father very ill. He asked the Lions to trade him to the Rams so he could be closer to his ailing father. The Lions refused and told Radovich he had no choice but to either play for them or play for no one.

He signed with the Los Angeles Dons of the AAAFC, Radovich was then offered a player-coach position with a minor league in Los Angeles. When the minor league team found out that Radovich had been blacklisted by the NFL—which the minor league was affiliated with—they rescinded the offer. This left Radovich to fend for himself.

Then he met Alioto, who happened to be a top antitrust attorney.

In 1957, Radovich v. National Football League was a landmark case in which the Supreme Court ruled in Radovich's favor. The court ruled that the Sherman Antitrust Act applied to the NFL.

The NFL owners were then faced with the prospect of accepting the National Football League Players Association or a lawsuit.

They accepted. Reluctantly.

Radovich's name is unknown to most fans, receiving a settlement of $45,000 for his troubles.

THE 2nd AMENDMENT

Pete Rozelle hired FBI agent Jack Danahy as head of NFL Security in 1968, a position he held until he resigned to go into private business in 1980.

Danahy was the guy who administered polygraph tests to numerous NFL owners about gambling and it was Danahy who interviewed Lenny Dawson before Super Bowl IV when the allegation of his ties to gamblers broke in the national press.

Danahy was an FBI agent from 1942-1968 and had quite a resume: he handled a German double-agent during World War II, he was the trial investigator for the Alger Hiss case, served as the supervisor for the Soviet Espionage Section of the FBI, he arrested the spy that was eventually swapped with the Russians in return for downed U2 pilots, personally handled a key Soviet defector, and it was Danahy who proposed the anti-organized crime squad that became the Federal Strike Force approved by RFK that aggressively went after racketeering.

When asked if there had been attempts to fix games under his watch, Danahy said that in his years in the league there were probably innumerable attempts to fix games. He said he would be a fool to think otherwise. But he also thought that most attempts were not reported by players because it would have been a hassle to do so. Danahy believed that most attempts were met with a cold shoulder by the players.

Nonetheless Danahy was at odds with what you might call "the underworld" and illegal gambling interests. It was his job to keep the NFL players, owners, officials, and the game honest.

He said he had no idea how much money was illegally wagered on football in a year and admitted it was probably an unknowable amount.

Once he was asked for information as to how many bookmakers were working in New York. He had no idea. However, instead of avoiding the issue and the question, he took the number of bars in New York, multiplied it by two, and told the curious party (presumably a journalist) 1,476. This seems to have satisfied the inquisitor.

Perhaps Danahy's position as NFL security chief and adversary of undesirable elements followed him once he was out of the NFL?

The year after he left the NFL to start his own security company, he was walking down a street in New York City and he was attacked. The assailant hit him violently, knocking him down. As he lay on the sidewalk the attacker continued to pummel him and he realized that he would not be able to get up to defend himself before his attacker had finished him off, which seemed to be the goal. As it turned out Danahy had a gun on him. So he took it out and shot and killed his "mugger."

This incident seemed to garner very little press and you can find very little info on this curious crime online.

Hmmm?

THE G.O.A.T.

The Super Bowl is a secular national holiday in the United States.

It has its own rituals like any holiday, such as where you watch the game, with whom will you watch the game, and what will you have to eat and drink.

Somewhere along the way the commercials that are now tailored by ad agencies in most cases just for the prime time impact of the games huge worldwide audience, became part of the ritual.

That somewhere is traced to January 22, 1984 when Apple Computer ran its "1984" ad to introduce its MacIntosh computer to the world.

Up until Super Bowl XVIII only one company had made a Super Bowl commercial especially for the Super Bowl.

Advertising Age in a poll it published named Apple's "1984" commercial the greatest TV commercial of all time.

It ran only once, sort of, and almost wasn't run at all.

Steve Jobs hired Chiat/Day to create and produce the ad. When Jobs showed it to Apple's Board of Directors, they hated it.

Apple had purchased ninety seconds on the Super Bowl telecast but would sell thirty seconds of the time to another firm after the board disapproved of the ad. Jobs and Steve Wozniak each agreed to pay half of the ad's cost if necessary. Apple did end up paying for the ad. It was a sensation.

It was perhaps the first time a Super Bowl ad caused such buzz and it set the standard that others have aimed for in their Super Bowl ads since.

The ad was created by a team of three: copywriter Steve Hayden, art director Brent Thomas, and creative director Lee Clow.

Ridley Scott, the director of *Blade Runner* directed the ad, which cost $900,000 to produce. Scott has gone on to be one of the finest directors in film having directed *Thelma and Louise*, *Gladiator*, *Kingdom of Heaven*, *Alien*, *The Martian* and many other films of note.

The ad is said to have only run that one time which has added to its legend.

Technically it was first run on TV in December 1983 at 1 am on a TV station KMVT in Twin Falls, Idaho right before sign off as to make it eligible for awards in 1984.

And it was later run before movies in theaters until April of 1984 when George Orwell's estate claimed copyright infringement and filed a cease and desist order.

But by then the commercial, which Jobs wanted to announce that his new product would change the world, also changed the Super Bowl, for as huge NFL fan Hunter S. Thompson might say, "for good or ill."

ROOM 990

In 1965 the AFL had scheduled its All-Star Game for New Orleans.

The main promoter of the game, Dave Dixon, had been tirelessly trying to get pro football in New Orleans for years, This game was to showcase the city which was a hotbed of football fans as has been borne out by the history of the New Orleans Saints. After Katrina, New Orleans—often described with the "small market" appellation—a city that was devastated like almost no other in American history, sold out season tickets to a team that many thought was about to abandon them in their hour of need. The Saints have been sold out ever since. And this is for a team that never won D#¢k.

Yet it was 1965 and this was the Deep South. In retrospect, the promoters of this game dropped the ball. Big Time.

The AFL had given many men a second chance or even a first chance at the pro football apple.

This goes for every demographic, but not least of all the African-American players.

When the AFL All-Stars descended on New Orleans the trouble was waiting at the airport.

There were laws in New Orleans, admittedly out of touch with the direction of race relations in the United States, and the men who promoted this game were men of the world and should have known better as to not smooth the way for what was about to happen.

At the airport taxis, according to law and certainly to the local attitude of m,any would not allow white taxi cabs to pick up African-Americans. As it turned out there was a loophole of some sort that would allow white taxis to pick up African-Americans if a white person hired the cab.

It may be hard to compute looking from the 21st century but this was the reality on the ground in New Orleans in 1965.

African-American players found they could not hire cabs, they could not go into clubs, and they could not patronize certain restaurants and bars.

On Bourbon Street players were even threatened at gunpoint when they tried to force themselves into a music club.

There were laws.

As unconstitutional as these laws were, they were still the law. Which put rank and file citizens in unwinnable situations.

The players, supposedly led by Cookie Gilchrist along with others, summoned each other to room 990 of The Roosevelt Hotel—at that time the premier hotel in the city and the hotel where players were staying—for a meeting.

The Roosevelt had been the headquarters of Louisiana's legendary governor Huey Long back in the day.

On the bus to practice that day, the white players noticed that there were no black players. Ron Mix and Jack Kemp went to speak to the black players.

The societal slights were as blatant as could be.

City leaders even sent Ernest "Dutch" Morial, then President of the New Orleans Chapter of the NAACP, to "reason" with the players. He asked for twenty-four hours to straighten the situation out. Morial would go on to become the first African-American mayor of New Orleans.

Long story short, the players voted to boycott the game and not play. The players then left New Orleans.

Hastily, the game was moved to Houston and played before a crowd of 15,000 plus.

In 1966, New Orleans got its NFL franchise.

The late Buddy D, an iconic sports journalist in New Orleans, often said on his radio show that one of the most important issues in regard to racial attitudes in the city was the Saints coming to New Orleans. It was a rallying point that all citizens could relate to and it was Buddy's contention that the Saints were one of the few things that got the races on the same page.

As such, Room 990 of the Roosevelt Hotel is a little-recognized landmark of the Civil Rights movement.

In 1925 C. C. Pyle, known to the world as "Cash-and-Carry" Pyle, a promoter extraordinaire signed Red Grange, the most famous football player in America to a three-year contract.

Grange and Pyle came to an agreement with Geroge Halas of the Chicago Bears to have Grange play with the Bears on a nineteen-city barnstorming tour.

After the tour's success, with over 65,000 people coming out to see Grange play in New York, Pyle wanted the NFL to grant him a new team that would feature Grange—the NFL's New York Yankees—but with Tim Mara's Giants already in New York, the NFL did not want another New York team and his request was denied.

So Pyle started his own league, the American Football League.

There were nine teams.

The New York Yankees with Grange; the Philadelphia Quakers, who would win the championship; the Boston Bulldogs, who folded after four games; the Brooklyn Horseman, which claimed Notre Dame's "Four Horsemen" as their main attraction, a team that folded into the already existing Brooklyn franchise in the NFL after four games; the Chicago Bulls, owned and operated by Joey Sternaman (the brother of Chicago Bears co-owner Dutch Sternaman); the Cleveland Panthers; the Los Angeles Wildcats, who did not play a game in Los Angeles but were a road team (almost all Wildcat players hailed from west of the Mississippi); the Newark Bears, whose backfield consisted of players that all played college football in Georgia; and the Rock Island Independents, who jumped from the NFL to join the American Football League.

Philadelphia and New York played before large crowds. The others? Not so much. The League folded after one season.

In 1926 there were twenty-six pro football franchises and by 1927 only twelve.

Pro football was such an under-the-radar enterprise for most of America—the college game being so wildly popular that when Red Grange and the Chicago Bears visited the White House and met president Calivn Cooloidge, Coolidge was informed that Grange was with the Chicago Bears and Coolidge answered, "I have always enjoyed animal acts."

Grange joined the Bears in 1927.

Pyle was quite a character. He designed a domed stadium in the early 20's that would be equipped with magnifying glasses that a spectator could bring up at his seat to get a closer look at the action like looking through a pair of binoculars.

He had a debilitating stroke which paralyzed him on one side.

Red Grange said Pyle showed up a couple of years later seemingly recovered from the stroke.

Pyle told him he had gone to a cottage in the woods of Wisconsin and built a pulley type contraption and paid kids to use the pulley to first exercise his arm every day and then his leg until he regained use of his extremities.

C. C. was quite an interesting guy.

GENTLEMAN, START YOUR AGREEMENT

In 1934 a Harlem businessman James Semler, in reaction to the exclusion of African-American players from the NFL after the 1933 season, organized a pro football team—the New York Brown Bombers, a team made up exclusively of African-American players.

The idea, among other things, was to showcase that there were indeed enough good African-American football players in America who could play at the highest level.

This seems self-evident today when the NFL is more than 70% African-American.

Nonetheless, this is now and sadly, that was then.

The team's coach was Fritz Pollard, an ex-NFL player who had played and starred in the first official NFL season—1920—for the undefeated champion Akron Pros. Pollard, who was the highest paid member of the Akron Pros, is the only member of the Akron team of 1920 who is in the NFL Hall of Fame. Pollard led the Pros to an undefeated season with a record of 8-0-3.

By the time he became coach of the Brown Bombers, Pollard was retired and running a newspaper in New York. He took the job with the Brown Bombers to help get African-Americans back into the pro football business.

Pollard assembled an all-star team of great African-American players, including: Joe Lillard, Duke Slater, and Sol Butler; gathering the bulk of his players from HBCU's (Historically Black Colleges and Universities) long before the NFL started to do so post-World War II.

The record of the Brown Bombers, named after heavyweight fighter Joe Louis, is elusive, as there are different tabulations of their win-loss record in the accounts of the team and found in online archives. Even in the Black press of the time, reporting of the teams games was spotty.

They played mostly what would be considered minor league teams as all NFL teams refused to play them.

The Brown Bombers played many games on the West Coast against white teams.

Pro football was not a big money-maker in those days and the team struggled to make ends meet and eventually this, along with the Great Depression, led the team to disband.

The team had mixed success on the field of play and while it's hard to pin down its actual record they did hold their own mostly and on some occasions defeated top minor league teams.

The so-called "gentlemen's agreement" that the NFL adopted after the 1933 season is in modern times blamed on George Preston Marshall, owner of the Redskins.

Pollard could attest to the fact that even in his day as a star at Akron and as the first African-American head coach in the NFL in the 1920's that he was subjected to vicious taunts from both players and spectators as well as the fact that opposing players would go out of the way to injure him. He knew full well what he was up against but was a pioneer who fought to include African-Americans in this part of American life through actions on the field and off as well as later with his newspaper.

He had started an all African-American team in Chicago, the Chicago Blackhawks—a team that predates the New York Brown Bombers—in an attempt to demonstrate not only the level of skill possessed by African-American players but that they could coexist on the field without causing riots and mayhem, one of the arguments used to keep them out of the league.

It was evident to most, even in the day when the twenty-one African-Americans who played in the NFL from 1920 to 1933 that societal and league forces were trying to minimize African-American participation.

Iowa All-American Oze Simmons and Pollard both claim that George Halas told them that he would love to have them on his team but that there was an unwritten agreement in the league not to allow them to play. To a question as to why African-American players didn't play in the 40's, Halas much later would only say that he really didn't know. That's about as lame an answer as you could come up with since Halas had been one of the most important constants in league matters throughout the history of the league.

In the 40's, Kenny Washington, the UCLA great, played in the College All-Star Game in Chicago and Halas told him he was trying to find a way to sign Washington but that an unwritten agreement prevented it.

In 1946, Washington became the first African-American to sign an NFL contract and join the Los Angeles Rams. By that time Washington was getting older and had had several knee operations. Although still a good player, his prime had passed.

The Rams signed Woody Strode shortly after signing Washington and the Cleveland Browns signed Bill Willis and Marion Motley soon after that same year thereby re-breaking the color line.

It is of some note that free enterprise or competition in the form of the All American Football Conference post-World War II and the formation of the upstart American Football League in 1960 was important in giving African-American players a place to display their talents and was in no small measure an accelerant to the ultimate embrace of African-Americans in the NFL.

George Preston Marshall, clearly a dedicated racist, gets most of the blame for keeping the NFL all white for the thirteen years between 1933 to 1946.

However Pollard blamed NY Giants owner Tim Mara, who refused to schedule the Brown Bombers, and George Halas for the "gentleman's agreement" and not Marshall.

The Brown Bombers hung on for a few seasons and never could make a financial go of it. One year, a second team in New York—also named the Brown Bombers and also exclusively African-American—was formed to compete for the same fanbase in New York City which didn't help matters.

The team was finally done in by the Great Depression and financial woes.

Fritz Pollard's name is not a household name in America like Jackie Robinson but Pollard is worthy of true iconic status.

All-American in 1919, first African-American player in the Rose Bowl, first African-American to be named to the prestigious Walter Camp All-American Team, star of the first NFL champion Akron Pros in 1920, first African-American head coach in the NFL. He was finally inducted into the NFL Hall of Fame in 2005.

Other greats like Joe Lillard (the last African-American NFL player in 1933), Duke Slater (NFL Hall of Famer in 2020) and Kenny Washington, (voted outstanding college player in 1940 and first NFL player signed to the NFL in 1946 to reintegrate the league) are now all but forgotten.

MUSIC MAN

Sam Spence, who died at the age of eighty-eight in 2016 in Longview, Texas, is one of the most unknown famous composers in American history.

In 1966 the radios of America were playing the Association's hit "Cherish" or the Righteous Brothers, "You're My Soul and Inspiration." Tunes that if you lived in that era you remember well.

But do you remember Sam Spence's music?

If you're an NFL fan you do.

In 1966 the embryonic *NFL Films* tapped Spence, an American composer living in Germany to compose the music to accompany the films.

Spence went on to compose numerous soundtracks to backup the NFL film images and narration by John Facenda and others.

In 1998 the compilation of his compositions was released, "The Power and The Glory the Original Music + Voices of NFL films."

The original choice of NFL films was a guy named Mahlon Merrick who was doing the music for the Jack Benny program and soon handed the NFL films gig to Spence.

Ed Sabol had preferred Spence's sweeping orchestration to Merrick's more march heavy approach.

Spence's success was not without its controversy over the years.

Some complain that bassoon drone, a timpani here, a woodwind there were healthy derivatives or at best homages.

They were Hollywood-esque but this is and what seems to have been needed here.

Steve Sabol said of the *NFL Films'* music: "I wanted music that would speak to the passion of the game and that would also be contemporary."

Spence made good use of folk songs, drinking songs and public domain traditional music.

His composition "Up She Rises" relies on a healthy dose of the tune in "Drunken Sailor" which is presumably why it has found its way into heavy use in the cartoon *SpongeBob Squarepants*.

Spence until the day he died had a dispute with the NFL over royalty payment for his work. It's simple he got none.

His version of the story is that early on he received a call from the NFL at his home in Germany informing him that his work was being ripped off and the NFL was going to go to court on his behalf. His NFL Film music the league told him was being used in the porn film *Deep Throat*.

Spence told the NFL not to worry as Germany had laws about such things and they would protect him. The NFL insisted and sent him a copy of *Deep Throat* which he watched in its entirety for legal purposes taking notes to mark the spots where his music was featured on the film's soundtrack.

Spence said he found not one note of his music in the porno flick.

The NFL tried again. They called him and said they were going to trial in two days and they needed him to sign a document to fight for his work in court. He said he did not want to sign the document they FedExed him. He was persuaded to sign it and gave it to the FedEx guy with a promise from the NFL that they would return the signed document as soon as the case was settled. They didn't.

So? No royalties ever,

You'll be hard pressed to find another story that includes the movie *Deep Throat*, the NFL, and Spongebob Squarepants.

GUERILLA TV

As time capsule's of the NFL experience go, the 1976 production of Super Bowl X by TVTV is a very wistful and interesting ride.

TVTV was a production company that started in 1972 with a mission. According to Wikipedia, the mission was to take advantage of new video technologies to change society and have a good time among other high and low purposes.

TVTV went on to cover and make documentaries of both the Democratic and Republican Conventions in 1972, cover the Oscars, and even a documentary of a Bob Dylan concert and eventually a PBS series. It appears they were well connected to get access to all those plum gigs.

TVTV's documentary of Super Bowl X at some point became "Super Bowl IX and Half" and features among the staff Bill Murray (newly minted member of *SNL* by that time), Christopher Guest, and Brian Doyle Murray. The production cast also included Harold Ramis (so that would be two Ghostbusters included in the Super Bowl documentary, for those counting).

TVTV had great access to the players even going into their hotel rooms, locker rooms before and after the game, interviews with Steelers wives, and a CBS-sponsored touch football game with short interviews with Phyllis George, Pat Summerall, and Johnny Unitas.

Unitas is offered a Chevy by Bill Murray in the short flippant interview and Unitas turns it down saying he prefers Pontiacs and Murray asks him why he prefers Pontiac and Unitas replies that he likes the Indian Hood ornament on the Pontiac.

Paul Hornung and Tom Brookshier are also seen at the touch football game along with George at that time a CBS TV personality.

There are cameos of and a brief appearance by Walter Cronkite in the Super Bowl crowd and a Steeler wife getting access to the Steelers locker area after the Steelers win by showing her marriage certificate to prove who she is.

There are three cuts of TE Jean Fugett that give a personal touch to the experience, one inside the Dallas locker room and introducing some of his teammates, a second on the sideline after a game ending injury and finally after the game reactions lamenting the loss and his inability to play in such a big game all of which gives a unique overview at the human and personal experience of a player.

Johnny Unitas, Bill Murray, Paul Hornung, Christopher Guest, Phyllis George, Pat Summerall, Steelers wives by the pool, and what appears to be Colts owner Bill Irsay making fun of the NFL union head Ed Garvey with explicit contempt.

All in all, a fascinating guerrilla documentary of the Super Bowl.

You can see it on YouTube.

THE NATIONAL ANTHEM

You just never know who you might see playing in an NFL game or what impact that person might have on the Earth.

November 9,1922 Paul Robeson scored both TD's in Milwaukee Badgers 12-0 victory over the Oorang Indians.

To call Paul Robeson, a former NFL player with the Akron Pros and Milwaukee Badgers in the first two NFL seasons, a renaissance man is to just scratch the surface.

Robeson was an NFL player, an All American at Rutgers,valedictorian at Rutgers, he excelled in other sports, he was a lawyer, a stage performer, and a film star, and of course a giant of the civil rights movement for no other reason than his high profile and steadfast support of the cause.

He became an international star with his singing of "Ole Man River" in the London premier of Showboat.

This gave him a powerful platform that he used all of his life.

Now to the national anthem.

No, not the Star Spangled Banner but the Chinese National anthem.

Say what?

"March of the Volunteers" was a song written by Nie Er with lyrics by poet Tian Han in the early 1930's. The song was for a theatrical production in support of the Chinese struggle against the Japanese invasion and conquest.

1932 saw Pathe records issue a gramophone that was available in China and then in 1936 the song was used by activist Liu Liangmo at large rallies and the song went as we say in this day an age 'viral'.

Liu Liangmo requested that Robeson record "The March of the Volunteers" and after a concert in New York City in which Robeson sang the song in both English and Chinese Robeson the recording was made and helped to popularize the song.

Robeson's stature around the world as an artist is given some credit for helping make the song internationally known.

The song became a rallying cry for Chinese freedom and was even recorded by the Air Force Choir as the opening music in part of the Why We Fight series that was supervised by famous Hollywood director Frank Capra, during World War II.

In 1949 "March of the Volunteers" became the National anthem of the People's Republic of China.

During the cultural revolution of 1966 it fell out of favor with Mao and its lyricist Tian Han was imprisoned without trial and later died in prison in 1968.

In 1982 the song was rehabilitated and became once again the national anthem of China. In 2002 it was given constitutional protection as the official Chinese National anthem.

Robeson's contribution to its popularity and impact was not insignificant and he is recognized by the People's Daily the official paper of the People's Republic of China Republic of China on many occasions with articles praising the American singers contribution to the cause of the Chinese people.

Robeson's accomplishment along with his significant connection to the national anthem of China make him arguably the most famous person ever to play in the NFL.

OORANG

Walter Lingo plunked down $100 to buy a franchise in the NFL in 1922.

Lingo was what you'd call an American entrepreneur of the highest order.

He had an affinity for the Native American culture he believed had flourished in the land around LaRue, Ohio, where he lived, and for his Oorang Airedales that he bred and sold.

He named his team the Oorang Indians and as he was a good friend of Jim Thorpe the great Native American athlete Thorpe was asked to help Lingo organize his team. He made a deal with Thorpe, whose job it was to assemble and coach the team and recruit an all Native American squad.

But the main raison d'etre of the Oorang Indians was to promote the sale of Lingo's Airedales.

The team worked at the kennel during the week and in the off-season, and played football on the weekends.

LaRue, Ohio, had a population of only about 1,000 and as such is the smallest town ever to have an NFL team.

Consequently, they played most of their games on the road.

The games also featured the birth of the halftime show. It is believed that the hawking of Airedales and the Indian skill exhibitions the team performed were the first real halftime shows.

Jim Thorpe would run the dogs through a series of tricks and the Indians would perform a kind of Wild West show by throwing tomahawks and knives and performing Indian dances.

The team had very little success on the field as many of the Native players were over 40.

The second season, 1923, they won very few games and were outscored 235-12.

The players were drawn from a wide variety of Native tribes such as the Cherokee, Blackfeet, Mohawk, Mission, Winnebago, Chippewa, Penobscot among others. A few had colorful Native names.

Joe Little Twig, Big Bear,Wrinklemeat, Red Fang,Gray Horse,Laughing Gas,Dick Deerslayer, Baptiste Thunder, Bear Behind the Woodchuck, Xavier Downwind, Arrowhead, War Eagle and Long Time Sleep.

The team lost some of its drawing power in the second season as the crowd appeal the second time around for the halftime show waned. The team folded after the 1923 season.

Mr. Lingo's Oorang Airedales, on the other hand, sold by the thousands in pre-depression America. They went for $150 apiece. One Airedale was worth more than the whole NFL franchise.

The Great Depression hurt Lingo's business but the kennel stayed in business into the 1960s.

WHAT'S THE POINT

One of the most influential fellows in the history of football is a guy you probably never heard of even if you are a HUGE football fan.

His name was Charles K. McNeil and he was once a mathematics teacher. One of his high school students was John F. Kennedy, ya know, the president guy.

Anyway, Charles was a gambler. And a good one. Actually a very very good one. So good that the bookies in Chicago where he was a security analyst would limit his bets.

He was so good at gambling he quit his job to gamble full time. Charles came up with an idea. It's called the point spread.

It was the 1940s and he was pissed about being limited by the bookies so he became a bookie and he introduced the spread to his customers. This was a system he had used himself to make his bets. He put his old bookie out of business.

He estimated that he won 25 out of 27 years, winning a bit over 60% of the time, and he said he won about $325,00 a year on average.

As in all stories that involve credit for the invention of anything from the wheel to television it is hard to pin down to a definitive moment or human who actually gets the whole credit for creation.

And so it is with Charles K.McNeil, it seems that the point spread was used by others in the 30's notably Karl Ersin and Darby Hicks guys who worked at the Minneapolis Star Tribune and a gambling newsletter the Minneapolis Gorham Press.

But it is recognized by almost all the big hitters in the gambling racket that McNeil was the guy who popularized the point spread and thereby is responsible for its toehold and subsequent success.

He was a legend. He hung around a place called the Gym Club in Chicago and is said to have had the fight song of the college team he had bet on that day played over the loudspeaker at the club.

Other men made their mark on the gambling racket besides Mr. McNeil.

Another titan of the "industry" is a dude named Ed Curd.

Ed was the guy who invented the "juice." You bet $11 to win $10.

But back to Charles K. McNeil, he was perhaps the most successful sports gambler of all time and when the mob wanted to partner up with him he just decided it was time to call it a career and he quit.

For better (or for bettor) or worse the game was changed by a math teacher. His name again, Charles K. McNeil.

His thoughts on successful gambling:

To be successful you had to have three things—money, guts and brains—and if you didn't have all three you would fail.

There should be a Hall of Fame for guys like Charles.

HALL OF FAME

Special Thanks to Sarah Burnette, Bob Detwiler, Christine Donnelly, Gina Ferrara, Karissa Kary, David Rowe, and Janis Turk.

And Tom Amoss, Larry Beron, Danny Burnstein, Joshua Clark, Jill Conner, Judy Conner, Jeff Duncan, Jo Gershman, Steve Grishman, Su Gonczy, Alden Hagardorn, Lew Lefton, John Travis, Angus Lind, Debbie Lindsey, Heidi Melancon, Philip Melancon, Rhonda Munsterman, Austin Niel, Daniel Nodurft, Ron Swoboda, Elizabeth Thompson, Robert Thompson, Ronnie Virgets.

And the crew at the Fairgrinds Coffeehouse in New Orleans and THE chair.

And a Very Special Thank You to Geoff Munsterman.